D0303954

what is this thing called philosophy?

'*What Is This Thing Called Philosophy?* is an impressive book. The range of topics is excellent and covers much that is both humanly engaging and philosophically important. There is great clarity and intellectual commitment in the writing – a fine resource for anyone new to philosophy.'

Stephen Hetherington, *UNSW, Australia*

'*What Is This Thing Called Philosophy?* is an excellent, wide ranging and stimulating textbook, written by first rate academics. Both deep and lively, it introduces the main contemporary issues in the major areas of philosophy and will no doubt be of great service to anyone approaching the field for the first time.'

Claudine Tiercelin, *Collège de France and Institut Jean Nicod, France*

What Is This Thing Called Philosophy? is the definitive textbook for all who want a thorough introduction to the field. It introduces philosophy using a question-led approach that reflects the discursive nature of the discipline. Edited by Duncan Pritchard, each part is written by a high-profile contributor focusing on a key area of philosophy, and contains three or four question-based chapters offering an accessible point of engagement.

The core areas of philosophy covered are:

- Ethics
- Political Philosophy
- Aesthetics
- Epistemology
- Philosophy of Mind

- Metaphysics
- Philosophy of Science
- Philosophy of Religion
- The Meaning of Life.

The accompanying Routledge companion website features valuable online resources for both instructors and students including links to audio and video material, multiple-choice questions, interactive flashcards, essay questions and annotated further reading. This is the essential textbook for students approaching the study of philosophy for the first time.

Contributors: Michael Brady, Berit Brogaard, Thom Brooks, Axel Gelfert, Tim Mawson, Thaddeus Metz, Kristie Miller, Duncan Pritchard, Kathleen Stock.

Duncan Pritchard is Professor of Philosophy at the University of Edinburgh, UK.

What is this thing called?

The Routledge 'What is this thing called?' series of concise textbooks has been designed for use by students coming to a core and important area of philosophy for the first time. Each volume explores the relevant central questions with clear explanation of complex ideas and engaging contemporary examples. Features to aid study include text boxes, chapter summaries, study questions, further reading and glossaries.

What Is This Thing Called Knowledge? third edition
Duncan Pritchard

What Is This Thing Called Philosophy of Language?
Gary Kemp

What Is This Thing Called Metaphysics? second edition
Brian Garrett

What Is This Thing Called Ethics?
Christopher Bennett

EDITED BY DUNCAN PRITCHARD

what is this thing called philosophy?

Routledge
Taylor & Francis Group

LONDON AND NEW YORK

First published 2016

by Routledge
2 Park Square, Milton Park, Abingdon, Oxon OX14 4RN

and by Routledge
711 Third Avenue, New York, NY 10017

Routledge is an imprint of the Taylor & Francis Group, an informa business

British Library Cataloguing in Publication Data
A catalogue record for this book is available from the British Library

Library of Congress Cataloging in Publication Data
Pritchard, Duncan.
What is this thing called philosophy? / Duncan Pritchard. -- 1 [edition].
pages cm. -- (What is this thing called?)
Includes bibliographical references and index.
 1. Philosophy--Introductions. I. Title.
BD21.P75 2015
100--dc23
2015021942

ISBN: 978-0-415-83976-1 (hbk)
ISBN: 978-0-415-83977-8 (pbk)
ISBN: 978-0-203-77100-6 (ebk)

Typeset in Berling LT Std
by Saxon Graphics Ltd, Derby

Printed and bound by CPI Group (UK) Ltd, Croydon, CR0 4YY

CONTENTS

BOXES

CONTRIBUTORS

Michael Brady, *University of Glasgow, UK*
Berit Brogaard, *University of Miami, USA*
Thom Brooks, *Durham University, UK*
Axel Gelfert, *National University of Singapore, Singapore*
Tim Mawson, *Oxford University, UK*
Thaddeus Metz, *University of Johannesburg, South Africa*
Kristie Miller, *University of Sydney, Australia*
Duncan Pritchard, *University of Edinburgh, UK*
Kathleen Stock, *University of Sussex, UK*

PREFACE
HOW TO USE THIS TEXTBOOK

The goal of this textbook is to provide an overview of all the main areas of philosophy: ethics, political philosophy, aesthetics, epistemology, philosophy of mind, metaphysics, philosophy of science, and philosophy of religion. There is also a concluding part on the meaning of life, a philosophical topic that cuts across several core areas of philosophy. Each part has been written by an expert in the field, and breaks the topic down into three questions that define that field, with a chapter devoted to exploring each question. Like all the other textbooks in Routledge's 'What is this thing called X?' series, this book has been designed to be as user-friendly as possible, and does not presuppose any prior background knowledge.

Each chapter closes with a summary of the main points made in that chapter and offers some questions for discussion. For those who wish to explore the topic discussed in that chapter in more detail, there is also a section recommending additional introductory and advanced readings. A further section identifies free internet resources that are relevant to that chapter. Within each chapter you'll find text boxes which give supplementary information relevant to what is being discussed in the main text, such as more information about an historical figure who has been mentioned.

Although terminology is avoided where possible, you don't need to worry if you come across a technical word that you don't understand, since all terminology is explained at the back of the book in a glossary. (Technical words that have corresponding entries in the glossary are identified in the text by being in **bold** at first mention.) There is also an introductory section on the nature of philosophy and at the back of the book you will find some practical advice about writing good philosophy essays. Finally, at the very end of the book, there is an index.

Duncan Pritchard

INTRODUCTION
DUNCAN PRITCHARD

• WHAT IS PHILOSOPHY?

Answering the question, 'What is philosophy?', is by no means straightforward. Indeed, it is arguably a philosophical task in itself. Part of the difficulty relates to the fact that philosophy has changed its meaning over the years. The first philosophers were the ancient Greeks, around the sixth century BCE. Indeed, the term 'philosophy' comes from the Greek – it means 'love of wisdom'. So construed, the philosopher in the ancient world was someone who was concerned with a range of questions, not all of them of a kind that we would these days think of as philosophical.

Consider the case of Aristotle (384–322 BCE), for example, who is arguably the greatest ancient Greek philosopher (if not of all time). He was engaged in a range of inquiries, including some that we would now categorise as straightforwardly scientific, falling under such subject areas as physics and biology. Indeed, the idea of an academic philosopher who is exclusively pursuing a distinctive set of philosophical questions is a relatively new invention, historically speaking. For instance, some of the most famous philosophers of the so-called 'early modern' period which saw an explosion in philosophical and scientific thought (very roughly, from 1500 to around 1800), such as Gottfried Leibniz (1646–1716) and René Descartes (1596–1650), were also prominent scientists and mathematicians. Conversely, some of the most famous scientists of that period also made contributions to philosophy, most notably Sir Isaac Newton (1642–1727). So the idea of philosophy as a completely distinct branch of knowledge-seeking is not something that would be recognisable to many of the most famous philosophers in history, and certainly not the ancient philosophers who invented the term.

Even so, that does not mean that there are no distinctively philosophical problems and questions, and here there is a clear continuity from the inquiries undertaken by the ancient Greek philosophers and those undertaken by philosophers working today. Indeed, many of the core problems of philosophy – a number of which are covered in this book – have been with us since the ancients, such as the epistemological problem of radical scepticism and the metaphysical problem of free will. What is it about these problems that makes them distinctively philosophical?

One way of thinking about this question is to regard the intellectual development made since the invention of philosophy over 2,000 years ago as a gradual carving-up of philosophical and non-philosophical questions. The lover of wisdom is interested in learning everything he or she can about our world and our place within it. In the absence of specialised branches of learning, the ancient Greek philosophers thus posed philosophical questions alongside other kinds of questions, ones that we would today classify as falling under the remit of, say, chemistry or psychology. But once those specialised branches develop, then the questions that belong to these branches become detached from the rest. The philosophical problems are thus the ones that cannot be 'farmed-off' into one of the other specialised branches of learning.

Although there is some truth in this way of thinking about philosophical problems, it is not the full story. For while it is quite right that philosophical problems do not neatly fall within the ambit of any other specialised field of study, to classify philosophical problems purely in terms of this negative criterion fails to capture the positive characteristics shared by such problems. For as you will see when you read this book, philosophical problems display a distinctive kind of generality that you don't find in other subject areas. For example, whereas modern cognitive science might ask questions about the nature of human cognition – such as concerning how it works, or how it might be improved – it takes a philosopher (of mind) to wonder how human cognition is possible at all. For instance, how did we come to have self-consciousness, and what is the nature of this self-consciousness? These are philosophical questions.

This point about the generality of philosophical problems is sometimes expressed by saying that philosophy is the 'queen of the sciences', in that it interrogates the underpinning intellectual framework which is taken for granted in specific subject areas. That is why philosophical problems are distinct from the kinds of problems that arise within particular fields, and it is also why philosophical problems have a special kind of generality. While there is something right about this way of thinking about philosophy, it is important not to construe this point as saying that philosophical inquiry should be completely divorced from other kinds of inquiry, much less should we conclude that while other subject areas can learn from philosophy, philosophy has nothing to learn from them.

A moment ago I compared the kinds of questions asked by cognitive scientists with the more general questions posed by philosophers of mind. Nonetheless, philosophers of mind should be very interested – and in practice *are* very interested – in the latest findings in cognitive science. Indeed, when properly done philosophy of mind can interact very closely with cognitive science. And this point is not confined to philosophy of mind, much less is it confined to philosophy's relationship to the sciences. All areas of philosophy can both learn from, and contribute to, other subject areas, and often these intellectual bonds will not just be with the sciences, but with non-scientific subjects too, such as history or literary theory.

The best way of getting to grips with philosophy is, however, to simply dive in and engage with a philosophical debate. This book has been designed with that purpose in mind. While it presupposes no prior knowledge of philosophy, it encompasses all the main areas of this field, and this means that it covers nearly all the core philosophical problems too. You'll be introduced to ethics, epistemology, philosophy of mind, metaphysics, philosophy of science, philosophy of religion, aesthetics, and political philosophy. And you'll engage with such perennial philosophical problems as the nature of knowledge and the meaning of life (a topic which is covered here within its own special section). Once you've read this book, you will know exactly what philosophy is, and will be well on the way to becoming a philosopher in your own right!

Part I

ethics

Michael Brady

The study and practice of philosophy is valuable for many reasons, and not least because it helps to foster *independent thinking*. And being an independent thinker seems especially valuable when it comes to dealing with *moral* or *ethical* questions, such as: How should I live my life? What kind of person should I be? One reason for this is that our moral opinions are largely *inherited* from our parents, peers, society at large. For example, most of us think that there is nothing wrong with using animals for food. Given that most of us have grown up eating meat in a society where nature is tailored for human needs, this is hardly surprising. But perhaps we *should* give more thought to our inherited views. After all, the fact that a belief is the product of upbringing and socialisation is no guarantee that it is correct – think, for instance, about moral views that at one time supported slavery. One reason to think philosophically about moral and ethical issues is, then, to ensure that we are not making similar mistakes. Another reason is that independent thinking about moral matters helps us to live an independent life: for thinking and deciding solely on the basis of values that we have inherited from others seems rather like living a life in accordance with what others *tell* you to do; and this isn't the best kind of life for a human being to live. So being an independent thinker about moral questions is especially valuable, if we want to avoid moral mistakes, and if we want to live our own life.

But how do we become independent thinkers about ethical issues? Indeed, what is it for something to *be* an ethical issue? In this Part I hope to answer these questions. I'll begin by saying a little about what ethics is, how it contrasts with other subjects, and about how it is done. I'll then take you on a tour of the three main types of moral philosophy, considering on the way some of the most important ethical issues and questions in each, outlining what some of the most famous moral philosophers have said about these, and explaining problems with and objections to what these philosophers have said. By organising the Part in this way I hope to illustrate that the path to independent thinking about moral issues isn't one that we take alone: good thinking, in morality as well as other subjects, is *guided by* the views of others. Nevertheless, by raising objections I also hope to illustrate that truly independent thinking begins when we start to question what others have said, and refuse to be guided by them alone.

1

what is ethics?

First, a terminological issue: in the introduction I sometimes referred to ethics and at other times to moral philosophy. Are these synonymous? Some would say not, holding that ethics is a broader subject than moral philosophy. But for most philosophers, the terms can be used pretty much interchangeably, and so in what follows I'll do so too.

So what is ethics? Very roughly, ethics is the study of the codes of conduct or systems of rules that govern our behaviour, especially as this affects people and other sentient beings. We can try to make this less abstract by contrasting ethics with other codes or systems. Law, for instance, is a system of rules that governs how we ought to act. What distinguishes ethics or morality from law? One difference is that ethical codes and laws can apply to different things: it is plausible to think that morality requires that I keep my promises; but I have no *legal* obligation to keep my promises, unless I'm on the witness stand, say. I might, conversely, be subject to laws that diverge from what I morally ought to do: suppose I live in a country where it is illegal to do something that isn't immoral, such as criticise the royal family. A second reason is that the sanctions for violations of rules and standards are different in each case. If I break my promise to Joe, then Joe might be upset with me, and tell others not to trust me. But this differs in kind from the kind of sanction the state imposes if I am caught violating its laws. A third reason is that our motives for abiding by morality and law are different: my conscience might motivate me to keep my promise to Joe; but people are law abiding usually for self-interested reasons.

There are also similarities between religious and moral codes. Both are broadly concerned with individual well-being and behaviour with respect to other people. And many of the things that we think are morally right (or wrong) are also claimed by religion to be right (or wrong). Nevertheless, many people want to separate morality from religion. One reason has, again, to do with motives: many people, believers and non-believers alike, are motivated to act morally without any thought about such conduct being commanded by God. Another reason, explained by Plato in the dialogue *Euthyphro*, is that the idea that morality upon God's commands faces a difficulty. For either God commands us to do things because they are right, in which case rightness is distinct from what God commands; or things are right only because God commands them, in which case God's commands appear to be arbitrary or made for no reason, which undermines the view of God as perfectly good.

BOX 1.1 THE EUTHYPHRO DILEMMA

In **Plato's** dialogue *Euthyphro*, the titular character claims that he knows what 'piety' is. Piety is nowadays a term for religious reverence. But for Plato it was a matter of fulfilling our duties with respect to the gods and other humans. We might think of it as 'morally right'. Euthyphro suggests that 'the pious is what all the gods love, and the opposite, what all the gods hate, is impious' (9e). At this point Socrates raises the dilemma, asking if 'the pious is loved by the gods because it is pious, or is something pious because it is loved by the gods?' (10a). The worry with the latter is that if God commands us to do things but not *because* they are right, then God is in a sense making up moral rules *for no moral reason*. This is problematic: why would a loving God do this? And why should we obey such rules, even if they stem from a loving God? Consider an analogy: suppose that loving parents command their children to do certain things, and forbid them from doing others, *for no good reason*. Why would loving parents do this? And why should children obey such commands, even if they are given by loving parents? If the former, then what is morally right is independent of what God commands. But then presumably the study of what is morally right should be independent of the study of what God commands. If so, then ethics and theology are distinct.

A more positive answer to our question is to list a number of things that are thought to be moral rules, and then say something about what these rules have in common. Traditional moral rules include 'negative' duties not to lie, steal, harm, manipulate, or maltreat others, and 'positive' duties to help those in need, to be honest, and promote justice. So we might say that morality is a system of rules *like these*. Do these rules have anything in common? On one account, a feature of moral rules is that they are 'overriding'. This means that when moral rules conflict with other things I have reason to do, the moral rules are the ones that we should follow. Suppose, for example, that I've promised to give Joe a lift, and so have a moral duty to do this. Suppose now that a more attractive option arises: that Jenny, whom I like a great deal, asks me to forget Joe and go out on a date with her instead. Most people think that despite the attractiveness of a date with Jenny, I should keep my promise to Joe, because moral considerations are more important than self-interested considerations. Another feature that moral codes are typically thought to have is 'universality'. This means that a moral rule is one that applies to *everyone* in the same circumstances; so if it is wrong for me to break my promise to Joe, then it would be wrong for *anyone* to break a promise in similar circumstances. A third feature is that our motives for abiding by moral rules are given by the rules themselves: I should keep my promise to Joe *because I promised*, rather than (say) because it will be good for me. So moral rules seem to be overriding, universal, and the kind of things one should obey *because* they are moral rules. And ethics is, again roughly, the study of such systems of rules.

We can say more than this, however, because moral philosophy can be divided up into three further subdisciplines: metaethics, normative ethics, and applied ethics. *Metaethics* is the study of moral practice itself. It is concerned with, and aims to understand, what exactly is going on when we engage in moral talk and behaviour. *Normative ethics* is concerned with different theories about what is right and wrong; these theories attempt to say what it is that right actions have in common, in virtue of which they count as right. And *applied ethics* focuses more on practice than theory, in that it is concerned with real-life and often controversial issues that humans face, such as capital punishment, euthanasia, animal rights, abortion, and famine. Applied ethics involves thinking about these issues, and in a way that is informed by the different normative theories. But the relation between theory and practical issues is not strictly one way. For as we'll see, applied issues provide test cases for moral theory.

• CHAPTER SUMMARY

- Ethics or moral philosophy is the study of codes of conduct that govern our behaviour.
- Morality can be distinguished from law; and moral rules are independent of religious commands.
- Moral rules are thought to be overriding, universal, and to be obeyed because they are moral rules.
- There are three subdisciplines in ethics: metaethics, normative ethics, and applied ethics.

• STUDY QUESTIONS

1 Give examples of things that are or have been illegal but are not immoral; and give examples of things that are immoral but are not illegal.
2 Explain in your own words why morality probably isn't based on religion.
3 Are there any other features – other than overridingness universality, and the connection to a particular motive – that make a rule a moral rule?
4 Explain in your own words the basic differences between metaethics, normative ethics, and applied ethics.

• INTRODUCTORY READING

Bennett, Christopher (2010) *What is this Thing Called Ethics?* (London: Routledge). [Another helpful introductory book on morality and moral thinking.]
Rachels, James and Rachels, Stuart (2011) *The Elements of Moral Philosophy*, 7th edn (New York: McGraw-Hill Publishing). [This thorough and comprehensive introduction has a helpful first chapter on defining 'morality'.]

2

what is metaethics?

- How do we do metaethics?
- Moral disagreement
- Moral rightness and wrongness
- Moral motivation

• HOW DO WE DO METAETHICS?

Philosophical methodology is puzzling to those who aren't philosophers, at least compared with other subjects, where we have a pretty good idea of what studying these involves. After all, historians have their texts to focus on, English students their novels, psychologists their brain scans. So how do we do **metaethics**?

To answer this question, note that morality has certain distinctive features, and those who study metaethics try to make the best sense they can of these. One is that people *disagree* about moral issues such as capital punishment, animal experimentation, and abortion. Another is that people seem to assume that moral issues are ones on which people can be *right* or *wrong*. These features are related: unless you think that you are right and the person you are arguing with is wrong, then why bother arguing with them? A third is that morality is closely tied to *behaviour*.

Metaethics is the attempt to make sense of a practice that has these (and other) features; and metaethical theories can be distinguished in virtue of the kinds of explanations of the features they offer. But this means that we can think of what metaethics *is* in terms of what metaethicists *do*. In what follows I'll illustrate this by showing how different theories fare when it comes to capturing these features.

• MORAL DISAGREEMENT

It is obvious that people disagree about moral issues. Some people think this casts doubt upon the idea that there is any such thing as 'objective moral truth'. An objective truth is one that depends upon the nature and feature of what the truth is about (the *object*) rather than upon the nature of the person who holds a particular view (the *subject*). Some truths are objective: suppose I say that broccoli is high in vitamin C. This is true, but its truth depends solely upon the nature of broccoli itself.

But suppose I say that I dislike broccoli: this is a subjective truth, since its truth depends upon a fact about me, namely that I find the taste of broccoli unpleasant. Now objective truths are the kinds of things that people tend to agree about, at least if they have enough information. But moral disagreement persists, even if people have access to all of the relevant information: this suggests that morality isn't objective, but is instead subjective.

This latter idea is very popular – hence the common refrain that morality is 'just a matter of subjective opinion'. A well-known and related position is **moral relativism**, which holds that morality isn't objective but is 'relative' to the dominant views within cultures, societies, or other such groupings. This means that a certain practice – such as female infanticide – might be morally right relative to the prevalent moral code of society A, but morally wrong relative to the prevalent moral code of society B. But there is no objective fact of the matter about the morality of female infanticide, independent of how the practice is viewed by different groups of people. And support for moral relativism comes from the obvious and undoubted fact that different cultures do hold different moral opinions and engage in different moral behaviour.

Despite its widespread acceptance, moral relativism is a deeply problematic metaethical view. For one thing, the fact that different cultures or groups disagree isn't enough to support, by itself, the idea that there is no objective truth. Groups, like people, can get things wrong. For another, the fact that people disagree actually seems *incompatible with* relativism. Suppose I claim that female infanticide is wrong, and you claim that it is sometimes morally permissible. If relativism is correct, then when we are faithfully reporting the dominant views in our respective cultures, both of our statements are true, and so we aren't really disagreeing after all. Moreover, relativism cannot explain the close connection between morality and motivation. If my moral judgements report the majority views in my culture, then this connection is broken, since there is no close or necessary connection between the majority views and my action: perhaps I think the majority of people in my culture stupid.

Subjectivism itself fares better than relativism. For the subjectivist, morality is a matter of subjective opinion, so that when someone says that it is wrong to break promises, she is reporting or expressing what she, *as an individual*, thinks about breaking promises. On this view, there is moral disagreement because different people have different subjective opinions. To this extent, morality is like other areas where we have subjective opinions and where we disagree, such as taste. And just as we use evaluative language when expressing our tastes – as when I say that the soup is horrible – so too we use evaluative language when expressing our moral opinions. Moreover, there is a strong link between our subjective opinions and our actions – if I don't like the soup, then I'm strongly motivated not to eat it – and so subjectivism can capture this connection better than relativism.

Nevertheless, subjectivism, at least in its basic form, doesn't have a *plausible* account of moral disagreement. For moral disagreement is very much different from disagreement about matters of taste – about, say, whether the soup tastes nice. The latter kind of 'disagreements' are soon admitted to be *simply* matters of opinion; I don't like the taste, you do, and ultimately that's all we can say about the matter. However, we know that moral disagreement is not like this: our discussion about whether female infanticide is ever permissible isn't the kind of thing that we quickly realise is just a matter of taste. Indeed, the discussion appears to have nothing really to do with me or you at the subjective level at all; instead, it has everything to do with the *practice* of female infanticide, and whether *it* is right or not.

Moral disagreement, unlike disagreement about tastes, is more about features of the *object* of disagreement than the *subjects* that are party to the disagreement, then. If so, then moral disagreement might show that objectivist views in metaethics are more plausible than it might initially appear.

• MORAL RIGHTNESS AND WRONGNESS

Objectivist views also seem well-placed to explain our second feature, namely that moral beliefs and claims can be true or false. For a moral belief is true insofar as it matches objective moral reality, and false otherwise.

However, many philosophers think that this kind of explanation is not plausible, since they find the idea of objective moral truths and features troubling and difficult to understand. Consider the moral property or feature of 'wrongness'. This doesn't seem to be a normal feature of our natural world, like redness or roughness or sweetness. Indeed, if you are asked to describe what wrongness is, you will probably struggle; for unlike shapes and sounds, colours and textures, wrongness doesn't seem to feel or look or sound any particular way. It is not, in other words, a *sensory* property, something we discover by using our senses. But then what kind of property could it be?

This is the kind of consideration that led David Hume, the great Scottish philosopher, to think that rightness and wrongness aren't objective features of the world after all. Hume asks us to consider an instance of murder, and to describe all of the objective facts of the matter. You might describe two people having an argument, blows being exchanged, a gun being drawn and fired, one person being hit and falling, and so on. But you won't include 'wrongness' as one of these facts. We only 'discover' the wrongness, said Hume, when we turn our gaze inwards and consider our *emotional* response to what happened. Morality is more a 'matter of the heart' rather than a feature of objective reality.

Perhaps the objectivist can reply to this criticism. Consider the property of 'dangerousness'. Certain things – like driving in fog, lion-taming – are objectively dangerous. But dangerousness isn't a property of driving in fog that is over and above the *natural* properties this has. Moreover, we don't literally see (or smell or hear) danger. If we were, to follow Hume, simply to describe the facts about a dangerous situation, then the feature of 'dangerousness' would not figure in our explanation. We'd say, for instance, that the fog descended, there was heavy traffic on the motorway, some people were driving without lights, and so on. Instead, to call something dangerous *just is* to say that it has these other, natural properties; dangerousness is identical with, rather than additional to, these other properties. So why can't moral properties be like this?

Unfortunately for the objectivist, the attempt to say that moral properties are identical with properties of the natural world faces a famous and devastating objection. This is known as the '**open-question argument**' and was made by the philosopher **G. E. Moore**. Moore was a *non-naturalist*: he thought that moral properties were features of the universe, but were not identical with the natural features of common-sense experience, or the kinds of things studied by the natural sciences. Now it is not at all easy to understand what a non-natural property is. But Moore thought we were pushed to accept the existence of such properties, since moral properties *couldn't be* defined in terms of natural properties. For suppose I said that rightness was the property that acts had when they are desired by me. Moore thought that we could admit that some act is desired by me, and yet still ask whether it was the right thing to do. This kind of question was, for Moore, 'open', a question that it made sense to raise; whereas it clearly doesn't make any sense to ask whether doing the right thing was the right thing to do. But if so, then the 'right thing to do' and 'desired by me' cannot mean the same thing or cannot refer to the same property. And Moore thought that this same argument will work against *any* suggested identification. Because of this, he concluded that rightness isn't a natural property at all.

Not everyone thinks that Moore's argument works – at least, in all its details. But most people think that it raises a very serious problem for objectivists, since they will have to identify rightness with a set of natural properties in a way that the open-question argument doesn't apply. And it is safe to say that all naturalist objectivist accounts to this point have failed to show any such thing. Moreover, since non-naturalist versions of objectivism are for many people too mysterious to take seriously – because non-natural properties aren't things that we can say much about, other than that they are not part of the natural world – then objectivism as a whole seems unable to give a good explanation of what it is that makes moral views right or wrong.

BOX 2.1 THE OPEN-QUESTION ARGUMENT

G.E. Moore's *Principia Ethica* was published in 1903. Moore was a philosopher at the University of Cambridge, and wrote widely in the philosophy of mind, epistemology, and moral philosophy. His 'open-question argument' was part of his general attack on 'naturalistic' accounts of morality – these seek to define moral terms using natural terms. For Moore, a term like 'good' is indefinable; as he says, 'If I am asked "what is good?", my answer is that good is good, and that is the end of the matter.' Although many people have found problems with Moore's version of the argument – some think that it simply begs the question against naturalistic accounts – the spirit of the argument remains, and still poses a genuine problem for those who think moral properties part of the natural world. For example, a new version of the argument holds that it is always possible for us to intelligibly ask why we should *care* about the fact that some act has some natural property, whereas it isn't intelligible to ask why we should care that it would be good. This shows, the argument continues, that no natural property can be identical with goodness.

• MORAL MOTIVATION

Objectivism is also thought to struggle with explaining our third feature, namely the close connection between morality and behaviour. To see this, note that if I sincerely hold that I ought to donate 5 per cent of my salary to Oxfam then, other things being equal, this is something that I'll do. And if I sincerely judge that I ought not to eat meat then, again if other things are equal, I won't eat meat. So there is a very close connection between holding a moral view and acting in accordance with that view. This is a view called '**internalism**', since a motive to act is supposed to be 'internal' to or 'part of' the moral judgement itself. However, objectivism seems in tension with internalism. This is because judgements about objects do not in general move us to act. Suppose I judge that a new VW Golf costs over £10,000. This alone won't motivate me to do anything; at least, I'd have to desire to buy a Golf for me to do something like start saving money. But if there is in general no close connection between judgements about the objective world and action, what is so special about judgements about objective *moral* properties? Objectivism has traditionally struggled to answer this question.

Subjectivism is in a better position to explain the relevant connection. Some philosophers think that the close connection between moral judgement and action shows that moral judgements do not *describe* objective features of the world, but instead *express* subjective states of the self that do have motivational force, such as desire or emotion. To see this difference, think about swearing. Imagine you are at a football match and hear someone shout 'the referee is a bastard'. It is possible that this person is using language in order to describe, literally, his views on the referee's parentage. But it is much more likely that the person is using language to express his anger at the referee for making a decision that goes against the person's team. And often language can be used for expressive, rather than descriptive, purposes. One form of subjectivism – called **expressivism** – holds that moral language has the function of expressing desires and feelings, rather than the function of describing the objective world. In this way expressivism can explain the close connection between moral judgement and motivation. This is because if my saying that 'I ought to keep my promise' expresses my desire to do so; and since a desire is the kind of state that causes me to act, then my moral judgement has a clear link with action. As a result, we might think that subjectivist accounts fare rather better when it comes to capturing the third feature that morality appears to have.

CHAPTER SUMMARY

- Metaethics is about the nature and practice of morality.
- Metaethical theories try to explain the essential features of morality. These include the fact that people disagree about moral matters, think that moral questions have right and wrong answers, and that morality and action are closely connected.
- The fact of moral disagreement seems to cast doubt upon the *objectivity* of morality, and favour some form of *subjectivism*. However, in fact, objective accounts are better placed to explain moral disagreement.
- Moral relativism holds that morality is relative to cultures or other groups; a different form of subjectivism holds that morality is a matter of subjective opinion.
- Objectivist accounts struggle to explain what rightness and wrongness are; these cannot be natural properties, and the idea that they are non-natural is mysterious.
- Objectivist accounts also struggle to explain the connection between moral judgement and motivation.

STUDY QUESTIONS

1 Give examples of some serious moral disagreements. What explanations can you give for why people disagree about these things?
2 What does moral relativism say about moral judgements? Are there any areas where our judgements are relative to the majority beliefs in our culture?
3 Explain in your own words what subjectivism says, and why it might be plausible. Can the subjectivist really account for moral disagreement?
4 Why can't moral properties be natural properties, according to G.E. Moore?
5 Explain in your own words why people think there is a link between morality and action. Why do objectivist accounts struggle to explain this link?

INTRODUCTORY READING

Kirchin, Simon (2012) *Metaethics* (Basingstoke: Palgrave Macmillan). [A clear, accessible, and thorough introduction to central questions in metaethics.]
Miller, Alexander (2013) *Contemporary Metaethics: An Introduction*, 2nd edn (Cambridge: Polity Press). [Both an excellent and comprehensive introductory text, and a rigorous and sophisticated discussion of contemporary debates.]

• ADVANCED FURTHER READING

Harman, Gilbert and Judith Jarvis Thomson (1996) *Moral Relativism & Moral Objectivity* (Oxford: Wiley-Blackwell). [A stimulating debate between two of the world's best moral philosophers, Harman putting the case for relativism, Thomson the case that morality is objective.]

Moore, G. E. (1903/1993) *Principia Ethica*, 2nd edn (Cambridge: Cambridge University Press). [Moore's classic and influential book, which presents his attack on naturalistic accounts of morality.]

Schroeder, Mark (2010) *Noncognitivism in Ethics* (London: Routledge). [An excellent overview of expressivist theories.]

Smith, Michael (1994) *The Moral Problem* (Oxford: Blackwell). [A splendid book covering many of the central issues in metaethics, and a particularly illuminating discussion of moral motivation.]

• FREE INTERNET RESOURCES

http://ethics-etc.com/about/ [A forum for discussing issues in ethics, with a section on metaethics.]

http://peasoup.typepad.com/ [Another good online discussion site, with a lot of discussion of metaethics.]

Sayre-McCord, Geoffrey, 'Metaethics', *Stanford Encyclopedia of Philosophy*, http://plato.stanford.edu/entries/metaethics/ [An excellent overview of central issues in metaethics.]

3

what is normative
ethics?

- How do we do normative ethics?
- Consequentialism
- Deontology
- Virtue ethics

• HOW DO WE DO NORMATIVE ETHICS?

Normative ethics is, roughly, the study of *theories* about morality. Moral theories are abstract structures that aim, amongst other things, to tell us what right (or wrong) things have in common in virtue of which they count as right (or wrong). How is this study to be conducted?

On one popular view, ethical theorising involves moving *from particular to general and back again*. That is: it starts off with our opinions or judgements about particular cases, and sees whether we can find any *general principles* that can explain these. (Compare this with scientific methodology, where we start with observations of particular phenomena and then see if we can find any scientific principles or theories to explain what we see.) If we can, such principles can form part of a more general theory about rightness and wrongness. But this isn't just one-way traffic. For we can always go back and test our general principles or rule against other particular cases. In this way moral theorising seeks a balance between the particular and general; and the best theories are the ones that achieve the best balance between these. Let's consider a real-life example to illustrate this methodology.

In 1884 a ship called the *Mignonette* set sail to explore the Great Barrier Reef. The captain was Thomas Dudley, the mates were Edwin Stevens and Edmund Brooks. The cabin boy was a 17-year-old called Richard Parker. The ship was 1,600 miles from land when it sailed into a hurricane, and Dudley, Stevens, Brooks and Parker boarded a lifeboat with only two small tins of turnips to eat. After nineteen days they were close to death, and Dudley considered drawing lots to choose a victim to feed the remaining crew. Brooks was against any killing, Stevens was indecisive, so Dudley killed Parker who was near to death. The three sailors survived by eating Parker's body for thirty-five days until rescued. Upon their return to England, Dudley, Stevens, and Brooks were each sentenced to six months' hard labour and then released.

This is an interesting, if rather gruesome, story. And it raises a question for moral philosophers: Did Dudley do anything *wrong* in killing Parker, or was he *justified* in killing him? I'm sure that most of you will have an opinion about this. Some will hold that what Dudley did was wrong, others that it was permissible; some of you might also be unsure. But another question can be asked of the former camps: *Why* do you think what he did was wrong (or permissible)? Again, some of you might hold that he acted wrongly because it is always wrong to kill an innocent person; others that he did something OK because in emergencies innocent people may be sacrificed so that more people might live. But note what has happened: in both cases, you are appealing to *reasons* and *principles* in order to support your opinions about the particular case. In the first case, the principle 'it is always wrong to kill innocent people'; in the second, the principle 'it is OK to kill innocent people in order to save more lives'. Discovering your views about particular cases, and coming up with reasons and principles in order to support them, is the starting point for theorising about ethics.

But of course moral thinking doesn't *end* here. For a further important question is this: which of our moral principles is *correct*? Note that the two moral principles cited above cannot both be true: for if it is *always* wrong to kill innocent people, then it cannot be OK to kill innocent people in any circumstances, even when more lives are at stake. So how can we go about discovering which one is correct?

It is at this point that the idea of a moral *theory* comes into play. For moral theories propose a moral principle that is claimed to be somehow *fundamental*, and so is the basis for all other moral principles. In addition, moral theories give some argument as to why this principle is true: typically, theorists argue that it explains our views about particular cases *better than any rival principle*, and should, for that reason, be the one we adopt. (In this way moral theorising once again mirrors scientific theorising: for scientific theories are to be believed insofar as they can explain observable phenomena better than any rival theories.) If one such argument is plausible, then that is the moral theory that we ought to accept.

In what follows I'll discuss three of the best-known moral theories, and say a little about why some people find them attractive and why other people think they are mistaken. The theories can be distinguished in virtue of which aspect of our *actions* they take to be most important in determining whether that action is right or wrong; and there are three such aspects. Whenever we act, there is (i) the motive or reason for why we did what we did; there is also (ii) the act itself; and finally there is (iii) the result or outcome of the action. The first moral theory we will look at, **consequentialism**, takes (iii) to be most important to rightness and wrongness. Our second moral theory, **deontology**, holds that it is (ii), although the motive typically counts as well; our third moral theory, **virtue ethics**, holds that it is (i) that really matters, although the nature of the act itself must also be taken into consideration. Let us look at these in turn.

• CONSEQUENTIALISM

Consequentialism holds that the outcomes or consequences of actions are the most important thing to consider when thinking about morality; as a result, actions are right or wrong in virtue of the value – that is, the goodness or badness – of the consequences that they bring about. Now consequentialism actually refers to a general type of moral theory, particular versions of which can be distinguished on the basis of how they answer two important questions: (a) what is it about some outcome that matters that makes it good or bad? And (b) how are actions to be related to outcomes, so that they count as right actions? Some consequentialist theories hold that what really matters is the effect that actions have on *human happiness*. Other consequentialist theories hold that other things than human happiness count to determine value. Some versions hold that an act is right when and because it brings about the *most* happiness. Other versions hold that right acts are ones which fit the best consequentialist rules, or which express the best consequentialist motives, where we figure out what the best rules and best motives are by (you guessed it) appeal to consequences. So there are many different versions of consequentialism. I'll look at the best-known of these, namely *Utilitarianism*, as proposed by its most famous advocate, John Stuart Mill.

I said above that moral theories typically identify a fundamental principle, and Mill's utilitarianism is a nice example of this. Mill calls his the 'Greatest Happiness Principle', and it states that 'Actions are right in proportion as they tend to promote happiness; wrong as they tend to produce the reverse of happiness. By happiness is intended pleasure and the absence of pain; by unhappiness, pain and the privation of pleasure' (*Utilitarianism*, ch. 2). Mill thought that the only thing that really matters in an outcome is pleasure and freedom from pain; these are the only things that we really find valuable, and everything else is valuable only as a means to these. Mill also thought that right actions are ones that promote happiness. This is usually understood in terms of bringing about as much pleasure as possible, or *maximising* pleasure. So on Mill's view, the right thing to do, of all of the options available to us, is the thing that will bring about the most happiness, understood as pleasure and freedom from pain, and where we consider the same kind of happiness of everyone equally. Any other action is wrong. So we must always bring about 'the greatest happiness for the greatest number', to use a well-known phrase.

Why might we be attracted to utilitarianism? One reason is pretty obvious: the consequences of actions do seem to matter morally! It is a terrible thing if an innocent person dies; but it seems much worse if 10,000 people die. I do a good thing if by donating to charity a child gets access to clean water and an education; I do a much better thing if by donating more money to charity 100 children get access to clean water and an education. Utilitarianism takes this simple idea and makes it the bedrock of the theory. Another reason is that the theory is simple: we have a way of telling, at least in principle, whether some action was right or wrong, and a way of working out, at least in principle, what we ought to do. A third reason is that it doesn't appeal to anything mysterious such as non-natural properties, or anything controversial like a divine lawgiver: everyone has a reasonable idea of what pleasure and pain are, and everyone agrees that pleasure is good and that pain is bad.

There are, however, some serious problems with the theory. The first is that more things seem to matter to the value of an outcome than pleasure and freedom from pain. Certain things are valuable for us in addition to, and independently of, pleasure: think, for instance, of values such as understanding, freedom, friendships, accomplishments. We don't want to have friends simply as means to the pleasure that they bring; if we did, we wouldn't be a very good friend! And freedom isn't just valuable as a way of getting pleasure. Imagine that you could get more pleasure if scientists tampered with your brain so that you always did what they decided. We wouldn't like to live that kind of life, because being free matters to us, even if by being free we get less pleasure.

A second problem is that sometimes utilitarianism will seem to demand that we do things that are morally wrong. Suppose I am the chief justice and could ensure that the murder rate in my city drops significantly by arranging the public torture and execution of a murderer in my charge, something that will be an effective deterrent and thus save future victims of murder. Ought I to do this? It seems that utilitarianism will say 'yes', as this is the act that will bring about the most happiness (or minimise pain and misery). But many people think that you must not torture and kill people, even if they are murderers, and even if this would save more lives. (If you are not convinced, suppose that the deterrent effect could be achieved by torturing and killing an *innocent* person.) There are many similar examples where happiness can be maximised by stealing, by lying, by breaking promises, indeed by violations of all of the moral rules and principles that we intuitively think we ought to live by. For many, this is good reason to reject utilitarianism.

A third problem is that utilitarianism requires us to *do* too much: it sets the bar for morally correct behaviour extremely high. Remember that according to utilitarianism, the right action is the one that maximises happiness; all other possible actions are *wrong*. That means, however, that if you do anything that doesn't maximise happiness, your behaviour is immoral and you are subject to moral criticism. But this means that we are subject to moral criticism for *a great many* of the things that we do in everyday life. Suppose you like listening to live music, and pay £15 for a ticket to see a band, then spend £10 on drinks, and then £5 on a taxi home. This would be a very enjoyable night for you, and certainly not extravagant in terms of cost. However, £30 sent to Oxfam could provide clean water for those without, or food for those who are starving, or cataract surgery so that someone doesn't go blind. Pleasant though it was, your night out isn't the best way for you to spend that money, from a utilitarian perspective. You should, instead, have given the money to Oxfam, or done something similarly worthwhile. The fact that you didn't means that you are immoral. Now this argument can be repeated; and if it is, you'll see that *most* of the things you do are immoral from the utilitarian perspective, since the money or time you spend doing those things could be better spent maximising happiness elsewhere.

Many people think that this makes utilitarianism too *demanding* a moral theory: it requires that you spend much more of your money and time helping others than you usually do, and holds that you are immoral when you don't do this. But these demands, and this kind of criticism, are too much; we don't think that we are required to spend nearly all of our time and money helping others, on pain of being highly immoral. Insofar as utilitarianism has these implications, people think that it is flawed as an ethical theory.

Utilitarians have a number of responses to these criticisms. Most of these consist in showing how the distance between utilitarian teaching and our intuitions about the above issues is much narrower than the criticisms imply. And it is fair to say, therefore, that the jury is still out on whether we should reject the theory on the basis of these criticisms. If, however, you do think that these criticisms are convincing, you might prefer to adopt a moral theory that doesn't succumb to them. If so, you might prefer to be a *deontologist*.

BOX 3.1 'THE EXPERIENCE MACHINE'

Mill thought that pleasure and freedom from pain were the only things that are intrinsically good. But is he right to think this? The philosopher Robert Nozick, in his book *Anarchy, State, and Utopia*, produced a famous hypothetical example that might make us doubt Mill's view; this is 'The Experience Machine'. Nozick asks us to imagine a machine that could stimulate the brain to give us pleasant experiences that are indistinguishable from those we get in real life. Would we want to swap our lives for life on the machine – say if we were promised much more in the way of pleasure if we swapped? Presumably, if pleasure is the only good, we should plug in. But Nozick thinks – and many people agree – that we would be reticent to do so. For more things matter to us than pleasure: we want to really do things and really have friends, and not just have the pleasant experiences of having done things or having had friends.

• DEONTOLOGY

Whereas consequentialists focus on the outcomes – and only on the outcomes – in their assessment of actions, deontologists think that it is the nature of the action, and (for some deontologists) the reason why someone acted, that are all-important. This isn't to say that deontologists think that consequences don't matter. But they are not the *only* things that matter. On this view, some things are right or wrong *regardless of* their consequences.

Deontological moral theories take their name from the Greek word *deon*, which can be translated as duty, and refers to what we are morally obligated to do, or what we must necessarily do if we are to act morally. Deontological theories are characterised by two things. The first is *constraints*: there are certain things that we have a duty not to do, even if the consequences are good. The second is *permissions*: although we have a duty to help others, we are not always morally required to do what will bring about the best outcome, and so have permission to act in other ways. Immanuel Kant is the most famous proponent and defender of a deontological moral theory, so it will prove useful to look at his views in more detail.

Kant's theory can be found in a book called the *Groundwork for the Metaphysics of Morals*, and here he proposes that constraints and permissions follow from requirements of *reason* rather than any desires or other motives we have. He starts by describing the morally good person, for him a person with a 'good will'. This person will do her duty *because* it is her duty. In our terms, we might say that the good person is someone who does the right thing because it is right. Suppose, to illustrate, you see someone slip and injure herself on an icy pavement. The right thing to do in this instance is to come to their aid. But different people might have different motives for doing this. You might help them just because you see that they are in need of help, and be moved to help by thoughts that this would be the right thing to do. I might help them, on the other hand, because (and only because) I find them attractive, and think that my offering assistance might result in a date. Kant would say – and most people would agree with him – that your action is morally praiseworthy in this instance, whilst mine is not. There is something morally lacking if I do the right thing, but only because *I* stand to benefit from it. So this is an anti-consequentialist point: the morality of our actions differs, *even though the consequences of our actions – namely, that the person is helped – are the same.*

But how can we tell what our duty is? Kant's view is that an action of ours is wrong if we couldn't rationally commit to *everyone* acting in a similar way. This is captured by *his* fundamental moral principle called the *Categorical Imperative*. In its most famous form, this states: 'Act only on that maxim that you can at the same time and without contradiction will that it should become a universal law.' Now the language and concepts here are not familiar, but the basic idea is: it is the same *kind* of idea (although different in important ways) that we find in the Golden Rule of Christian morality, which enjoins us to treat others as we would like to be treated. To illustrate, suppose that I'm planning to cheat on my taxes, so that I get the benefits from other people paying and also get the benefits from spending the money I save on myself. And suppose, for the sake of argument, that I am devious enough to get away with the plan. Is this something that it would be morally OK for me to do? For Kant, the answer is 'no'. For I cannot rationally will that my plan be a 'universal law' – that is, something that everyone else does – since their acting in this way will undermine my plan. If *no-one* paid their taxes, then my plan is scuppered: I can't get the benefits from other people paying if no-one pays. My plan thus fails the Categorial Imperative test. And this is a good thing, since we think that such 'free-riding', which involves using double standards, is wrong.

Nevertheless, critics of deontology have raised problems for Kant's views in particular, and for deontological accounts in general. One problem is that it is not clear whether the Categorical Imperative does rule out immoral actions. Suppose I plan not to pay my taxes, but *only on condition that* most other people are paying theirs. This could be a 'universal law' without a problem, since people can only follow this if enough other people are paying taxes, and so my plan to take advantage of this isn't undermined. So I can in this case be a free-rider, provided that I formulate my plan carefully. Another problem concerns Kant's views about the strength of the duties or obligations. For Kant, lying is morally wrong. But Kant thought that we have a 'perfect duty' not to lie, which means that we can *never* lie under any circumstances – even to save a life. And this seems too extreme. As with consequentialism, Kantian moral philosophers have smart and sophisticated responses to these objections. But as with consequentialism, the jury is still out on whether such defences are successful.

There are more general worries with deontological theories. The first is that deontologists must justify constraints and permissions. If certain acts are prohibited, then we have to be told *why* they are prohibited. But this might be a difficult story to tell. For suppose that a deontologist picks a particular feature of actions that makes them wrong: they involve using people against their will, for example. But if there is something particularly bad about using people in this way, then the right thing to do will be to *minimise* occurrences of such behaviour. And this just means that consequentialism is true after all.

A second problem is that there seem to be limits on constraints, such that if enough is at stake then we can break them. For instance, lying is OK to save someone's life. But what seems true about lying also seems true about killing. Most people will think that at some point it is morally permissible to kill someone. What if the population of Europe depended upon the life of one innocent person? But if we do think this, then pressure can be put on the deontologist to explain, in a non-arbitrary way, when stakes are high enough to justify breaking constraints. If it is OK to kill an innocent to save the population of Europe, why isn't it OK to kill an innocent when 1,000 lives are at stake, or 100, or 10, or even 2? The deontologist needs to tell a story here; but it is not obvious what kind of story they can consistently tell.

In light of these and other problems faced by consequentialism and deontology, there has in recent years been a move back towards a more ancient form of moral theory that many people now think was unduly neglected. This theory is **virtue ethics**.

• VIRTUE ETHICS

Virtue ethics holds that moral thinking and theorising should be much more focused on people, their characters and motives, than it is on actions or consequences. As with our other theories, virtue ethics comes in various versions. On one account, an act is right if it expresses virtuous motives, and wrong if it expresses vicious motives. Think, to illustrate, of the difference between two apparently similar actions in an earlier example: helping someone who has fallen on the ice. You help this person because she is in need of help; whereas I help her only because I find her attractive. Although the actions are apparently the same, most people will agree that only your act was morally praiseworthy, and this is because only your act is *kind*. I'm not morally praiseworthy because my action is *sleazy*. So in this example we might think that the morality of what we do depends upon the motive involved; here it is a virtuous motive that makes an act right.

On another version, virtue ethics holds that virtue is important in order for us to 'see' the right thing to do in our circumstances. This kind of virtue ethics rejects the idea that there is any principle or formula – like the Greatest Happiness Principle or the Categorical Imperative – that we can use in order to figure out what we should do in particular cases. Moral truth and moral thinking are much more complicated than this, and it is only the virtuous person who has a grasp of the full complexity of value and circumstances and who, as a result, can figure out how we ought to act. This requires a particular kind of sensibility and training. To use an analogy, experts in chess-playing, unlike novices, don't follow explicit rules. Instead, experts have the capacity to just 'see' what the right move is. Virtuous people are like expert chess-players in this regard.

But what *is* virtue, and who counts as a virtuous person? This is a question that occupied one of the greats of ethical thinking, the Greek philosopher Aristotle. Aristotle was concerned with the question of how we should live, and in his major work in moral philosophy, the *Nicomachean Ethics*, sought to answer this question. The answer he gave was 'virtuously', since he thought that the virtuous life was the best and happiest life for human beings. Now for Aristotle, each moral virtue is a 'mean' between two 'extremes' of feeling or desire. For example, *courage* is a mean between cowardice (being afraid of the wrong thing, and afraid too much) and rashness (not being afraid enough of things which are fearful); *temperance* is a mean between intemperance (too susceptible to pleasures) and insensitivity (not susceptible enough). Operating over all of the virtues of character and intellect is the 'executive' virtue of practical wisdom, the excellence that enables a person to pick out what is really valuable in life and what ought to be pursued: this is the virtue that enables them to 'see' the right thing to do. So Aristotle's basic picture is that having a virtuous character is to be disposed just right, so that one can both see the right thing to do and be motivated accordingly. And you can see why, on this view, Aristotle thought that the good life was the virtuous life: for there seems to be a strong connection between being courageous, temperate, generous, and wise, and attaining those goods that make up a flourishing human life.

Even if this is true, however, some might worry about whether Aristotle's picture of the virtues, and virtue ethics in general, is ultimately satisfactory as an ethical theory. Aristotle's account is often criticised on the grounds that it is too *egoistic*: on his view, we should do the right thing because this is what virtue requires, and we should be virtuous because ultimately this makes us happy. But some think that this is the wrong kind of justification for acting morally: we should do the right thing, as Kant thought, because it is the right thing, and not any ulterior motive. We should, in other words, be virtuous, even if by being virtuous we make ourselves worse off. We think that morality should win out over self-interest in these circumstances, and this is something that a virtue ethics based upon individual flourishing might struggle to accommodate.

There are other worries with virtue ethics. One is that a theory that makes the rightness of actions depend upon the goodness of motives cannot capture the distinction between doing the right thing, and doing the right thing for the right reason. Even when I help someone who has fallen because I'm attracted to her, then my *action* would seem to be right, even though my motive is dubious. Another is epistemological: how are we to tell who the virtuous person is? This is important, if virtue ethics is supposed to give us practical advice. Suppose that you are faced with a particular moral problem: should you bring your children up to be vegetarian? Here the instruction 'do what the virtuous person would do' is of little help, unless you have some idea of who the virtuous person is and some indication of what in fact they would do in these circumstances. But how can we tell whether someone is virtuous or not? External behaviour might not help, since as we saw we can do the right thing from the wrong kind of motives. Indeed, it seems very difficult to identify anyone who would count as a moral expert or someone whose views on morality is authoritative, someone whose advice one might reliably seek. (If someone thinks that such moral expertise is to be found amongst moral philosophers, then I'd suggest that they haven't met many moral philosophers.) If so, however, then virtue ethics might not prove to be a useful ethical theory; and if an ethical theory is of little use in our moral thinking about how we should act, we might think that it is a pretty bad theory.

Normative ethics concerns which of these theories, amongst others – for there are other possibilities here too, including *contractarian*, *divine command*, and *egoistic* moral theories – is correct. Each theory has sophisticated supporters and opponents, and each of the various theories has a good deal of plausibility – and a good deal that seems wrong with it. But this isn't a source for pessimism about the prospects for arriving at the right theory about moral matters. It is, instead, exactly what one would expect, given how large and important and complicated the questions generated by moral thinking are. As with other areas of philosophy, progress will be slow and painstaking, precisely because of the importance and difficulty of the questions with which philosophers deal.

This doesn't mean that we give up on moral thinking and theorising either; in fact, we don't have that as an option, given that we are faced with moral questions and problems daily. This is the province of practical or applied ethics (here too I'll use the terms interchangeably), a subdiscipline that is of importance and interest in its own right, but also because thinking about practical issues can, as we have seen all along, help us to think better about theoretical matters.

• CHAPTER SUMMARY

- Ethical theorising moves from the particular to the general, and back again.
- We appeal to general principles and rules in order to explain our opinions about particular cases; but particular cases can also be used to 'test' moral principles.
- Consequentialism is a moral theory that makes the rightness of an action depend solely upon the value of its consequences.
- Utilitarianism holds that pleasure and the absence of pain are the only things intrinsically valuable, and that we should aim to maximise pleasure in our actions.
- Utilitarianism has been criticised for allowing immoral actions, and for demanding too much.
- Deontology is characterised by constraints and permissions.
- Kant's fundamental moral principle is the Categorical Imperative, and holds that wrong actions are ones that we cannot rationally will that everyone perform.
- Deontology has been criticised for being absolutist, and for failing to explain why we have constraints and permissions.
- Virtue ethics holds that morality should be much more focused on people, their motives, and their character.
- Aristotle thought that the best way to live was virtuously; and virtues are a mid-point between excesses of feeling and desires.
- Virtue ethics has been criticised for being too 'egoistic', and for being unclear as to how we identify the virtuous person.

• STUDY QUESTIONS

1 Think of examples of particular moral views you hold, and examine the reasons why you hold them. Can you arrive at a fundamental or basic reason?
2 What are the components of action, and how can we distinguish normative theories by appeal to these components?
3 What is consequentialism? What reasons are there to take the theory seriously?

4 Explain in your own words the main idea behind Mill's utilitarianism. What problems does his theory face?
5 Explain in your own words Kant's Categorical Imperative. Think of how the Categorical Imperative could be used to show that murder, stealing, and lying are wrong.
6 What is a virtue? Why does acting in accordance with the virtues promise to lead to a happy life?

• INTRODUCTORY READING

Driver, J. (2006) *Ethics: The Fundamentals* (Oxford: Wiley-Blackwell). [A clear and accessible overview of the main moral theories.]
Timmons, M. (2002) *Moral Theory: An Introduction* (Lanham, MD: Rowman & Littlefield). [Another helpful and comprehensive survey of normative theories.]

• ADVANCED FURTHER READING

Baron, M., Pettit, P. and Slote, M. (1997) *Three Methods of Ethics* (Oxford: Wiley-Blackwell). [An excellent three-way discussion from major proponents of Kantian deontology, consequentialism, and virtue ethics.]
Kamm, F. M. (1993– 6) *Morality, Mortality*, 2 vols (New York: Oxford University Press). [An important and comprehensive defence of deontological constraints and application of deontological thinking to practical matters.]
Parfit, D. (2011) *On What Matters*, 2 vols (Oxford: Oxford University Press). [A massive and very important work from one of the world's most prominent moral philosophers.]

• FREE INTERNET RESOURCES

Aristotle, *Nicomachean Ethics* (350 BC) Aristotle's classic work in moral philosophy, available here. http://www.classics.mit.edu/Aristotle/nicomachaen.html
Kant, I., *Groundwork for the Metaphysic of Morals* (1785) Kant's classic work in moral philosophy, available from a site edited by the philosopher Jonathan Bennett. http://www.earlymoderntexts.com/pdfs/kant1785.pdf
Mill, J. S., *Utilitarianism* (1863) Mill's statement and defence of his utilitarian theory. https://www.ebooks.adelaide.edu.au/m/mill/john_stuart/m645u/

There are also excellent entries on consequentialism, deontology, and virtue ethics at the *Stanford Encyclopedia of Philosophy*: http://plato.stanford.edu/.

4

what is applied ethics?

- How do we do applied ethics?
- Euthanasia
- Animal rights

• HOW DO WE DO APPLIED ETHICS?

Sometimes moral philosophers think about the nature of morality itself. Sometimes they think about which moral theory is the best. But at other times they look in detail at particular practical issues and the philosophical problems these generate. One common way of thinking about applied ethics is that it is the application of moral theory to practical problems – such as **animal rights**, abortion, the environment, conduct in warfare, and the like. There is something right about this; without some knowledge of the theoretical considerations that underlie our everyday moral thinking, debates about moral issues will end up simply as a clash of basic moral opinions and intuitions, and there's not much progress to be made if our discussion consists of you saying that (e.g.) capital punishment is never justified, and me saying that sometimes it is the right thing to do. But there is something wrong about this view as well, insofar as it implies that we do practical ethics by surveying what each moral theory says about various practical issues, and leaving it at that. There won't be much progress either if you say 'as a deontologist, capital punishment is never justified', while I reply 'as a utilitarian, it sometimes is'. Indeed, it is not obvious that what we are doing is in fact disagreeing in this latter case, rather than stating our adherence to a moral theory and saying what this theory says about a practical issue.

A better account of what goes on in practical ethics is this: practical issues generate problems for us, and some of these are unavoidable. Take diet, for instance. The meat industry raises and kills millions of animals for consumption by human beings each year. Given that we have to eat, we face a decision: should we eat meat, and in doing so support the meat industry? Or consider the issue of how we should spend our money. It is very rare for people in the UK to starve to death, since either people in the UK have a decent enough income to provide for themselves, or there are social services and charities to provide food for those in need. But things are very different in other parts of the world, where thousands of people die from starvation each day. Given that we have an income and that we are, relatively speaking, much better off than such people, do we have an obligation to give some of our money to help them? Or is it morally OK for us to spend all of our money on ourselves and those close to us?

As I said, moral thinking about these issues isn't simply the application of theory to them. Instead, it often takes the form of looking closely at the issue and trying to identify the relevant moral questions it raises. Close and careful scrutiny is very important in order for us to understand what is at stake. For practical issues that generate moral problems are very complicated, since they are often closely related to other moral issues, involve appeal to different values, sometimes have moral and legal aspects, and do not admit of easy or straightforward answers. To see how this works, let us look closely at two practical issues: euthanasia, and animal rights.

• EUTHANASIA

Everyday discussions of euthanasia – like everyday discussions of many moral issues – are often rather crude, and involve appeal to slogans to carry the day. So some people argue that euthanasia is a good thing, because 'it is right for people to die with dignity'. Other people argue that euthanasia is morally problematic, because it's 'what the Nazis did'. The philosophical questions of what euthanasia *is*, of the values involved, of the distinction between morality and legality, and of the relation between euthanasia and other closely related moral questions, are rarely discussed. But these issues are central to the question of the morality of euthanasia; and we can make moral progress on the issue only if we stop sloganeering and look more closely at these aspects.

So: what is euthanasia? Euthanasia involve the death of a person, where in some sense the death of the person *is for the person's own good*. This is an essential feature of euthanasia, but is ignored by those who simply equate euthanasia with murder, since murder involves bringing about the death of a person but not for the person's own good. (The Nazis didn't engage in euthanasia, since their motives were not to benefit the people they killed.) There are, in addition, different types of euthanasia: we can distinguish voluntary, nonvoluntary, and involuntary euthanasia. Voluntary euthanasia involves bringing about someone's death at their request – either verbally, or through a 'living will'. Nonvoluntary euthanasia occurs when a secondary party – usually a family member – requests that the person is killed, when the person is unable now or in the future to consent. Involuntary euthanasia occurs where someone is killed and yet has expressed the wish to continue living, or is able to consent but is not consulted. This still counts as euthanasia, if the motive of the person doing the killing is that it was for the person's own good.

Another important distinction concerns *how* the death is brought about. Active euthanasia involves doing something that results in death, such as giving the patient a lethal injection. Passive euthanasia involves medical staff failing to take measures to save the person's life, such as continuing with life-saving treatment, with the result that the person dies. The distinction between active and passive euthanasia cuts across the distinction between voluntary, nonvoluntary, and involuntary euthanasia, so there are active and passive versions of each of these three types.

This kind of close scrutiny of euthanasia is important for moral thinking about practical issues; for once these distinctions are made, people might be reticent to think that all cases are either wrong or permissible. Those in favour of euthanasia will be hard pressed to support *involuntary* euthanasia, since killing someone against their will seems at the heart of what is wrong with murder. Those against euthanasia will probably oppose active euthanasia more than passive. And most people will think that it is difficult to find a moral difference between voluntary passive euthanasia and abiding by a patient's request that doctors do not resuscitate her if this will prolong her suffering. In this case, both of these might seem morally permissible.

In a sense, then, applied ethics shows how complicated the issue of euthanasia is; but by showing the complexity of the issue the subject *clarifies* the issue. We get a better grasp and understanding of the issue by realising that there are important distinctions here that everyday thinking about euthanasia fails to make. But a second way in which applied ethics 'clarifies by complicating' is by showing that there are a whole range of different values in play when we think about the morality of euthanasia; and once we realise this, we might make progress by thinking about which of these we take to be most important. Consider, for instance, reasons that people have given in support of euthanasia. *Autonomy* is an important value; and one reason to think euthanasia can sometimes be justified is that it promotes a person's autonomy, by giving them control over an important aspect of their life. *Suffering* is an obvious disvalue; another reason in favour of euthanasia is that it is a way to relieve someone's suffering, and things which relieve suffering are, other things being equal, thought to be good things. A third reason is based upon the suffering of others: the fact that someone continues to live in agony can be very distressing for their family and friends.

But there are considerations that speak against the practice. One is the potential for abuse – by family, by doctors. Another is the possibility of mistaken diagnoses. But a third consideration – raised by the philosopher J. David Velleman in his paper 'Against the Right to Die' – is that legalising euthanasia might increase someone's autonomy, but in a bad way. Having the choice to end your life, when you previously didn't have any such choice, might put pressure on the ill, elderly, and infirm, to opt for euthanasia because they don't wish to be a burden on family, friends, and hospital resources. But this might mean that some people ask to be killed, not because they really want this, but because they think that others want this. It would be better for patients, in these circumstances, not to have the option, and not to thereby be liable to such pressures. (Here the patient is like the bank employee who doesn't have the freedom to open the safe; this person is better off because she isn't a potential target of threats from bank robbers.)

Which of these values is most important? How can we rank values, or determine which should take precedence here? How does our moral thinking affect our thinking about the legality of euthanasia, and how do the potential negative consequences of legalising euthanasia affect our views about its morality? These are all extremely difficult, very complicated, and challenging questions. But they are the kinds of questions we must ask and deal with if we are to have even the chance of making the right kind of decision in such cases. Applied ethics brings all of these questions and distinctions to light, and in this is very different from the simple application of theory to a practical issue.

• ANIMAL RIGHTS

A second important applied issue is that of animal rights. Everyone agrees that we have, sometimes, obligations or duties towards other people: we should treat people with respect, not harm them, help them when they are in need, consider their interests when we are deciding how we should act, and so on. However, it is much less clear whether we have moral obligations towards non-human animals. Moreover, even if we do have such obligations, it is not obvious how strong these obligations are. If we have a duty not to harm other human beings, do we have an equally strong duty not to harm animals?

An extreme position is that we have no moral duties towards animals, because animals have no 'moral status' in themselves. However, we can have *indirect* duties or obligations to animals, in virtue of the fact that our (mis)treatment of them can affect the welfare of other human beings. To support this extreme position, someone might rehearse various arguments. One would hold that animals do not feel pain. Another would hold that animals do feel pain but that only human pain matters. A third would hold that moral duties and obligations are a human construct, resulting from a *contract* between human beings, aimed at promoting the welfare of all. Since animals are not or cannot be a party to any such contract, we have no duties towards them directly.

The first argument here isn't very plausible. Many animals display the kinds of pain behaviour that other human beings display when they are in pain; if such behaviour is good enough evidence to think that other humans suffer, then it should be good enough evidence to think that animals suffer as well. The second argument saddles its proponent with an explanatory burden: *why* is it that only human pain matters? The third argument is a bit better, but still not convincing: after all, we have direct obligations to young children and to other humans who, through lack of mental capacity, are also unable to form a contract.

Suppose, therefore, that animals have *some* moral standing, and that we have some duties to them. Our question now is: how much consideration do we owe them? A consequentialist philosopher called Peter Singer has famously advanced an argument that we owe animals and humans *equal* consideration. Singer urges, in a paper called 'All Animals Are Equal', 'that we extend to other species the basic principle of equality that most of us recognize should be extended to all members of our own species'. This doesn't mean that humans and animals have equal *rights*, only that we give equal consideration to human and animal interests in deciding how we should act.

Why does Singer think this? His basic thought is that the many and obvious differences between humans and animals do not justify giving them unequal consideration; for the many and obvious differences between human beings do not justify giving more consideration to some humans than others on this basis. We don't, for instance, think that some humans have higher standing than other humans in virtue of greater intelligence, or moral capacity, or physical strength. So for Singer, *actual* differences between humans do not warrant unequal consideration and unequal treatment. Equality between humans is for him a *moral ideal*, not something that is grounded in actual equality in intelligence and the like. But if this is the case, then why should differences in moral capacity or intelligence justify unequal consideration when it comes to animals? He writes: 'If possessing a higher degree of intelligence does not entitle one human to use another for his own ends, how can it entitle humans to exploit nonhumans?' Instead, what gives a creature the right to equal consideration is its *capacity for suffering and enjoyment*. We should give equal consideration to animals because animals can, like us, suffer pain and enjoy pleasure. He thinks that any other basis for concern – for example, intelligence or rationality – is arbitrary, and no better as a criterion for determining consideration than characteristics of race or gender.

If Singer is right, this would have significant effects on certain practices that involve giving unequal consideration to humans and non-humans. Consider raising and killing animals for food. This involves sacrificing the most important interests of animals – not to be mistreated, not to be killed – so that relatively trivial human interests – in eating meat – are satisfied. By the same token, animal experimentation – in the name of science, or to test whether certain substances are safe for humans – also involves giving unequal consideration. This is because we wouldn't perform similar experiments on human beings – such as orphaned infants – who have levels of intelligence and moral capacity below that of animals we do experiment on. So animal experimentation is impermissible.

Many people have found something persuasive in Singer's argument, so much so that it has played a central role in the animal rights movement – giving the lie to the common but mistaken claim that philosophers never contribute anything of practical value to the world! But it should not be surprising that some have found his argument, and certainly his conclusions about the possibility of experimentation on human infants, problematic. One criticism is that Singer's view isn't really a view about animal *rights* at all; instead, it proposes that we give to animals equal consideration, but allows (in line with consequentialist thinking on other matters) that the welfare

BOX 4.1 THE REPLACEABILITY ARGUMENT

In the nineteenth century an English philosopher called Leslie Stephen wrote: 'Of all the arguments for vegetarianism none is so weak as the argument from humanity. The pig has a stronger interest than anyone in the demand for bacon' (*Social Rights and Duties*, 2 vols (Cambridge: Cambridge University Press, 2011) [originally published in 1896]). This presents a rationale for eating meat on the grounds that the meat industry in fact *benefits* animals. For if people didn't eat meat, then the numbers of animals in existence would be drastically reduced: without the demand for bacon, many of the pigs currently alive would never have lived at all. So meat-eating is a benefit to the animals it brings into existence, assuming that they have a pleasant life on the whole. (This is why the argument only supports free-range farming, since factory-farmed animals have, we can assume, miserable lives.) This benefit balances out the loss that an animal that is killed suffers. So animals on this view are *replaceable*, without moral loss. Singer himself presents this argument in his book *Practical Ethics*, and (as you might imagine) raises objections to it. One is that it seems to imply that we have an obligation to bring (happy) human beings into existence, on the grounds that this benefits them. Another, more controversial, objection is that the same argument would seem to support the replaceability of human beings who are at a similar mental level; if so, then there is something seriously wrong with the argument itself.

of some animals can be overridden if the consequences are good enough. A different view, defended by the deontological philosopher Tom Regan in a book called *The Case for Animal Rights*, maintains that animals have *inherent value* or *worth*. For Regan, humans and animals alike have inherent value: for 'we are each of us the experiencing subject of a life, a conscious creature having an individual welfare that has importance to us whatever our usefulness to others' (1983:111). This means that animals must be treated with respect and as independently valuable, rather than as objects that can be used or exploited by humans, or sacrificed when some greater good is at stake. Such protection from harm by others, even when a greater good is at stake, is after all part of what it *means* to have a right. Those wishing to defend the idea that animals have genuine rights against mistreatment might therefore prefer to adopt a view like Regan's, rather than a view like Singer's.

A criticism that might be levelled against both Singer and Regan is that human life seems on the whole to be considerably more valuable than animal life, along a host of dimensions: our lives, but not theirs, include deep personal relationships, jobs, hobbies, cultural pursuits, sports, intellectual development, travel, and the like. And it can't be claimed that this is simple discrimination by the part of humans against animals. After all, it is plausible to claim that not all *animal* life has equal value;

dolphins seem more valuable than krill, for example. Finally, many people argue that Singer's conclusions about the practical implications of his argument do not follow. (You might want to ask yourself whether a similar argument can be made against a deontological perspective like Regan's.) Some propose that free-range animals are in fact *benefited* by the meat industry, since they are brought into existence as a result of the demand for meat; and it is better for an animal to have a few years of pleasant existence before death, than not to have ever existed at all. This is known as the 'replaceability argument' for continuing to eat meat. Moreover, since humans are in general more valuable than animals, this might warrant sacrificing animals through medical experiments when the interests of many more humans are at stake.

There are, of course, many other perspectives that are relevant to the debate about animal rights – just as there are, of course, many different considerations and arguments that are applicable to debates about euthanasia. However, one thing that I hope is again apparent, from the brief discussion of animal rights above, is that our thinking about this important issue will involve thinking about a whole host of important but difficult other moral issues: about the relative values of humans and animals, or about whether sentience is the only thing that really matters in a determination of moral duties and obligations. Here too applied ethics promises to clarify what is at issue in this debate, to direct our thinking in the right kinds of ways, and focus our deliberation on the right kinds of questions. It is difficult to see how this won't enable us to arrive at better answers to these and other moral questions. For we can only arrive at better answers if we understand what it is we are thinking about; and here, as elsewhere, moral philosophy is of the utmost importance.

• CHAPTER SUMMARY

- Applied ethics involves the close scrutiny of particular issues, rather than simply applying different normative theories.
- Questions in applied ethics are difficult, since they involve understanding the issue at hand, comparison of different values in play, and the relation between the issue and others in the subject.
- Euthanasia involves ending someone's life for that person's sake.
- We can distinguish voluntary, nonvoluntary, and involuntary euthanasia; we can also distinguish active and passive euthanasia.
- The relief of suffering and the promotion of autonomy speak in favour of some forms of euthanasia; but autonomy might also count against the practice.
- We owe some direct moral consideration to animals, since they are capable of feeling pain.
- Peter Singer argues that we own animals *equal* consideration, and that we should therefore stop eating meat and stop experimenting in animals.

• STUDY QUESTIONS

1 Why does applied ethics involve more than the simple application of normative theories to practical questions?
2 How does euthanasia differ from murder? How does it differ from suicide?
3 Is there any real moral difference between active and passive euthanasia?
4 Explain Singer's argument that 'all animals are equal' in your own words.
5 Is it morally permissible to eat free-range meat? If so, why? If not, why not?

• INTRODUCTORY READING

Glover, Jonathan (1990) *Causing Death and Saving Lives* (Harmondsworth: Penguin). [A clear, accessible, and provocative look at life-and-death moral issues and choices.]
Singer, Peter (1993) *Practical Ethics*, 2nd edn (Cambridge: Cambridge University Press). [Singer's popular and very clear introduction to some of the main issues in applied ethics, including his own views on animal rights.]

• ADVANCED FURTHER READING

Kuhse, Helga and Peter Singer (eds) (2006) *Bioethics: An Anthology*, 2nd edn (Oxford: Wiley-Blackwell). [A comprehensive and excellent collection of articles covering a wide range of bioethical topics, including abortion, euthanasia, and cloning.]
LaFollette, Hugh (ed) (2006) *Ethics in Practice*, 3rd edn (Oxford: Wiley-Blackwell). [Excellent anthology of classic papers on practical issues, with a helpful introduction. Features J. David Velleman's important paper 'Against the Right to Die'.]
Light, Andrew and Holmes Rolston III (eds) (2003) *Environmental Ethics: An Anthology* (Oxford: Wiley-Blackwell). [Another comprehensive collection from Blackwell, containing both classic and new essays, and covering central issues in environmental ethics.]
Regan, Tom (1983) *The Case for Animal Rights* (Oakland, CA: University of California Press). [An important and ground-breaking defence of the idea of animal rights from a deontological perspective.]
Singer, Peter (1975/1995) *Animal Liberation* (New York: Random House). [Singer's most popular book, arguing in favour of the ethical treatment of animals, and one of the main influences on the animal rights movement.]

• FREE INTERNET RESOURCES

A comprehensive list of links to work in applied ethics can be found at the site maintained by Chris MacDonald: http://users.ox.ac.uk/~worc0337/phil_topics_ethics.html.

The Utilitarianism website has links to a lot of Peter Singer's work to 2007 here: http://www.utilitarianism.net/singer/. News of his latest research can be found at his personal website: http://www.princeton.edu/~psinger/.

The *Stanford Encyclopedia of Philosophy* also has a number of excellent entries on issues in applied ethics: http://plato.stanford.edu/.

Part II
political philosophy

Thom Brooks

Political philosophy is a branch of philosophy that focuses on the power and institutional relations between individuals and groups. This Part looks at three essential areas within political philosophy presented in this Part's chapters. These are on freedom, justice and global justice.

The first chapter is about freedom. What does it mean to be *free*? We examine ideas concerning how we might understand ourselves to be free – where the results may be surprising. We next consider three different theories about how freedom should be understood. These are the ideas of positive freedom where to be free is to achieve some end or goal, negative freedom where to be free is to not be coerced or interfered with and republican freedom where to be free is to not be subjected to the domination of another. We also look at the idea of paternalism and what limits might be justified on our freedom, such as the risk of causing harm to others. The chapter closes by considering the relevance of our being alienated to our being free.

The second chapter focuses on justice. Justice concerns ideas about just distributions of things we value. This is clearly connected to ideas of freedom: just distributions are designed to be consistent with our freedom – so which view of freedom we support can impact on our favoured view about justice. The chapter begins by examining debates over whether our political obligation stems from our agreeing some kind of a 'social contract'. We next examine the most influential account of justice: John Rawls's justice as fairness. We then turn to critical alternatives. The first are the capabilities approaches by Amartya Sen and Martha Nussbaum. A second is feminism: we examine the perspectives of liberal feminists and radical feminists. A third is the multiculturalism of Bhikhu Parekh. The capabilities advocates claim Rawls works with an incomplete view about freedom. Multiculturalists argue philosophers like Rawls are wrong to see our differences as problems, but instead should embrace them. The chapter closes by considering once again the potential relevance of alienation for our theories of justice. Does and should it matter?

The final chapter in this Part examines the topic of global justice. This field in political philosophy has exploded in recent years and the area attracting the most attention. Whereas most, but significantly not all, theorising about justice in the history of political philosophy concerns justice within the state, there is increasing interest today in exploring justice beyond the state in international justice. We examine the views of statists and nationalists who argue that our group membership can have normative importance for us: how we came to be a member may have arisen arbitrarily, but the special connections we have to fellow group members can yield special duties that apply to co-members alone. This perspective is compared with cosmopolitans who argue that borders are arbitrary and mask the moral equality of individuals across states. The chapter closes with a look at climate change justice. We consider conservationist approaches, such as the idea of the ecological footprint and the polluter pays principles. These proposals aim to solve the problem of climate change by reducing emissions to a sustainable level. We also examine adaptation views which argue the problem is best solved through improved technology. If climate change is happening, which approach is best? The answer may be surprising.

The chapters in this Part can be read in any order. Each is also self-standing and does not presuppose you have any background knowledge of the topic gained beforehand. The topics are presented through questions and considered in a conversational style. My task is to inform you of key definitions, leading figures as well as ideas, and to clarify why the ideas considered are ideas worth considering. No effort is spent on listing concepts or dropping names in some ready list for their own sake. Instead, my goal is to inform *and interest* you, the reader, in political philosophy through considering freedom, justice and global justice. Your task – should you choose to accept it! – is only to reflect on the points raised as they arise. Don't skim or rush your way through. Philosophical ideas make best sense and easiest to remember when the ideas come *alive*. So let them and enjoy!

5

what is freedom?

- Introducing freedom
- Are we free – and how do we know it?
- Freedom and options
- Positive freedom
- Negative freedom
- Republican freedom
- The harm principle
- Freedom and alienation

INTRODUCING FREEDOM

This chapter focuses on the idea of **freedom**. What is it and how should it be understood? We begin by considering how we might know ourselves to be free, which is examined by Immanuel Kant. We also think about whether freedom is about having options or having options we prefer. This opens an interesting debate about whether we might be free to choose where our choices are second best or worse. We next critically examine three different theories of freedom: positive freedom (we are free when we can achieve some goal or end), negative freedom (we are free when we are *not* coerced or interfered with) and republican freedom (we are free when not subjected to the domination of others). You have to consider for yourself which is best! We then turn to John Stuart Mill's harm principle and ask if it provides a justified limit on the exercise of our freedom. The chapter closes considering the relevance of our being alienated to our being free.

ARE WE FREE – AND HOW DO WE KNOW IT?

So are *you* free? Think about it and what this question means. Some people might answer yes and others no. Those who argue might say that they do what they please without interference from others. This runs together two *different* ideas about what freedom is: the idea of *positive freedom* (that freedom is about our ability to achieve some goal) and the idea of *negative freedom* (that freedom is about our *not* being coerced or interfered with by others). So which might it be? And those who argue they aren't free might say it's because they feel trapped, but don't deny they make choices for themselves. This raises a third idea about what freedom is: the idea of *republican freedom* (that freedom is about our not coming under the domination of others). These are three different definitions about freedom that are important and we'll examine them more closely below. However, they don't address our more *fundamental* question: are we free – and how do we know we are free?

This question can be pursued from two perspectives. The first is historical. Benjamin Constant (1767–1830) distinguished between the *freedom of the ancients* versus the *freedom of the moderns*. The freedom of the ancients refers to the time of ancient Greece and the Roman Empire about 2,000 years ago. Constant argues that freedom was understood in a non-individualistic way. We would not talk about *my* freedom, but *our* freedom as a city. Freedom was secured by groups as a group. The freedom of the moderns refers to our modern understanding of freedom more recently. This is the idea that freedom is to be understood individually. So we talk today about individual freedom and not the freedom of the whole.

Constant's point is that today we think about freedom as moderns and not ancients – and there is no turning back. We understand freedom as the freedom of individuals not groups. We might talk loosely about *our* freedom together, but we are talking about the freedoms of our individual members as individuals. There's no turning back – or so Constant argues – because once this view of the moderns is adopted it permanently shapes our perspective and so even the intuition of freedom of and for a group is lost to us today.

Constant's distinction between the freedom of the ancients and the freedom of the moderns is useful for two reasons. The first is it helps us understand better the development of freedom in the work of philosophers over time. Plato and Aristotle didn't only present different arguments for freedom from contemporary philosophers, but these arguments have a different character altogether. Or so Constant argues. This can make it easier to grasp philosophical changes over time in your reading of the history of philosophy.

The second reason this distinction is useful is because it helps highlight the idea that freedom for us today – whatever else it may be – is a concept that applies to individuals. So when we think about what freedom is and whether we are free, it should be approached from the perspective of the individual. But this still doesn't tell us how we know we are free. Instead, Constant only says that freedom is understood by us as individual freedom. He's right, but we must probe deeper.

Think about freedom and how it might apply to you. Consider an exercise developed by Immanuel Kant (1724–1804). He examined the limits of what he called 'pure reason', exploring the boundaries of what rationality could achieve. Kant focuses on what he identifies as 'antinomies' of pure reason: instances where the use of reason alone cannot confirm or deny a particular state of affairs. One of these antinomies concerns freedom and Kant's analysis is as fascinating as it might be surprising.

Kant asks us first to consider the claim that we are free. This is the idea that we are each the cause of our own activities. You are reading this sentence now. But *what* is the cause of your doing this? Kant's first perspective on freedom is that we are free because we can assume we are the cause of what we do. Kant claims that through the use of our reasoning alone it cannot be denied that we are our own cause.

Kant next considers a second claim that states the opposite. This is the idea that there is no freedom. Instead, every action occurs according to laws of nature. We are not the cause of our activities, but rather they are natural reactions to the world around us. We might perceive directly this is true, but can it be absolutely ruled out 100 per cent through the use of our reason alone? Kant argues it cannot. This creates his antinomy: pure reason alone cannot prove with certainty that we are the cause of our freedom or rather that our freedom is an illusion. So which side should we choose?

We might go even further with this thought experiment. Suppose someone said to you that everything that happens in the world happens for a reason or that everything that takes place is pre-determined in advance by God. Could you disprove it? Kant's point is we cannot – or at least not through the use of our reasoning alone. Perhaps things do happen for a reason even though we don't always know what that reason is. Or maybe there is a divine plan we each act out in our lives: we think we're choosing our lives for ourselves, but really they have been decided for us. We could possibly argue back and forth seemingly forever about whether we are free to choose for ourselves or whether our freedom is an illusion. And this is Kant's point. But this doesn't mean he lacks an answer for how we should resolve this problem.

Kant argues that because reason alone cannot confirm with certainty our freedom we must use a second test. This is to ask ourselves: which perspective makes the world more intelligible? First imagine a world without freedom. Every action is not the responsibility of individuals, but the result of nature or it is pre-determined. Perhaps we cannot absolutely rule it out as a possibility through thought alone, but does it make best sense? Second, compare this with a world of freedom where individuals choose their actions and so might be accountable for the choices they make. Which perspective makes best sense *to you*? Consider an example: Cain stabs Abel and Abel dies. In a world without freedom, Cain might claim he could never be blamed for killing Abel or anyone else. He is unfree because his actions were not the result of his choice and so he should not be held responsible for Abel's death. But in a world with freedom where we assume we are each the cause of our actions, Cain can be blamed for killing Abel where he chose to do so. This is because he is exercising his freedom as the cause of his actions.

Kant's point is that our freedom must be assumed. This is because we cannot confirm or deny it through the use of reason alone. We then ask which perspective makes the world most intelligible. Kant argues our world is most intelligible when we assume individuals are free and not when we assume they lack freedom. Our assumption might turn out to be wrong, but it makes best sense of the world given the limits of our reasoning. We are free – we are the cause of what we do – and our freedom is assumed.

• FREEDOM AND OPTIONS

If we are free because it makes the world more intelligible, then what are we free to do? It is common to believe that we have freedom where we have *options*. This is the claim that freedom requires choice. If we do not have options to choose from, then we cannot be free. Imagine Alice is in a bank to withdraw cash from her account. A gunman enters the bank and threatens Alice by saying 'either hand me all of the cash from your account or you will be killed!'. Most of us probably agree that Alice has no choice: her only option is to agree to the gunman's threat. Alice lacks options and so is not free to act in this case.

There is a famous counterexample by Thomas Hobbes (1588–1679). Suppose sailors find themselves on a sinking ship. The only way they can save themselves from drowning and safely reach shore is by throwing their valuable cargo overboard. This would make the boat less heavy and save their lives. After they reach the shore, the ship's owner asks about what happened to the missing cargo. The sailors say they had to throw it overboard because they had no choice. In short, the sailors say they were unfree. Why? Because they had no option but to get rid of the cargo so they could avoid drowning.

Hobbes argues the sailors are wrong and that, in fact, they are free to do otherwise. Hobbes's point is that the sailors *did* have options: they could throw the cargo overboard and save their lives *or* they could not have done so and risk drowning at sea. Freedom is about our having options whatever they might be. Perhaps the sailors only valued one option, namely, to save their lives and avoid drowning. Hobbes doesn't disagree that one option is more preferable to the other. Nor is it disputed that many, if not all of us, would do the same in that situation. But his point is that freedom is about *having* options and not *what* the options are.

Let's think again about Alice and the gunman in the bank. We might think that Alice is unfree and has no choice: if she does not obey the gunman, then she risks his making good on his threat to kill her. But Hobbes's claim is that Alice is free because she has alternative possibilities. She might obey the gunman, but she can also do otherwise. Alice has a choice. It may not be a good choice. Both options might be awful and non-ideal. But there are options and where there are options then there is freedom. Alice is free even in a situation like that.

Hobbes's claim is controversial. It runs against our common intuitions about what freedom should look like. Moreover, we often link freedom with *responsibility*, which we saw already in our discussion of Kant on freedom. To understand an individual as free is to see them as having choices and so having some responsibility for the choices they make. Legal systems typically would find someone under duress innocent of most crimes largely because duress can significantly limit the responsibility – and so significantly limit the freedom – of affected individuals.

But Hobbes's view is also controversial because when we think about freedom as our having options we have a tendency to assume the options that count are those worth choosing. Not all options are the same. Sailors on a sinking ship have options in theory, but we might think they don't in practice. This is because they – as well as you and I – would only ever choose to save our lives and never opt to drown if given that choice. Likewise, a gunman in a bank gives us an option strictly speaking – 'your money or your life!' – but we would only choose to hand over our money and not opt to risk death in that situation. Options matter, but we often believe some options count more than others. But how or why?

Imagine you want to purchase a particular car and have the money to pay for it. You are provided with two or three options that include the particular car you want to own. Are you free to choose? Yes, and it is because the particular car you want is an option. Now imagine the same situation, but you lack the ability to pay for the particular car you want. You might think your freedom is curtailed because your options are non-ideal and the particular car you most value is now out of reach. Should it matter which options we have for freedom?

Harry Frankfurt (1929–) examines the relation between freedom and the options we can choose. Sam is an addict. He must feed his addiction daily and he lacks the ability to stop without intervention by others. Sam's addiction looks like a clear case of someone without freedom. He has one, and only one, option: to satisfy his addiction each day.

But suppose that Sam is a happy addict. He cannot choose to act differently. He has only one option and that is to feed his daily addiction. Nevertheless, Sam would not choose a different option even if he could do so. So Sam has one, and only one, option and it is the only option he wants. Is Sam free to continue his addiction even though he cannot do otherwise? Does it even make sense to say we can be free without having another choice?

Frankfurt's famous example of the happy addict highlights serious questions about freedom and options. Freedom is often thought to be about our having alternative possibilities to choose from – freedom is having options. But we also often give greater weight to options that matter for us. So it's not simply a matter of having choice, but the choices we have to pick from. This is a subject for much debate in philosophy and I won't take a side in it here. But it is helpful – and challenging – to reflect more carefully on what *you* believe matters for freedom, and the hypothetical examples of sinking ships and the happy addict may help us sharpen our own view about how we should think about this.

BOX 5.1 WHICH OPTIONS COUNT?

Freedom is often thought to be about options, but which options should count? Suppose you are comparing supermarkets looking to purchase ice cream. One supermarket has five different flavours of ice cream to choose from. The second supermarket has six different flavours. The second supermarket has more options than the first. So are you freer in choosing ice cream at the second supermarket? Think about it. Does freedom consist in having more options or should it matter which options you have? Imagine you're looking specifically for cookie dough ice cream and only the first supermarket has it. Are you freer at the first supermarket because it has the one option you most want? Or suppose a third supermarket opens that carries only one variety of ice cream – and it's cookie dough ice cream. Do you have equal freedom in either the first and third supermarkets?

I list these questions to make you *think* about your own intuitions regarding freedom. If freedom is about our options, then we must come to some view about whether more options means more freedom or not. We must also consider whether some options might count for more than others and why. Is it because some options achieve more important ends or satisfy certain desires? Or should such considerations not count? If you only prefer one option, is freedom satisfied where it is available? Or not? Freedom and options raise important questions about everyday concerns like our freedom to buy goods or our freedom to choose universities for further study. What do you think about it?

• POSITIVE FREEDOM

We now turn to the three leading views about freedom: positive freedom, negative freedom and republican freedom. We start with **positive freedom**. This is the idea that freedom is about achieving some goal or end. It is a *positive* view of freedom insofar as it is about the ability to make an achievement. For example, we might say that we each have a 'freedom to an education' or 'freedom to health care'. These claims state we are free to achieve an education or receive health care. A freedom to vote entails the ability to vote.

T. H. Green (1836–82) is the most influential defender of positive freedom. He says freedom is 'a positive power or capacity of doing or enjoying something worth doing or enjoying' (1986: 199). Positive freedom is not the ability to do *anything* or make any choice, but rather the ability to achieve goals and ends worth achieving. It matters which options we have and what they can permit us to do.

Green argues our individual freedom should not be considered separately from the freedoms of others in society. All freedom is the freedom of individuals, but each person shares a set of goals and ends which Green calls their *common good*. Think about it. Everyone might want to exercise freedoms to education, health care or play sport in different ways. Green doesn't deny this. His point is that each expresses differently similar kinds of freedoms, such as the freedom to education and so on. This means that if these freedoms are commonly shared (even if expressed in different ways by each individual), and they are positive freedoms worth achieving, then they require some means of protection. This guarantees their availability for all.

This leads Green – controversially – to argue that our individual freedom is best promoted within a state. It may seem counterintuitive to say the state can be necessary to ensure we are each free. After all, many criticise the state for infringing the freedoms of individuals. The state seems only a source of limiting freedoms and not promoting them. But Green is no fan of an activist state: in fact, he supports a minimal state. His claim is not that the state knows best, but that together our shared social and political institutions can achieve what we cannot individually: secure the promotion of our individual freedom by protecting our shared, common good through the law and social institutions. The state can have a role to play in ensuring our positive freedom flourishes.

BOX 5.2 WHO IS T. H. GREEN?

Thomas Hill Green (1836–82) was a moral and political philosopher at the University of Oxford more famous for what he brought about than credited. Green was a founding figure in British Idealism, a movement dominant in Britain from the late nineteenth century until about the First World War. Green and other British Idealists were the first to teach and advocate the work of Immanuel Kant and G. W. F. Hegel to an English-speaking audience. Today, Kant and Hegel are widely viewed as canonical figures in Anglo-American philosophy, but the role of British Idealists in bringing this about is rarely recognised.

Green attempted to develop ideas from Kant's and Hegel's philosophies in his own work and life. He took seriously the need for philosophy to be alive to present concerns and connect with others. This led Green to become the first Oxford don to run and win election on Oxford's city council. He became famous as an advocate for temperance and claimed that banning the sale of alcohol would help all citizens achieve positive freedom.

Green's conviction that ethics and political philosophy were not only about how we should *think* about such issues in the seminar room, but about what we must *do* about them in wider society is a perhaps all too rare example of how academic philosophers can and perhaps should make philosophy more accessible and relevant.

• NEGATIVE FREEDOM

The leading alternative to positive freedom is **negative freedom**. This is the idea that freedom is our *not* being coerced or interfered with by others. Negative freedom defines itself *negatively* in terms of what it is *not*. (This is opposite from how positive freedom views itself: as a *positive* source of achievement.) Negative freedom is easiest to remember as a concept of freedom that identifies what it is through what it isn't.

Negative freedom's most influential defender is Sir Isaiah Berlin (1909–97). He argues:

> I am normally said to be free to the degree to which no man or body of men interferes with my activity. Political liberty in this sense is simply the area within which a man can act unobstructed by others…You lack political liberty or freedom only if you are prevented from attaining a goal by human beings.
>
> (Berlin 1969: 122)

Let's unpack this quotation. Berlin claims to be appealing to our common-sense intuitions about what freedom is about. Imagine a case of someone *lacking* freedom. Think about what freedom *is not*. Berlin bets that at its heart we think about freedom as our *not* being constrained. Freedom is not being handcuffed or tied to a tree. And so freedom is about not being fettered in these kinds of ways in general. To talk about freedom without reference to coercion – as Berlin claims is the case with positive freedom – is to miss something significant about what we immediately consider freedom to be.

Berlin argues that we are free when others do not coerce or interfere with us. To be coerced or interfered with is not to be free. Note the importance of viewing freedom's limits, where others intervene on our ability to choose for ourselves. It is where other people constrain us that freedom ends. This has some intuitive appeal. Few would argue that if a police officer handcuffs a criminal the criminal is somehow free. Instead, we'd say the criminal's freedom is constrained because his or her freedom of movement is interfered with by the actions of the police officer. It doesn't matter if the criminal is in fact innocent: either way the person lacks freedom because of coercion or interference by another.

But how important is it that our freedom is limited by other people? Imagine you're walking through a park and come across a narrow path. The wind is so strong that you're unable to cross it – each time you attempt it the wind knocks you down and forces you backwards. So are you *free* to enter through the path? This seems to cause a problem for negative freedom if you accept what Berlin suggests above that coercion or interference must come from another person. But there seems no compelling reason to argue for this. Your movement *is* interfered with – by the strong winds – and so, if negative freedom is about freedom as *not* coercion or interference, it seems clear that case should count as a kind of non-freedom.

There is a final point. Berlin criticises positive freedom's defenders for advocating a view of freedom contrary to our common-sense intuitions and which fails to account sufficiently for coercion. But he also claims positive freedom is mistaken because it runs together different concepts under the single umbrella conceptual term 'freedom' and so make a conceptual mistake. Berlin says: 'Everything is what it is: liberty is liberty, not equality of fairness or justice or culture, or human happiness or a quiet conscience' (1969: 125). When positive freedom's defenders talk about a freedom to education *as a kind of freedom* why do they say this? Is it because doing so renders us more equal? Or is it more fair and just? Or will it lead to greater happiness? Berlin argues these may each be noble ends and valuable to achieve. But our understanding of one should be considered separately from the others. Perhaps education for all is what we should accomplish as a community. But this is not about freedom *per se* or maybe not at all. Berlin demands that we separate our study of freedom from other concepts in order to understand freedom much better. He does not argue that freedom is not related to concerns about education, health care and other issues. Instead, Berlin is only claiming that positive freedom's view of freedom is too wide because it considers much more than freedom alone, and so is conceptually incoherent.

But is positive freedom counterintuitive and incoherent? Consider one consequence for Berlin's position on negative freedom. We can be free to receive an education – according to Berlin's idea of negative freedom – even where it is impossible for us to achieve it. Does this make sense? Suppose education is free for everyone in your country. There is nothing to pay and places in schools will always be made available. But all the schools are located so far away in a distant city that you're unable to travel to them daily to receive the education available for you because of the costs. No one is coercing you or interfering with your freedom. Negative freedom is not compromised: in fact, the option is available to you. But it is an option you could never exercise and so cannot choose even if you wanted to. Does it make sense to say you are free to do something forever beyond your reach? Or would you argue – as Green might – that you are not free to enjoy this education because you are unable to achieve it? Which side do you find most compelling? Can you see why philosophers continue to debate which is preferable?

• REPUBLICAN FREEDOM

Let us now consider a third view of freedom: **republican freedom**. Note immediately that this is about republicanism with a lower case 'r': it is not the republicanism of the Republican Party in the United States. It isn't about any political party. Republicanism is 'republican' in the sense that it derives from a view of freedom found originally in ancient Rome.

Philip Pettit (1945 –) defines republican freedom by citing the influential eighteenth-century work *Letters of Cato*: 'Liberty is, to live upon one's own Terms; Slavery is, to live at the mere Mercy of another' (Pettit 1999: 33). Pettit defends republican freedom as a theory about freedom as non-domination. He considers the different ways in which freedom is *not*. Pettit agrees with negative liberty proponents that coercion can be a limit on our freedom. But Pettit rejects the idea that every coercion renders us unfree. For example, the law prohibits murder. Anyone who commits murder will be convicted and sentenced. Imprisonment is a clear case of coercive interference on individual freedom. But are we limiting the freedom of murderers when we imprison them?

Pettit argues that in cases like this the limits we impose on our individual activities may be coercive, but they need not be understood as interfering with our freedoms. We should decide such cases through public deliberation: we engage with each other using reasons for one policy or another. This active sense of democracy is an activity where we can together come to shared views about agreed limits to the exercise of freedom. These limits are not so much interferences with our freedom, but rather define the boundaries of what we are free and not free to do. So interference with our actions can be a violation of our freedom, but not all interferences are. It depends on what activity we're talking about. Which we select can change over time and depends on what our common agreement is. Pettit's emphasis on the importance for deliberation is what he calls our discursive control – our control over policy outcomes through public deliberation.

The importance for Pettit's republican theory of freedom is that it spells out an alternative to positive and negative conceptions of freedom. Positive freedom is about what we can achieve. Negative freedom is about our being free when *not* coerced or interfered with by others. In contrast, republican freedom is about non-domination. Pettit's argument is that domination takes place where power is exercised over us arbitrarily. A tyrant (and enemy of republics) is a clear example. The tyrant exercises domination over his subjects by enforcing any law at any time and in any way. His subjects lack a say over the laws that govern them and how they are administered. This form of dominion is an evil that republican freedom opposes.

Freedom as non-domination is not about the absence of law or governments. Instead, it is about the people subjected to the law having a say about it and its exercise. Republican freedom is about the people having discursive control through public deliberation over the ways in which their freedoms are defined. The fact that the law may forbid me from doing one thing or another is not a case of non-freedom *if, and only if*, that law is a product of our discursive control over what the law is. To be non-dominated is not to live without a rule of law, but have a rule of law that is not arbitrarily imposed from above.

● THE HARM PRINCIPLE

So what is the proper boundary for where our freedom begins and ends? Republicanism has offered one view – freedom as non-domination – but is there another way to think about this? This leads us to consider *paternalism* more widely. Paternalism is about justified interferences with our freedom.

The best known and influential view of paternalism is presented by John Stuart Mill (1806–73) in his famous **harm principle**. Mill argues:

> The object of this essay is to assert one very simple principle...That principle is that the sole end for which mankind are warranted, individually or collectively, in interfering with the liberty of action of any of their number is self-protection. That the only purpose for which power can be rightfully exercised over any member of a civilised community, against his will, is to prevent harm to others. His own good, either physical or moral, is not a sufficient warrant.
>
> (1989: 13)

Mill defends this idea in his essay *On Liberty*, published originally in 1859, which is devoted to examining the harm principle and its application. Mill views the harm principle as a 'simple' principle at its heart: the only legitimate justification for restraining freedom is to prevent harm to others. That's it.

Mill argues that the prevention of harm to others trumps other possible justifications. These possibilities include the idea that limiting another's liberty – where no one is clearly otherwise harmed by it – is for his or her own good. Part of the reason for this is that there is such wide disagreement about what constitutes the good for every individual. For liberals like Mill valuing individual freedom most highly, no single individual's idea of the good is intrinsically more valuable than the considered judgement of any other individual. So it is best to leave it to each individual to determine his or her own good for his or her own self. Others may provide useful advice, but they should not be in any position to limit how we each determine our own good for ourselves.

But this freedom to choose our own good for ourselves is subject to a condition. If our activity should cause or threaten to cause harm to others, then this is not permitted and so beyond the boundaries of the permissible exercise of our individual freedom. This is meant to leave open sufficiently widely the large range of ways in which we might pursue our own distinct understanding of our individual good.

The main concern to be raised though is about what constitutes a 'harm'. Mill believes he offers us a clear justifiable limitation, but can we discover where we should draw the line? One distinction to draw is that not all harms to others should be prevented. I'm 100 per cent against boxing: I'd like to see it banned, in part because of the harm inflicted on boxers by each other. But I'm in a small minority. Many people may not like boxing or claim it's their favourite sport, but relatively few call for it to become illegal. Boxing is an example of where harm to others should not be prevented, or so most people think. If this is correct, then limiting freedom to where it may cause harm to others is too wide because it will include cases, such as boxing, that we wouldn't want covered.

Another way of thinking about harm is harm to morals. It may seem to make sense: many of the things we ban are often viewed as immoral. Few think murder and theft are always justified: instead, these are cases of actions that many of us are happy to be treated as illegal precisely because they are wrongs. But Mill is critical of this perspective for good reason. Whose view of what is moral should count? Perhaps we generally agree on the wrongness of murder and theft, but what about other crimes? Mill's point is that our individual decisions about our individual good should be reserved to our individual conscience. It's only where it may cause or threaten to cause harm to others that we should agree this is a step too far. To argue harm to others should take the form of harm to the *morals* of others appears to be outside what Mill has in mind.

Perhaps a better way of understanding the harm principle is not as a harm to others *in general* or a harm to the *morals* held by others, but instead as a harm to the *autonomy* of others. Reconsider the example of boxing. The reason why many would permit boxing – and what makes this kind of harming more acceptable – is because its participants *consent* to it. So perhaps there is a real risk of physical injury. What matters most is whether we consent to this risk or not. If we do, then any harm that takes place may seem of less importance.

This idea that consent matters for thinking about harm is consistent with Mill's insistence that our conscience is for each one of us to decide for ourselves. This not only helps us make sense of how the harm principle could permit harms arising in contact sports, but also other activities from surgery to ear piercings and tattoos. The fact that an injury might arise need not entail there is no freedom to run its risk. Even if we accept the harm principle, what matters is whether there is a harm to autonomy and the autonomous decisions of others. The line may still be difficult to draw, but we can have a clearer idea about what kind of line we're drawing.

BOX 5.3 WHICH HARMS COUNT?

Mill argues for a harm principle that claims the justified limit on our freedom is where it causes or threats to cause harm to others. It seems a simple idea, but is it?

There are several ways we might think about *harm*. The first is harm to others. The question is: what harms should count? It is clear that many different kinds of harms are widely permissible, from harms arising in contact sports to piercing. So we should try to narrow our understanding of harm.

A second way to think about harm is as a harm *to the morals* of others. The questions here are: *which* morals and *who* decides? It is easy to find much overlap. We widely agree that some actions can be violations of morality, such as murder or theft. But what about others, especially more controversial cases like drug use or prostitution?

A third way to think about harm is as a harm *to the autonomy* of others. We now consider the role that *consent* plays in determining whether someone is subjected to harm. If they have consented to it, then their autonomy may not be harmed and so the harm principle does not apply. This opens up questions about what can and cannot be consented to: for example, could we ever consent to give up our autonomy permanently by agreeing to become someone else's slave? Most argue that you cannot. In any event, harm to autonomy can make better sense of why consensual participation in contact sports or body piercing is not a kind of harm we should prevent.

Finally, keep in mind that Mill is talking about *harm to others*. This is sometimes referred to as other-regarding harms. These are the harms that one person does or threatens to another. Most harms we think about take that form: murder and theft are two examples. But there is also *harm to self* or self-regarding harms. These include suicide and self-injury. These are not directly included by Mill's harm principle because they are about harming ourselves whereas the harm principle focuses on harm to others. The question for *you* to consider is: should harm to self count, too?

Mill challenged utilitarianism from within. He argued that not all pleasures were equal because some were more important, or 'higher', than others. Better to be a dissatisfied Socrates than a satisfied pig, or so he once claimed.

BOX 5.4 WHO IS J. S. MILL?

John Stuart Mill (1806–73) is one of the most influential philosophers of the nineteenth century. He was the son of James Mill, who was a close associate of Jeremy Bentham who founded utilitarianism. Utilitarians like Bentham and Mill's father argued that public affairs should be based on the Greatest Happiness Principle. They claimed people calculated the *utility* arising from their decisions to maximise their happiness and minimise their pain.

Mill's most influential contribution is his harm principle: the idea that harm to others is the only justified interference on our freedom. He advocated this in numerous forums. Mill briefly served as a Member of Parliament in the UK – failing to win re-election after about three years in office – and his best-known speech was in favour of capital punishment. Part of Mill's argument is that the death penalty is justified because it would deter potential murderers from performing murder. This would both maximise the freedom of all and even that of potential murderers because they would become more likely not to carry through on their intention to kill another.

• FREEDOM AND ALIENATION

Let us close by considering something a final issue. This is the relation between freedom and alienation. Can we be free and yet feel alienated from others? Usually, we might think of being free as something positive (even if not positive freedom) or perhaps enjoyable. So can we have freedom but be alienated from others?

The problem of alienation is not usually considered or even recognised by most philosophers on freedom. Nor is its connection to freedom obvious. Perhaps the best depiction of alienation and the issues it raises for freedom are captured by G. W. F. Hegel (1770–1831). He says:

> When a large mass of people sinks below the level of a certain standard of living…that feeling of right, integrity and honour which comes from supporting oneself by one's own activity and work is lost. This leads to the creation of a *rabble*.
>
> (1991: 266)

The rabble are characterised by a feeling of disconnection. They lack a sense of self-worth and this arises through the poverty of their living standards. Hegel appears to connect living in poverty with a sense of alienated discontent for the have-nots.

This passage has led many to refer to this as Hegel's so-called problem of poverty. But it is a mistake to think the central issue is our material wealth (or its lack). Hegel continues: 'Poverty in itself does not reduce people to a rabble; a rabble is created only by the disposition associated with poverty, by inward rebellion against the rich, against society, the government, etc.' (Hegel 1991: 266). Hegel is clear: it is not our material circumstances that make us members of a rabble, but instead our *convictions* about how we relate to others in our community. Individuals lacking material wealth may be more likely to view themselves as members of a rabble, but anyone rich or poor could join it.

Hegel considers the rabble's alienation as a conviction about the self and others. It is a view that believes that I will not be heard no matter how loud my voice and that my contribution will be ignored no matter my efforts. To be alienated is to possess a conviction about one's separation from others and to not identify oneself with others: the alienated are the preyed upon and the acted upon.

Note that the rabble may be wrong about their disconnection. I might have a conviction that my voice will never be heard, but this is not to say I lack opportunities to try. I might simply fail to notice the ways in which my voice is heard. We can be alienated even if others in our society do not actively promote or desire it.

So how does this relate to freedom? Consider republican freedom and its idea that freedom is non-domination. I am free where I have opportunities to deliberate publicly with others about the laws and policies that govern us. This makes the laws and policies chosen as non-arbitrary and so non-dominating: they may limit the exercise of our freedom, but only to map out freedom's boundaries as we – the community's members – see fit.

Now suppose I have the conviction that I am alienated from the community. I have the option to participate in public deliberations, but know (or at least have a firm conviction about knowing) that my say will count for little and be fruitless. I'm wasting my time and will not – even cannot – influence outcomes. Republicans would see such a person as free. No one forces anyone to take part in public deliberation. But so long as it is genuinely open to all, those who fail to participate have only themselves to blame. Republicans can say that those who are alienated – who have a conviction that society is run by others, for others and unresponsive to my input – are free. Even if they are convinced they are not. This is likewise true for negative freedom's defenders. So long as no one is coercing me or interfering with my activities, I am free even if I have a conviction about my alienation.

Positive freedom seems different. If freedom is about what we can achieve and I have a conviction about my alienation from others, then this may place limits on what I can achieve because of my alienation. It may not be too surprising to find positive freedom potentially more responsive to this problem raised by Hegel given that positive freedom's best known defender, Green, was an advocate of Hegelian philosophy!

But this final point remains. There are different ways of characterising freedom. Each has its merits and limitations. The question to consider is: does our conviction matter for freedom? How we think about freedom will shape the answers we give – and possibly help us understand freedom from new perspectives.

● SUMMARY

- Are we essentially free or are our actions determined? Immanuel Kant argues that the use of pure reason alone cannot answer this question. Our freedom should be assumed because this makes best sense of our relations with others.
- There is a debate over the relation of freedom and options. Thomas Hobbes claims we are free so long as we have options to choose from. But some argue that to be free we must have options worth choosing from.
- Positive freedom understands freedom as the ability to do or achieve something.
- Negative freedom claims freedom consists in our *not* being coerced or interfered with by others.

- Republican freedom says we are free when we are not dominated. This is understood in terms of our having discursive control.
- John Stuart Mill argues that the harm principle is a compelling limit on the exercise of freedom. The principle claims we are not free to harm others for any reason.
- The problem of alienation can have some importance for freedom. This is because to be free is not only to have an option to choose from, but the conviction that there are options available.

• STUDY QUESTIONS

1 How do *you* know yourself to be free?
2 Does freedom require we have *any* options or only the options we *prefer*?
3 Is freedom best understood as what you are able to achieve (positive freedom) or the absence of coercion (negative freedom)?
4 How is republican freedom different from negative freedom?
5 Are there any justified limits on our freedom, such as the harm principle?

• INTRODUCTORY FURTHER READING

Carter, I., M. Kramer and H. Steiner (eds) (2006) *Freedom: A Philosophical Anthology* (Oxford: Blackwell). [The most comprehensive collection of readings on liberty available.]

Mill, J. S. (1989) *On Liberty and Other Writings* (Cambridge: Cambridge University Press). [Defends one of political philosophy's most well-known and influential ideas: the harm principle.]

Miller, D. (ed.) (2006) *The Liberty Reader* (London: Paradigm). [Excellent introduction and key readings on liberty by contemporary and historical features. Essential readings on this topic.]

• ADVANCED FURTHER READING

Berlin, Isaiah (1969) *Four Essays on Liberty* (Oxford: Oxford University Press). [Ground-breaking work in the philosophy of freedom both influential and controversial.]

Dimova-Cookson, M. (2003) 'A New Scheme of Positive and Negative Freedom: Re-constructing T. H. Green on Freedom', *Political Theory* 31: 508–32. [Excellent analysis of positive and negative freedom that defends a revised view of Green's theory of freedom.]

Frankfurt, H. (1969) 'Alternate Possibilities and Moral Responsibility', *Journal of Philosophy* 66: 829–39. [Classic essay exploring whether freedom consists in our having options or having the option we desire.]

Green, T. (1986) *Lectures on the Principles of Political Obligation and Other Writings* (Cambridge: Cambridge University Press). [The key defence of the positive theory of freedom and leading alternative to negative theories of freedom.]

Hegel, G. W. F. (1991) *Elements of the Philosophy of Right* (Cambridge: Cambridge University Press). [Hegel is widely regarded as one of the most important, yet also one of the most difficult, philosophers in the canon. His Philosophy of Right develops a philosophy of freedom and how it informs our views of self, other and community. A major contribution to how we might understand alienation as a problem for freedom.]

Kant, I. (1996) *Critique of Pure Reason* (Indianapolis: Hackett). [A complex and significant contribution to our understanding of several areas of philosophy. Claims our freedom is intelligible, but cannot be confirmed through pure reasoning alone.]

Pettit, P. (1999) *Republicanism: A Theory of Freedom and Government* (Oxford: Oxford University Press). [Major philosophical contribution to republican theories of freedom. Defends republican freedom as a theory of non-domination.]

• FREE INTERNET RESOURCES

Carter, I. (2012) 'Positive and Negative Liberty', *Stanford Encyclopedia of Philosophy*, http://plato.stanford.edu/entries/liberty-positive-negative/. [An excellent overview of both positive freedom and negative freedom.]

Dworkin, G. (2014) 'Paternalism', *Stanford Encyclopedia of Philosophy*, http://plato.stanford.edu/entries/paternalism/. [Useful overview and critical examination of different views about paternalism, including the harm principle.]

Lovett, F. (2014) 'Republicanism', *Stanford Encyclopedia of Philosophy*, http://plato.stanford.edu/entries/republicanism/. [Accessible introduction to republican theories of freedom both past and present.]

O'Connor, T. (2010) 'Free Will', *Stanford Encyclopedia of Philosophy*, http://plato.stanford.edu/entries/freewill/. [Recommended introduction to issues concerning the nature of freedom and how freedom might be understood.]

6
what is justice?

- Introducing justice
- The social contract
- Rawls's principles of justice
- Political liberalism
- The capabilities approach
- Feminism
- Multiculturalism
- The stakeholder society

INTRODUCING JUSTICE

This chapter examines the topic of **justice**. But what is it? Justice is about ideas regarding legitimate distributions of things we value. Justice and freedom are connected: which distribution we find most compelling will vary depending on our favoured view about freedom. The idea of a social contract creating duties binding on all contracting individuals is historically a venerable view of political obligation that remains so today. Perhaps the most influential contemporary view of justice is defended by John Rawls. We examine his claims about which principles should count as principles of justice. We also consider how his idea of political liberalism meant to account for the pluralist nature of contemporary societies.

Not everyone is convinced by Rawls's account. We look at three groups of critics. The first group consists of advocates of the capabilities approaches defended in different ways by Amartya Sen and Martha Nussbaum. The second group consists of feminists and we will examine liberal feminists and radical feminists. The third group comprises multiculturalists such as Bhikhu Parekh who see our differences as something that should be embraced and not a problem. We close our analysis by considering anew the problem of alienation and its potential relevance for how we think about justice.

● THE SOCIAL CONTRACT

What justifies political obligation? Put simply: why should citizens obey the state? The most famous answer is because we have agreed to obey through a **social contract**. The idea of the social contract has a long history in philosophy and can be traced back to Plato. However, the best-known defence of the social contract is offered by Jean-Jacques Rousseau (1712–78).

Rousseau begins from the premise that every person is born free. The problem is that conflicts will arise over time between individuals ranging from questions of who might owe what to whom to more substantial matters concerning the proper relations between individuals living in community. This cannot be left to each person to decide for himself or herself. This is because we might pursue only our private self-interest, which is arbitrary and applied haphazardly. Instead, we must try to find some principled way of forging agreement among citizens whereby each has his or her own private interests.

Rousseau argues that each individual should agree to *not* determine disputes from the vantage point of private interest, but instead all should accept a social contract binding on everyone that commits its members to abiding by a *general will*. The general will is the substantive interest shared by every citizen in the community. Because it is shared by everyone, it can serve as a common basis for resolving disputes.

The general will is distinguished from a common will. The common will is determined by asking citizens to vote for the option that best satisfies their private self-interest. Perhaps one option receives more votes than another. This can only be justified as a legitimate obligation on all members if, in fact, the winning option is determined by its connection to the general will that everyone shares.

So when do we have a decision consistent with the general will or common will? This can be difficult to tell. Rousseau argues that a majority vote can *usually* indicate that is the view of the general will on an issue, but it is open to error. The people who decide are you and me – those citizens with a voice. The problem is we must each separate our private self-interests from our collective, general will. I should only vote for tax cuts where it benefits the substantial interest of all and not because I will benefit personally from it. But nor is the general will meant to be idealised. It is not about choosing what the community *should* obligate its members to do en route to creating a paradise on Earth, but addressing the general will *as it is* (and not how it should be) *here and now*.

Rousseau's idea of the general will speaks to debates concerning representation. Should elected representations for a particular community try to gain the best deal for their community possibly at the expense of others? This is closer to following the common will. Instead, the general will perspective supports representatives who may vote for measures that address the shared, common good of all and even where it might undermine the community they represent. In short, the general will is about remaining concerned with the whole rather than only its parts in isolation from the whole.

The idea of the social contract has been influential because it grounds our political obligation on *consent*. The reason why we should obey our state is because we consent to its having the authority to do so. We must all consent to this arrangement in order to be bound to it. So if we don't accept a social contract and refuse to consent to it, then we should move to another community which has a social contract we can consent to. But whatever problems we might have in distinguishing the general will from particular self-interest, this claim that the law binds us because we consent to it is a powerful one.

It also has its critics. One concern is that a social contract might have been agreed at some time in the past giving rise to a new political community. But then why should you and I today – people who weren't there at the state's founding – be obligated by the consent of our ancestors to a past agreement? A second concern is the form consent should take: what does it mean to consent to a social contract? Must there be words said or some special ceremony in some explicit declaration? Or should our consent be *implied* in virtue of our living in a community – so the bare fact we live *here* justifies our having obligations to our community? Another concern is that social contract theorists – often called *contractarians* – often speak about the social contract as a specific document. The problem is that philosophers, like Rousseau, appealing to the idea of a social contract argue for a useful fiction: we should view ourselves *as if* we consented to a contract binding each of us together in a social contract. But where can we find this hypothetical contract?

So perhaps the social contract is a useful thought experiment that provides one claim about political obligation – that it is derived from individual consent – it might not be more than that. Or is it?

BOX 6.1 DO SOCIAL CONTRACTS EXIST?

Social contract theories are often criticised for their being hypothetical constructs. Some contractarians build influential theories about justice on the foundation of some past, long-ago imaginary meeting that never happened. So it's tempting – at least from one level – to write off social contract theories as implausible or worse.

But this could be a mistake. It is true the idea of the social contract is a powerfully influential idea and this has led to some attempts to put this idea into practice. There are several examples. Perhaps one is the Magna Carta (1215). This 'Great Charter' limited the powers of the king through a declaration of publicly acknowledged rights and liberties that was signed by many of those directly affected.

Other examples come from the United States, such as the Declaration of Independence and US Constitution. We might find most constitutions examples of social contracts: they spell out our political and legal agreement by common consent and command our obedience in light of the consent they are granted.

• RAWLS'S PRINCIPLES OF JUSTICE

John Rawls (1921–2002) is the most influential political philosopher from the last century. His work developing a new theory of justice – which Rawls calls **justice as fairness** – and building on insights from earlier philosophers literally revolutionised the field and sparked new interest in political philosophy that has continued since. What importance is given to political philosophy today is in no small measure a product of Rawls's contribution to the subject.

Rawls begins from a similar starting point as Rousseau. How to understand a just society for all? What fair system of cooperation over time could deservedly win the acceptance of citizens? Rawls accepts the need for a social contract, but he develops it with a twist. While Rousseau appeals to a hypothetical contract agreed at some time in the past, Rawls uses a simple thought experiment that you and I can engage with at any time which can make the idea of a social contract more relevant and alive to our present concerns.

Rawls asks us to *imagine* we're in the original position. There is no set number, but there are several of us present. Our goal in the original position is to agree principles of political justice that will constrain the legitimate activities of our community. Rawls says nothing about how many they might be or what they are in advance. But before continuing, pause and consider this question: which, if any, principles of justice do *you* think should be agreed?

One challenge for Rousseau's conception of the social contract is its claim that we should follow the general will. The problem is it's difficult to steer clear of private self-interest. Rawls proposes a solution to this problem. He asks us to imagine ourselves in the original position with others, but behind a *veil of ignorance*. The veil of ignorance is symbolic. We are to have no knowledge of features about ourselves that are arbitrary from a moral point of view. So what kinds of features are morally arbitrary? These are to include our age, gender, wealth, sexual orientation and particular talents. Everyone in the original position is to be ignorant about which might apply to them when they lift the veil of ignorance, leave the original position and enter their shared political community.

The purpose of the veil of ignorance is that it forces us to think about which principles of justice we might all endorse if we did not know certain morally arbitrary features about ourselves. If we knew that we were male or wealthy, then we would run the risk of supporting principles of justice favouring rich men because of our private self-interest. But this would be contrary to identifying what satisfies a general will that is common to all. Instead, we are to choose principles without knowing whether we will benefit from them or not. This is because our morally arbitrary features are hidden from us.

The veil of ignorance forces us to think more carefully about the reasons for which principles of justice we would endorse. Of course, you and I are here and now. We know our age, gender and other morally arbitrary features about ourselves. Yet, Rawls demands that these factors cannot weigh into how we decide which principles to choose.

The principles we choose are to be decided unanimously. This is an important condition. It is because they are to be binding on all. Rawls accepts the idea that all must be bound by a social contract, but disagrees with Rousseau about how we should do it. Instead of a fictional past contract agreed by others, Rawls's thought experiment is something we can do at any time to confirm and reaffirm which principles we would choose.

The principles chosen unanimously are to apply to what Rawls calls *the basic structure*. This refers to constitutional essentials of most states, such as their political institutions, the judiciary and holders of public offices among others. Principles apply to the basic structure only largely relating to the public sphere and not the private sphere (although there are some exceptions we'll come to below).

Rawls argues we would choose two principles of justice:

a Each person has the same indefeasible claim to a fully adequate scheme of equal basic liberties, which scheme is compatible with the same scheme of liberties for all; and
b Social and economic inequalities are to satisfy two conditions: first, they are to be attached to offices and positions open to all under conditions of fair equality of opportunity; and second, they are to be to the greatest benefit of the least-advantaged members of society.

(Rawls 2001: 42–3)

The first principle of justice is that each individual has the same set of 'equal basic liberties'. None should have more than any other. In the original position and behind a veil of ignorance, we would affirm unanimously that each of us should have an equal share of basic liberties.

The first principle has priority over the second, and the latter concerns a particular circumstance. This is the justification of socio-economic inequality. Rawls's claim is that we must each have an equal share of basic rights and liberties no matter what. If we don't have that, then our political arrangement is unjust. But if we do enjoy equal liberties, then socio-economic inequality *can* be justified should certain conditions be satisfied. This is what Rawls means when he says the first principle of justice has lexical priority over the second.

The second principle of justice should be understood in two parts. The first part is that we must each enjoy fair equality of opportunity. Someone occupying a public office, such as a President or Prime Minister, can enjoy more privileged opportunities than many other citizens. Rawls claims this inequality *can* be justified *if* everyone has the same equal share of basic liberties *and* each one of us has the same fair equality of opportunity to become President or Prime Minister. Otherwise, this privileged difference is unjust.

The second part of the second principle is more controversial. This is the claim that socio-economic inequalities can be justified where they are to the greatest benefit of the least-advantaged. Rawls calls this his *difference principle*. Let me clarify it through an example. Suppose the most-advantaged in society are the most wealthy and the least-advantaged the most poor. The government wants to reduce taxes for the most wealthy. So what does the difference principle require? It would permit a reduction on taxes for the most wealthy, but only if the relative reduction for the most poor is equal to or greater than enjoyed by the most wealthy. You might think about the difference principle as being a claim that the differences between the most-advantaged and least-advantaged should *not* increase through adopting new policies.

Finally, we might wonder: so how poor can the least-advantaged be in Rawls's theory of justice? His answer is that everyone must be above a 'social minimum' of rights and liberties, including income and wealth as well as self-respect. Rawls does not put a figure on how much might be enough. But it is clear that it is whatever makes it possible for each citizen to have a decent life with self-respect.

The evidence for Rawls's two principles of justice is simple: close your eyes, put yourself in the original position behind a veil of ignorance and see if you can confirm that everyone would agree to these two principles in this way. Much of the criticism directed to Rawls's theory is that people argue they'd come to different conclusions. Rawls believes we would be somewhat risk adverse in the original position: this is why he thinks we would unanimously permit socio-economic inequality, but a guarantee of a social minimum. Others claim we would either reject a social minimum or approve of a more strongly redistributive system of economic justice. If you were in the original position, what principles do you think would be unanimously agreed? Do you agree with Rawls?

BOX 6.2 WHO IS JOHN RAWLS?

John Rawls (1921–2002) is the dominant political philosopher of the last century. He spent virtually all of his career at Harvard University.

Rawls revolutionised the field of political philosophy. He argued for a new theory of justice as fairness. Rawls ingeniously brought together insights from leading moral and political philosophers in the history of philosophy and reworked them into a novel and distinctive view that remains the most influential theory of justice today. If it were not for his achievements, then political philosophy might not have enjoyed the resurgence it experienced since the publication of his *A Theory of Justice* in 1971.

It is also significant that Rawls not only developed his own new theory of justice, but he also popularised the work of Kant, and so launched a serious interest that has since long overtaken utilitarianism as a dominant force in contemporary political philosophy.

• POLITICAL LIBERALISM

In his later work, Rawls admits his theory of justice suffers from a serious problem: the problem of political stability. Suppose we agree principles of justice that attach to the basic structure and govern the constitutional essentials of our political community. Can this be enough to yield political justice over time?

Rawls's recognition of the problem of political stability takes the following form. He claims we most of us endorse different reasonable comprehensive doctrines. These doctrines are philosophical or religious in character and include all major world religious and philosophical views for a start. Members of our community accept different comprehensive doctrines from Kantianism, Hegelianism and utilitarianism to Catholicism, Judaism and Hinduism and beyond. Each provides us with a view of value and meaning.

Now think about their relation to political justice. The more common way to think about disagreement in political affairs is to hold a vote, but one potential problem is that one group representing a particular comprehensive doctrine can outnumber others and so come to dominate decision-making with preferences more closely aligning themselves to their particular doctrine.

Rawls wants to guard against this because the *differences* we have are *reasonable differences*. We might prefer one doctrine over others, but Rawls's point is that accepting any of them is reasonable. Citizens have reasonable differences over the reasonable doctrines they endorse.

Rawls also maintains that each citizen should be conceived as free and equal. This highlights the real importance of guarding against one reasonable doctrine dominating over others. This is because it would undermine the equality of citizens. So what we require is some means to accommodate the equality of citizens with the reasonable differences they will have about the comprehensive doctrines they support. Rawls calls this the fact of reasonable pluralism and he argues that every society is characterised by this difference.

It's also worth noting that he's ruling out *unreasonable* comprehensive doctrines. These are doctrines about value and meaning that are *not* reasonable. Rawls also identifies a couple, like white supremacy and fascism. What makes each unreasonable is that they fail to recognise the fact of reasonable difference in every community. Instead, they claim that they – and they alone – should dominate others. Not only is this unreasonable, says Rawls, but it also denies the equality of citizens. So unreasonable comprehensive doctrines like these should not be left out of the process of public deliberation altogether.

So what to do? Rawls argues for the idea of public reason. Public reason is a reason that is *public* in the sense that it is available to all no matter which reasonable comprehensive doctrine is supported. Non-public reasons pertain only to one or a few such doctrines. The standard example of a non-public reason is that we should endorse a particular stance on euthanasia because it is the view of a specific religious group.

We consider public reasons as *real people* and no longer in the original position. The original position is where we determine the principles of justice that *rationally* constrain our political constitution, but public reasons are a *reasonable* constraint on our policies within this – and from the perspective of you and I here and now as people who know their age, gender and other features unlike those before in the original position.

Public reasons can appeal to anyone irrespective of their reasonable comprehensive doctrine, such as to the idea of human dignity. In order to accept their normative force, we are not required to accept any particular doctrine. So an appeal to human dignity concerning euthanasia might serve as a kind of public reason whereas an appeal based on the authority of a religious figurehead's declaration would not. It is important that public reasons *can* be endorsed by anyone irrespective of their reasonable comprehensive doctrine and not that they *are* so endorsed. Rawls is not looking for unanimous agreement.

Rawls argues that we should use public reasons to forge an overlapping consensus. Only public reasons can figure into this account and so non-public reasons are discarded. This is because an overlapping consensus can form a connection between our different comprehensive doctrines and render political stability over time more possible. We are to use public reasons in deliberating public affairs and to weigh them in favour of or against policies. The idea is that even if we are convinced by the public reasons behind adopting a policy we can at least access the reasons – as *public* reasons – behind a decision.

The use of public reasons to form an overlapping consensus ensures that no one comprehensive doctrine dominates others. What rules is a consensus supported by reasons accessible to all, even if they do not accept them. In this way, Rawls argues he can achieve political stability for the right reasons. In other words, political stability can be achieved in other ways, such as a brutal dictatorship with a tight grip on its power. However, such a form of government would deny the equality of persons and the fact of reasonable pluralism. An overlapping consensus can overcome these problems.

Rawls calls his views on public reason and an overlapping consensus *political liberalism*. It has attracted criticism. Some argue that an overlapping consensus is not required for political stability. They claim that if we wish to achieve political stability through forging a connection with others, then we already do so through commonly agreeing to two principles of justice. Others argue that the overlapping consensus is too fragile a basis to secure political stability over time. The public reasons we are permitted to use may not be the reasons that command our substantial support. This could mean that any consensus can fail to connect to the reasons that we find most persuasive and so Rawls's solution to the problem of political stability requires more work. Do *you* think there is a fact of reasonable pluralism that poses a problem for political stability? How else might you address it without undermining the equality of citizens?

• THE CAPABILITIES APPROACH

One important alternative to Rawls's theory of justice is the '**capabilities approach**'. A capability is the ability to do or be in respect to some thing. In other words, capability is about our freedom. The most frequent example to explain capabilities is the difference between starving and fasting. Consider someone who is starving and another fasting. Both have the same *actual functionings*: they each lack food. Their difference is not in their actual functioning, but in the capabilities. This is because the person starving does so involuntarily. However, the person fasting has the capability to eat, but chooses not to exercise it. And this is how capabilities are about freedom. Capabilities mark out the importance of our ability to do or be and claim this importance should receive appropriate support from the state. However, our having a capability to do or be in relation to some thing is not a requirement that we must exercise our capabilities at every waking hour. Instead, it is to say all are important and we should be able to exercise any and all whenever we wish, but we need not do so. We are free to exercise – or not exercise – our capabilities.

This approach has two major figures defending different understandings of it. Amartya Sen (1933 –) refers to capability as a continuum where our focus is on how overall capability can be increased. He has argued that the best measure of well-being is capabilities, not resources (Sen 1999). This is confirmed when we consider how people across different countries perform in relation to various capability indicators, such as health, longevity and infant mortality. We soon discover that wealth is an unreliable guide and that famines are caused by a lack of political freedom, not lack of food. As Sen argues, no democracy has suffered or is likely to suffer a famine. This is because democracy is a form of government consistent with securing freedoms for its citizens. The capability approach is meant to help capture this dimension.

Sen is critical of Rawls's theory of justice, but one central concern is that Rawls's understanding of socio-economic justice is driven too much by resources rather than well-being. Sen argues that his idea of capability should become part of Rawls's theory.

The other leading figure defending this approach is Martha C. Nussbaum (1947 –). She argues not for a *capability* approach like Sen, but a *capabilities* approach that makes clear the plurality of capabilities we have. She claims there are ten capabilities ranging from life and bodily health to practical reason and affiliation (Nussbaum 2000). These capabilities are non-competitive and so cannot be traded off one another: we cannot have less of one and more than another to compensate for it. Our capabilities should be guaranteed over a threshold that – like Rawls's idea of the social minimum – marks out a minimally decent life.

Nussbaum is also critical of Rawls's theory of justice. She is especially concerned by his adherence to a social contract theory. The problem is that contractarian theories of justice make assumptions about the people who are party to them: and this tends to be able-bodied people without learning disabilities, and frequently men. A social contract could only work if everyone engaged from similar circumstances, but our world is not like that. The problem is that social contract theories, with their assumptions about the contracting parties, will disadvantage further less dominant groups such as minorities. The best way to overcome such problems is to avoid the use of social contract theories as a basis for determining justice and, instead, adopt the capabilities approach.

• FEMINISM

Another critical voice directed at Rawlsian justice is **feminism**. There is no one 'feminism' and it is perhaps best characterised as a diverse tent. If there is a single thread that speaks to most, if not all, versions of feminism, then it is a concern about power and equality between men and women. A *feminist* analysis of justice is one that examines the potential power inequalities between genders to expose them and point to their change. There are two leading feminist groupings I explore here: radical feminists and liberal feminists.

Radical feminists call themselves radical: this is more a badge of honour than a criticism. Radical feminists, such as Andrea Dworkin (1946–2005) and Catharine MacKinnon (1946 –), focus on gender inequalities and how they are essentially problematic. For example, Dworkin and MacKinnon famously argue for the banning of pornography.

The problem with it is that women may lack consent to participate, they can be abused, and pornography sends a symbolic message that women are second-class citizens where men are the actors and women are the acted-upon. Dworkin and MacKinnon argue that unless we ban pornography these problems will continue.

Liberal feminists, such as Nussbaum and Susan Moller Okin (1946–2004), share a different view of feminism. They also focus on gender inequalities, but from a liberal perspective that prioritises the importance of individual freedom and consent. Liberal feminists can accept that the way much pornography is produced and distributed is deeply flawed. But many liberal feminists stop short of calling for a ban. This is because they argue that while much pornography *can* be problematic it is not *essentially* problematic. It is possible to regulate the industry differently to ensure consent is acquired and abuses avoided.

Radical and liberal feminists also differ on other issues, such as prostitution. Radical feminists generally reject prostitution and highlight the problems associated with women lacking consent, abuse and risk of serious infection. Liberal feminists don't deny these problems, but argue that – as with pornography – we need not ban prostitution because it may be possible to secure individual rights and consent for all – not least for women – through better regulation rather than a ban.

These debates between feminists are meant to highlight the key differences between feminism as it is understood today, and to show some of its diversity. It is untrue that all feminists approach issues of justice from the same angles and reach the same conclusions in every case.

Feminists have been critical of Rawlsian justice for failing to do justice to these issues. Rawls may argue for equal basic liberties and fair equality of opportunity in the *public* realm. Feminists are often concerned by the absence of the *private* realm, such as the home, that can be a site for real concerns. For example, Rawls did not originally claim principles of justice related to the family because he did not think the family was part of the basic structure of society.

Rawls's mind changed on this issue, but only thanks to the work of the liberal feminist Okin. She claimed that principles of justice should apply to the family. Part of the reason is that many women are denied the same opportunities as men in public affairs because they are expected to maintain the home. The family should not then be structured however private individuals want because it has an effect on the life changes and publicly available opportunities of women. This is one of a very, *very* long list of feminist contributions at the very heart of political philosophy.

• MULTICULTURALISM

Rawls focuses on the problem of political stability as an issue. What is the issue to be overcome? People have differences about value and meaning. This is a concern for

Rawls because he is looking to provide a single structure to manage and govern disputes. But why have one structure?

Multiculturalism is another wide tent encompassing many different views. Many of its proponents argue that group differences can justify differences in public treatment. In other words, rules can and should apply differently depending on the groups we belong to. Famous examples include a general law that everyone must wear a crash helmet when using motorcycles, but with a special exemption for Sikhs provided they wear a turban.

Okin (1999) provides the most-discussed essay on multiculturalism and she links it with feminism. She notes the dual tendencies – often progressive in their aspirations – to better accommodate multicultural differences while also accommodating feminism. Instead of everyone becoming part of a melting pot where differences disappear, we should be seen as part of a salad bowl: a health mix of difference that can work well together while respecting our differences.

The problem is we cannot do both at the same time. This is because many of the rights that some multiculturalists claim are damaging for women. So the special exemptions concern different clothing only for women, different rules governing education or marriage for women and practices like female genital cutting. Permitting multicultural *differences* renders women more *unequal*. This is because much of the effect of greater multiculturalism is further domination of women by men.

Okin does not reject multiculturalism in principle and she argues that not every multicultural practice is problematic. However, part of our test for whether it can be permissible to consider granting some new exemption based on multiculturalism is to ask if it respects the equal rights of men and women. Is multiculturalism bad for women? Yes, but only where it undermines gender equality – and this is how a liberal feminist would see this issue.

Perhaps the most respected defender of multiculturalism – and a philosopher who shares Okin's concerns – is Bhikhu Parekh (1935 –). He rejects the idea of our cultural differences as a problem to be overcome as Rawls can sometimes appear to suggest. Instead, Parekh views our differences as something to be embraced. Our project should not be to end our differences, but to celebrate them.

This perspective does not deny the need for us to share some common commitments. But Parekh (2006) highlights that the ties that should bind each citizen should be connections that all might share. If we defined citizenship or political inclusion with reference to certain religious customs or distinct cultural practices, then this can exclude fellow citizens and so should be avoided.

Instead of creating an overlapping consensus, we should instead seek to discover principles that all might claim in common. These might include principles of respect, dignity and equality. This should be the basis for our common bonds of citizenship because they can be supported by all. But rather than seek to move away from our cultural differences towards an overlapping consensus, we engage each other from our cultural differences with tolerance, respect and new understandings forging a common political life together.

What is sometimes overlooked is Okin's claim that multiculturalism and feminism are often not talking about different things. She argues that *multicultural* issues are frequently *feminist* issues. Make a list of issues flagged as falling under multiculturalism, such as the veil, polygamy and female genital cutting. How many on your list are about regulating the freedoms of women versus men? Is multiculturalism about the domination of women? If not, then what is Okin failing to appreciate?

• THE STAKEHOLDER SOCIETY

We considered the idea of Rousseau's social contract, its recasting in Rawls's theory of justice and political liberalism, and their critique by capability theorists, feminists and multiculturalists. I conclude by examining once more a concept that has received no mention thus far in this chapter: political alienation.

The previous chapter concluded by noting the problem of alienation as depicted by Hegel. This is the idea of people having a conviction about their disconnection from others. Hegel viewed this as the big issue of modern life. Perhaps it still is. But what should be proposed in terms of a view *of justice* concerning individuals who are alienated from society? Can we have political justice in a world where many of our fellow citizens feel alienated from each other?

Let me outline a possibility. The problem of alienation is that individuals fail to see themselves as having a stake in society; they lack the conviction of themselves as stakeholders. This problem may be the fault of the other members of the community for allowing some members to become disconnected in this way.

The relevance of this idea is: can we have justice when we are alienated? This is not a problem for Rousseau: alienated individuals need not politically engage for political justice to flourish. Nor is it a problem for Rawls: so long as the two principles of justice are not breached and public debate is engaged through public reasons there is no requirement we would, in fact, engage in any debate.

But what kind of justice is a community where some of its members have a conviction of permanent separation? If stakeholding is a view that those who have a stake should have a say, then this perspective seems compatible with what we've seen from Rousseau, Rawls and others. What is different is the claim that stakeholders must not only have a stake, but share a conviction of themselves as stakeholders. In other words, they must not only identify with others as fellow citizens in their minds, but also in the hearts. So a question to reflect on is: should political justice take the form of a stakeholder society? Should our convictions about self and other count when weighing up the relative merits of theories of justice?

• SUMMARY

- The social contract is thought to be a source for political obligations because we have consented to them. Social contract theorists are called contractarians.
- The most famous contemporary social contract theory is Rawls's theory of justice.
- Rawls defends two principles of justice that we can discover through entering an original position behind a veil of ignorance. The first principle is that each person must have an equal share of basic rights and liberties. The second principle states that any socio-economic inequalities can only be justified if the first principle is satisfied *and* every person enjoys a fair equality of opportunity in addition to the difference principle. These principles are rational constitutional constraints.
- Rawls's political liberalism develops his ideas on justice, including the claim that we should deliberate publicly through the use of public reasons that any individual endorsing any reasonable comprehensive doctrine could, but might not, accept. These reasons can build an overlapping consensus making possible political stability despite our many differences over which view of the good is best.
- Capabilities theorists criticise Rawls for having an impoverished view of freedom. A capability is the ability to do or be. Sen argues we should think about capability along a single metric and it could fit within Rawls's views on principles of justice. Nussbaum claims there is more than one capability and offers a list of ten capabilities. She argues that we must each ensure every person can enjoy all capabilities above a threshold and that it can form an overlapping consensus.
- Multiculturalists, such as Parekh, reject the idea that pluralism in society is a problem. Parekh is critical of Rawls's claim that we can and should distinguish between the private and public spheres in the way that Rawls does. Parekh argues differences are to be embraced.
- Can we be alienated in a just society? One idea is that this is impossible and to live in a just society is to be at home in it. An example is the claim that citizens are stakeholders where they should have a say over decisions where they have a stake *and* possess a conviction of themselves as stakeholders. Justice may require fairness, but it might also concern belonging as well.

• STUDY QUESTIONS

1 Do our political obligations stem from a social contract?
2 What is Rawls's theory of justice – and is it convincing?
3 What is the difference between Sen and Nussbaum over capabilities?
4 Is multiculturalism compatible with justice?
5 Should justice account for stakeholding?

• INTRODUCTORY FURTHER READING

Rawls, J. (2001) *Justice as Fairness: A Restatement* (Cambridge, MA: Harvard University Press). [This book is Rawls's lectures about his theory of justice that brings together his earlier work and more accessible.]

Sandel, M. (2009) *Justice: What's the Right Thing to Do?* (Harmondsworth: Penguin). [An excellent, accessible introduction to the idea of justice covering the leading figures and ideas.]

• ADVANCED FURTHER READING

Brooks, T. (2012) *Punishment* (London: Routledge). [A comprehensive examination of the philosophy of punishment and defence of a unified theory of punishment bringing together multiple penal purposes. But it also argues for the idea of a stakeholder society and why this matters for political justice.]

Brooks, T. and M. Nussbaum (eds) (2015) *Rawls's Political Liberalism* (New York: Columbia University Press). [A recent contribution by leading figures delivering a timely reassessment of Rawls's theory of justice.]

Nussbaum, M. (2000) *Women and Human Development: The Capabilities Approach* (Cambridge: Cambridge University Press). [A highly influential account revising Sen's work on capabilities.]

Okin, S. (1999) *Is Multiculturalism Bad for Women?* (Princeton: Princeton University Press). [An excellent essay with a series of critical responses that reflects on possible conflict between feminism and multiculturalism – and what we should think about it.]

Parekh, B. (2006) *Rethinking Multiculturalism: Cultural Diversity and Political Theory*, 2nd edn (Basingstoke: Palgrave Macmillan). [The most significant contribution to our understanding of multiculturalism richly informed by a leading statesman.]

Plato (1992) *The Republic* (Indianapolis: Hackett). [Perhaps the best-known work in philosophy and a crucial early contribution to our understanding of justice.]

Rousseau, J.-J. (1997) *The Social Contract and Other Later Political Writings* (Cambridge: Cambridge University Press). [The most important text in the history of philosophy defending the idea of a social contract.]

Sen, A. (1999) *Development as Freedom* (Oxford: Oxford University Press). [A key statement by this Nobel Prize winning economist about his novel capability approach and its relevance for justice within and beyond states.]

• FREE INTERNET RESOURCES

Baehr, A. (2013) 'Liberal Feminism', *Stanford Encyclopedia of Philosophy*, http://plato.stanford.edu/entries/feminism-liberal/. [An accessible introduction to this influential view of feminism and its critics.]

Cudd, A. (2012) 'Contractarianism', *Stanford Encyclopedia of Philosophy*, http://plato.stanford.edu/entries/contractarianism/. [An excellent overview of social contract theories in political philosophy.]

Human Development and Capability Association, https://hd-ca.org/. [An important resource for information and links about capability approaches.]

Song, S. (2010) 'Multiculturalism', *Stanford Encyclopedia of Philosophy*, http://plato.stanford.edu/entries/feminism-liberal/. [A useful examination of multiculturalism, its issues and challenges.]

Wenar, L. (2012) 'John Rawls', *Stanford Encyclopedia of Philosophy*, http://plato.stanford.edu/entries/rawls/. [The best introduction to Rawls's justice as fairness available.]

7

what is global justice?

- Introducing global justice
- Statism and nationalism
- Cosmopolitanism
- Climate change and conservationism
- Climate change and adaptation

• INTRODUCING GLOBAL JUSTICE

This chapter examines the topic of **global justice**. So then what *is* global justice? While more general theories about justice focus on justice within a particular community, global justice focuses on justice among and across states. This field has exploded in recent years: perhaps no other area in political philosophy receives as much attention. Global justice is about justice across states internationally. Most theorising about justice in the history of philosophy looked only at justice within a state. Global justice explores justice beyond the boundaries of the state. We examine the views of statists and nationalists first. They argue that our group membership can give rise to special duties binding only on group members. We next consider their opponents: the cosmopolitans. They argue that such groups are arbitrary and mask the moral equality of individuals, which should matter most.

The chapter closes by looking at the issue of climate change – perhaps the area within global justice receiving the most attention at present. We consider conservationist approaches, such as the idea of the ecological footprint and the polluter pays principle. These proposals aim to solve the problem of climate change by reducing emissions to a sustainable level. We also examine adaptation views, which argue the problem is best solved through improved technology. If climate change is happening, which approach is best? The answer may be surprising because these proposals get their target wrong.

BOX 7.1 ARE JUSTICE AND GLOBAL JUSTICE DIFFERENT THINGS?

Historically, philosophers have focused almost exclusively on questions of domestic justice rather than global justice. The few exceptions that can be found in antiquity on the whole devoted little space to the subject matter.

Where global justice is addressed, the focus is usually on defining and exploring the conditions for a just war, such as its having a just cause and being fought in a just way.

It is not until more recently that serious attention was brought to bear on global justice. Much original theorising treated states as if they were persons. But now there is a wider recognition that such analogies can miss their mark and international justice is more complex.

• STATISM AND NATIONALISM

One set of related perspectives on global justice concerns **statism** and **nationalism**. They argue that our membership in groups can give rise to special duties to co-members that do not extend to non-members. Special duties should be contrasted with general duties. General duties extend to everyone while special duties might only relate to fellow members of a family or state.

For example, consider the case of a missing child. It could be argued that we all may have some duty to aid rescue efforts to locate the missing child. This would be a kind of general duty: it is general because it universally applies to everyone. It does not matter who the child is. Now consider the case of *our* missing child. Would you have the same duty to aid rescue efforts for your own child than you have for someone else's child? It's likely you would accept your duty is greater, or more stringent: it might be wrong to disobey a general duty, but violating a duty in this case may intuitively seem even worse. The greater duty we might have to our own children is a kind of special duty: a duty that can apply to some, but not everyone. What matters is the kind of relationship we share.

David Miller (1946 –) is the leading philosopher defending a form of nationalism he calls *ethical nationalism*. Ethical nationalism is a nationalism based on ethical considerations. It is not a nationalism based on ethnicity. Miller (2008) argues that our relationship to each other in groups can be ethically significant. This requires, for example, our group membership to be of intrinsic importance to ourselves and other group members. Miller claims that the borders that should count for global justice are the borders around the individuals within groups, or what he calls (ethical) 'nations'.

This leads Miller to defend a distinctive view of global justice. While he accepts that all persons everywhere share in moral importance, Miller highlights the importance of our connections to one another as ethically significant. Suppose a tsunami strikes a country on the other side of the world from where you read this sentence. The effects are devastating and people live in severe poverty as a result.

Miller argues that we have remedial responsibilities. These are our responsibilities to remedy others. He understands these responsibilities in terms of groups: our *nation* may have a responsibility to remedy the suffering in another. We should decide by taking into account different considerations pertaining to our relations. So we ask if a given nation was morally or at least causally responsible for the need for a remedy. We ask if a nation is able to provide some means of remedy. We consider the possible historical and cultural ties that may exist between nations, including whether there is a shared border or language. We weigh up these connections nation by nation to select those nations that should provide assistance to others.

Criticisms of this approach include questions about why the *nation* or the *state* should count. Others worry that Miller provides a useful analysis for how to decide *now* which nations might assist others to address immediate problems, but there is no clear plan over time. For example, what if some nations are always chosen to provide remedy – why should they bear all the costs? If each connection is weighed equally with none having priority, then it is possible that nations *responsible* for problems elsewhere are never properly held to account.

The difference between Miller's ethical nationalism and *statism* is that the latter claims that state membership can give rise to special duties not unlike ethical national membership, and for similar reasons. A common criticism of statist views is that the borders are more arbitrarily drawn. Historical accident or a large body of water separating different land masses can explain how some state boundaries came to be formed. While not everyone disputes that state membership can yield special duties to co-members, this is sometimes viewed as more problematic than nationalism because of the concern about boundaries.

BOX 7.2 CITIZENSHIP TESTS

Recent years have seen a proliferation of citizenship tests. These tests are typically requirements for new migrants wanting to become citizens of their adopted country.

These tests can take different forms. Some are like a bridge to citizenship: the test is easily passed and a formality where new citizens declare their commitment to their new country.

Others, such as the UK test, act more like a barrier to citizenship where the test is more difficult and an obstacle to citizenship (Brooks 2013).

Should citizenship tests act like a bridge or barrier for new migrants? What kinds of information should be found on these tests – historical and cultural trivia or affirmation of principles?

• COSMOPOLITANISM

Cosmopolitanism is the leading alternative approach to nationalism and statism. The classic statement of cosmopolitanism is the famous declaration by Seneca (4 BC–65 AD) that he is 'a citizen of the world' and so not belonging exclusively to any one state. Where nationalists and statists highlight the importance of *particular* group memberships, cosmopolitans focus on the importance of our *universal* group membership as fellow human beings. They claim our national and state identities are arbitrary from a moral point of view. This is because we could have been born somewhere else. So why should the bare fact that we happened to be born *here* matter for why I might be owed *additional* special duties? This is especially problematic where my national membership is not a product of free choice, but instead of habit or compulsion.

So what does cosmopolitan justice look like? The one article that helped launch contemporary work by political philosophers on global justice is Peter Singer (1946 –): it is as well known as it is controversial. Singer uses a hypothetical example of a child drowning in a shallow pond. He argues: 'If it is in our power to prevent something bad from happening, without thereby sacrificing anything of comparative moral importance, we ought, morally, to do it' (Singer 1972: 231). We weigh the *moral* cost of our action against the *moral* cost of our inaction to others. If saving a child from drowning in a shallow pond ruins my expensive suit, then the *monetary* cost of my action is high. But this is not the *moral* cost – and this is the only one that should count. The moral cost of my acting is negligible: I'll become wet and somewhat inconvenienced. The moral cost to the drowning child is much greater: the child would drown. When we weigh these costs, we should conclude we have a duty to save the drowning child.

The importance of this one example is the consequences that almost cascade from it. If Singer is correct, then the *identity* of who we save is irrelevant. If the moral cost to us in acting is less than the moral cost to others of our inaction, then we should act. It does not matter if the person is our child, neighbour or stranger. This is one immediate sense in which Singer's argument is *cosmopolitan*: it is an argument about universal justice irrespective of our national identities. Singer's point is that our special relations need not matter at all.

A second consequence concerns *distance*. Again, if the moral cost of our action is less than the moral cost to another of our inaction, then we should act. The point to be made here is that it does not then matter what distance is between the rescuer and the rescued. Suppose it does not cost much financially to save another from severe poverty, but I'd rather spend the money on a new electric guitar. I'd get real enjoyment from owning the guitar and the hours I'd spend playing music. But if the moral cost of spending the money on my guitar is that those in need might endure severe hardship or perish from my inaction, then the money for my guitar should be spent on others instead. We may well have a moral duty, if Singer is correct, to give larger sums to charities than we often do.

A final consequence concerns *motivation*. Singer's argument (remember it now?) is a claim about our *positive duties*. These are duties we owe to others irrespective of our responsibility for their situation. For example, we should save the drowning child because of the relatively lower moral cost to ourselves. It does not matter how the child got there. Maybe someone left the child there by accident. Or maybe on purpose. Either way, our motivation to help is rooted in the fact that we have a moral obligation arising from a positive duty. We act because we can do so. It is our ability to act because we can that makes this duty *positive*.

Thomas Pogge (1953 –) defends a very different reason for providing remedy to those in need. He argues that we have not a positive duty, but rather a *negative duty* to do so. Negative duties arise in relation to our bearing some responsibility for the situation of need that others find themselves in.

Pogge (2008) argues that persons living in affluent states have a negative duty to assist people in severe poverty. He claims it is because 'we' in affluent states knowingly, foreseeably and avoidably maintain an international order that perpetuates severe poverty. The causal chain is the following. 'We' in affluent states live in democracies and we vote for our political representatives. These representatives – either personally or someone appointed on their behalf – engage in supporting policies and institutions, such as protectionism that benefits the affluent over others, organisations like the IMF and World Bank that render developing economies more easily exploited by developed countries, and the international resource privilege where affluent states permit political leaders – often in despotic regimes – to sell off their country's natural resources held in common for their own personal profit. Pogge's argument is that citizens in affluent states have a negative duty to people in severe poverty because these citizens elect politicians and their representatives who maintain this exploitative global order that perpetuates severe poverty.

This is also a cosmopolitan view sharing several points with Singer: our responsibility is as individuals to individuals elsewhere. Our nationality and their nationality are unimportant. Every person is of equal moral concern.

So while Singer argues that we have a positive duty to help others in virtue of our ability to help (and irrespective of the reasons others may have for requiring help), Pogge claims we have a negative duty to help others because we share some responsibility for their requiring help. These are their differences, but what about possible concerns?

One criticism of Singer's view is that maybe it does matter *why* someone requires rescue. Should it matter that individuals are in severe poverty because of choices they made? Or do you think we should save the lives we can because we can?

A second criticism is that Singer's famous example is a poor analogy. Real world global justice is not finding children drowning in shallow ponds. Some even object to the idea that those in need are akin to children unable to help themselves whereas we are the big, strong adults empowered to save lives at will. Global justice concerns problems of greater complexity that are very different. So maybe if Singer's example was closer to the situation we find ourselves in it would serve as a more powerful case for positive duties. But because it is a poor analogy it is self-undermining.

Finally, some criticise Singer's reliance on positive duties as a faith in human charity. If we have a moral duty to help others if we can, then who will know and how might it be enforced? It appears we must simply grasp the positive duty and we should then be compelled to act. But not everyone will possess this motivation. Plus, our charitable action is for us to provide: positive duties flow from one individual to another. But why think that ending severe poverty should take this form and not be coordinated by states to states?

Now consider Pogge's defence of negative duties. Criticisms of it focus on two areas. The first is whether it is a negative duty. So we vote for politicians and they appoint representatives onto global institutions, like the IMF, that create the problems that Pogge claims. Why blame the voter? It is arguable that voters may have little, if any, idea about how their vote could be linked in this way. Instead, we might think the negative duties are not ours, but belong to the relevant politicians and/or their appointees for their decisions. If there is a negative duty to assist others (and we should emphasise *if*), then perhaps the duty is not for us but others.

A second area of criticism is a belief that all *existing* severe poverty can be imputed to problems arising from a coercive institutional order that is knowingly, foreseeably and avoidably maintained by affluent states. Let's grant for the sake of argument that much, if not most, severe poverty is perpetuated, at least in part, by the global order. If the order is not to be blamed for all of it, then why is there a negative duty on all those who maintain the global order to end it altogether? Moreover, can we honestly say that *all* cases of severe poverty are the result of human decisions?

Recall Miller's arguments about an ethical nationalist approach to global justice. Miller considers cases such as tsunamis causing severe poverty. It is not difficult to imagine natural disasters causing such problems and through no fault of any government or global order. If Miller is correct about this, then Pogge is incorrect to claim non-human causes cannot be blamed for severe poverty in any case.

Miller's arguments here are interesting for another reason. Singer defends a view of (cosmopolitan) global justice based on positive duties. Pogge argues for a view of (cosmopolitan) global justice grounded in negative duties. But Miller's explicitly non-cosmopolitan view brings both kinds of duties together in requiring us to consider various factors mentioned above, including a nation's ability to provide remedy to others (addressing the potential for fulfilling positive duties) and a nation's possible moral and/or causal responsibility for severe poverty elsewhere (addressing possible negative duties). If we do not wish to choose either positive duties or negative duties, then Miller provides one illuminating account of how they could work together in tandem.

This discussion brings us full circle. Theories of global justice focus on justice between and among states. The two leading approaches are nationalism/statism and cosmopolitanism. Each defends a distinctive perspective. I examined their leading defenders and their interrelation. But it's important to note something further.

Nationalists, like Miller, may argue that co-membership in a group can and should give rise to special duties under certain conditions. But he does not reject general duties for all. And to that degree this claim to a non-cosmopolitan theory of global justice appears somewhat hybrid. Likewise, cosmopolitans, such as Pogge, might emphasise the moral equality of individuals internationally. However, he also does not reject our having special duties provided, in his view, that we do not fail to observe a general duty to someone as a result.

There are subtle differences that begin to appear, but the central point I want to raise is that nationalists and cosmopolitans may each claim different positions for themselves. Nonetheless, there is increasingly closer overlap between the two. To different degrees, most philosophers in global justice accept some elements from nationalists or statists and others from cosmopolitans.

BOX 7.3 WHAT ARE POSITIVE AND NEGATIVE DUTIES?

Positive duties are duties to others irrespective of our responsibility for their plight. They are often characterised as charitable acts. We help those in need for the reason that we can. Positive duties may play on our good will, but not everyone feels their motivational force.

Negative duties are duties we owe to others because of our responsibility for their plight. These duties are thought to be more stringent in focusing on the more narrow idea of harm. This is also believed to give negative duties greater motivational force.

Positive duties and negative duties speak to different dimensions, but can come together and are not mutually exclusive.

If we had to choose between our fulfilling a positive duty or a negative duty, which would you choose?

• CLIMATE CHANGE AND CONSERVATIONISM

Perhaps the single biggest topic of concern for philosophers working on global justice today is climate change. The most popular approach is what we might call **conservationism**. This is the general idea that the just response to what to do about climate change is to conserve through reducing carbon emissions and the like.

It is important to note some background to the debate. Read my words: there is a clear and unambiguous global scientific consensus that confirms climate change is taking place. The Intergovernmental Panel on Climate Change produces regular substantial assessment reports examining the science and, more recently, the ethics of climate change. These reports confirm that climate change is happening with human activities a major factor for them. Climate change is a major problem because it contributes to increasing threats to coastal communities due to rising sea levels, an increasing likelihood of drought, a greater risk of more extreme weather and the spread of tropical diseases to new areas.

Conservationist approaches aim to solve the problems associated with climate change by reducing our carbon emissions to sustainable levels so that future climate change – and its associated dangers – do not occur. These reductions can take multiple forms, including greater energy efficiencies, lifestyle changes and increased use of renewable energy sources.

One conservationist approach is the *ecological footprint* (Wackernagel and Reiss 1996). An ecological footprint is a measure of the Earth's carrying capacity at a sustainable level. We divide this carrying capacity by the number of human beings on the planet. This yields our ecological footprint – and an indicator of the limits for our consumption and carbon emissions at sustainable levels.

The ecological footprint is popular with many political philosophers as a fair and equal principle. The footprint is equal because everyone's footprint is to be the same size. It does not matter where you live or who you are – and this leads many to affirm its fairness. Climate change is a problem for us all: we're all in this together. Everyone must live within the same-sized footprint and together we can end future climate change.

This view of conservationism is so popular that many concerns we might have are not often raised. For example, should ecological footprints be equal? Different people have different resource needs because of age or pregnancy. These differences between people and over time should count against any one-size-fits-all approach that the ecological footprint offers. Furthermore, individuals have different resource needs depending on where they live. The resource needs of Connecticut, Arizona and County Durham – to name only three places I've lived in – are very different from one another.

Perhaps the biggest worry is to imagine all governments agree to limit their resource usages to within a *per capita* ecological footprint. Every country would tackle climate change on the same footing, right? Wrong: the concern is that more affluent states can better manage a shift to living within an ecological footprint because they are more technologically advanced than the global poor. So while the ecological footprint claims to promise equality and fairness, it now appears that it might be unfair and treat people unequally. Additionally, it might ossify the relative positions of rich versus poorer states. We get conservationism, but at a high cost.

The leading alternative conservationist approach to the ecological footprint is the *polluter pays principle* (Caney 2005). This principle says that polluters should pay because they pollute. The reason is because polluters have a negative duty to do so. Polluters release carbon emissions that contribute to climate change which, in turn, contributes to the serious problems arising from climate change. Polluters should be targeted to make the situation much better.

The polluter pays principle is conservationist for two reasons. First, it is designed to increase the price of oil to incentivise carbon emission reductions. Typically, the polluter pays principle advocates defend a tax of between \$2 and \$3 per barrel of oil. The increased costs make using oil more expensive and so encourage alternatives to it leading to overall carbon emissions falling below a sustainable level.

The second reason the principle is conservationist is that the principle is not only designed to reduce our carbon emissions, but also to generate much-needed revenue that can be used to compensate for damage already done. The idea is that those contributing to climate change-related damage should pay for it.

There are several serious concerns with this proposal as well. The first is identifying the polluters: we are all the polluters and victims of pollution. So who should pay whom? Carbon emissions can last several decades in our atmosphere: the activities of people now long dead can impact on future generations. If polluters should pay, then the problem is that not all polluters are still alive.

A second serious problem concerns the polluter pays principle as a *conservationist* principle. The principle claims that a higher tax will yield the benefit of sustainable levels of carbon emissions. While higher prices contribute to fewer emissions, it is unclear if any reasonable price rise might bring about the desired effect. Targeting individual behaviour might not reduce global emissions overall to sustainable levels and so the polluter pays principle could still contribute to further climate change problems.

A related problem is in the name: the *polluter pays principle*. If costs are raised on how much polluters must pay, then the polluter can still pollute so long as he or she can pay for it. Essentially, the polluter pays principle may be more of a polluters can pay as much as they are able to principle. Not only might the principle fail to reduce climate change, it might make it worse.

A final problem concerns compensation. The polluter pays principle says that those who pollute should pay and this income be used to compensate others for the damage caused. Putting aside serious questions about how this income is collected and distributed, this claim assumes that environmental damage can be compensated for. But how much should it cost to compensate for making a species extinct? This appears to be a case of a non-compensatory good, for which no compensation is relevant.

This overview of conservationist approaches to tackling climate change does *not* challenge the scientific consensus about climate change or its potentially catastrophic effects. We critically examined two perspectives developed and defended by political philosophers: the ecological footprint and the polluter pays principle. Each is not without fundamental concerns. How might you improve these accounts?

● CLIMATE CHANGE AND ADAPTATION

Our final examination focuses on the leading alternative to conservationist approaches. This is **adaptation**. The idea is that another way to solve the problem of how to live with climate change is to adapt ourselves to it. This is captured well by the statement: 'We will save ourselves by adapting to our ever-changing circumstances…At the end of the day, the story will have a happy ending' (Kahn 2010: 7, 12).

The adaptation measures considered are largely technological. So where rising sea levels threaten coastal communities, then we should build new flood defences. Where there is drought endangering food production, we should create more weather-resistant genetically modified crops. The problems of climate change can be managed through adapting to mitigate their potentially harmful effects.

Earlier in this chapter it was noted that theories of global justice share an increasing amount of overlap. Statists and cosmopolitans emphasise different goals, but each shares much in common. Likewise, most conservationists accept the need for at least adaptation measures. This is because climate change has already taken place. Adaptation proponents also tend to agree we require some conservationist reduction in carbon emissions, but this is because it will make the climate easier to adapt to. So there is some overlap here as well.

There are several fundamental concerns about adaptation as an acceptable alternative to conservationism. First, it tends to downplay risks. Climate change is not bad for everyone: the Maldives might not exist if sea levels continue to rise, but a warmer planet renders more of the US state of Alaska's tundra farmable. Should this be alarming?

A related concern is that adaptation proponents put too much trust in future scientific advancement. They believe as a matter of faith that technology will save us. This is even though it does not yet exist and may not even be conceived. Worse still: while there is a wide scientific consensus that climate change is happening, the models are less precise about the exact state of the planet in future. Call it a known unknown: we know that we don't know exactly what future we must adapt to. This makes it all the more difficult to have real confidence that unknown future scientific advancements will satisfactorily address an uncertain future. Some fear the risk of getting it badly wrong is environmental catastrophe. But is this fear justified as a reasonable precaution? What do *you* think?

Adaptation proponents also claim – like defenders of the polluter pays principle – that climate changes can be compensated for. Again, it is unclear that environmental damage is a compensatory good. But more fundamentally: if we know others may contribute to an activity with potentially harmful effects, then why think this is legitimate where this harm is later compensated for? Think about it: do we permit individuals knowingly and avoidably to endanger others knowing they can easily afford compensating them for it? This may seem a very counterintuitive view of justice.

So while conservationist proposals can be subjected to serious criticisms, so too can adaptation. This does not mean we should reject either as it stands, but it does impress upon us the need to consider these concerns.

But there is one final point worth raising. Neither side seems to address the real challenge of climate change. Conservationists claim that if carbon emissions are brought under a sustainable level – whether through an ecological footprint or polluter pays principle – then we can have a sustainable forever after. Adaptation proponents argue that we can adapt our way to a sustainable future. Both claim environmental catastrophe will be avoided if only our impact on the planet is better managed.

This overlooks too readily the fact that environmental catastrophes have happened long before human beings walked the Earth. A future ice age or other natural calamity won't be stopped because we reduce our impact or because such events have happened when we had no impact at all. This raises the issue of whether climate change is a problem to be solved or only managed. It also raises the question: why save the planet if catastrophe might happen in future no matter our efforts? I think it's safe to say that there is much more to be said on climate change and global justice – and political philosophers are at its frontier.

• SUMMARY

- Global justice is about justice between individuals and states internationally.
- Statism is the view that co-membership in a group can give rise to special duties to co-members that do not extend to non-members. So state boundaries can matter for global justice.
- Nationalism (or 'ethical' nationalism) is the view that co-national membership in a group gives rise to special duties to co-nationals. The boundaries that matter here are around individual members of a group and not lines on a map.

- Cosmopolitans largely reject the idea that group memberships can legitimate differences in justice for some and not others because these differences are often arbitrary. Cosmopolitans argue justice should be more universal.
- Climate change concerns global justice because human-caused climatic change gives rise to important questions concerning who or which state has obligations to others in light of the problems climatic changes have for humans and the natural world alike.
- Conservationists, such as advocates of the ecological footprint and polluter pays principle, claim we can solve climate change by reducing our carbon emissions within some sustainable limit.
- Adaptation proponents claim we can solve climate change through advances in scientific technologies that will allow us to enjoy a sustainable tomorrow by adapting to future changes.

• STUDY QUESTIONS

1 Can and should our group memberships, as co-citizens or co-nationals, give rise to special obligations binding only to fellow group members?
2 Should we accept the cosmopolitan view that justice should be universal?
3 Do you find statism more convincing than cosmopolitanism? Is there a middle ground between them?
4 Which do you prefer – the ecological footprint or the polluter pays principle?
5 If we could adapt to future climate changes, should we do it?

• INTRODUCTORY FURTHER READING

Brooks, T. (ed.) (2008) *The Global Justice Reader* (Oxford: Blackwell). [The most comprehensive collection of contemporary and historically influential work on global justice available.]

Gardiner, S. (2004) 'Ethics and Global Climate Change', *Ethics* 114: 555–600. [A comprehensive overview of the research and ethics of global climate change. Essential reading for a fuller understanding of the subject.]

Singer, P. (1972) 'Famine, Affluence, and Morality', *Philosophy and Public Affairs* 1: 229–43. [The article that effectively launched contemporary work in global justice. Powerful and controversial defence of positive duties and global justice.]

• ADVANCED FURTHER READING

Brock, G. (2009) *Global Justice: A Cosmopolitan Account* (Oxford: Oxford University Press). [A major contribution to cosmopolitan theories of global justice and how they can interact with non-cosmopolitan approaches.]

Caney, S. (2005) 'Cosmopolitan Justice, Responsibility and Global Climate Change', *Leiden Journal of International Law* 18: 747–75. [Influential argument in favour of the polluter pays principle. Excellent critical examination of this principle and its critics.]

Kahn, M. (2010) *Climatopolis: How Our Cities Will Thrive in the Hotter Future* (New York: Basic Books). [An economist providing an argument for adaptation instead of conservationism in addressing climate change.]

Kant, I. (1991) *Political Writings* (Cambridge: Cambridge University Press). [In his *Perpetual Peace* essay, Kant sets out a highly influential account of cosmopolitanism and without a world-state.]

Miller, D. (2008) *National Responsibility and Global Justice* (Oxford: Oxford University Press). [The leading statement of ethical nationalism and anti-cosmopolitanism. Contains fascinating analysis of what a just non-cosmopolitan distributive justice should look like.]

Pogge, T. (2008) *World Poverty and Human Rights*, 2nd edn (Cambridge: Polity). [Influential cosmopolitan argument for viewing global justice through the lens of negative duties.]

Wackernagel, M. and W. Reiss (1996) *Our Ecological Footprint: Reducing Human Impact on the Earth* (Gabriola Island: New Society Publishers). [The key work behind the idea of the ecological footprint. Highly influential for many working in environmental ethics.]

• FREE INTERNET RESOURCES

Blake, M. and P. Smith (2013) 'International Distributive Justice', *Stanford Encyclopedia of Philosophy*, http://plato.stanford.edu/entries/international-justice/. [Excellent overview of global justice and issues of international distribution.]

Brooks, T. (2013) *The 'Life in the United Kingdom' Citizenship Test: Is It Unfit for Purpose?* Durham: Durham University, http://papers.ssrn.com/sol3/papers.cfm?abstract_id = 2280329. [The only comprehensive report into the UK citizenship test available. Influential and repeatedly cited in Parliamentary debates.]

Intergovernmental Panel on Climate Change, http://www.ipcc.ch/. [Home webpage for the IPCC and its scientific and ethical assessment reports. Essential reading on climate change.]

Kleigeld, P. and E. Brown (2013) 'Cosmopolitanism', *Stanford Encyclopedia of Philosophy*, http://plato.stanford.edu/entries/cosmopolitanism/. [Accessible and comprehensive coverage of cosmopolitanism that is a necessary starting point for anyone coming to the topic for the first time.]

Part III

aesthetics

Kathleen Stock

Etymologically, the term 'aesthetics' derives from the Greek for 'perceptible to the senses'. In this broad sense, aesthetics as an academic discipline might be taken to concern issues surrounding perceptual experience generally. However, this is not how it is used in analytic philosophy in the Western tradition: insofar as aesthetics is concerned with perceptual experiences at all, it is more narrowly focused on issues concerning the sorts of perceptual experiences we get from artworks, or from beautiful objects, man-made or natural. Over time, the scope of aesthetics has also broadened to concern questions which on the face of it look less directly related to perceptual experience: questions about the nature of art and the nature of aesthetic judgement, as well as more 'local' investigations into the nature of particular art forms and critical questions concerning them. The result is what can seem a rather tangled field.

To help us make sense of it, we can say that roughly speaking, aesthetics is concerned with two sorts of philosophical questions: questions about art, on the one hand, and questions about **aesthetic experience** and **aesthetic judgement** on the other. These questions are connected, insofar as art is usually thought to be one of the primary sources of aesthetic experience and judgement. In Part III, I'll tackle some of the most basic philosophical questions in these areas. In chapter 8, we will consider the nature of art, looking at some of the challenges that developments in art history, and particularly the **avant-garde**, have posed for attempts to define the concept. In chapter 9, I'll move on to discuss the nature of 'aesthetic experience': this is usually thought to be a sort of experience one characteristically gets from artworks, but also from some objects in the natural world, and possibly other objects too. I'll discuss how positive accounts of the nature of aesthetic experience have been challenged by the assumption that art should be a primary source of such experience, in conjunction with developments in art history. Finally, in chapter 10, I'll examine the notion of an 'aesthetic judgement', and certain historically important questions concerning it; namely: can there be a standard of correctness for such judgements? Are there rules governing the application of aesthetic judgements? And is it ever appropriate to believe an aesthetic judgement about an object, based on the testimony of someone else, without having seen it oneself? In addressing these issues, two important names will recur repeatedly in discussion: the Scottish Philosopher David Hume (1711–76) and the German Philosopher Immanuel Kant (1724–1804).

8

what is art?

• INTRODUCTION

Lots of people are interested in what art is. For some, an investigation into the nature of art might be a practical exercise; they investigate by trying to make art. For others, it might take the form of close, careful engagement with particular artworks, as a viewer or listener. For philosophers, it has often taken the form of an attempt to offer a definition of the general category, art, in terms of a set of conditions that govern application of the concept *art* (italicised because the concept is being referred to). In this chapter, we will investigate some prominent approaches to this quest for a definition, both positive and negative, and explore their respective virtues and drawbacks.

• WHAT A GOOD DEFINITION WOULD LOOK LIKE

For philosophers committed to the enterprise of defining *art*, the holy grail would be a set of conditions, each of them individually necessary for *art*, and all of them taken together jointly sufficient for it. Necessary conditions of *art* would be conditions that all artworks *had to* satisfy, to count as art at all. Sufficient conditions of *art* would be conditions that, if all of them were satisfied by an object, would be *sufficient* or *enough* to qualify that object as an artwork. As necessary conditions, the conditions would say what all artworks had in common; as jointly sufficient ones, they would say what distinguished artworks from all other things. But some are pessimistic that this goal is attainable, preferring to focus only on finding a set of individually necessary conditions of *art* (sometimes referred to as art's 'essence').

So: philosophers bent on defining *art* aim to say, at least, what all artworks have in common; and perhaps, more ambitiously, what differentiates art from all other things as well. A further constraint usually endorsed upon any definition is that it be in tune with widespread current art-historical and critical practice. This is sometimes called the 'critical practice constraint'. It would not be convincing to say, for instance, that all artworks are necessarily made in studios, or that all art is made to look pretty. To say this would be to ignore the vast number of artworks, standardly accepted as such by artistic critics and other relevant experts, which are made outdoors, or made to deliberately look ugly.

These are artificial examples, since to my knowledge no one has ever offered them as conditions. But they demonstrate the point that successful definitions of art should accommodate at least most, and ideally all, of the objects about whose art-status there is consensus in the community of art experts.

• THE DIVERSITY OF EXISTING ARTWORKS

On the face of it, this makes the task of the would-be definer of art very difficult, in conjunction with a further fact: there is an apparently vast and diverse range of objects counted by experts as artworks.

Let's start with the traditional **'fine arts'** – painting, sculpture, architecture, music, and poetry, which, according to a famous text by Paul Kristeller, 'The Modern System of the Arts' (1951), were identified for the first time as a significant group in the eighteenth century. Take one famous object from each group: Botticelli's painting *La Primavera*; Rodin's sculpture *The Kiss*; Wren's St Paul's Cathedral; Bach's *Brandenburg Concerti*; and Sylvia Plath's poem *Lady Lazarus*. If one's focus is on the perceptible and manifest properties of such works, as experienced by a viewer or listener engaged with them, it already appears difficult to find properties common to all of these objects. After all, they cross sense modalities (vision, hearing, touch), media (canvas, marble, paper), and systems of representation (written language, musical notation, depiction).

Relatively recent events in art history make the task yet more difficult. In the twentieth century there was an explosion in the development of new art forms, and movements acknowledged as important by the artistic community. Partly these were driven by technological development: for instance, in the case of photography and cinema. Partly they were driven by recognition that the formation of the traditional artistic 'canon' has been influenced by prejudicial factors, such as the devaluation of the experiences and activities of women and people of colour. For instance, it was noticed that items traditionally considered, in virtue of their useful functional role, to be 'craft' objects, and so disqualified as art, were often those most likely to be made and used by women; women whose historical confinement to the home had deprived them of the time, economic means or social influence needed to produce objects destined for galleries and concert-halls. Observations such as this led to an expansion of accepted artforms, to include many craft objects and decorative items formerly excluded in principle. A notable example is quilts.

Most challenging of all for the would-be definer of art, however, is the fact that in the twentieth century the development of new art forms and movements was partly driven by the avant-garde. That is, artists often sought self-consciously to make objects that acted as counterexamples to prior artistic traditions, often reacting to and rejecting dominant views on the nature of the art form in which they were working. So for instance (very crudely): mass-produced 'readymades' were presented as artworks as a reaction to the idea of the artist as highly skilled artisan; conceptual art, including the use of performances and of textual descriptions, was developed in order to undermine the idea that an artwork must be a perceptible material object; the development of atonal music was a rejection of historically dominant Western norms governing classical music composition; and symbolism was developed as a contrast to the dominant naturalistic and realist aspirations of French literature at the time.

The result of all this is the existence of an apparently vast range of objects standardly agreed by art experts to belong to the class of artworks; and which, thanks to avant-garde movements, includes many objects deliberately intended to constitute counterexamples to prominent views on the nature of art. As long as the quest is for a set of common *perceptible* or *manifest* properties, the prospects of finding any common set of properties shared by all has looked hopeless. In relatively recent times, a different tack has been taken to the task of definition, which I shall now explore.

• FROM MANIFEST TO NON-MANIFEST PROPERTIES

Generally speaking, the properties that any physical object has can be divided into two broad categories: manifest properties (those one can perceive) and non-manifest ones (those one can't). In the latter category fall many relational properties: properties constituted by the object's standing in relation to other entities. For instance, Jamie possesses the non-manifest, relational property of *being from Aberdeen* – this is a property constituted by his standing in a particular relationship to Aberdeen. That Jamie possesses this property is normally not something you could tell by looking at him.

In the past, would-be definers of *art* have concentrated on trying to define art in terms of conditions pertaining to *manifest* properties. This is perfectly understandable, given the traditionally privileged relationship between art and the senses: historically speaking, art has been thought of as something that gives us valuable perceptual experiences (see chapter 9). But as the type of artworks critically received as such has expanded, philosophers have moved to considering non-manifest, relational properties as definitive of *art* instead.

• FUNCTIONAL AND PROCEDURAL DEFINITIONS OF ART

Broadly speaking, two sorts of non-manifest, relational properties have been considered. The first are functions. Functional definitions of art say, roughly, that art is that which has a particular function, or restricted set of functions. Functions are non-manifest properties, because you can't always tell by perceiving a thing what its function is. They are relational properties because what function(s) a thing has usually depends on either (a) a relation to the intention its maker had in making it, with respect to its use; or (b) a relation to its actual use by people; or both.

Unfortunately, like other definitions before them, functional definitions of *art* tend to be hampered by the wide variety of objects counted as art by experts. This diversity means that whatever function is offered as necessary for art, it must be suitably generally characterised, so as to fit all the objects. However, this can give rise to a problem: for the more general any function offered as necessary conditions for art is, the less suitable it is likely to be as a sufficient one (since generally characterised functions tend to be fulfilled by non-artworks too). For instance, one well-known functional definition, offered by Monroe Beardsley in 'Redefining Art' (1982), suggests (in broad terms, leaving aside detail irrelevant for our purpose here) that art is that which is intended to provide 'an experience with marked aesthetic character', valuable in virtue of that character. How this definition should be read depends, of course, on the meaning of 'marked aesthetic character' (see chapter 9 for related discussion). If 'marked aesthetic character' is construed very broadly – say, as a 'pleasurable perceptual experience' – the definition seems to apply to table settings, Christmas wreaths, and haircuts, and so include too much; if it is construed more narrowly (say, in the way Beardsley in fact defines it, as involving things like emotional distance, the active discovery of connections, and a sense of integration with the object) the definition seems to exclude many twentieth-century art objects, such as readymades and some conceptual artworks, which have been deliberately made to be 'anti-aesthetic', having no aesthetically significant perceptible properties at all. Beardsley bites this bullet (that is, accepts this unpalatable consequence), denying that many readymades and conceptual works are really art at all. Others have thought this a big problem with the definition, given the aforementioned desire to fit with standard critical practice.

The second sort of non-manifest, relational property in terms of which philosophers have attempted to define *art*, is *standing in relation to some sort of procedure*. **Procedural definitions of art** say, roughly, that art is that which has undergone a particular procedure. This is a non-manifest property because you usually can't tell by perceiving a thing what procedures it has undergone.

• DICKIE'S INSTITUTIONAL DEFINITION OF ART

The most well-known procedural definition, George Dickie's institutional definition of art, says that an artwork is an artefact which has had a particular status conferred upon it – the status of being 'a candidate for appreciation'. Moreover, this status must have been conferred by some person(s) acting on behalf of an institution: the institution of 'the artworld'.

An analogy: what makes certain bits of paper *money*? The rough answer is that they have had a certain status conferred upon them – the status of being legal tender – via a certain sort of procedure – being designed, printed and released for use in a certain way – where this procedure is carried out by people legitimately acting in certain defined roles, on behalf of a certain institution (the Bank of England, in the case of Sterling).

Another example: ordinary wine becomes *sacramental wine* via a procedure of ecclesiastical certification, and a ritualistic use at a certain point in a mass, by people suitably ordained in the Roman Catholic Church.

According to Dickie, artworks owe their status to an analogous procedure. Roughly, members of the artworld confer upon **artefacts** the status of 'candidates for appreciation', i.e. put them forward as the sort of thing that should be considered as worthy of appreciation (whether or not they actually turn out to be so worthy). This procedure, when carried out with respect to artefacts, is both necessary and sufficient to make an object an artwork. Because this procedure is so generally characterised, without much specific detail at all, Dickie's definition apparently overcomes the problem of artistic diversity: no matter whether the case concerns a painted canvas, a mass-produced urinal, a poem, a sonata, a performance, or a film, arguably there is an artefact which has been presented by someone responsible for it as a candidate for appreciation. (Admittedly, to make this stick in every case, some manipulation of the traditional notion of an artefact as a material object will be required, but let that pass.)

Dickie's institutional definition apparently depends on the coherency of thinking of the artworld as a genuine institution, akin in relevant ways to the Bank of England and the Roman Catholic Church. These institutions are centrally organised; have clearly defined roles, established in a hierarchical relationship to one another; and have agreed formal procedures for acceding to these roles, and for leaving them. The artworld, composed of visual artists, dancers, film-makers, musicians, curators, film producers, spectators, museum owners, cinematographers, poets, theatre managers, critics, novel readers, gallery-goers, set designers, costumiers, architects, and so forth, is not centrally organised, contains far fewer defined hierarchies – many of them discrete from one another – and the conditions of membership of many of these roles is very vague (*a gallery-goer* looks like it might be anyone who wanders into a gallery; *a visual artist* might be any one who picks up a paint brush). This is one worry about Dickie's definition: does the artworld have the formal structure to count as an institution, properly speaking, and so to bestow on its members the power of giving objects a genuine 'status' (as opposed to just calling them *art* and acting as if they are art)?

Another worry originates with the famous art theorist, philosopher and critic Richard Wollheim, in his book *Art and its Objects*. He presents Dickie with a dilemma: that is, with two possible consequences of the institutional definition, each of which are apparently unpalatable, and which together are supposed to exhaust the available options. The first option is that there are good independent reasons for members of the artworld to present a given object as a candidate for appreciation (etc.), so

BOX 8.1 RICHARD WOLLHEIM

The author of a powerful attack on the Institutional Theory, Richard Wollheim (1923–2003) was a British philosopher and one of the most well-known and influential people working in philosophical aesthetics in the twentieth century.

Amongst his books on art, he wrote *Art and Its Objects*, *Art and the Mind*, and *Painting as an Art*. His analysis of pictorial experience in terms of the notion of 'seeing-in' is of lasting significance and relevance to contemporary discussion of pictures. His knowledge of art and art history was immense, and, as well as works in philosophy, he wrote many influential critical pieces and reviews. He was well known for his enthusiasm for painting, in particular – in one work, he describes his habitual practice of staring at individual paintings for up to three hours at a time, to better discern their true meaning.

Wollheim's teaching career started at University College London in 1949, where he eventually became the Grote Professor of Mind and Logic, and continued later in the United States at Columbia, Berkeley and UC Davis. In an earlier life, he was a soldier in the Second World War, and participated in the liberation of the concentration camp Bergen-Belsen, an experience which he wrote about in a memoir 'A Bed Out of Leaves', for the *London Review of Books*. One of the surrealist things he describes there is being commanded to organise a dance between newly liberated, massively traumatised female camp survivors and British soldiers; an event which, predictably, ended in confusion and panic. He had a deep interest in and enthusiasm for psychoanalysis, and both his philosophical writing and his acclaimed autobiography *Germs: A Memoir of Childhood* are often infused with this perspective. He died in 2003, leaving a legacy of great work on painting, aesthetics generally, and philosophy of mind behind him.

rendering it, according to Dickie, as an artwork. These might be reasons that pertain to the object's intrinsic nature, the experiences it gives rise to and the quality of thought it provokes, or whatever. If this option is the case, the objection goes, we do not need to refer to the fact that the artworld designated the object an artwork to explain why it counts as such; we can refer to the prior reasons instead. In this case, the artworld is simply drawing attention to a pre-existing fact.

The other option, according to Wollheim, is that there are *no* good independent reasons for members of the artworld to call a given object an artwork. Wollheim thinks this option is unpalatable too. For if artworks count as such for no good reason, then effectively we lose any connection between what makes an artwork an artwork at all, and what makes an artwork a *good* artwork. On this horn of the dilemma, even if an artwork happens to provide valuable experience or thought, as many do, this is not the reason it counts as an artwork. This seems strange, Wollheim thinks, given the actual importance and value that art tends to have in our lives.

Procedural definitions generally, and the institutional definition in particular, cannot seem to explain the value of art, given that the conditions they focus upon are a matter of certain procedures being carried out, which have no intrinsic value in themselves. In contrast, whatever other problems they have, functional definitions are well placed to give an account of the value of art, in terms of the value of whatever function they state is definitive of art. But this does not worry Dickie, who bullishly proclaims it a virtue of his account that it does not make value a defining feature of art, arguing that this enables his account to accommodate very bad art, which has no apparent value at all but which still is counted as art nonetheless.

• ANTI-ESSENTIALISM

Not all philosophers of art have thought defining *art* to be a feasible or even coherent project. One sort of worry builds on Wollheim's earlier objection to Dickie and to procedural definitions generally. That is, first, that in order to illuminate genuinely the nature of art, an account of *art* should capture the (good) reasons for which some objects get designated as artworks, and others rejected. Procedural definitions do not appear to do this. In focusing on the mere fact of the process by which artworks get classified, they miss the point of that process, and so have nothing to say about any essence of *art* in a meaningful or interesting sense. The objection continues (now departing from Wollheim): in fact, when we look and see, we see that there *is no* single set of general reasons for which artworks count as such. There are good reasons why particular artworks count as such, but these differ from case to case. To argue thus is to be an **anti-essentialist** about art: to think that there is no interesting set of necessary conditions which all artworks fulfil, and no interesting limited set of sufficient ones.

One ground for being an anti-essentialist in this vein is to think that *art* is a concept derivative upon the prior concepts of individual art forms, such as painting, sculpture, music, and theatre. Granted, it is necessary and sufficient for an object counting as an artwork that it be a member of an individual art form; but this is a wholly uninteresting definition of *art* barely worthy of the name, in that it throws the explanatory burden back a stage, and demands prior definitions of individual art forms to be truly informative. This is where the interesting definitional work gets done, it is assumed. The contemporary aesthetician Dominic Lopes has argued for this sort of position, assuming that individual art forms can be interestingly defined in terms of necessary and sufficient conditions, and that art is just the sum total of everything that falls into an individual art form.

A more radical ground for anti-essentialism is to think that even individual art forms cannot interestingly be defined. This sort of position is advanced in a well-known article by Morris Weitz, written in the 1950s (chronologically prior to Dickie's

BOX 8.2 TRACY EMIN

Tracy Emin (1963–) is a British artist who has become famous for the challenging and controversial nature of the art she produces. One famous piece, 'My Bed' (1998), consists of the bed she had previously been using in her London flat, transported to a gallery, complete with objects from her life at the time on and around it, including condoms, slippers, and soiled sheets. 'My Bed' perplexed many people who saw it in the gallery. They ask themselves how a 'real' object, which was produced with no special skill, or even apparent care for its aesthetic effect, could count as art. They wondered whether this counted as a representation of something, or as the thing itself. They reflected on the fact that, had they themselves produced something similar, it would not have been counted as important art or of any real financial value (a point satirically echoed by a former partner of Emin, Billy Childish, who claimed he had another old bed of Emin's in his shed, and offered to sell it for a high price). In 2014 'My Bed' was sold by Christies for over £2.5 million.

Institutional Theory). Weitz was influenced by the later Wittgenstein in his *Philosophical Investigations*, who was sceptical generally of concepts being definable in terms of sets of individually necessary and jointly sufficient conditions. Weitz argues that *art*, like other concepts according to Wittgenstein, is a **family resemblance concept**: that is to say, some artworks have properties in common with certain other artworks, but there are no properties common or necessary to all artworks. (Weitz thinks this is also true of art form concepts, so would presumably reject Lopes's account for this reason.) According to Weitz, each time the concept of *art* is extended to cover new cases, it is extended via a practical decision made on the basis of similarity to some other established artworks but not all of them, rather than more automatically by reference to a fixed set of necessary and sufficient conditions which all artworks must fulfil.

Earlier I described the 'critical practice constraint' often taken to be operative on successful definitions of art: namely, that successful definitions must accommodate the wide variety of artworks thought of as such by art critics, artists and other relevant experts in the artistic community. Despite being a constraint upon definitions, it seems that this constraint has the effect of motivating anti-essentialism of the variety espoused by Weitz. For the critical practice constraint forces the would-be definer to focus upon the actual classificatory practices of the artistic community. Meanwhile, in the course of those classificatory practices, members of the artistic community don't consult a single definition during decisions to class new objects as 'art'. Rather it seems that they make decisions with respect to individual avant-garde cases on the basis of resemblance to some existing artworks. It would be too much to expect that despite the multiplicity of conscious grounds upon which relevant individuals make decisions with respect to new cases, nonetheless identification of some deep shared function or other shared property (manifest or relational) is motivating those decisions.

The result is a family resemblance account of *art*. Given the critical practice constraint, the only alternative to anti-essentialism seems to be to do as Dickie effectively does and focus on, as the defining property of *art*, the fact that classification by members of the artistic community occurs at all (that objects are 'presented as candidates for appreciation' etc). Yet this attracts other problems, some of which we have seen.

What to do? One might drop the critical practice constraint, and argue that what counts as art may be something that many members of the artistic community can be wrong about, in principle. Alternatively one might keep the constraint and remain relaxed about the anti-essentialism about art that seems thereby supported. One might think that art is primarily a social practice of making and appreciating, guided by individual conscious choices and by evolving conventions, rather than a natural kind whose essence remains fixed. One might also recall that it is unclear in any case what positive work even a widely accepted definition of art would do, given that it seems we don't need one to be able to tell what counts as art or not; or at least, we have done without one up until now, without apparent problem.

● CHAPTER SUMMARY

- Philosophers have sought to define the concept *art*, as a means of understanding what art is. They have aimed to do this by offering either a limited set of individually necessary and jointly sufficient conditions of *art*; or, less ambitiously, a set of necessary conditions only.
- They have also aimed to offer definitions that satisfy the 'critical practice constraint'; i.e. accommodate current classificatory practices within the community of artists, critics, and other relevant experts. This has proved challenging, given the wide diversity of entities classified by that community as artworks.
- This diversity has caused theorists in recent times to focus on searching, not on manifest properties shared by all artworks, but non-manifest ones, and more specifically, non-manifest relational ones. Two important definitions of art that focus on non-manifest relational properties of objects are (a) functional definitions and (b) procedural definitions.
- George Dickie's institutional definition is a famous version of the latter. Amongst others, it faces worries about whether the artworld counts as a genuine institution with the power to transform objects into artworks in the way required by the definition. It also faces worries about whether it can account for the value of art in our lives.
- A different approach is to reject the search for a definition of art altogether, and argue that art is not governed by any (interesting) necessary conditions. This anti-essentialism about art might be motivated by the thought that individual art

forms, rather than the general category of art, are the important explanatory unit; or by the thought that art is a family resemblance concept. The latter view looks to be supported by the critical practice constraint alluded to earlier.

• STUDY QUESTIONS

1 Make sure you understand the difference between necessary and sufficient conditions. Try to work out: what are the necessary conditions of being a traffic warden? What are the sufficient conditions?
2 Make a list of as many different artworks as you can think of. Include items from the visual, literary, and performative arts. Look at your list. Are there any manifest, perceptible properties common to all such items? If so, are these properties of any help in attempting to formulate a definition of *art*?
3 Now consider whether the items on your list share any particular function, and if so, whether that is of any help in formulating a definition of *art*.
4 Earlier I suggested that Dickie's institutional definition of art was unable to account for the (good) reasons for which individuals classified certain items as artworks. Do you think a successful definition ought to be able to account for such reasons?
5 Do you think a successful definition ought to be able to accommodate most or even all of the items currently classified as artworks by artists, critics and other members of the artistic community? Why/why not?
6 If it were true that no necessary conditions governed the concept of *art*, would it follow that there was no such thing as art?

• INTRODUCTORY FURTHER READING

Carroll, Noel (ed.) (2000) *Theories of Art Today* (Madison: University of Wisconsin Press). [A good collection, with entries from many prominent recent contributors.]
Danto, Arthur (2013) *What Art Is* (New Haven: Yale University Press). [A recent introductory work by a historically influential figure in the field.]
Davies, Stephen (1991) *Definitions of Art* (Ithaca, NY: Cornell University Press). [A comprehensive and useful orientation to the debate on the nature of art.]
Freeland, Cynthia (2002) *But is it Art?* (Oxford: Oxford University Press). [Introduction focusing on the avant-garde as an issue for defining art, and as a stimulus for development.]
Kristeller, Paul (1951) 'The Modern System of the Arts', *Journal of the History of Ideas* 12(4): 496–527 [Classic art-historical account of how the modern concept of 'the fine arts' emerged.]

● ADVANCED FURTHER READING

Beardsley, Monroe (1982) 'Redefining Art', in M. J. Wreen and D. M. Callen (eds) *The Aesthetic Point of View* (Ithaca, NY: Cornell University Press), pp. 298–315. [Contains a relatively succinct statement of Beardsley's functionalist definition of art.]

Dickie, George (1969) 'Defining Art', *American Philosophical Quarterly* 6(3): 253–56. [An early statement of Dickie's influential Institutional Theory.]

Lopes, Dominic (2008) 'Nobody Needs a Theory of Art', *Journal of Philosophy* 105(3): 109–27. [An ingenious and persuasive attempt to argue that the project of defining art as a general category is an uninteresting one.]

Weitz, Morris (1956) 'The Role of Theory in Aesthetics', *Journal of Aesthetics and Art Criticism* 15(1): 27–35. [An influential anti-essentialist paper, and the spur to Dickie's attempt to define art in terms of relational properties.]

Wollheim, Richard (1980) 'The Institutional Theory of Art', in *Art and its Objects* (Cambridge: Cambridge University Press), pp. 157–66. [Makes a powerful objection to Dickie's Institutional Theory.]

● FREE INTERNET RESOURCES

Adajian, Thomas (2012) 'The Definition of Art', *Stanford Encyclopaedia of Philosophy*, http://plato.stanford.edu/entries/art-definition. [A useful overview of issues surrounding the question of the definition of art.]

9

˙what is aesthetic experience?

• INTRODUCTION

The term 'aesthetic experience' has a complex history and is used in lots of apparently different contexts. Its primary context of use seems to be in relation to artworks, but it is also used in relation to the natural world, both on a large scale (e.g. landscapes) and a small one (e.g. pebbles, flowers, driftwood, coral). In this chapter, I'll examine some of the most prominent attempts to give a positive characterisation of it. I'll also further examine the relation between aesthetic experience and experience of art.

• AESTHETIC EXPERIENCE: THE PROBLEM(S)

Imagine you're on an evening stroll in the Alps, staring at mountains silhouetted against the stars. Or imagine that you're staring with fascination at the delicate patterns on a starfish, washed up on a white sand beach in the Tropics. Or imagine that you're in the Tate Modern in London, mentally absorbed by the gentle washes of colour in an abstract painting; or at a performance by your favourite band, energised by the rhythm of a drum beat and its interaction with the melody. These all look like examples of 'aesthetic experiences'. Such experiences look, on the face of it, like valuable and life-enhancing ones. However, it can often seem difficult to capture what they have in common. One might even wonder if there really is one sort of thing involved in all these examples. In this section I'll discuss several issues that arise with respect to the notion of aesthetic experience.

As just suggested, philosophers have wondered whether there is really one genuine and unified kind of experience – 'aesthetic experience' – rather than just a collection of further different sub-kinds of experience. Speakers can apply terms loosely in ways that mask underlying differences, some of them significant. To take an example from geology: people historically have used the term 'jade' to refer to what they originally thought of as one single kind of thing, a precious green stone. However, closer analysis with modern tools has shown that 'jade' is used to refer to two similar-looking but geologically distinct substances, jadeite and nephrite. One, though not the only, way to look at this would be to say that whether something is 'jade' or not is wholly dependent on whether that thing falls into the more basic sub-kinds, nephrite and jadeite. On this view, the term 'jade' does not pick out a genuine, unified kind of thing. Analogously, one might wonder: is 'aesthetic experience' a genuinely unified kind of thing, which can be had in relation to landscapes, paintings, music and other types of object; or is it merely a relatively loose collection of further more basic sub-kinds? (See 'What are Emotions?' in chapter 16, for an analogous discussion about kinds of emotion.) This is not to suggest that aesthetic experiences might fall into sub-kinds identifiable by scientific method: the analogy with jade is not supposed to go this far. The pertinent question is rather: are there interesting features that all aesthetic experiences have, in their own right? Call this 'the question of unification'.

Some have given a positive answer to the question of unification. Yes, there is a genuine unified kind, *aesthetic experiences*; all such experiences share certain common features in their own right, definitive of membership, and irrespective of what further sub-kinds they may belong to. As we'll see, a positive view usually identifies some distinctive relation(s) to other mental states as definitive of aesthetic experience. On the other side of the debate are those who think that there is no genuinely unified kind of thing, and that the term 'aesthetic experience' refers only to several more basic sub-kinds. I'll look at this 'deflationary' approach briefly later on.

Let's assume for the moment a positive view is the right one. Then a new set of questions arises, with respect to the relation between 'aesthetic experience' and art. Traditionally, art has been seen as a primary source of aesthetic experience, whatever that turns out to be. But as we will see, a lot of art doesn't look like a very good fit for those positive characterisations of aesthetic experience that have been offered; equally, those characterisations will also seem to apply to lots of things which are not art (nor even landscapes or natural objects). We will examine these issues under the heading 'the relation to art'.

• THE QUESTION OF UNIFICATION

This section asks: does 'aesthetic experience' refer to a single unified kind of thing or merely to a collection of further and more basic sub-kinds? Those who offer what I'm calling a 'positive' view say 'yes'. Aesthetic experiences all have certain features in common, whether or not they belong to further sub-kinds. The features typically cited are distinctive relations to further mental states.

In order to understand this debate, we need to understand something about its history. Eighteenth-century philosophers – such as the Earl of Shaftesbury, Francis Hutcheson, David Hume and Immanuel Kant – were greatly interested in the nature of *beauty*. Those accounts also tried to characterise the experience of beauty in terms of its allegedly distinctive relations, or lack of relations, to other named mental states. Speaking very roughly, and ignoring important differences between the various views, common ground in those earlier discussions included: that the experience of that beauty was (a) an experience which fundamentally depended on perception; which was also (b) pleasure-involving; (c) non-cognitive (roughly, was immediate and didn't involve any kind of rational inference or other computation); (d) non-practical (roughly, it did not meet any practical need or desire); and (d) was valuable simply 'for its own sake', not because it led to some other valuable goal.

Gradually, however, the conversation shifted towards a wider class of experience than just that of beauty. One reason for this was because of a continuing focus throughout the eighteenth century on the fine arts (painting, sculpture, music, poetry, architecture and dance), and the language we use to describe and critically engage with them. This language contains more than the adjective 'beautiful' to describe art. It includes adjectives such as 'graceful'; 'balanced'; 'dainty'; 'delicate'; 'bold'; 'muscular'; 'flowing'; 'lively'; 'charming'; and 'harmonious'. Equally, not all works amongst the fine arts are beautiful, and not even all works up until the eighteenth century: the history of painting, for instance, has always included disturbing and ugly imagery as well as the beautiful. 'Aesthetic experience' came to designate, more inclusively, the group of experiences that lead to the application of all these different adjectives, used in criticism and appreciation of the arts.

BOX 9.1 CLIVE BELL

Clive Bell (1881–1964) was a British art critic and member of the 'Bloomsbury group', an early twentieth-century group of intellectuals, artists and writers, based in London and Sussex, whose members included the writers Virginia Woolf and Lytton Strachey, and the painters Dora Carrington, Roger Fry and Duncan Grant. Bell was married to Woolf's sister, Vanessa, also a painter. Clive Bell was responsible, with Fry, for the championing of the 'post-impressionist' movement in painting – including artists such as Manet, Gauguin, Degas, Cezanne and Van Gogh – to an initially sceptical British public. As part of this effort, they attempted to provide an art-theoretical framework which would allow people to see post-impressionism as a natural part of the development of art history, generally. 'Aesthetic formalism' was the result: a theory that attempted to analyse aesthetic experience as responding only to manifest, perceptible properties of objects such as shape, colour, line and texture, all elements strongly emphasised, often at the expense of clear representation, in post-impressionist work. Though aesthetic formalism has since taken a drubbing from philosophers as a general theory of aesthetic experience, it remains an important and influential venture in the history of painting.

However, even though emphasis shifted away from experiences of beauty to a wider notion of aesthetic experience, and remains there today, it was and is still thought by many that a positive account of an *aesthetic experience*, more generally, can be produced by characterising it in terms borrowed from discussions of beauty: namely, as essentially (a) perceptual; (b) pleasure-involving; (c) non-cognitive, (d) non-practical and (e) valuable 'for its own sake'. Contemporary commentators still often discuss it in these terms. I'll now examine each of these supposedly identifying characteristics of aesthetic experience in more detail.

A note: sometimes people talk of aesthetic experiences as the experience of aesthetic 'properties'. Though this raises questions about the metaphysical status of these alleged properties (are they really 'in the world', like scientifically identifiable properties such as weight and volume?), for the purposes of this section it does no harm to speak like this.

● IS AESTHETIC EXPERIENCE FUNDAMENTALLY DEPENDENT ON THE PERCEPTUAL?

It is often claimed to be a basic fact about aesthetic experience that it is fundamentally dependent on the having of perceptual experience (an experience of seeing, hearing, smelling, touching, tasting). (See chapter 15, 'What is Perception?' for general discussion concerning perception.) This is not just to say that it is an experience caused by perceiving something in particular: many experiences are caused by perceiving something, without fundamentally depending on perception in the relevant sense. To say that a type of experience is fundamentally dependent on perceptual experience is to say that it could not be the type of experience it was, if it did not involve perceiving.

Another way this point is sometimes put is that aesthetic 'properties' necessarily depend, at least in part, on properties perceived by the senses. That is, whether an object has the property of *beauty*, or *elegance*, or *boldness*, or *balance* or *charm*…(etc.) depends on what other, usually more basic, properties one perceives it as having (for instance, its shape, its colour, its proportion, its weight, its textures, its line, its melody, its rhythm, and so on).

One radical view, '**aesthetic formalism**', says that aesthetic experience *exclusively* depends on properties perceived by the senses (e.g. shape, colour, line, rhythm, tone, texture, and so on). This restrictive view seems unable to accommodate, most obviously, the fact that, in the context of art, aesthetic appreciation is very often directed to representations of objects – pictures or sculptures or 'sound portraits' – whose internal aim is not just to produce an experience of aesthetically pleasing basic sensory properties, but also to represent objects in the world, and to be recognised and appreciated for doing so.

We can make the point with a thought experiment of Arthur Danto's in his book *The Transfiguration of the Commonplace* (1981). He asks us to imagine several canvases all exactly the same, in terms of their manifest perceptual properties: all rectangular canvases of the same size, painted the same shade of homogenous red. One is called *The Israelites Crossing the Red Sea* and depicts the moment after they had crossed, and their pursuers were drowned. Another is not an artwork at all, but merely a primed canvas, awaiting an artist's marks. Yet both provide exactly the same perceptual experiences, at whatever level of complexity of content these are described. This seems to show that being a representation is a matter not only of looking (or sounding) a certain way, but also a matter of being produced by a person with a certain cognitive set, including an understanding of representational systems, and the intention to use or adapt them to convey some meaning or other.

It seems that we need to retreat to a more moderate claim about the relation between aesthetic and perceptual experience: namely, aesthetic experience of an object at least *partly* depends on the perceptual experience of its properties. Yet even this looks problematic to some, given the assumption that aesthetic experience should be the sort of experience provided by art, plus the fact that in recent times, art has included conceptual art, and the production of 'non-perceptual' artworks. (See 'The Problem of Non-Perceptual Art' (2003) by James Shelley for the response that one can have non-perceptual aesthetic experiences.)

• ARE AESTHETIC EXPERIENCES ESSENTIALLY PLEASURABLE?

Probably because of the aforementioned historical connection with discussions about the nature of beauty, a strong emphasis tends to be placed in discussions of aesthetic experience on a connection to pleasure. It is undoubtedly true that paradigmatic aesthetic experiences involve pleasure – looking at beautiful paintings or landscapes, listening to stirring symphonies or limpid piano sonatas, eating wonderful meals, and so on. However, as with the previous discussion, the supposed connection between aesthetic experience and art, plus development of the concept of *art* to cover a wide range of cases, poses a problem for a conception of aesthetic experience as essentially pleasurable.

Earlier I described how great painting often focuses on ugly and disturbing scenes. Equally, a major genre in the theatre, tragedy, represents harrowing events. Spectators of such works undoubtedly often have an experience of value, but it is not obvious that they must be enjoying themselves in a pleasurable way as they do so (not all valuable experiences are pleasurable at the time). Adjectives such as 'agonising', 'gut-wrenching', 'visceral', and 'devastating' are not infrequently appropriately applied to experiences of theatrical performances of tragedies. These look difficult to reconcile with the spectator being in a pleasurable state. Yet these look to many like 'aesthetic experiences' too.

One response would be to insist that such experiences, though on the face of them unpleasant, may also have pleasurable elements. One might add, why else would the spectator willingly pay money to have such experiences? One might also add that whatever harrowing effects a tragedy has on a spectator, these are usually short-lived, and indeed, sometimes even compatible with eating ice-cream at intervals, chatting with one's companions, and so on. One might make an analogy with fearful experiences that are also pleasurable for some, such as bungee-jumping. Here too we have an apparently normally unpleasant experience, felt as pleasurable; the analogy with theatre is further strengthened by noting that both in bungee-jumping and in theatre-going, the situation is controlled and largely predictable. (This is not the only possible response: Hume attempts a different and more complex explanation of this 'unaccountable' pleasure in his essay 'Of Tragedy' (1777).)

A more basic problem for the association between aesthetic experience and pleasure is raised by experiences of art that are *neither* valuable *nor* pleasurable. One might cite experiences of *ugliness*, *decay*, *disharmony*, and *lack of balance*, where these are ascribed as signs of failure in a work or object. Do these descriptions, and the experiences that underpin them, also count as aesthetic? If so, the thought that aesthetic experiences are pleasurable ones has met an obviously problematic sort of case. Certainly, the language of art criticism is centrally concerned with such adjectives, since it is not only focused on what succeeds but also on what fails. The question then becomes: to what extent must the class of aesthetic experiences coincide with the sorts of experience that form the basis for art criticism? Clearly, given the history of the discussion, the two must overlap; but this leaves room for the overlap to be only partial. Whether or not it makes sense to class both pleasurable and displeasurable experiences of art works into one single class of aesthetic experiences will depend on whether any further features, apart from pleasure, are found to unite the class.

● ARE AESTHETIC EXPERIENCES ESSENTIALLY NON-COGNITIVE?

I turn now to another popular candidate for a feature uniting aesthetic experiences as a class: that they are 'non-cognitive'. The term 'cognitive', broadly speaking, is used to refer to that which has to do with the concept-using, intellectual, or reasoning part of the mind. To suggest that aesthetic experiences are *non*-cognitive is to suggest that in some significant sense they do *not* involve this part of the mind.

For Kant, whose 'Analytic of the Beautiful' (the first section of his *Critique of Judgement*) has been hugely influential in discussions of aesthetic experience, the experience of beauty must be non-cognitive in at least the following sense. When one looks at an object and finds it beautiful, this 'evidence' for the thing's beauty is not recognition of the object as falling under some concept (as recognising the object, say, as a *Lalique vase*, or as a *Monet watercolour*, or as a *landscape formed by glaciation*). Nor is one's pleasure at the experience of beauty caused by any such conceptual classification.

With respect to the last point, Kant makes a distinction between an experience of 'free' beauty – which we can think of as 'true' beauty – and an experience of 'dependent' beauty. Seeing something as 'dependently' beautiful involves thinking of it as something like a perfect or very successful instance of the thing it is supposed to be. So one might find a Lalique vase 'dependently' beautiful. This would involve consciously considering the thing in question as falling under the concept *Lalique vase*, and taking pleasure in how the thing fulfils the very high standards of artistry we would expect of this type of object. In contrast, seeing something as 'freely beautiful' is not like this: no consideration of what the thing is supposed to be is involved as a 'ground' of the experience.

Some commentators have interpreted Kant as saying that in order to see objects as 'freely' beautiful, one cannot employ concepts at all: that somehow one must switch off one's cognitive abilities – one's knowledge of the history of the objects one is looking at, and even of what the objects are – in order to experience them aesthetically. Effectively, when extended to aesthetic experience more generally, this is to make the Kantian position very close to the aesthetic formalist position we looked at above. For if, in true aesthetic experience, one cannot utilise conceptual or empirical knowledge of objects, then it seems there is nothing left but to rely on information about the objects' perceptible properties, brought solely via one's senses. A moderate interpretation of Kant's view is that a person's pleasure in the beauty of a thing should not in any way be caused by the recognition that the thing falls under some concept, where this is compatible with concept application occurring during the relevant experience. (See Christopher Janaway's 'Kant's Aesthetics and the "Empty Cognitive Stock"' (1997) for this interpretation.)

A different way of making the claim that aesthetic experiences are 'non-cognitive' has its roots in the British Empiricist tradition. On this sort of view, the emphasis is on the immediate, non-inferential, non-reasoning nature of aesthetic experiences. That is, one does not *work out* whether something satisfies a particular aesthetic adjective or not; one does not apply principles, or examine evidence, and then make inferences to that conclusion. Rather one's experience comes to one immediately, without intellectual effort, just as perceptual experiences do. Saying this looks wholly compatible with allowing that aesthetic experiences may involve the application of concepts; equally, it allows that aesthetic experiences may draw upon background understanding and knowledge for their existence in particular cases. What is disallowed, rather, is the *effortful* application of concepts, understanding or knowledge to experience, as a result of reasoning. This seems preferable to the view that no background knowledge should be called upon, for reasons already touched upon in criticising the aesthetic formalist position: namely, that it seems to drive a wedge between experience of art grounded in critical appreciation and aesthetic experience. Critical appreciation of the arts is fundamentally grounded in knowledge and experience. We wouldn't trust a critic who didn't know what sort of object she was discussing; who didn't know who made it, or when; what artistic movements it belongs to; what interesting comparisons it makes with other artworks, and so on. If reliable aesthetic experiences of artworks depend on this sort of knowledge, then any account of aesthetic experience that excludes it looks suspect. (If, on the other hand, you are suspicious of the whole notion of a 'reliable' aesthetic experience, knowledgeable or not, then save your suspicions for chapter 10, where the issue will be discussed in more detail.)

• ARE AESTHETIC EXPERIENCES ESSENTIALLY NON-PRACTICAL?

We have just looked at a negative association traditionally made between aesthetic experiences and what might broadly speaking be called 'cognition'. A different negative association traditionally made, also with roots in Kant, is between aesthetic experiences and 'practical interest', or, even more generally, desire. Often this alleged feature of aesthetic experience is referred to by saying it is 'disinterested', though this usage tends to be loose and, as we'll see, covers a range of different-looking cases.

One version of this claim says that to count as such, properly speaking, aesthetic experiences must *not* be grounded in pleasure derived from the thought of the attainment of practical goals. This view is usually bound up with the view, discussed earlier, that aesthetic experience must be pleasurable. Lots of experiences are pleasurable, not all of them aesthetic, so we need some way of distinguishing the pleasure which is distinctively associated with aesthetic experiences from other kinds. The claim being considered is that aesthetic pleasure towards an object is *not* a pleasure based on the thought of that object's helping one to achieve certain useful ends.

We find a variant of this view in Kant, who in the 'Analytic of the Beautiful' argues that true aesthetic pleasure is disconnected from practical desire altogether. Some pleasures – for instance, pleasure in what is morally good, according to Kant – come with a desire (other things being equal) to act so as to bring the good state of affairs about, or at least to maintain it. For Kant, aesthetic pleasure has no accompanying desire to commit some further action (see Shelley 'The Concept of the Aesthetic' (2013) for discussion). It is purely 'contemplative'.

As we saw earlier, some might be uncomfortable about too strong a connection being made between aesthetic experience and pleasure. Sometimes the claim that aesthetic experience is disinterested instead becomes the claim that aesthetic experience, whether pleasurable or not, should not be *motivated* by practical interest, including self-interest. This is a claim, not so much about any pleasure supposedly involved in aesthetic experience, but rather about the motives for which one might seek aesthetic experience.

It is true that often one enters art galleries or concert halls without any thought about how what one is about to experience will help one achieve some further end. Thus, it is not usually in doubt that *some* aesthetic experiences may be motivated non-instrumentally. What seems less secure is that *all* must be. In a famous article called 'The Myth of the Aesthetic Attitude' (1964), George Dickie argues that the type of motive accompanying the seeking-out of aesthetic experiences need not affect what kind of experience it turns out to be, in terms of the quality of its attention to an object, its felt pleasure and/or its value. In responding to the same painting, two people might have the very same high-quality aesthetic experience, and yet one of them be motivated instrumentally (say, because she wants to improve her aesthetic education, in order to move into a certain social clique) and the other non-instrumentally. Of course, sometimes certain motives will make us distracted, or only focused on particular details at the expense of others. Dickie discusses the examples of a jealous spouse attending a play in which his partner acts, in order to assess behaviour towards fellow cast members. But these sorts of case don't show that *all* instrumentally motivated experiences involve imperfect or incomplete attention to an object. It remains possible, according to Dickie, that one might be instrumentally motivated in pursuing what nonetheless turns out to be a very valuable and/or pleasurable aesthetic experience, involving full attention to all aspects of the thing being contemplated, without any effect on the quality of the experience itself. If this is granted, then it seems *ad hoc* to insist that true aesthetic experiences be non-instrumentally motivated.

The claim that aesthetic experience is entirely separate from practical interests implies that it is separate from moral interests, since moral interests look like a species of practical interests (see p. 10, 'Moral Motivation'). This position is called 'radical autonomism'. Radical autonomism, too, has been heavily criticised. As is by now familiar, the trouble stems from the close historical association between aesthetic experience and art. Narrative artworks such as novels and films often ask of the reader a particular moral response: the condemnation of villainous behaviour; the approval of virtuous character. So it seems that, for as long as we characterise aesthetic experiences as closely connected to the experiences provided by artworks, aesthetic experiences will often involve moral responses. Radical autonomism cannot accommodate this, apparently.

• IS AESTHETIC EXPERIENCE 'VALUABLE FOR ITS OWN SAKE'?

Sometimes the claim that aesthetic experience is 'disinterested' is connected to a further claim: that aesthetic experience has only intrinsic value, and not instrumental value. It is valuable, not because of any further desires or goals it promotes, but simply 'for its own sake'. Oscar Wilde expresses a version of this view when he claims, at the beginning of *The Picture of Dorian Gray*, that 'All art is quite useless' (assuming, of course, as Wilde does, that art is a major resource for aesthetic experience).

Though at first it looks like there is one, the supposed connection between aesthetic experience being non-instrumentally motivated, and its being intrinsically valuable, is harder than one might think to recover. Say that I enter an art gallery with no motive other than to enjoy its paintings (a case of non-instrumental motivation). The first point to make is that, of course, my experience might not be valuable at all. But even if it is, it doesn't seem to follow from my being motivated non-instrumentally that any value I derive from the experience won't be instrumental. It might so happen that the experience I get there unexpectedly helps me in some further goal of mine. Nor does my experience being non-instrumentally valuable even follow from the fact that the pleasure I feel, in looking at the paintings, is not pleasure at the thought of any instrumental goal being satisfied by my doing so. For pleasure and value are different things: the value of an experience might emerge only on reflection, after the pleasure of the experience has ended, and turn out to be instrumentally valuable after all.

In any case, why should we accept that aesthetic experience cannot be instrumentally valuable? This is much stronger than to say that it cannot be *only* instrumentally valuable (that there must be some intrinsic value as well). I've already discussed the possibility of someone who has what looks like a very high-quality, fully attentive aesthetic experience, yet who was motivated to seek out that experience for instrumental reasons (e.g. for self-improvement, for some further end). In that case, should her experience in fact fulfil her further instrumental ends, and be valuable on that basis, it would seem churlish to disallow that the experience count as properly aesthetic, so long as the subject also got some value that was non-instrumental out of the experience too.

It seems, then, that the claim under consideration is best interpreted as that aesthetic experience must not *only* be instrumentally valuable; it must *also* be intrinsically valuable. Though this is harder to deny, it does exclude from the class of aesthetic experiences those subject only to negative evaluation, in terms of properties like *ugliness*, *decay* and *disharmony*. Perhaps this is not too high a price to pay. In any case, assuming that many experiences in life are intrinsically valuable, including moral ones, this falls far short of offering us any distinctive characteristic of aesthetic experience as a genuine class, as we might have hoped for.

• A DEFLATIONARY APPROACH TO AESTHETIC EXPERIENCE

In the face of limitations of the various characterisations of aesthetic experience considered so far, one alternative 'deflationary' approach is to give a list of certain properties and objects, and then characterise aesthetic experience as whatever

BOX 9.2 SHERRI IRVIN

In her article 'The Pervasiveness of the Aesthetic in Everyday Experience' (2008), the American contemporary philosopher Sherri Irvin, working out of the University of Oklahoma, discusses a range of activities and states which have not been traditionally associated with the aesthetic, and yet which seem to her to be cases of aesthetic experience. These include drinking tea out of her favourite mug; resting her cheek on her hand as she looks at the ducks in the pond outside her window; petting her cat and smelling its fur; and fiddling distractedly with her wedding ring. If Irvin is right, then these examples pose a much stronger challenge to traditional notions of the aesthetic than the experience produced by any avant-garde artworks, for they include everyday activities with no associated physical object, and even action and events of which one might be, by Irvin's own admission, 'hardly conscious'. Irvin goes on to develop an account of aesthetic experience based on the work of John Dewey. Irvin's provocative attempt to root the notion of aesthetic experience in ordinary life rather than exalted cultural settings is an intriguing one that raises several questions for the traditional view.

experiences are had in relation to these sorts of properties and objects. For instance, in 'Aesthetic Experience Revisited' (2000), Noel Carroll identifies a selection of properties, including form, design, symmetry or the lack of it, mass, expressive (emotion-arousing) properties, and aesthetic properties such as *unity* and *gracefulness*, and then identifies the class of aesthetic experiences as whatever attentive experiences are had in relation to those properties, and their interaction. This is presented as a way of saving the class of aesthetic experience, but it is not clear that it really does. As he himself admits, to say this is to admit that there is no one kind of aesthetic experience. Hence it does not seem we have a genuinely interesting class after all. Granted, this is not the most sceptical position on aesthetic experience one might take here: he is not saying, for instance, that our use of the term 'aesthetic experience' is completely randomly applied. This is still a class with somewhat predictable membership. However, on Carroll's view, there is nothing interesting about the class in its own right; membership is entirely determined by belonging to some sub-class of experience (e.g. attentive experience in relation to design properties; attentive experience in relation to expressive properties).

• THE RELATION TO ART

It is notable that many of the putative positive characterisations of aesthetic experience described above apparently failed because of a bad fit with some group of artworks. For instance, the claim that aesthetic experience was essentially perceptual was challenged by the existence of non-perceptual conceptual art. The claim that aesthetic experience was essentially pleasurable was challenged by art that seeks to shock and disturb. The claim that it is essentially detached from the practical is challenged by representational art that seeks to educate morally and to thereby change behaviour. Given the great diversity of objects which are now counted as artworks (see chapter 8) this problem seems likely to reoccur wherever 'aesthetic experience' is considered near-identical to 'experience appropriately had in relation to artworks'.

One way to deal with these problems is to argue that the link between aesthetic experience and art should be weakened. It should not be a constraint on an adequate account of aesthetic experience that it fits with our experience of all paradigmatic artworks. Instead, we might suggest, aesthetic experience is appropriately produced by *a significant number of, but not all*, artworks, and by some things that are not artworks too (indeed, this was conceded from the beginning, when it was admitted that natural objects could provide aesthetic experiences). Certain artworks provide valuable experiences that are not aesthetic. On this view, aesthetic experience is a central but not an essential product of art, and does not exhaust everything valuable about it.

However, one problem with this sort of move for the views we have looked at is that some of them seem hard pressed to accommodate even *a significant portion* of artworks. For instance, as we've seen, the claim that aesthetic experience is non-cognitive seems to exclude from consideration any representational artwork; or even any artwork at all, proper appreciation of which requires the application of knowledge about its provenance and context. This is surely the vast majority of them. The insistence that aesthetic experience be non-practical in some sense, meanwhile, seems to exclude all artworks which seek to influence moral, political or religious opinion or behaviour, or to teach anything whatsoever. Again, this is a large proportion of them.

One significant group of artworks that might seem to fit the prescriptions that aesthetic experience be perceptual, non-cognitive, and non-practical, is that of *abstract visual artworks* such as paintings by Rothko, Pollock, Klee and Kandinsky. One might defend a characterisation of aesthetic experience in the relevant terms, additionally arguing that the production of aesthetic experience, thus construed, is the special provenance of abstract visual artworks as well as objects in the natural world, but not artworks generally. See 'In Defence of Moderate Aesthetic Formalism' (2000) by Nick Zangwill for some related claims.

Whether or not this works for abstract art, a potential obstacle here, at least with respect to natural objects, is that there are those who think that even the aesthetic experience of the natural world is appropriately infused with cognitive knowledge. For instance, Allen Carlson has argued that appropriate appreciation of the natural world is cognitive, requiring application of knowledge about scientific categories. According to him, knowledge of such categories determines what on a large scale to perceive (e.g. not just the pebble in isolation from its environment, but the pebble as situated on the hillside, and the relation between it and the terrain around it); and what to notice in detail (e.g. the patterns on the pebble as produced by weather-erosion on limestone). To fail to pay attention to this information is to distort the phenomenon in question, according to Carlson.

A different approach to the problematic relation between aesthetic experience and art, meanwhile, is to widen out the conditions upon aesthetic experience to the point at which it seems difficult to see how experiences of artworks could fail to meet them. One thinker who provides material for this sort of approach is John Dewey. The details of Dewey's view are not always easy to extract, but it seems clear that for Dewey, an aesthetic experience is a particularly intense, emotionally integrated portion of consciousness, marked out from the rest of experience by having some sort of unified structure, with its internal parts experienced as standing in relation to one another. It is experienced as having something like a beginning, a middle and an end, where the end brings some sort of closure or completion. It also involves a balance of activity and passivity. There is no suggestion here that the experience has to be perceptual, non-cognitive or non-practical: Dewey apparently allows that intellectual and practical experiences can exhibit aesthetic character. Nor apparently need it be pleasurable: he cites a 'rupture of friendship' as an experience with potential aesthetic character. As well as potentially applying to experiences of all artworks, this sort of view clearly allows for all sorts of objects to count as sources of aesthetic experiences, and not just artworks: Dewey cites memorable meals, and storms, as two possible sources.

• CHAPTER SUMMARY

- There is controversy about whether 'aesthetic experience' is a genuinely unified class, or simply a class defined by membership of further sub-kinds.
- Attempts have been made to show that aesthetic experience is a genuinely unified class by characterising it in terms of being essentially (i) perceptual, (ii) pleasurable, (iii) non-cognitive, (iv) non-practical, (v) valuable for its own sake.
- Most of these attempts have encountered obstacles, given a prior assumption of a close connection between 'aesthetic experience' and 'experience appropriately produced by artworks', plus the diversity of objects in the class of artwork.
- Possible responses include: (i) denying aesthetic experience is a genuinely unified class after all; (ii) weakening the connection between 'aesthetic experience' and 'experience appropriately produced by artworks' so that only some artworks appropriately produce aesthetic experience; or (iii) widening the account of aesthetic experience even further so many sorts of objects can produce it, including nearly all artworks.

• STUDY QUESTIONS

1 From memory, consider times in your life where you had what might be classed as a powerful aesthetic experience. These might be when you were listening to great music, looking at paintings, reading a poem, or standing looking at a beautiful landscape or sunset. If you can, write down descriptions of your experience – feelings and thoughts – in each case.

2 Now consider whether your experiences in these cases had anything in common, and specifically, whether they share any of the features discussed as common to aesthetic experience in this chapter. Specifically: were they all pleasurable? Were they all in any sense non-cognitive? Were they motivated for practical ends? Were they valuable 'for their own sake'? Doing this will help you critically reflect on the truth or otherwise of the claims being considered, by having concrete cases to consider.

3 As we've seen, many philosophers have rejected the idea that the value of aesthetic experience (and art, in fact) comes from its being instrumentally valuable, i.e. its leading to further valuable goals. Do you agree with them?

4 Consider the 'deflationary' account, according to which there is no distinctive kind of thing that is aesthetic experience, over and above membership in various sub-kinds. What are the considerations in favour of this position, if any?

5 Dewey suggests that aesthetic experience is not just appropriately had in relation to artworks and landscapes, but may also be had in relation to things like storms, meals, and quarrels. Do you agree? If so, what account of aesthetic experience does this imply? Contrast to the traditional view.

• INTRODUCTORY FURTHER READING

Carroll, Noel (2000) 'Art and Ethical Criticism: An Overview of Recent Directions in Research', *Ethics* 110(2): 350–87. [Survey, including the debate on the relation between ethical judgement and aesthetic experience.]

Danto, Arthur (1981) *The Transfiguration of the Commonplace* (Cambridge, MA: Harvard University Press), ch. 1 ('Works of Art and Mere Real Things'). [Classic text in which Danto introduces the thought experiment of 'indiscernibles' in order to discredit aesthetic formalism, among other things.]

Dickie, George (1964) 'The Myth of the Aesthetic Attitude', *American Philosophical Quarterly* 1(1): 56–65. [Accessible and influential attack on the notion of a positive characterisation of aesthetic experience.]

Hughes, Fiona (2009) *Kant's Critique of Aesthetic Judgement* (London: Continuum). [Helpful and detailed interpretation of Kant's difficult '3rd Critique', including the 'Analytic of the Beautiful'.]

Irvin, Sherri (2008) 'The Pervasiveness of the Aesthetic in Everyday Experience', *British Journal of Aesthetics* 48: 29–44. [An interesting and accessible attempt to explain Dewey's view, and to develop it into one which fully captures the aesthetic experience of the everyday.]

• ADVANCED FURTHER READING

Carroll, Noel (2002) 'Aesthetic Experience Revisited', *British Journal of Aesthetics* 42(2): 145–68. [Recent defence of a 'deflationary' approach to aesthetic experience.]

Dewey, John (2009) *Art as Experience* (New York: Perigee). [Dewey's stimulating and idiosyncratic contribution to the discussion about aesthetic experience and art, originally published in 1934.]

Janaway, Christopher (1997) 'Kant's Aesthetics and the "Empty Cognitive Stock"', *Philosophical Quarterly* 47(189): 459–76. [Accessible interpretation of Kant on the supposed non-cognitive nature of aesthetic experience.]

Shelley, James (2003) 'The Problem of Non-Perceptual Art', *British Journal of Aesthetics* 43(4). [An intriguing defence of the idea that aesthetic experience is not essentially grounded in perceptual experience.]

Zangwill, Nick (2000) 'In Defence of Moderate Aesthetic Formalism', *Philosophical Quarterly* 50(201): 476–93. [Provocative attempt to resurrect the unfashionable position of aesthetic formalism for a restricted range of cases.]

• FREE INTERNET RESOURCES

Carlson, Allen (2010) 'Environmental Aesthetics', *Stanford Encyclopaedia of Philosophy*, http://plato.stanford.edu/entries/environmental-aesthetics/. [Overview, including discussion from a partisan perspective of Carlson's own view that aesthetic experience of the natural environment is importantly cognitive.]

Ginsborg, Hannah (2013) 'Kant's Aesthetics and Teleology', *Stanford Encyclopaedia of Philosophy*, http://plato.stanford.edu/entries/kant-aesthetics/. [A detailed and helpful account of Kant's position on beauty and aesthetic experience.]

Hume, David (1777) 'Of Tragedy', in *Four Dissertations*, http://www.davidhume.org/texts/fd.html. [Essay in which Hume attempts to explain the origin of the 'unaccountable pleasure' of viewing harrowing tragedies on stage.]

Kant, Immanuel 'Analytic of the Beautiful', trans. James Creed Meredith, originally published by Oxford: Clarendon Press, 2011, http://www.sophia-project.org/uploads/1/3/9/5/13955288/kant_beautiful.pdf. [Difficult but massively influential section of Kant's *Critique of Judgement*.]

Leddy, Tom (2013) 'Dewey's Aesthetics', *Stanford Encyclopaedia of Philosophy*, http://plato.stanford.edu/entries/dewey-aesthetics/. [A useful attempt to systematise Dewey's sometimes confusing theory.]

Shelley, James (2013) 'The Concept of the Aesthetic', *Stanford Encyclopaedia of Philosophy*, http://plato.stanford.edu/. [A good historical overview of the development of the concept, and its philosophical consequences.]

10

what is aesthetic judgement?

• INTRODUCTION

In this final chapter, I will be concerned with some questions about the nature of aesthetic judgements. These are best characterised, at least initially, by example. Aesthetic judgements about an object would include: that it is *ugly*, that it is *graceful*, that it is *dainty*, that it is *dynamic*, that it is *pretty*, that it is *pallid*, that it is *bland*, that it is *vivid*, that it is *unbalanced*…and so on. In other words, aesthetic judgements about an object are those evaluative judgements often invoked in artistic and literary criticism, but also in the assessment of landscapes, the physical attributes of people and animals, fashion, food, craft objects, and home decoration as well. Often they pertain to the physical appearance of an object but not always, as in the claim that a novel is *well-composed*. They can include claims about 'expressive' aspects of objects, for instance that a piece of music is *sad* or *angry*, or that a painting is *tranquil*. A judgement that something is *beautiful* is also an aesthetic judgement – perhaps the central case.

In this chapter I'll be introducing three questions concerning aesthetic judgements. Namely, are there standards of correctness for aesthetic judgements? Are there rules connecting aesthetic judgements with non-aesthetic properties? And: are aesthetic judgements transmissible via testimony? First, however, I'll briefly connect the questions of this chapter to those of the last.

• AESTHETIC JUDGEMENT AND AESTHETIC EXPERIENCE

What is the relation between aesthetic judgements and aesthetic experience? Presumably, those who think that aesthetic experience is a genuine entity (see chapter 9), think of this sort of experience as underpinning at least some aesthetic judgements. To say this wouldn't be to say that experiences identical in every respect underpin such judgements – after all, the judgements described are diverse and each apparently pick out genuinely different properties (*beauty* is different from *grace* is different from *balance* etc.). (See 'What are Properties?' in 'What is Metaphysics?' for general discussion of properties.) The claim would be, rather, that broadly speaking, the experiences which (supposedly) underpin such judgements have certain features in common which entitle us to classify them as a group under the heading 'aesthetic experience' – perhaps, being perceptually based, pleasure-involving, non-cognitive, non-practical, and/or valuable for their own sake.

Against this, we can note at this stage that some of these characterisations apparently fail to fit some of the examples of aesthetic judgements just cited. For instance, some of those judgements (e.g. that something is *ugly*, or *unbalanced*) seem to be based on an unpleasant experience, not a pleasurable one, and nor is it clear that they imply value, though they do imply valuation. Others apparently involve concept-application and some degree of understanding, a point famously spelled out in an article by Kendall Walton, 'Categories of Art' (1970). For instance, when assessing an object in terms of such judgements, what counts as *graceful* or *tranquil* or *dynamic* or *unbalanced* might be relative to the category to which the object belongs. What counts as *dynamic* paintwork for cubist paintings, as a category, might be different from what counts as *dynamic* paintwork for eighteenth-century British watercolour still-lifes. Assessing this difference seems to involve knowledge of what is normal for the relevant category

Maybe a single characterisation of aesthetic experience eventually will be offered to accommodate this diversity of judgement. Or maybe it will turn out that there is no single sort of experience, positively characterised, which might plausibly underpin all these types of judgements but not other non-aesthetic judgements. Leaving this matter aside, I turn now to three questions about aesthetic judgement which do not depend directly on an answer to this matter.

• ARE THERE STANDARDS OF CORRECTNESS FOR AESTHETIC JUDGEMENTS?

Let's make what looks like a reasonable and minimally committed assumption: aesthetic judgements are partly based on some sort of 'subjective' evaluative response – something like approval or disapproval. Nearly all the examples of aesthetic judgements given so far seem, in their characteristic uses, to indicate either approval – e.g. *graceful, delicate, pretty, vivid* – or disapproval – e.g. *ugly, unbalanced, bland*. To say this is obviously not to make the stronger claim that pleasure must be involved, though very often, of course, it will be.

The apparent subjectivity of aesthetic judgements makes it look as if there can't be any standard of correctness governing them. If it is partly a matter of personal preference whether a thing counts as *graceful*, or *ugly*, then it seems there can be no fact of the matter here. However, also note that we often act as if there *were* facts about aesthetic judgements' correctness or incorrectness. We might get into arguments with others about whether a particular view is *beautiful*, or building *graceful*, or piece of music *dynamic*. This seems to imply we think there are standards of correctness about such judgements – otherwise, why would we bother arguing? But then there looks like a tension here.

One famous attempt to resolve this tension is given by David Hume in his essay 'Of the Standard of Taste' (1757). Hume starts with an assumption: that certain properties ('forms or qualities') in the world are naturally fitted to promoting pleasurable or displeasurable responses in human beings who perceive or otherwise interact with them. The standard of correct aesthetic judgement towards an object, in a particular case, coincides with whatever these natural responses are towards that object, fully perceived or cognised. Hume concedes, however, that in many cases a person is not in the right situation to access what the natural response is to an object. She might be unperceptive, inattentive, biased against the object for personal reasons, have no real experience with such objects or know what they are normally like, be drunk, or tired, and so on. Additionally, Hume notes certain 'blameless' factors which inevitably colour judgement: culturally acquired, age-based, or simply personal preferences for some kinds of thing over another. Some people like comedy, some like tragedy, some like neither – these are not universal human preferences, but derive from individual idiosyncrasies.

Despite the probability of such factors colouring an individual's judgement, Hume gives us two methods to work out what the standard of correctness for aesthetic judgements is. The first method is to find cases where there is a near-universal response to an object, either of approval or disapproval. Hume tells us that the works of Homer, for instance, are admired across most cultures and historical periods. Cross-cultural and pan-historical convergence of opinion is a good indicator that a natural, and so on Hume's terms 'correct', response is being given, free of distorting or local influences. We might be able to explain away the convergence of a few people's judgements in terms of 'local' distorting factors such as lack of experience; we might even explain away the agreement of an entire cultural group in terms of shared cultural and social influences; but the wider and more diverse the sample, the less readily such explanations are available.

Most judgements don't converge near-universally, however, and for those that don't, we need a different method to reach a standard of correctness for aesthetic judgement. Here Hume idealises the notion of a critic, and gives a list of characteristics that the ideal critic would have. She would be one whose judgements suffer from none of the local distorting influences mentioned earlier, such as bias, inattention, or lack of experience. Her perceptive faculties would be alert, and tuned finely enough to pick out all the details of an object, and not miss any. Thus characterised, an ideal critic would be someone more likely than the average person to 'channel' the natural human response to an object and what aesthetic adjectives should be applied to it. This would not yet be enough though to ensure that her judgement on an object would meet standards of correctness, because she might still be subject to some of the 'blamelesss' preferences just listed – e.g. she might prefer tragedy to comedy, or have specific preferences common to her cultural background. So Hume invokes, not just the judgement of one ideal critic, but the 'joint verdict' of several; assuming as before, that the more widely shared a critical response (this time, amongst ideal critics) the less likely it is to have been influenced by distorting factors. This, then, is the second method for deriving a standard of correctness for aesthetic judgement – the 'joint verdict' of ideal critics.

Aside from interpretation of Hume's view itself, some of which is controversial and which I have simplified here, the view, thus expressed in a nutshell, has been subject to a large amount of criticism, both historical and contemporary. One prominent historical critic is Kant, who in his 'Analytic of the Beautiful' effectively complains that Hume's theory doesn't so much genuinely describe how to derive a *standard* for aesthetic judgement, so much as just describe what most people, or certain special people – ideal critics – tend to like. Kant thinks that making an aesthetic judgement – or at least, a judgement that something is beautiful, which is his principal concern – does not just imply that people *will* make the same judgement, if they are in the right sort of circumstance; but more strongly, that they *should* make the same judgement; that they are getting something wrong if they don't.

Contemporary critics of Hume have focused on other aspects of the view. One source of discussion is how imperfect ordinary people can recognise ideal critics; or even if such ideal critics exist at all. If we can't, or they don't, then in that case, he seems to be at most declaring the *possibility* of a 'standard' of correctness for aesthetic

---

BOX 10.1 DAVID HUME

The Scottish philosopher David Hume (1711–76) had a great influence in aesthetics, but an equal one in metaphysics, epistemology, philosophy of mind and moral philosophy. He was also a well-known historian and essayist. He was born in the Scottish Borders, attended Edinburgh University around the age of 10, and travelled extensively around Europe in his lifetime, working as the private secretary of soldiers and politicians alongside writing the masterworks which would make him famous.

Hume was famously an empiricist, meaning that he placed a great emphasis in his arguments upon what can be ascertained via observation and evidence. He also was a naturalist, preferring to root explanations in a notion of human nature rather than appeal to supernatural influence or other unobservable postulates. It is no surprise, then, that his theory of aesthetic judgement offers an empirically observable standard of correctness, grounded in what it is (he thinks) natural for human beings to respond.

judgements in cases where there is not already strong critical convergence, rather than giving us an actual practical guide to making such judgements. Another controversial issue is Hume's assumption of general facts about human responses to objects – that if we could strip away what was culturally specific or idiosyncratically individual, we would be left with something common to all. And still others – most notably Jerrold Levinson in 'Hume's Standard of Taste: The Real Problem' (2012) – have worried about what reason the average person – who does not share the ideal critic's sensibilities, experience and sensitivity – has for trying to acquire these aspects and so 'correct' her judgement, especially if she is already deriving a lot of pleasure from her own, 'incorrect' aesthetic enthusiasms.

However such questions are answered, it remains the case that Hume's ingenious essay is of exceptional interest to anyone interested in how apparently subjective judgements of liking or disliking can be genuinely subject to criticism. Below, I turn to a different question about aesthetic judgement, on which Hume's essay also effectively takes a view: whether there could be rules linking certain non-aesthetic properties of objects with certain aesthetic judgements.

• ARE THERE AESTHETIC RULES LINKING NON-AESTHETIC PROPERTIES WITH AESTHETIC ONES?

It is usual to think that aesthetic judgements are not totally random; that where a person makes an aesthetic judgement about an object, she does so in response to the perception of more basic, non-aesthetic properties of that object. So, for instance, where I make a judgement that a particular painting is *vibrant* and *dynamic*, I do so in response to the perception of underlying colour, shape and textural properties of the canvas.

'Non-aesthetic properties' could be interpreted really generally as any property that was not an aesthetic one. On this interpretation, they might include such properties as moral ones, chemical ones, or biological ones. However, this is not how 'non-aesthetic properties' is usually interpreted in this context. Rather, it is characteristically taken to refer to perceptible physical properties of objects, to do with, for instance, their dimensions, shape, colour, shade, texture, tempo, pitch, tone, rhythm, flavour, or scent. (One popular way of identifying this class of properties is to say that they are the sorts of properties 'anyone' with working senses could perceive; the implication being that aesthetic properties require some further skill or training to detect.)

Given the assumption that aesthetic judgements are made in response to the detection of non-aesthetic properties in this sense, this then raises a question for those who already think that there are standards of correctness for aesthetic judgements: could there be formulable rules, linking certain aesthetic judgements (e.g. it is *pallid*) with combinations of underlying non-aesthetic properties (e.g. it is curved, it is pale pink, it is 2 foot high)? (See p. 198, 'What are Properties?' for relevant discussion.)

It seems to Hume that there could be, in principle. Admittedly, these would not be *a priori* rules, according to him; that is, they would not be rules derivable prior to seeing what aesthetic judgements people actually made in practice. So they would not be like mathematical rules, or logical rules, for instance, which are formulated independently of how people actually count, or reason. But as I have presented him, Hume thinks that, via his first method of ascertaining a standard of correctness for aesthetic judgement – that is, via looking at judgements where critical response converges, pan-historically and cross-culturally – we can work out which non-aesthetic features of an object are causally responsible for the positive response. We can then make a rule linking these non-aesthetic properties with the relevant aesthetic judgements: wherever these non-aesthetic features occur, the relevant aesthetic response will be appropriate. Hume's aesthetic rules, in other words, would be empirical.

Kant, on the other hand, denies that there are either *a priori* or empirical rules connecting aesthetic judgements with underlying non-aesthetic properties. Empirical 'rules', as we have already heard, would not for Kant have the required universal force – they would merely record what people do or have liked, not what they should like. Meanwhile *a priori* rules which connect aesthetic concepts with non-aesthetic concepts cannot exist, according to Kant, because of his explanation of how aesthetic judgement is derived: because the pleasure supposedly involved is not a result of the application of any concepts at all (see Fiona Hughes' *Kant's Critique of Aesthetic Judgement* (2009) for elaboration).

Kant's rejection of *a priori* aesthetic rules is grounded in what many consider to be an unattractive metaphysics of mind. A British philosopher from the twentieth century, Frank Sibley, gives us a different reason to think that there can't be either *a priori* or empirical rules connecting aesthetic concepts with non-aesthetic ones, in isolation from their context. He argues that the application of an aesthetic judgement to an object is sensitive to *all* of the non-aesthetic properties of the object. No non-aesthetic property can be ruled out in advance as irrelevant. Because of the essentially contextual nature of aesthetic concept application, we cannot even say with confidence that a particular non-aesthetic property inevitably counts in favour of a particular aesthetic judgement. For according to Sibley, the very same non-aesthetic property (say, a curved line in a pale shade of grey on a canvas) may either count for the ascription of a normally 'positive' aesthetic adjective (e.g. *delicate*) or for the ascription of a negative one (e.g. *insipid*), depending on what other non-aesthetic properties are also present. If this is right, then at most we can make defeasible generalisations linking aesthetic judgements with non-aesthetic properties, but never exceptionless rules. The most we can say for sure is that something with exactly the same non-aesthetic properties as the thing we are currently judging, would have the same aesthetic properties. Conversely, if two objects differ in their aesthetic properties, there must be some corresponding difference in their underlying non-aesthetic properties.

If Sibley is right, it seems we can't make *a priori* rules describing the conditions which govern aesthetic concepts in terms of certain isolated non-aesthetic properties. And in fact, against Hume, we can't even empirically work out rules associating certain natural or habitual aesthetic judgements with the occurrence of certain isolated non-aesthetic properties, because to describe some non-aesthetic properties of an object in isolation without giving a complete account of them may well alter what aesthetic judgement is appropriate in that particular case.

One way of describing the relationship between non-aesthetic and aesthetic properties which Sibley describes is that it is a **supervenience** relation: aesthetic properties supervene on non-aesthetic ones (see chapter 19, 'Is Our World Structured?' for relevant discussion). On the face of it, it makes aesthetic properties look metaphysically quite peculiar. They are in some genuine sense grounded in underlying non-aesthetic properties, and so not just projected randomly onto objects: two objects with the identical underlying non-aesthetic properties will share identical aesthetic properties. But at the same time they can be realised in otherwise physically very different objects – plausibly, a painting, a sonata and a building could all realise the aesthetic property of being *bold*, for instance. Those puzzled by this may be reassured to find that supervening properties occur in many areas, not just aesthetics: for instance, arguably moral properties supervene on physical properties, as do mental properties on physical properties of the brain.

It seems clear that in referring to 'non-aesthetic' properties in making his claim, Sibley had in mind only manifest, perceptible properties of physical objects such as shape, colour, texture, volume, tempo, pitch and so on. But, amongst the non-aesthetic properties relevant to aesthetic judgement, those philosophers who have rejected aesthetic formalism (for instance, Danto, as discussed earlier) have included non-manifest properties: for instance, relational properties to do with the history of an object (e.g. who made it, in what historical context, with what intentions, and with what techniques). If this is right, then Sibley's claim can be extended to the claim that a particular aesthetic judgement about an object potentially depends on a complete specification, not just of the objects' perceptible properties, but also relational ones too.

• ARE AESTHETIC JUDGEMENTS TRANSMISSIBLE VIA TESTIMONY?

The final issue I'll describe in this chapter concerns whether aesthetic judgements are appropriately transmitted by testimony, from one person to another. When a belief that something is the case is appropriately transmitted by testimony, a person appropriately adopts that belief on the basis that someone else tells them so. In non-aesthetic domains there is often appropriate transmission of belief via testimony of others: for one, it would be inefficient to insist that people ascertain the truth of all their beliefs for themselves. When, for instance, someone is telling you about what

BOX 10.2 'OF THE STANDARD OF TASTE'

In his essay 'Of the Standard of Taste', Hume introduces us to the notion of an ideal critic, embodying characteristics that make her aesthetic judgement especially reliable. One thing that distinguishes the ideal critic from others, according to Hume, is her 'delicacy of taste': 'where the organs are so fine, as to allow nothing to escape them; and at the same time so exact, as to perceive every ingredient in the composition'. If a critic can perceive every small detail of an object, then her aesthetic judgements in response to those details will be more complete, says Hume. He goes on to exemplify delicacy of taste with a story from *Don Quixote*, in which two men taste wine from a barrel; the first pronounces it to be tainted by the taste of leather; the other pronounces it to be tainted by the taste of iron. The barrel is then emptied and a key on a leather thong is found at the bottom of it.

Hume's use of this story has proved strangely prescient, given recent scientific findings. Scientists have discovered that some people are 'supertasters', meaning that they have a heightened ability to taste intensely, and to discriminate between different taste stimuli. This ability is often correlated with a larger than usual number of tastebuds on the tongue. Scientists have also discovered that a high percentage of wine critics are supertasters. It seems, then, that there is a class of people better able to ascertain the basic flavours of wine than most, and that those whose job it is to make aesthetic judgements about wine often fall into this class.

happened to her yesterday, it is normally appropriate to believe her about the facts she relates, even though you didn't witness the events yourself (see p. 138, 'The Statues of Daedalus' for relevant discussion).

In contrast to these ordinary cases, some philosophers have found reason to deny that aesthetic judgements are appropriately transmissible via testimony. Often, they endorse the so-called 'acquaintance principle', which says that a person making an aesthetic judgement about an object must do so in a way that is based on her first-hand perception of that object; it follows that it may not be appropriately based upon the mere testimony of someone else. For instance, even if someone I normally trust and find reliable tells me that a painting in a gallery they have seen is dynamic and vibrant, it is inappropriate for me to believe her on this basis. The acquaintance principle requires that I perceive it myself.

Many have found the acquaintance principle compelling. They feel it captures something intuitive about aesthetic experience: that in matters of aesthetic judgement, first-hand experience is often to be preferred over second-hand. One challenge for those who advocate it is to explain how it is compatible with our practices of art, music and literary criticism. For in effect, the acquaintance principle looks like an attack on the role of the critic.

The arguments of the last two sections seem either to endorse the role of the critic (Hume) or, at least, to leave it largely intact (Sibley). If Hume is right, critics – at least, if they are in the ideal circumstances, with the right sort of sensibilities and training – can be a guide to the 'right' aesthetic judgements about objects. Meanwhile, if Sibley is right, and we cannot extrapolate rules associating certain aesthetic judgements with certain non-aesthetic properties taken in isolation, we could still assent to a critic's aesthetic judgement about an object on the basis of her testimony; in fact, in a sense, we might be all the more dependent on critics, in the absence of any such rules. But against this, the acquaintance principle makes it look as if the practice of listening to and being influenced by art, musical and literary criticism is misguided: for what else is criticism, but the attempt to transmit aesthetic judgements via testimony, which the acquaintance principle apparently rules out?

The challenge for anyone who wants to salvage the role of the critic and so reject the acquaintance principle is to explain away its apparent attraction in a way which doesn't undermine the enterprise of aesthetic judgement altogether. One natural move against the principle is to argue that there are no reasons special to the aesthetic realm which require aesthetic judgement to be made on the basis of first-hand experience; rather, there are certain contingent circumstances, potentially occurring in the case of *any* testimony, that often make second-hand experience and subsequent testimony about aesthetic judgement unreliable. In this vein, one might cite the supposed fact that few people are suitably qualified to make aesthetic judgements; the harder it is to achieve, the less reliable second-hand judgements will be. A slightly different approach would be to focus on the difficulty, not of being suitably qualified, but of working out who is suitably qualified; which judges are specially reliable. We might, with Hume, be able to identify the characteristics of 'ideal' judges, in theory, but it is a further step to identifying actual examples of people who possess them, as critics of Hume have complained. A third approach would be to say that there is social pressure on people to give culturally mandated aesthetic judgements, and this encourages unreliability about their own native responses to objects.

However, a problem with all of these variants is that they seem also to undermine the validity of first-hand aesthetic judgements, and so can't account for the apparent attraction of the acquaintance principle in the first place. For if I can't tell what good aesthetic judgements are, or who is specially reliable at making them, there seems little reason to put faith in my own judgements over those of others, since presumably I won't be able to tell whether my own judgements are sound or reliable either. Equally, if social pressure encourages others to respond unreliably, presumably it may well encourage me to become out of touch with my own responses too, in a way which may not be apparent to me, given humans' familiar capacity for self-deception generally.

A different line of attack against the acquaintance principle is simply to argue that there is no good reason to hold it. The principle doesn't obviously follow simply from

Sibley's claim that there are no rules connecting the aesthetic and non-aesthetic. Sibley's view rules out *inferring* an aesthetic judgement, on the basis of an incomplete description of only some of the non-aesthetic properties of the object. One might indeed go further than this, and say that even *as complete a description as possible* of the non-aesthetic properties of an object would not permit one to make an aesthetic judgement about the object, without having perceived it oneself. This seems plausible, given the further plausible assumption that descriptions are never fine-grained enough to convey fully all the non-aesthetic properties of an object. A description 'slightly curved' does not suggest how exactly the object is curved; a description 'palest pink' does not convey the exact shade. Arguably, a description could not in principle convey all the information relevant to whether an aesthetic concept should be applied or not. All this seems plausible, perhaps, but still does not imply the acquaintance principle: because even so, one might still be able to depend on the expertise of someone else to make the right aesthetic judgement, when confronted with an object, and then to simply reliably pass that judgement on. This is what is sometimes called 'pure' testimony: testimony in the absence of any accompanying offering of evidence for a judgement. Many cases of ordinary belief transmission are acceptably like this. As yet we've found no reason to think aesthetic judgement might not be transmitted that way too.

It might seem that the acquaintance principle follows from the claim that aesthetic experience/judgement essentially requires perception. However, this is not obvious. The acquaintance principle goes further than the claim that aesthetic experience is essentially perceptual, and says that it essentially requires *your* perception, and not someone else's. Analogously, colour experience/judgement essentially requires perception at some stage, but I can appropriately judge that an object is red, based on testimony of someone else, having never seen the object.

Sometimes – as in Kant's endorsement of it in the 'Analytic of the Beautiful' – motivation is offered for the acquaintance principle via the thought that aesthetic judgement essentially involves some sort of pleasurable response. But again, one might question why my making such a judgement required *me* to have had the hedonic response in question, at first hand, rather than simply being informationally related in the right way to *someone* who had.

Perhaps, instead, the pleasure involved in many aesthetic judgements, in tandem with the non-practical nature of many of them (see chapter 9), is responsible, not for the truth of the acquaintance principle itself, but, more mundanely, for its apparent psychological attraction. For simply to take the associated aesthetic judgement about an object on the say-so of someone else may well be to miss out on the pleasure associated with making the judgement oneself, without any additional practical gain. This looks like a relatively undesirable state of affairs. It's more fun, perhaps, to perceive the object at first-hand, and experience the pleasure oneself.

• CHAPTER SUMMARY

- As well as talking about 'aesthetic experience', philosophers talk about aesthetic *judgements*: judgements about whether objects satisfy adjectives such as 'is ugly'; 'is graceful'; 'is dynamic'; 'is pretty', and so on.
- Aesthetic judgements may or may not be underpinned by a single kind of experience, 'aesthetic experience', as examined in chapter 9.
- Philosophers have also differed about whether there is any standard of correctness for aesthetic judgements. In his essay 'Of the Standard of Taste' Hume offers us two methods for deriving such a standard.
- Kant has criticised Hume's theory for failing to capture the supposed universality of aesthetic judgements. Hume and Kant consequently differ on whether there are rules connecting aesthetic judgements and non-aesthetic properties. Both agree that there are no such *a priori* rules; Hume thinks there are empirical rules but Kant denies this, again on the grounds that they would not have the required universal force.
- Sibley offers a theory according to which there are neither *a priori* nor empirical rules, on the grounds that aesthetic judgements about an object are sensitive to the complete set of non-aesthetic properties of that object.
- A further matter of controversy concerning aesthetic judgement is the 'acquaintance principle', which says that aesthetic judgements about an object must be made on the basis of first-hand experience of that object.

• STUDY QUESTIONS

1 As we've seen, Hume offers two methods for supposedly deriving a standard of correctness for aesthetic judgements, both rooted in 'natural' responses of human beings. What do you think of this suggestion?

2 Kant criticises Hume for not capturing the supposed 'universality' of aesthetic judgement. He thinks that when we call something beautiful, effectively we are saying that others *should* agree with us, not just that they *will*. Do you agree with him?

3 Do you agree with Sibley that *the very same set of* non-aesthetic property might give rise to two different and contrasting aesthetic judgements, depending on the context of what other non-aesthetic properties are also present? Think of examples which support your position.

4 Do you share the sense of many that in order to make an aesthetic judgement about an object, only first-hand experience of that object will do? That is, do you endorse the 'acquaintance principle'? Why/why not?

• INTRODUCTORY FURTHER READING

Hughes, Fiona (2009) *Kant's Critique of Aesthetic Judgement* (London: Continuum). [Helpful and detailed interpretation of Kant's difficult '3rd Critique', including the 'Analytic of the Beautiful'.]

Robson, Jon (2012) 'Aesthetic Testimony', *Philosophical Compass* 7(1). [Sensible, accessible overview of what can be a quite technical debate.]

Shelley, James (1994) 'Hume's Double Standard of Taste', *Journal of Aesthetics and Art Criticism* 52(4): 437–45. [Scrupulous and insightful interpretation of Hume's 'Of the Standard of Taste'.]

• ADVANCED FURTHER READING

Levinson, Jerrold (2002) 'Hume's Standard of Taste: The Real Problem', *Journal of Aesthetics and Art Criticism* 60(3): 227–38. [Provocative challenge to Hume's theory, focusing on what reason the non-ideal judge has to become more like the ideal one.]

Sibley, Frank (1959) 'Aesthetic Concepts', *Philosophical Review* 68 (4): 421–50. [Important essay in the history of aesthetics, rejecting the idea of general rules connecting aesthetic judgements with non-aesthetic properties.]

Walton, Kendall (1970) 'Categories of Art', *Philosophical Review* 79 (3): 334–67. [Ground-breaking paper attacking aesthetic formalism and promoting the importance of historical and other relational properties, as well as manifest perceptual properties, in grounding aesthetic judgements.]

• FREE INTERNET RESOURCES

Gracyk, Ted (2011) 'Hume's Aesthetics', *Stanford Encyclopaedia of Philosophy*, http://plato.stanford.edu/entries/hume-aesthetics/. [A comprehensive overview of Hume's theory of aesthetic judgement.]

Hume, David (1757) 'Of the Standard of Taste', in *Four Dissertations*, http://www.davidhume.org/texts/fd.html. [Classic essay offering a naturalistic theory of correctness for aesthetic judgements.]

Kant, Immanuel (2011) 'Analytic of the Beautiful', trans. James Creed Meredith, originally published by Oxford: Clarendon Press, http://www.sophia-project.org/uploads/1/3/9/5/13955288/kant_beautiful.pdf [Difficult but very influential section of Kant's *Critique of Judgement*.]

Zangwill, Nick (2014) 'Aesthetic Judgement', *Stanford Encyclopaedia of Philosophy*, http://plato.stanford.edu/entries/aesthetic-judgment/ /. [Useful introduction to some of the key issues, though with a strong slant towards the author's own preferred theory.]

Part IV

epistemology

Duncan Pritchard

Although **epistemology** is one of the core areas of philosophy, the term itself only came into existence relatively recently (it was coined by the nineteenth-century Scottish philosopher, James Frederick Ferrier (1808–64)). Nonetheless, even though the term is quite new, the cluster of philosophical questions that it describes goes right back to antiquity, to the birth of philosophy itself.

So what is epistemology? Well, it is essentially the theory of knowledge. Epistemologists are concerned with such questions as 'What is the nature of knowledge?', and 'How is knowledge acquired?'. They are also interested in a range of concepts which are closely related to knowledge, such as truth, rationality, understanding, and wisdom. So while our focus in the chapters that make up this section will be on the nature, value, and extent of our knowledge, we will also encounter some of these other epistemological concepts too.

In chapter 11 we will consider the question of what knowledge is, and in doing so we will consider the role that such notions as truth, belief, and justification have to play in a theory of knowledge. In chapter 12 we will ask what the value of knowledge is, and consider the proposal that it is not of any special value. Finally, in chapter 13, we will consider whether we have any knowledge; that is, whether our widespread belief that we know a great deal about the world around us is just an illusion.

Part IV

epistemology

Duncan Pritchard

11
what is knowledge?

- Knowledge, truth, and belief
- Knowledge versus mere true belief
- The classical account of knowledge
- The Gettier problem
- Responding to the Gettier problem

KNOWLEDGE, TRUTH, AND BELIEF

Think of all the things that you know, or at least think you know, right now. You know, for example, that the earth is round and that Paris is the capital of France. You know that you can speak (or at least read) English, and that two plus two is equal to four. You know, presumably, that all bachelors are unmarried men, that it is wrong to hurt people just for fun, that *The Godfather II* is a wonderful film, and that the moon is not made of cheese. And so on.

But what is it that all these cases of knowledge have in common? Think again of the examples just given, which include geographical, linguistic, mathematical, aesthetic, ethical, and scientific knowledge. Given these myriad types of knowledge, what, if anything, ties them all together?

In all the examples of knowledge just given, the type of knowledge in question is what is called **propositional knowledge**, in that it is knowledge of a **proposition**. A proposition is what is asserted by a sentence which says that something is the case – e.g. that the earth is flat, that bachelors are unmarried men, that two plus two is four, and so on. Propositional knowledge will be the focus of this section of the book, but we should also recognise from the outset that it is not the only sort of knowledge that we possess.

There is, for example, **ability knowledge**, or *know-how*. Ability knowledge is clearly different from propositional knowledge; I know how to swim, for example, but I do not thereby know a set of propositions about how to swim. Indeed, I'm not altogether sure that I could tell you how to swim, but I do know how to swim nonetheless (and I could prove it by manifesting this ability – by jumping into a swimming pool and doing the breaststroke, say).

Ability knowledge is certainly an important type of knowledge to have. We want lots of know-how, such as to know how to ride a bicycle, to drive a car, or to operate a personal computer. Notice, however, that while only relatively sophisticated creatures like humans possess propositional knowledge, ability knowledge is far more common. An ant might plausibly be said to know how to navigate its terrain, but would we want to say that an ant has propositional knowledge; that there are facts which the ant knows? Could the ant know, for example, that the terrain it is presently crossing is someone's porch? Intuitively not, and this marks out the importance of propositional knowledge over other types of knowledge like ability knowledge, which is that such knowledge presupposes the sort of relatively sophisticated intellectual abilities possessed by (mature) humans.

Henceforth, when we talk about knowledge, we will have propositional knowledge in mind. Two things that just about every epistemologist agrees on are that a prerequisite for possessing knowledge is that one has a belief in the relevant proposition, and that that belief must be true. So if you know that Paris is the capital of France, then you must believe that this is the case, and your belief must also be true.

Take the truth requirement first. In order to assess this claim, consider what would follow if we dropped this requirement. In particular, is it plausible to suppose that one could know a false proposition? Of course, we often *think* that we know something and then it turns out that we were wrong, but that's just to say that we didn't really know it in the first place. Could we genuinely know a false proposition? Could I know, for example, that the moon is made of cheese, even though it manifestly isn't? I take it that when we talk of someone having knowledge, we mean to exclude such a possibility. This is because to ascribe knowledge to someone is to credit that person with having got things right, and that means that what we regard that person as knowing had better not be false, but true.

Next, consider the belief requirement. It is sometimes the case that we explicitly *contrast* belief and knowledge, as when we say things like, 'I don't merely believe that he was innocent, I know it', which might on the face of it be thought to imply that knowledge does not require belief after all. If you think about these sorts of assertions in a little more detail, however, then it becomes clear that the contrast between belief and knowledge is being used here simply to emphasise the fact that one *not only* believes the proposition in question, but *also* knows it. In this way, these assertions actually lend support to the claim that knowledge requires belief, rather than undermining it.

As with the truth requirement, we will assess the plausibility of the belief requirement for knowledge by imagining for a moment that it doesn't hold, which would mean that one could have knowledge of a proposition, which one did not even believe. Suppose, for example, that someone claimed to have known a quiz answer, even though it was clear from that person's behaviour at the time that she didn't believe the proposition in question (perhaps she put forward a different answer to the question, or no answer at all). Clearly we would not agree that this person did have knowledge in this case. Again, the reason for this relates to the fact that to say that someone has knowledge is to credit that person with a certain kind of success. But for it to be your success, then belief in the proposition in question is essential, since otherwise this success is not creditable to you at all.

• KNOWLEDGE VERSUS MERE TRUE BELIEF

It is often noted that belief *aims* at the truth, in the sense that when we believe a proposition, we believe it to be the case (i.e. to be true). When what we believe is true, then there is a match between what we think is the case and what is the case. We have got things right. If mere true belief suffices for 'getting things right', however, then one might wonder why epistemologists do not end their quest for an account of knowledge right there and simply hold that knowledge is nothing more than true belief (i.e. 'getting things right').

There is in fact a very good reason why epistemologists do not rest content with mere true belief as an account of knowledge, and that is that one can gain true belief entirely by *accident*, in which case it would be of no credit to you at all that you got things right. Consider Harry, who forms his belief that the horse Lucky Lass will win the next race purely on the basis of the fact that the name of the horse appeals to him. Clearly this is not a good basis on which to form one's belief about the winner of the next horse race, since whether or not a horse's name appeals to you has no bearing on its performance.

Suppose, however, that Harry's belief turns out to be true, in that Lucky Lass *does* win the next race. Is this knowledge? Intuitively not, since it is just a matter of *luck* that his belief was true in this case. Remember that knowledge involves a kind of success that is creditable to the agent. Crucially, however, successes that are merely down to luck are never credited to the agent.

In order to emphasise this point, think for a moment about successes in another realm, such as archery. Notice that if one genuinely is a skilled archer, then if one tries to hit the bull's-eye, and the conditions are right (e.g. the wind is not gusting), then one usually *will* hit the bull's-eye. That's just what it means to be a skilled archer. The word 'usually' is important here, since someone who isn't a skilled archer might, as it happens, hit the bull's eye on a particular occasion, but she wouldn't *usually* hit the bull's-eye in these conditions. Perhaps, for example, she aims her arrow and, by luck, it hits the centre of the target. Does the mere fact that she is successful on this one occasion mean that she is a skilled archer? No, and the reason is that she would not be able to repeat this success. If she tried again, for example, her arrow would in all likelihood sail off into the heavens.

Having knowledge is just like this. Imagine that one's belief is an arrow, which is aimed at the centre of the target, truth. Hitting the bull's-eye and forming a true belief suffices for getting things right, since all this means is that one was successful on that occasion. It does not suffice, however, for having knowledge any more than hitting the bull's-eye purely by chance indicates that you are skilled in archery. To have knowledge, one's success must genuinely be the result of one's efforts, rather than merely being by chance. Only then is that success creditable to one. And this means that forming one's belief in the way that one does ought usually, in those circumstances, to lead to a true belief.

Harry, who forms his true belief that Lucky Lass will win the race simply because he likes the name, is like the person who happens to hit the bull's-eye, but who is not a skilled archer. Usually, forming one's belief about whether a horse will win a race simply by considering whether the name of the horse appeals to you will lead you to form a false belief.

Contrast Harry with someone who genuinely knows that Lucky Lass will win the race. Perhaps, for example, this person is a 'Mr Big', a gangster who has fixed the race by drugging the other animals so that his horse, Lucky Lass, will win. He knows that the race will be won by Lucky Lass because the way he has formed his belief, by basing it on the special grounds he has for thinking that Lucky Lass cannot lose, would normally lead him to have a true belief. It is not a matter of luck that Mr Big hits the target of truth.

The challenge for epistemologists is thus to explain what needs to be added to mere true belief in order to get knowledge. In particular, epistemologists need to explain what needs to be added to true belief to capture this idea that knowledge, unlike mere true belief, involves a success that is creditable to the agent, where this means, for example, that the agent's true belief was not simply a matter of luck.

• THE CLASSICAL ACCOUNT OF KNOWLEDGE

So it seems that there must be more to knowledge than just true belief. But what could this additional component be? The natural answer to this question, one that is often ascribed to the ancient Greek philosopher **Plato** (*c*. 427–*c*. 347 BC), is that what is needed is a *justification* for one's belief, where this is understood as being in possession of good reasons for thinking that what one believes is true. This proposal is known as the **classical account of knowledge**. (It also sometimes referred to as the 'tripartite' – i.e. three-part – account of knowledge.)

Consider again the case of Harry, who believes that Lucky Lass will win the race because he likes the name, and Mr Big, who forms the same belief on the grounds that he has fixed the race. As we noted, although both of these agents believe truly, only Mr Big intuitively has knowledge of what he believes. The claim that it is justification that marks the difference between knowledge and mere true belief accords with this assessment of our two agents' beliefs. Mr Big, after all, has excellent reasons in support of his true belief, since he is aware that the other horses have been drugged and so don't have a hope of winning (unlike the undrugged Lucky Lass). Harry, in contrast, can't offer any good reasons in support of his belief. That he happens to like the name of a horse is hardly a good reason for thinking that this horse will win a race!

Plausibly, then, the missing ingredient in our account of knowledge is justification, such that knowledge is justified true belief. Indeed, until relatively recently most epistemologists thought that this theory of knowledge was correct. Unfortunately, as we will now see, the classical account of knowledge cannot be right, even despite its surface plausibility.

BOX 11.1 PLATO (*C.* 427–*C.* 347 BC)

> Bodily exercise, when compulsory, does no harm to the body;
> but knowledge which is acquired under compulsion obtains no hold on the mind.
>
> Plato, *Republic*

Plato is one of the most influential philosophers who ever lived. He resided for most of his life in the Greek city of Athens, which is where he came under the influence of Socrates (470–399 BC) and where he in turn influenced the philosophical development of Aristotle (384–322 BC). After Socrates' death – an account of which is offered in Plato's book, the *Phaedo* – Plato founded 'The Academy', a kind of early university in which a range of topics, but most centrally philosophy, were taught.

Plato's writing was often in the style of a dialogue between Socrates, the mouthpiece of Plato, and an imagined adversary (or adversaries) on topics of vital philosophical importance. In the *Republic*, for example (perhaps his most famous work), he examines the question, central to political philosophy, of what the ideal political state is. Of more interest for our purposes, however, is his book the *Theaetetus*, in which he discusses the nature of knowledge. For as we have seen in this chapter, it has been suggested that in this work Plato was offering us an early version of the classical tripartite account of knowledge, whereby knowledge is understood as justified true belief. This account of knowledge was to be the dominant view in philosophy until the late twentieth century, when Edmund Gettier came along with his short, but devastating, article detailing the now infamous Gettier counterexamples to this proposal.

• THE GETTIER PROBLEM

The person who demonstrated that the classical account of knowledge is untenable was a philosopher named Edmund Gettier (1927–). In a very short article – just two-and-a-half pages in length – he offered a devastating set of counterexamples to the classical account: what are now known as **Gettier cases**. In essence, what Gettier showed was that you could have a justified true belief and yet still lack knowledge of what you believe because your true belief was ultimately gained via luck in much the same way as Harry's belief was gained by luck.

We will use a different example from the ones cited by Gettier, though one that has the same general structure. Imagine a man, let's call him John, who comes downstairs one morning and sees that the time on the grandfather clock in the hall says '8.20'. On this basis John comes to believe that it is 8.20 a.m., and this belief is true, since it *is* 8.20 a.m. Moreover, John's belief is justified in that it is based on excellent grounds. For example, John usually comes downstairs in the morning about this time, so he knows that the time is about right. Moreover, this clock has been very reliable at telling the time for many years and John has no reason to think that it is faulty now. He thus has good reasons for thinking that the time on the clock is correct.

Suppose, however, that the clock had, unbeknownst to him, stopped 24 hours earlier, so that John is now forming his justified true belief by looking at a stopped clock. Intuitively, if this were so then John would lack knowledge even though he has met the conditions laid down by the classical account of knowledge. After all, that John has a true belief in this case is, ultimately, a matter of luck, just like Harry's belief that Lucky Lass would win the 4.20 at Kempton.

If John had come downstairs a moment earlier or a moment later – or if the clock had stopped at a slightly different time – then he would have formed a false belief about the time by looking at this clock. Thus we can conclude that knowledge is not simply justified true belief.

There is a general form to all Gettier cases, and once we know this we can use it to construct an unlimited number of them. To begin with, we need to note that you can have a justified false belief, since this is crucial to the Gettier cases. For example, suppose you formed a false belief by looking at a clock that you had no reason for thinking wasn't working properly but which was, in fact, and unbeknownst to you, not working properly. This belief would clearly be justified, even though it is false. With this point in mind, there are three stages to constructing your own Gettier case.

First, you take an agent who forms her belief in a way that would usually lead her to have a false belief. In the example above, we took the case of someone looking at a stopped clock in order to find out the time. Clearly, using a stopped clock to find out the time would usually result in a false belief.

Second, you add some detail to the example to ensure that the agent's belief is justified nonetheless. In the example above, the detail we added was that the agent had no reason for thinking that the clock wasn't working properly (the clock is normally reliable, is showing what appears to be the right time, and so on), thus ensuring that her belief is entirely justified.

Finally, you make the case such that while the way in which the agent formed her belief would normally have resulted in a justified false belief, in this case it so happened that the belief was true. In the stopped clock case, stipulating that the stopped clock just happens to be 'telling' the right time does this.

Putting all this together, we can construct an entirely new Gettier case from scratch. As an example of someone forming a belief in a way that would normally result in a false belief, let's take someone who forms her belief that Madonna is across the street by looking at a life-sized cardboard cut-out of Madonna which is advertising her forthcoming tour, and which is posted just across the street. Forming one's belief about whether someone is across the street by looking at a life-sized cut-out of that person would not normally result in a true belief. Next, we add some detail to the example to ensure that the belief is justified. In this case we can just stipulate that the cut-out is very authentic-looking, and that there is nothing about it which would obviously give away the fact that it is a cardboard cut-out – it does not depict Madonna in an outrageous costume that she wouldn't plausibly wear on a normal street, for example. The agent's belief is thus justified. Finally, we make the scenario such that the belief is true. In this case, for instance, all we need to do is stipulate that, as it happens, Madonna *is* across the street, doing some window-shopping out of view of our agent. *Voilà*, we have constructed our very own Gettier case!

BOX 11.2 GETTIER'S AMAZING ARTICLE

The tale behind Edmund Gettier's famous article on why the classical three-part, or *tripartite*, account of knowledge is unsustainable is now part of philosophical folklore. So the story goes, Edmund Gettier was a young US philosopher who knew that he needed to get some publications under his belt if he was to get tenure in his job (in the US, junior academic appointments are usually provisional on the person publishing their research in suitably high-profile journals). Spurred on by this consideration, he looked around for something to write about, something which was interesting, publishable, and, most of all, something which could be written-up very quickly.

While it is said that he had no real interest in epistemology at that time (and, as we will see, he has shown little interest since), he was struck by the prevalence of the justified-true-belief account of knowledge in the literature, and believed it to be fatally defective. In a quick spurt of activity, he wrote a short three-page article outlining his objection to the view, and sent it to the highly regarded philosophy journal *Analysis*, which specialises in short papers of this sort. It was duly published in 1963 and created quite a storm.

Initially, there were several responses from philosophers who felt that the problem that Gettier had highlighted for the classical account of knowledge could be easily resolved with a mere tweak of the view. Very soon, however, it became apparent that such easy 'fixes' did not work, and quickly a whole industry of papers on the 'Gettier problem', as it was now known, came into being.

The most incredible part of this story, however, is that Gettier, having written one of the most famous articles in contemporary philosophy, never engaged at all with the vast literature that his short paper prompted. Indeed, he never published anything else in epistemology. The paper he'd written had gained him the tenure that he wanted, and that, it seems, was enough for him as far as publishing in epistemology was concerned.

Gettier is presently Professor Emeritus in Philosophy at the University of Massachusetts, USA. In 2013 the University of Edinburgh hosted an international conference in honour of the 50th anniversary of Gettier's famous article, with many of the world's leading epistemologists in attendance. Needless to say, it wasn't possible to persuade the man himself to participate in this event.

• RESPONDING TO THE GETTIER PROBLEM

There is no easy way to respond to the Gettier cases, and since Gettier's article back in 1963, a plethora of different theories of knowledge has been developed in order to offer an account of knowledge that is Gettier-proof. Initially, it was thought that all one needed to do to deal with these cases was simply tweak the classical account of knowledge. For instance, one proposal was that in order to have knowledge, one's true belief must be justified and also not in any way based on false presuppositions, such as, in the case of John just described, the false presupposition that the clock is working and not stopped. There is a pretty devastating problem with this sort of proposal, however, which is that it is difficult to spell out this idea of a 'presupposition' such that it is strong enough to deal with Gettier cases and yet not so strong that it prevents us from having most of the knowledge that we think we have.

For example, suppose that John has a sister across town – let's call her Sally – who is in fact at this moment finding out what the time is by looking at a working clock. Intuitively, Sally *does* gain knowledge of what the time is by looking at the time on the clock. Notice, however, that Sally may believe all sorts of other related propositions, some of which may be false – for example, she may believe that the clock is regularly maintained, when in fact no one is taking care of it. Is this belief a presupposition of her belief in what the time is? If it is (i.e. if we understand the notion of a 'presupposition' liberally) then this false presupposition will prevent her from having knowledge of the time, even though we would normally think that looking at a reliable working clock is a great way of coming to know what the time is.

Alternatively, suppose we understand the notion of a 'presupposition' in a more restrictive way such that this belief isn't a presupposition of Sally's belief in the time. The problem now is to explain why John's false belief that he's looking at a working clock counts as a presupposition of his belief in the time (and so prevents him from counting as knowing what the time is) if Sally's false belief that the clock is regularly maintained is not also treated as a presupposition. Why don't they *both* lack knowledge of what the time is?

If this problem weren't bad enough, there is also a second objection to this line of response to the Gettier cases, which is that it is not clear that the agent in a Gettier case need presuppose *anything* at all. Consider a different Gettier case in this regard, due to Roderick Chisholm (1916–99). In this example, we have a farmer – let's call her Gayle – who forms her belief that there is a sheep in the field by looking at a shaggy dog, which happens to look just like a sheep. As it turns out, however, there is a sheep in the field (standing behind the dog), and hence Gayle's belief is true. Moreover, her belief is also justified because she has great evidence for thinking that there is a sheep in the field (she can see what looks to be a sheep in the field, for example).

Given the immediacy of Gayle's belief in this case, however, it is hard to see that it really presupposes any further beliefs at all, at least unless we are to understand the notion of a presupposition *very* liberally. And notice that if we do understand the notion of a presupposition so liberally that Gayle counts as illicitly making a presupposition, the problem then re-emerges of how to account for apparently genuine cases of knowledge, such as that intuitively possessed by Sally.

The dilemma for proponents of this sort of response to the Gettier cases is thus to explain how we should understand the notion of a presupposition broadly enough to be able to apply it to the Gettier cases while at the same time understanding it narrowly enough so that it doesn't apply to other non-Gettier cases in which, intuitively, we would regard the agent concerned as having knowledge. In short, we want a response to the problem, which explains why John lacks knowledge in such a way that it doesn't thereby deprive Sally of knowledge.

Once it was recognised that there was no easy answer to the problem posed to the classical account of knowledge by the Gettier cases, the race was on to find a radically new way of analysing knowledge which was Gettier-proof. One feature that all such accounts share is that they understand the conditions for knowledge such that they demand more in the way of co-operation from the world than simply that the belief in question is true. That is, on the classical account of knowledge there is one condition which relates to the world – the truth condition – and two conditions that relate to us as agents – the belief and justification conditions. These last two conditions, at least as they are usually understood in any case, don't demand anything from the world in the sense that they could obtain regardless of how the world is. If I were the victim of an hallucination, for example, then I might have a whole range of wholly deceptive experiences, experiences that, nonetheless, lead me to believe something and, moreover, to justifiably believe it. (For example, if I seem to see that, say, there is a glass in front of me, then this is surely a good, and thus justifying, reason for believing that there is a glass in front of me, even if the appearance of the glass is an illusion.) The moral of the Gettier cases is, however, that you need to demand more from the world than simply that one's justified belief is true if you are to have knowledge.

In the stopped-clock Gettier case, for example, the problem came about because, although John had excellent grounds for believing what he did, it nevertheless remained the case that he did not know what he believed because of some oddity in the world – in this case that the normally reliable clock had not only stopped but had stopped in such a way that John still formed a true belief. It thus appears that we need an account of knowledge, which imposes a further requirement on the world over and above the truth of the target belief – that, for example, the agent is, *in fact*, forming his belief in the right kind of way. But specifying exactly what this requirement involves is far from easy.

● CHAPTER SUMMARY

- Epistemology is the theory of knowledge. One of the characteristic questions of epistemology concerns what all the myriad kinds of knowledge we ascribe to ourselves have in common: *What is knowledge?*
- We can distinguish between knowledge of propositions, or propositional knowledge, and know-how, or ability knowledge. Intuitively, the former demands a greater degree of intellectual sophistication on the part of the knower than the latter.
- In order to have knowledge of a proposition, that proposition must be true, and one must believe it.
- Mere true belief does not suffice for knowledge, however, since one can gain mere true belief purely by luck, and yet you cannot gain knowledge purely by luck.
- According to the classical (or tripartite) account of knowledge, knowledge is understood as justified true belief, where a justification for one's belief consists of good reasons for thinking that the belief in question is true.
- Gettier cases are cases in which one forms a true justified belief and yet lacks knowledge because the truth of the belief is largely a matter of luck. (The example we gave of this was that of someone forming a true belief about what the time is by looking at a stopped clock, which just so happens to be displaying the right time.) Gettier cases show that the classical account of knowledge in terms of justified true belief is unsustainable.
- There is no easy answer to the Gettier cases; no simple way of supplementing the classical account of knowledge so that it can deal with these cases. Instead, a radi-

cally new way of understanding knowledge is required, one that demands greater co-operation on the part of the world than simply that the belief in question be true.

• STUDY QUESTIONS

1 Give examples of your own of the following types of knowledge:

   - scientific knowledge;
   - geographical knowledge;
   - historical knowledge;
   - religious knowledge.

2 Explain, in your own words, the distinction between ability knowledge and propositional knowledge. Give two examples of each kind of knowledge.

3 Why is mere true belief not sufficient for knowledge? Give an example of your own of a case in which an agent truly believes something, but does not know it.

4 What is the classical account of knowledge? How does the classical account of knowledge explain why a lucky true belief doesn't count as knowledge?

5 What is a Gettier case, and what do such cases show? Try to formulate a Gettier case of your own.

6 In what way might it be said that the problem with Gettier cases is that they involve a justified true belief which is based on a false presupposition? Explain, with an example, why one cannot straightforwardly deal with the Gettier cases by advancing a theory of knowledge which demands justified true belief that does not rest on any false presuppositions.

• INTRODUCTORY FURTHER READING

Annas, Julia (2003) *Plato: A Very Short Introduction* (Oxford: Oxford University Press). [This is a succinct and very readable introduction to Plato's philosophy.]

Pritchard, Duncan (2013) *What is this Thing Called Knowledge?*, 3rd edn (London: Routledge). [See chapters 3–4 for further introductory-level discussion of the nature of knowledge.]

• ADVANCED FURTHER READING

Hetherington, Stephen (2010) 'The Gettier Problem', in S. Bernecker and D. H. Pritchard (eds) *The Routledge Companion to Epistemology* (London: Routledge), ch. 12. [A very useful and completely up-to-date survey of the main issues raised by Gettier-style examples.]

Pritchard, Duncan (2015) *Epistemology* (Basingstoke: Palgrave Macmillan). [This is an advanced textbook in epistemology. Chapters 1–4 offer a critical overview of some of the main analyses of knowledge in the contemporary literature.]

Shope, Robert K. (2002) 'Conditions and Analyses of Knowing', in P. K. Moser (ed.) *The Oxford Handbook to Epistemology* (Oxford: Oxford University Press), pp. 25–70. [A comprehensive treatment of the problem posed by Gettier cases and the various contemporary responses to that problem in the literature. The discussion that starts on page 29 is most relevant to this chapter. Note that as this chapter develops it becomes increasingly more demanding.]

Steup, Matthias, Turri, John and Sosa, Ernest (eds) (2013) *Contemporary Debates in Epistemology*, 2nd edn (Oxford: Blackwell). [See the exchange between Duncan Pritchard and Stephen Hetherington on whether there can be lucky knowledge (§7).]

Zagzebski, Linda (1999) 'What is Knowledge?', in J. Greco and E. Sosa (eds) *The Blackwell Companion to Epistemology* (Oxford: Blackwell), pp. 92–116. [A very thorough overview of the issues surrounding the project of defining knowledge, especially in the light of the Gettier cases.]

• FREE INTERNET RESOURCES

Chappell, Tim (2009) 'Plato on Knowledge in the *Theaetetus*', *Stanford Encyclopedia of Philosophy*, http://plato.stanford.edu/entries/plato-theaetetus/. [An excellent overview of Plato's view of knowledge, as expressed in his book, the *Theaetetus*.]

Gettier, Edmund (1963) 'Is Justified True Belief Knowledge?', *Analysis* 23: 121–3 (freely available on-line here: http://www.ditext.com/gettier/gettier.html). [The article which started the contemporary debate about how best to define knowledge and which contains, by definition, the first official Gettier cases.]

Hetherington, Stephen (2005) 'Gettier Problems', *Internet Encyclopaedia of Philosophy*, http://www.iep.utm.edu/g/gettier.htm. [An excellent overview of the Gettier problem, and the main responses to it, by one of the leading epistemologists.]

Ichikawa, Jonathan and Steup, Matthias (2012) 'The Analysis of Knowledge', *Stanford Encyclopedia of Philosophy*, http://plato.stanford.edu/entries/knowledge-analysis/. [An excellent and comprehensive overview of the issues regarding the project of defining knowledge.]

Kraut, Richard (2011) 'Plato', *Stanford Encyclopedia of Philosophy*, http://plato.stanford.edu/entries/plato/. [A very good overview of the life and works of Plato.]

Perseus Archive (Tufts University), http://www.perseus.tufts.edu/hopper/. [This is a fairly comprehensive archive of ancient Greek and Roman texts, including the works of Plato.]

Truncellito, David (2007) 'Epistemology', *Internet Encyclopaedia of Philosophy*, http://www.iep.utm.edu/e/epistemo.htm. [Read up to the end of §2.b for more on the basic requirements for knowledge.]

12

is knowledge valuable?

- Why care about knowledge?
- The instrumental value of true belief
- The value of knowledge
- The statues of Daedalus
- Is some knowledge non-instrumentally valuable?

WHY CARE ABOUT KNOWLEDGE?

Why should we care about whether or not we have knowledge? Put another way: is knowledge valuable and, if so, why? The importance of this question resides in the fact that knowledge has traditionally been the primary focus of epistemological theorising. Hence, if knowledge is not valuable then that should give us cause to wonder whether we should rethink our understanding of the epistemological enterprise.

In this chapter we will examine this issue in more detail and discover, perhaps surprisingly, that the value of knowledge is far from obvious.

THE INSTRUMENTAL VALUE OF TRUE BELIEF

One way of approaching the topic of the value of knowledge is to note that one can only know what is true, and truth in one's beliefs does seem to be valuable. If truth in one's beliefs is valuable, and knowledge demands truth, then we may be at least halfway towards answering our question of why knowledge is valuable.

Truth in one's beliefs is at least minimally valuable in the sense that, *all other things being equal at any rate*, true beliefs are better than false ones because having true beliefs enables us to fulfil our goals. This sort of value – a value, which accrues to something in virtue of some further valuable purpose that it serves – is known as **instrumental value**.

Think, for example, of the value of a thermometer. Its value consists in the fact that it enables us to find out something of importance to us (i.e. what the temperature is). This is why a working thermometer is valuable to us, but a broken thermometer isn't (unless, of course, it serves some other purpose, such as by being a handy paperweight). In contrast, some things seem to be of **non-instrumental value**, in that they are valuable *for their own sake*, and not simply in terms of some further useful purpose that they serve (like thermometers). Friendship, for example, is valuable in this way. For while friendship is undoubtedly useful, and therefore of instrumental value, one would be missing out on something important if one didn't appreciate the fact that having friends is good for its own sake. Indeed, someone who only values their friends because it serves their wider interests arguably doesn't have any real friends.

In order to see the instrumental value of true belief, think about any subject matter that is of consequence to you, such as the time of your crucial job interview. It is clearly preferable to have a true belief in this respect rather than a false belief, since without a true belief you'll have difficulty making this important meeting. That is, your goal of making this meeting is best served by having a true belief about when it takes place rather than a false one.

The problem, however, lies with the 'all other things being equal' clause, which we applied to the instrumental value of true belief. We have to impose this qualification because sometimes having a true belief could be unhelpful and actually impede one's goals, and in such cases true belief would lack instrumental value. For example, if one's life depended upon it, could one really summon the courage to jump a ravine and thereby get to safety if one knew (or at least truly believed) that there was a serious possibility that one would fail to reach the other side? Here, it seems, a false belief in one's abilities would be better than a true belief if the goal in question (jumping the ravine) were to be achieved. So while true belief might *generally* be instrumentally valuable, it isn't always instrumentally valuable.

Moreover, some true beliefs are beliefs in trivial matters and in this case it isn't at all clear why we should value such beliefs at all. Imagine someone who, for no good reason, concerns herself with measuring each grain of sand on a beach, or someone who, even while being unable to operate a telephone, concerns herself with remembering every entry in a foreign phonebook. In each case, such a person would thereby gain lots of true beliefs but, crucially, one would regard such truth-gaining activity as rather pointless. After all, these true beliefs do not obviously serve any valuable purpose, and so do not seem to have any instrumental value (or, at the very least, what instrumental value these beliefs have is vanishingly small). It would, perhaps, be better – and thus of more value – to have fewer true beliefs, and possibly more false ones, if this meant that the true beliefs that one had were regarding matters of real consequence.

At most, then, we only seem able to marshal the conclusion that some true beliefs have instrumental value, not all of them. As a result, if we are to show that knowledge is valuable then we need to do more than merely note that knowledge entails truth and that true belief is instrumentally valuable. Nevertheless, this conclusion need not be that dispiriting once we remember that while knowledge requires truth, not every instance of a true belief is an instance of knowledge (as we saw in the previous chapter, for example, some true beliefs are just lucky guesses, and so not knowledge at all). Accordingly, it could just be that those true beliefs that are clearly of instrumental value are the ones that are also instances of knowledge.

The problem with this line of thought ought to be obvious, since didn't our 'sand-measuring' agent *know* what the measurements of the sand were? Moreover, didn't our agent who was unable to jump the ravine because she was paralysed by fear fail to meet her goals because of what she *knew*? The problems that afflict the claim that all true beliefs are instrumentally valuable therefore similarly undermine the idea that all knowledge is instrumentally valuable. There is thus no easy way of defending the thesis that *all* knowledge must be valuable.

There is also a second problem lurking in the background here, which is that even if this project of understanding the value of knowledge in terms of the value of true belief were to be successful, it would still be problematic because it would entail that knowledge is no more valuable than mere true belief. But if that's right, then why do we value knowledge more than mere true belief?

• THE VALUE OF KNOWLEDGE

So we cannot straightforwardly argue from the instrumental value of true belief that *all* knowledge must therefore be instrumentally valuable. That said, we can perhaps say something about the specific value of knowledge that is a little less ambitious and which simply accounts for why, in general and all other things being equal, we desire to be knowers as opposed to being agents who have mostly true beliefs but lack knowledge (or, worse, have mostly false beliefs). After all, if we want to achieve our goals in life then it would be preferable if we had knowledge, which was relevant to these goals since knowledge is very useful in this respect. The idea is, therefore, that while not all knowledge is instrumentally valuable, in general it is instrumentally valuable and, what is more, it is of *greater* instrumental value, typically at least, than mere true belief alone (thus explaining our intuition that knowledge is of more value than mere true belief).

Consider the following case. Suppose I want to find my way to the nearest restaurant in an unfamiliar city. Having mostly false beliefs about the locale will almost certainly lead to this goal being frustrated. If I think, for example, that all the restaurants are in the east of the city, when in fact they are in the west, then I'm going to spend a rather dispiriting evening trudging around this town without success.

True beliefs are better than false beliefs (i.e. are of more instrumental value), but are not as good as knowledge. Imagine, for instance, that you found out where the nearest restaurant was by reading a map of the town which is, unbeknownst to you, entirely fake and designed to mislead those unfamiliar with the area. Suppose further, however, that, as it happens, this map inadvertently shows you the right route to the nearest restaurant. You therefore have a true belief about where the nearest restaurant is, but you clearly lack knowledge of this fact. After all, your belief is only luckily true, and as we saw in the last chapter, you can't gain knowledge by luck in this way.

Now one might think that it is neither here nor there to the value of your true belief whether it is also an instance of knowledge. So long as I find the nearest restaurant, what does it matter that I don't know where it is but merely have a true belief about where it is? The problem with mere true belief, however, is that, unlike knowledge, it is very *unstable*. Suppose, for example, that as you were walking to this restaurant you noticed that none of the landmarks corresponded to where they ought to be on the fake map in front of you. You pass the town hall, for instance, and yet according to the map this building is on the other side of town. You'd quickly realise that the map you're using is unreliable, and in all likelihood you'd abandon your belief about where the nearest restaurant was, thereby preventing you from getting there.

In contrast, imagine that you form your belief about where the nearest restaurant is by looking at a reliable map, and thereby *know* where the nearest restaurant is. Since this is genuine knowledge, it would not be undermined in the way that the mere true belief was undermined, and thus you'd retain your true belief. This would mean that you would make it to the restaurant after all, and thereby achieve your goal. Having knowledge can thus be of greater instrumental value than mere true belief since having knowledge rather than mere true belief can make it more likely that one achieves one's goals.

• THE STATUES OF DAEDALUS

The previous point picks up on a famous claim about knowledge made by Plato (*c.* 427–*c.* 347 BC), whom we came across in the last chapter. In his book, *The Meno* (see §§96d–100b), Plato compares knowledge to the statues of the ancient Greek sculptor Daedalus which, it is said, were so realistic that if one did not tether them to the ground they would run away. Plato's point is that mere true belief is like one of the untethered statues of Daedalus, in that one could very easily lose it. Knowledge, in contrast, is akin to a tethered statue, one that is therefore not easily lost.

The analogy to our previous discussion should be obvious. Mere true belief, like an untethered statue of Daedalus, is more likely to be lost (i.e. run away) than knowledge, which is far more stable. Put another way, the true belief one holds when one has knowledge is far more likely to remain fast in response to changes in circumstances (e.g. new information that comes to light) than mere true belief, as we saw in the case just described of the person who finds out where the nearest restaurant is by looking at a reliable map, as opposed to one who finds out where it is by looking at a fake map.

Of course, knowledge isn't *completely* stable either, since one could always acquire a false, but plausible, piece of information that seems to call one's previous true information into question; but this is less likely to happen when it comes to knowledge than when it comes to true belief. In the example given earlier, suppose that the map is indeed reliable, and thus that you do know where the nearest restaurant is. Nevertheless, there might still be further misleading counter-evidence that you could come across which would undermine this knowledge, such as the testimony of a friend you bump into who tells you (out of mischief) that the map is a fake. In the light of this new information, you'll probably change your belief and so fail to get to the restaurant after all.

Even so, however, the fact remains that knowledge is more stable than mere true belief. In the case just described, for example, the fact that the map had been working so far would give you good grounds to continue trusting it, and so you might naturally be suspicious of any testimony you receive to the contrary. Suppose a perfect stranger told you that the map was a compete fake. Would that lead you to change your belief given that it has been reliable so far? Probably not. A friend's testimony carries more weight than a stranger's, but even this testimony might be ignored if you had reason to think your friend might be playing a trick on you.

If you merely had a true belief about where the nearest restaurant is, in contrast, and had no good reason in support of that true belief, then all kinds of conflicting information would undermine that belief. As we saw, as soon as you start walking on your journey and you notice that none of the landmarks correspond to their locations on the map, then you would be liable to tear the map up in despair, even if the map is, in the one respect that is important to you (i.e. in terms of how to get to the nearest restaurant), entirely reliable.

There is a good reason why knowledge is more stable than mere true belief, and this is because knowledge, unlike mere true belief, could not easily be mistaken. Imagine, for instance, that a doctor diagnoses a patient by (secretly) tossing a coin, thus leading the patient to form a particular belief about what is wrong with her. Suppose further that this diagnosis is, as it happens, correct. Clearly the doctor does not know what is wrong with the patient, even though she happened to get it right on this occasion, and neither does the patient know what is wrong with her given that she acquired her belief by listening to the doctor. The problem here is that it was just a matter of luck that the doctor chanced upon the right answer, and thus it is also a matter of luck that the patient formed a true belief about what was wrong with her. In both cases they could so easily have been wrong.

Compare this scenario, however, with that in which a doctor forms her diagnosis of the patient's illness in a diligent fashion by using the appropriate medical procedures. This doctor will (in most cases at least) end up with the same correct diagnosis as our irresponsible doctor, and thus the patient will again acquire a true belief about the nature of her condition. This time, though, the doctor and the patient will know what the correct diagnosis is. Moreover, there is no worry in this case that this verdict could so easily have been mistaken; given that the doctor followed the correct procedures, it is in fact very *unlikely* that this diagnosis is wrong. Here we clearly have a case in which our goal of correctly determining the source of someone's illness is better served by the possession of knowledge rather than the possession of mere true belief because of the instability of mere true belief relative to knowledge (i.e. the fact that mere true belief, unlike knowledge, could so easily be wrong). In this sense, then, knowledge is more valuable to us than true belief alone.

For the most part, then, if one wishes to achieve one's goals it is essential that one has, at the bare minimum, true beliefs about the subject matter concerned. True belief is thus mostly of instrumental value, even if it is not always of instrumental value. Ideally, however, it is better to have knowledge, since mere true belief has an instability that is not always conducive to success in one's projects. Since knowledge entails true belief, we can therefore draw two conclusions. First, that most knowledge, like most mere true belief, is of instrumental value. Second, and crucially, that knowledge is of greater instrumental value than mere true belief.

BOX 12.1 TWO DISTINCTIONS IN VALUE

In this chapter we have come across the distinction between instrumental value and non-instrumental value. As we have seen, to value something instrumentally is to value it as a means to something else. Money, for example, is usually only of instrumental value, in that we value it only because it is an effective means to something else we desire (i.e. what we can purchase with the money). In contrast, to value something non-instrumentally is to value it for its own sake. We noted that friendship is a good example of something which is non-instrumentally valuable, in that although having friends is useful in many ways (and so instrumentally valuable), it is also the kind of thing that one should value for its own sake (i.e. regardless of whether the friendship in question happens to be useful). As the example of friendship illustrates, something can be *both* instrumentally *and* non-instrumentally valuable.

The instrumental/non-instrumental value distinction is thus a distinction in how we value things. Note that for our purposes we are really interested in whether someone *rightly* values something instrumentally or non-instrumentally. The miser, for example, is someone who values money for its own sake. But this is clearly a mistake, as money is only normally of instrumental value. Similarly, some people may only value friendship instrumentally – i.e. in virtue of what having friends can get them. But this is again a mistake, in that there is more to the value of friendship than its instrumental value. When we talk, for example, of the instrumental value of knowledge, we are not just talking about how we happen to value knowledge (i.e. whether rightly or wrongly), but rather making a claim about how we *rightly* value knowledge.

There is another distinction about value that we can draw, and which is arguably orthogonal to the instrumental/non-instrumental value distinction. This is the distinction between extrinsic and intrinsic value. To say that something is intrinsically valuable is to say that it is valuable in its own right – i.e. because of its *intrinsic properties*, the properties which are specific to the thing in question. In contrast, to say that something is extrinsically valuable is to say that it *isn't* valuable in its own right, but only because of its relationship to things external to it (i.e. because of its extrinsic, or relational, properties). Often, the distinction between extrinsic/intrinsic value maps onto the distinction between instrumental/non-instrumental value. So, for example, money is instrumentally valuable, as we have noted. It is also extrinsically valuable, in that we do not normally care about money in its own right, but only because it stands in a particular relationship to other things (i.e. that it enables us to purchase things). But some philosophers have argued that these two distinctions in kinds of value do not always map onto one another.

Consider, for example, the first book printed on the first-ever printing press. We would surely regard such an item as being of great value. Moreover, although this book would have a lot of instrumental value – it would be worth a lot of money, for example – we would also think that it was of non-instrumental value too, in that it is the kind of thing that one should value for its own sake and not simply because of its instrumental value. Crucially, however, this book does not seem to be of intrinsic value, in that its non-instrumental value rather concerns its relational properties (in particular, how it was produced). For example, an exact replica of such a book, which was produced by a machine rather than by the first ever printing press, would probably not be non-instrumentally valuable. But if that's right, then it seems that there can be items that are non-instrumentally valuable (i.e. valuable for their own sake) even though they are not intrinsically valuable (because their non-instrumental valuable is in virtue of their relational properties).

• IS SOME KNOWLEDGE NON-INSTRUMENTALLY VALUABLE?

At this point we might wonder whether the value of knowledge is only ever instrumental. That is, we might wonder whether the value of knowledge is always dependent upon what further goods, such as gaining relief from your illness, knowledge (in this case of the correct diagnosis of your illness) can help you attain. Are there kinds of knowledge which have non-instrumental value (i.e. the kind of value that we saw friendship as having above)?

In order to see how knowledge could be non-instrumentally valuable, think of those types of knowledge which are very refined, such as *wisdom* – the sort of knowledge that wise people have. Wisdom is clearly at least instrumentally valuable since it can enable one to lead a productive and fulfilled life. Crucially, however, it seems that knowledge of this sort would still be valuable even if, as it happens, it *didn't* lead to a life that was good in this way. Suppose, for instance, that nature conspires against you at every turn so that, like the biblical character Job, you are subject to just about every dismal fate that can befall a person. In such a case one's knowledge of most matters may well have no instrumental value at all because one's goals will be frustrated by forces beyond your control regardless of what you know.

Nevertheless, it would surely be preferable to confront such misfortune as a wise person, and not because such wisdom would necessarily make you feel any better or enable you to avoid these disasters (whether wise or not, your life is still wretched). Instead, it seems, being wise – like friendship, as we noted above – is just a good thing, regardless of what further goods it might lead to. That is, it is something that is good *for its own sake.* And notice that this claim marks a further difference between knowledge and mere true belief, since it is hard to see how mere true belief could ever be of non-instrumental value.

There may be stronger claims that we can make about the value of knowledge, but the minimal claims advanced here suffice to make the study of knowledge important. Recall that we have seen that knowledge is at least for the most part instrumentally valuable in that it enables us to achieve our goals, and that it is generally more instrumentally valuable in this respect than true belief alone. Moreover, we have also noted that some varieties of knowledge, such as wisdom, seem to be non-instrumentally valuable. Clearly, then, knowledge is something that we should care about. Given that this is so, it is incumbent upon us as philosophers to be able to say more about what knowledge is and the various ways in which we might acquire it, and this is something that epistemology aims to do.

BOX 12.2 KNOWLEDGE AND THE 'GOOD LIFE'

In this chapter we noted the possibility that at least certain kinds of knowledge, such as wisdom, might be non-instrumentally valuable, in that we would value such knowledge regardless of whether it had any practical use. This issue is related to one of the most ancient questions in epistemology, which is the role that knowledge plays in a good life. Notice that the notion of a 'good life' that is in play here is quite specific. The word used by the ancient Greek philosophers to capture this notion was that of '*eudaimonia*', which roughly means a life of flourishing. A good life, in this sense, is not necessarily a happy life (though happiness may be part of it), in that in order to flourish properly it could be that one needs to overcome challenges and adversity, which might involve suffering.

Moreover, it would be a mistake to think of the goodness of a good life purely in terms of someone following a moral code. For although being moral may be part of a good life, the ancient Greeks also thought that a good life exhibited lots of other features too, such as a life rich in cultural, social and political engagement.

The good life is meant to be something which is non-instrumentally valuable, in that it is valuable for its own sake, and not merely because of whatever instrumental value might be generated by living such a life. So even if one valued the good life because it made you feel good, or helped you to be successful, if you were wise you would also recognise that this is something to be valued regardless of its practical utility. Indeed, in principle at least, it could be that the good life is worth living even if it lacked any instrumental value. The death of Socrates is a case in point, in that in living what he took to be the good life he thereby ensured his own trial and execution.

However the good life is to be understood, it ought to be clear that knowledge – or, certain kinds of knowledge anyway – is bound to be very important to such a life. In order to live such a life, one needs to know what kinds of things are valuable and so worth pursuing, and one must also have the practical wisdom (or *phronesis*, as the ancient Greeks called it) to know how to acquire these goods. Knowledge is thus arguably at least a necessary condition for living a good life. But on many classical conceptions of the good life, knowledge plays an even more central role in *eudaimonia*, in that it is often claimed that some kinds of knowledge, such as the practical wisdom just described, are in fact not merely necessary conditions for living the good life, but rather constitutive components of it. If that's right, then the case for thinking that this kind of knowledge is non-instrumentally valuable is very strong indeed.

• CHAPTER SUMMARY

- One of the central tasks of epistemology is to explain the value of knowledge. But while it is obvious that we do value knowledge, it is not obvious why this is the case, nor what the nature of this value is.
- One way of accounting for the value of knowledge is to note that if you know a proposition, then you have a true belief in that proposition, and true beliefs are clearly useful, and therefore valuable. In particular, true belief has instrumental value in that it enables you to achieve your goals.
- One problem with this proposal is that it is not obvious that *all* true beliefs are instrumentally valuable. For one thing, some true beliefs are so trivial that it seems that they have no value at all. For another, sometimes it is more useful to have a false belief than a true belief.

- Moreover, even if one could evade this problem, another difficulty would remain, which is that, intuitively, knowledge is *more* valuable than mere true belief. If this intuition is right, then we need to say more than simply that knowledge entails true belief and that true belief is instrumentally valuable.
- One option is to say that knowledge is of greater instrumental value than mere true belief, since it is more useful to us (it enables us to achieve more of our goals than mere true belief alone). Part of the explanation one might offer for this could be that there is a 'stability' to knowledge which is lacking in mere true belief in that in knowing that something is the case one couldn't have easily been wrong.
- We also explored another suggestion, which was that *some* knowledge is of non-instrumental value, i.e. is valuable for its own sake. The example we gave here was that of *wisdom*. The idea, then, is that while knowledge is generally of greater instrumental value than mere true belief, some knowledge is also, in addition, non-instrumentally valuable (unlike mere true belief, which is never non-instrumentally valuable).

• STUDY QUESTIONS

1 What does it mean to say that something has instrumental value? Explain your answer by offering two examples of your own of something that is instrumentally valuable.

2 Is true belief always instrumentally valuable? Evaluate the arguments for and against this claim, paying attention to such issues as the fact that sometimes false beliefs can be useful (as in the case of the person trying to jump a ravine), and that true beliefs can sometimes be entirely trivial (as in the case of the person who measures grains of sand).

3 Is knowledge of *greater* instrumental value than mere true belief, insofar as the latter is indeed generally instrumentally valuable? Consider some cases in which one person has a mere true belief while someone else in a relevantly similar situation has knowledge. Is it true to say that the latter person's knowledge is of more instrumental value than the former person's mere true belief?

4 What does it mean to say that something has non-instrumental value? Explain your answer by offering two examples of your own of things that are non-instrumentally valuable, and in each case give a brief explanation of why you think they are non-instrumentally valuable.

5 Is knowledge *ever* non-instrumentally valuable? Evaluate this question by considering some plausible candidates for non-instrumentally valuable knowledge, such as the knowledge possessed by the wise person.

• INTRODUCTORY FURTHER READING

Annas, Julia (2003) *Plato: A Very Short Introduction* (Oxford: Oxford University Press). [This is a succinct and very readable introduction to Plato's philosophy.]

Greco, John (2010) 'Epistemic Value', in S. Bernecker and D. H. Pritchard (eds) *The Routledge Companion to Epistemology* (London: Routledge), ch. 21. [An accessible and completely up-to-date survey of the main issues as regards epistemic value.]

• ADVANCED FURTHER READING

Kvanvig, Jonathan (2003) *The Value of Knowledge and Pursuit of Understanding* (Cambridge: Cambridge University Press). [A very influential contemporary discussion of the value of knowledge.]

Pritchard, Duncan, Millar, Alan and Haddock, Adrian (2010) *The Nature and Value of Knowledge: Three Investigations* (Oxford: Oxford University Press). [The most up-to-date contribution to the debate about the value of knowledge. Note that it is quite demanding.]

Zagzebski, Linda (1996) *Virtues of the Mind: An Inquiry into the Nature of Virtue and the Ethical Foundations of Knowledge* (Cambridge: Cambridge University Press). [A clear, challenging and historically orientated account of knowledge which pays particular attention to the issue of the value of knowledge, including those types of knowledge, like wisdom, that might plausibly be regarded as non-instrumentally valuable.]

• FREE INTERNET RESOURCES

Chappell, Tim (2009) 'Plato on Knowledge in the *Theaetetus*', *Stanford Encyclopedia of Philosophy*, http://plato.stanford.edu/entries/plato-theaetetus/. [An excellent overview of Plato's view of knowledge, as expressed in his book, the *Theaetetus*.]

Kraut, Richard (2011) 'Plato', *Stanford Encyclopedia of Philosophy*, http://plato.stanford.edu/entries/plato/. [A very good overview of the life and works of Plato.]

Perseus Archive (Tufts University), http://www.perseus.tufts.edu/hopper/. [This is a fairly comprehensive archive of ancient Greek and Roman texts, including the works of Plato.]

Pritchard, Duncan and Turri, John (2012) 'The Value of Knowledge', *Stanford Encyclopedia of Philosophy*, http://plato.stanford.edu/entries/knowledge-value/. [A very up-to-date and thorough overview of the debate regarding the value of knowledge.]

Schroeder, Mark (2012) 'Value Theory', *Stanford Encyclopedia of Philosophy*, http://plato.stanford.edu/entries/value-theory/. [A comprehensive and completely up-to-date survey of the main philosophical issues as regards value.]

Zimmerman, Michael (2010) 'Intrinsic Versus Extrinsic Value', *Stanford Encyclopedia of Philosophy*, http://plato.stanford.edu/entries/value-intrinsic-extrinsic/. [A great survey of the literature on intrinsic (e.g. non-instrumental) and non-intrinsic (e.g. instrumental) value.]

13

do we have any knowledge?

- The radical sceptical paradox
- Scepticism and closure
- Mooreanism
- Contextualism

• THE RADICAL SCEPTICAL PARADOX

As it is usually understood in the contemporary debate, **radical scepticism** is not supposed to be thought of as a philosophical position (i.e. as a stance that someone adopts) as such, but rather it is meant as a challenge which any theorist of knowledge must overcome. That is, radical scepticism is meant to serve a *methodological* function. The goal is to show that one's theory of knowledge is scepticism-proof, since if it isn't – if it allows that most knowledge is impossible – then there must be something seriously wrong with the view. Accordingly we are not to think of the 'sceptic' as a person – as someone who is trying to convince us of anything – but rather as our intellectual conscience which is posing a specific kind of problem for our epistemological position in order to tease out what our view really involves and whether it is a plausible stance to take.

There are two main components to sceptical arguments, as they are usually understood in the contemporary discussion of this topic. The first component concerns what is known as a **sceptical hypothesis**. A sceptical hypothesis is a scenario in which you are radically deceived about the world and yet your experience of the world is exactly as it would be if you were not radically deceived. Consider, for example, the fate of the protagonist in the film *The Matrix*, who comes to realise that his previous experiences of the world were in fact being 'fed' into his brain whilst his body was confined to a large vat. Accordingly, whilst he seemed to be experiencing a world rich with interaction between himself and other people, in fact he was not interacting with anybody or any *thing* at all (at least over and above the tubes in the vat that were 'feeding' him his experiences), but was instead simply floating motionlessly.

BOX 13.1 *THE MATRIX*

The Matrix, a 1999 movie starring Keanu Reeves, is the first part of a famous film trilogy which explores sceptical themes. The film follows the story of a computer hacker called Neo, played by Reeves, who discovers that his experiences of the world are in fact entirely artificial, and that he is instead floating in a vat of nutrients and being 'fed' his experiences. In this nightmarish scenario, supercomputers have enslaved the human race and now use the 'essences' of humans as a power source. Neo escapes from the vat in which he has been floating and leads a rebellion against the supercomputers.

The problem posed by sceptical hypotheses is that we seem unable to know that they are false. After all, if our experience of the world could be exactly as it is and yet we are the victims of a sceptical hypothesis, then on what basis could we ever hope to distinguish a genuine experience of the world from an illusory one? The first key claim of the sceptical argument is thus that we are unable to know that we are not the victims of sceptical hypotheses.

The second component of the sceptical argument involves the claim that if we are unable to know the denials of sceptical hypotheses, it follows that we are unable to know very much at all. Right now, for example, I think that I know that I am sitting here at my desk writing this chapter. Given that I do not know that I am not the victim of a sceptical hypothesis, however, and given that if I were the victim of a sceptical hypothesis the world would appear exactly the same as it is just now even though I am *not* presently sitting at my desk, then how can I possibly know that I am sitting at my desk? The problem is that, so long as I cannot rule out sceptical hypotheses, I don't seem able to know very much at all.

We can roughly express this sceptical argument in the following way:

1 We are unable to know the denials of sceptical hypotheses.
2 If we are unable to know the denials of sceptical hypotheses, then we are unable to know anything of substance about the world.
3 Hence, we are unable to know anything of substance about the world.

Two very plausible claims about our knowledge can thus be used to generate a valid argument, which produces this rather devastating radically sceptical conclusion. In this sense, the sceptical argument is a **paradox** – i.e. a series of apparently intuitive premises which validly entail an absurd, and thus unacceptable, conclusion.

One might think that the weakest link in this argument is the second premise, on the grounds that it is far too much to ask of a knower that she be able to rule out radical sceptical hypotheses. Why should it be, for example, that in order to be properly said to know that I am sitting at my desk right now I must first be able to rule out the possibility that I am not being 'fed' my experiences by futuristic supercomputers that are out to deceive me? Surely all that I need to do in order to have knowledge in this case is to form my belief in the right kind of way and for that belief to be supported by the appropriate evidence (e.g. that I can see my desk before me). To demand more than this seems perverse, and if scepticism merely reflects unduly restrictive epistemic standards then it isn't nearly as problematic as it might at first seem. We can reject *perverse* epistemic standards with impunity – it is only the *intuitively correct ones* that we need to pay serious attention to.

Nevertheless, there is an additional way of motivating premise 2, one that makes its truth seem entirely uncontentious. Consider the **closure principle** for knowledge:

The closure principle

If I know one proposition, and I know that this proposition entails a second proposition, then I know the second proposition as well.

For example, if I know that I am sitting here in my office right now, and I also know that if I am sitting in my office right now then I can't be standing up next door, then it seems that I must also know that I am not standing up next door. So expressed, the principle seems entirely unremarkable.

Notice, however, that it follows from the fact that one is seated at one's desk in one's office that one is not encased in a large vat being 'fed' the experiences as if one were sitting at one's desk (aside from anything else, if one were in the vat then one wouldn't be *seated* at all, but *floating* in the nutrients contained therein). Accordingly, given the closure principle, it follows that if I know that I am currently seated in my office then I also know that I am not encased in a large vat being 'fed' experiences that are designed to deceive me. However, as the sceptic points out in premise 1 of her argument, that seems precisely the kind of thing that I could never know. As a result, concludes the sceptic, it must be that I don't know that I am presently seated in my office either.

In effect, what the sceptic's use of the closure principle does is make knowledge of normal 'everyday' propositions (i.e. the sort of propositions which we would usually regard ourselves as unproblematically knowing) contingent upon knowledge of the denials of sceptical hypotheses. Moreover, since the principle is so plausible, it makes this connection seem entirely intuitive. That is, the demand that I should know the denials of sceptical hypotheses seems now to be the product of entirely reasonable epistemic standards, not perverse ones. The trouble is, of course, that with this demand in place, the sceptical conclusion appears irresistible.

BOX 13.2 G. E. MOORE (1873–1958)

> I can prove…that two human hands exist. How? By holding up my two hands, and saying, as I make a certain gesture with the right hand, 'Here is one hand', and adding, as I make a certain gesture with the left, 'and here is another'.
>
> Moore, 'Proof of an External World'

G. E. Moore was a distinguished British philosopher – he spent his entire academic career at Cambridge University – who was very influential within twentieth-century philosophy. His work influenced both Ludwig Wittgenstein (1889–1951) and Bertrand Russell (1872–1970), two of the most prominent philosophers at the time. Moore's philosophical approach, however, unlike those of Wittgenstein and Russell, was very much to defend common sense rather than advance any grand philosophical theses. In epistemology this manifested itself with Moore's astonishingly direct response to the problem of radical scepticism. In ethics, another area of philosophy where his work has had long-lasting impact, his common-sense approach led him to claim that goodness could not be defined, contrary to the many definitions of goodness offered by ethicists.

• SCEPTICISM AND CLOSURE

What is one to do about this sceptical argument? One possibility might be to respond by rejecting the closure principle, although this is easier said than done. After all, how could such a plausible principle be false? How could it be that I could know one proposition, know that it entails a second proposition, and yet fail to know that entailed proposition? Indeed, the only instances where this kind of principle seems at all problematic is when it is employed in sceptical arguments, and this suggests that perhaps the reason why we find the closure principle problematic here is simply that it is helpful to the sceptic. If this is right, then the move to deny this principle smacks of desperation.

Nevertheless, there are motivations that can be offered in defence of rejecting this principle, at least as the sceptic employs it. One way in which some have gone about rejecting the closure principle is by appeal to the intuition that in knowing something I only need to be able to rule out all *relevant* possibilities of error, and don't have to rule out *all* possibilities of error. To suppose otherwise seems to be to endorse an unduly demanding conception of knowledge, one on which in order to acquire knowledge one should form one's belief in such a way that there is simply no possibility that it could have turned out false (this view is known as **infallibilism**). My failure to know that I am not a victim of a sceptical hypothesis entails that there is a possibility that my beliefs about whether, for example, I am presently seated could be false. But on the train of thought in play this is not meant to be a bar to knowledge that one is seated. Accordingly, insofar as the closure principle demands that in order to know everyday propositions, such as that one is seated, I should be able to rule out far-fetched – and thus, intuitively, *irrelevant* – error possibilities, such as sceptical hypotheses, then we should reject this principle as inherently suspect.

Although superficially appealing, this line of argument is not that persuasive on closer inspection. For notice that the closure principle is entirely compatible with the rejection of infallibilism. This principle does not demand that you know that all error possibilities are false, but only those error possibilities which are known to be incompatible with what you know, which is a much weaker claim. One cannot therefore reject the closure principle solely on the grounds that it leads to infallibilism, since it doesn't.

Everything thus rests on the further claim being made here about relevance: that sceptical hypotheses are far-fetched and therefore of their nature irrelevant. The problem with this suggestion is that it is hard to see just what, besides a blank statement of intuition, could justify the thought that sceptical hypotheses are irrelevant. Indeed, why doesn't the fact that we know that they are inconsistent with our everyday beliefs, such that those beliefs cannot be true if the sceptical hypotheses obtain, make them relevant?

A different tack that has been taken to attack the closure principle has been to suggest that the mark of knowledge is that one has a true belief which satisfies the following **sensitivity principle**:

The sensitivity principle

If an agent knows a proposition, then that agent's true belief in that proposition must be *sensitive* in the sense that, had that proposition been false, she would not have believed it.

For example, consider a case in which no one thinks that the agent has knowledge, such as a Gettier case like the 'stopped clock' example we looked at in chapter 11. In this case, we have an agent who forms a true belief about what the time is by looking at a stopped clock, one that just happens to be showing the right time. The agent in this case clearly doesn't know what the time is, even if her belief is justified, since it's just a matter of luck that her belief is true. One way of fleshing out this idea that the belief in this case is just too luckily true to count as knowledge is to notice that it is a belief which is insensitive. After all, had what the agent believed been false – if the time had been a minute earlier or later, for example, but everything else had stayed the same – then she would have carried on believing what she does regardless, even though it is no longer true. In contrast, someone who finds out what the time is by looking at a working clock will form a sensitive belief about what the time is, since were the time to have been different (but everything else had stayed the same), then the clock would have displayed a different time and the agent would therefore have formed a different (and likewise true) belief about what the time is. In short, a sensitive belief is one that changes as the facts change so that one does not end up with a false belief, while an insensitive belief is one that doesn't so change.

What is interesting about the sensitivity principle is that while most of our everyday beliefs are sensitive to the truth, our anti-sceptical beliefs, such as our belief that we are not brains in vats, are not sensitive. My belief that I am presently sitting at my computer writing this, for example, is sensitive since, were this to be false, but everything else the same – such as if I were standing up next to my computer, for example – then I wouldn't any longer believe that I was sitting; I'd believe that I was standing instead. In contrast, think of my belief that I am not a brain in a vat. Were this belief to be false – so that I was indeed a brain in a vat – then I would carry on believing it regardless. Indeed, it is explicitly part of how we characterise sceptical hypotheses that our beliefs in their falsehood are insensitive in this way.

If the sensitivity principle captures something essential about knowledge, then we can account for why we feel that we can know an awful lot of propositions that we think we know even while failing to know the denials of sceptical hypotheses. Of course, this would necessitate denying the closure principle, and that's a high price for any theory of knowledge to pay – perhaps *too* high – but notice that we would at least have *motivated* the denial of this principle in terms of how it conflicts with another epistemological principle (i.e. the sensitivity principle), which we have also seen is quite intuitive.

• MOOREANISM

A very different sort of response to this argument might be to try to use the closure principle to your own anti-sceptical advantage. The general idea is that one can employ the closure principle in order to show that we do know the denials of sceptical hypotheses after all, because we know lots of mundane claims, which entail the falsity of these hypotheses.

For example, I seem to be sitting at my desk right now and everything appears to be entirely normal. In these circumstances we would typically grant, provided that what I believe is true of course, that I do know that I am seated at my desk. As noted above, however, if we grant knowledge in this case then it follows, given that I know that I cannot be both sitting at my desk and floating in a vat of nutrients, that I must know that I am not floating in a vat somewhere being 'fed' misleading impressions of the world. The anti-sceptical thought that might arise at this point is thus to contend that, despite first impressions, we *do* know that we are not the victims of sceptical hypotheses after all and, moreover, we know this precisely *because* of our knowledge of rather mundane things (such as that we are seated) and the truth of the closure principle. Something like an anti-sceptical argument of this form is often associated with the remarks made about scepticism by **G. E. Moore** (1873–1958), and thus this approach to scepticism is often referred to as **Mooreanism**.

This way of trying to turn the closure principle back against the sceptic is really quite dubious, however. For one thing, what is at issue is whether we do know anything of substance, and thus it seems somewhat question-begging to make use of an instance of knowledge in order to show that we can know the denials of sceptical hypotheses after all, especially since we have already seen that the sceptical claim that we cannot have such knowledge is very plausible.

Moreover, given the plausibility of the sceptical premise regarding our inability to know the denials of sceptical hypotheses, the current state of play seems to be less a victory to Mooreanism rather than a further problem for one's theory of knowledge that needs to be resolved. How could it be that we can know the denials of sceptical hypotheses given that there appears to be nothing in our experiences which could possibly indicate to us that we are not in such a scenario? The Moorean cannot simply assert that we have such knowledge without also explaining how such knowledge could come to be possessed – but that is far more difficult than it might at first seem.

The challenge for Mooreans is to show how we can know the denials of sceptical hypotheses even though we are unable to tell such cases apart from counterpart non-deceived cases. One way they might do this is to propose the following **safety principle** as a condition on knowledge:

> **The safety principle**
>
> If an agent knows a proposition, then that agent's true belief in that proposition must be *safe* in the sense that it couldn't have easily been false (alternatively: were the agent to continue believing that proposition in similar circumstances, then the belief would almost always still be true).

Informally, the idea behind the safety principle is to capture the intuition that knowledge cannot be lucky. Think of the example of the skilled archer that we looked at in chapter 11. What constitutes such a skill is that the archer can usually hit the target in a wide range of relevant conditions. That is what sets a skilled archer apart from someone who only just happens to hit the target by luck. We noted above that we could think of knowledge in terms of this metaphor, where the arrow is belief and the target is truth. The idea is that knowledge arises when our beliefs hit the target of truth through skill and not through luck.

The safety principle offers a way of cashing-out this archery analogy. After all, one way of expressing the difference between the skilled archer who hits the target and the clumsy archer who hits the target is that the clumsy archer (but not the skilled archer) could very easily have missed. (Alternatively: there are lots of similar circumstances in which the clumsy archer misses the target, while only very few in which the skilled archer misses the target.) Similarly, someone who genuinely knows, rather than someone who merely happens to have a true belief, has a belief that could not have easily been false (were that belief to be formed in similar circumstances, then it would usually still be true).

In order to see this, contrast someone who finds out what the time is by looking at a reliable working clock with someone who finds out what the time is by looking at a broken clock, albeit one which, as it happens, is showing the right time. In the first case, the true belief is safe in that a belief about the time formed in similar circumstances (e.g. where the time was slightly different) would continue to be true. In contrast, the true belief in the second case is unsafe, since there are lots of similar conditions in which the agent forms a belief about the time and yet her belief is false (e.g. situations in which the time is slightly different).

What is interesting about the safety principle from our point of view is that it lends some support to the Moorean claim that we are able to know the denials of sceptical hypotheses. Even though I may lack any good reason for thinking that I'm not a brain in a vat – I wouldn't be able to tell the difference between being a brain in a vat and not being a brain in a vat after all – just so long as circumstances are pretty much as I take them to be, then my true belief that I'm not a brain in a vat won't be unsafe. This is because there won't be any similar circumstances in which I form this belief and my belief is false for the simple reason that if the world is pretty much as I take it to be then there are no similar circumstances in which I am a brain in a vat – this sort of thing only happens in circumstances that are very different from the ones I'm in. If this line of thought is granted, then it might be possible to allow that we can know the denials of sceptical hypotheses, even though we lack good grounds for these beliefs. If that's right, then the motivation to deny the closure principle as a way of dealing with the sceptical problem subsides.

One might want to object to this line of thought by saying that we can't simply presuppose that the world is pretty much as we take it to be, since once we presuppose that then we've already sidestepped the sceptical problem. This presupposition is not nearly as contentious as it might at first seem, however. To begin with, notice that no one disputes that if we are victims of sceptical hypotheses then we don't know very much. The interesting question is whether, *even if we're not so deceived*, we are able to know very much. To this question the sceptic replies negatively. The sceptic is therefore claiming that *whatever* circumstances we find ourselves in, we are unable to know very much (including that we are not the victim of a sceptical hypothesis); if this is right, it follows that we can assume anything we like about what circumstances we are in without dodging the sceptical challenge.

Even if this objection is not fatal, however, one might still worry about the idea that we can possess anti-sceptical knowledge in this way. After all, the analogy with the skilled archer suggests that we gain knowledge in virtue of forming beliefs in a way which involves being responsive to how the world is, and yet on this view anti-sceptical knowledge seems to be gained even though there is no responsiveness to the world at all. (Remember that the Moorean grants that we can't tell the difference between everyday life and a sceptical hypothesis.) In short, the worry one might have regarding such knowledge is that it involves no skill at all, and thus is in this sense only luckily true, even though it may well involve a safe true belief.

• CONTEXTUALISM

One final anti-sceptical theory that we will look at is **contextualism**. This view holds that the key to resolving the sceptical problem lies in recognising that 'knowledge' is a highly context-sensitive term. Think for a moment about other terms that we use that might plausibly be thought to be context-sensitive, such as 'flat' or 'empty'. For example, if, in normal circumstances, I tell you that the fridge is empty, then you will understand me as saying that it's empty of food, and not that it's empty of *anything* – it contains air, after all. Similarly, if, in normal circumstances, I tell you that the table is flat, I mean that it's not especially bumpy, and not that there are no imperfections *whatsoever* on the surface of the table. In different contexts, however, the applicable standards for terms like 'flat' or 'empty' could change. When a scientist requests a 'flat' table to put her highly sensitive instrument on, for example, she probably has in mind something an awful lot flatter than the sort of table that we would normally (correctly) classify as 'flat'.

Suppose for a moment that 'knows' is also context-sensitive in this way. One way in which this might have import for the sceptical problem could be if the sceptic was using the term in a more demanding way than we usually use it, just as the scientist is using a more demanding conception of what counts as a 'flat' surface in the above example. In this way, just as we can consistently grant that a table is 'flat' by our everyday standards even though it might not meet the scientist's more exacting standards, so we can, it seems, grant that we 'know' an awful lot relative to our everyday standards even though we may not count as knowing very much relative to the sceptic's more exacting standards.

More specifically, the contextualist thought is that whereas in normal contexts we count an agent as having knowledge just so long as she is able to rule out mundane non-sceptical possibilities of error, what the sceptic does is raise the standards for knowledge such that in order to count as having knowledge, the agent must in addition be able to rule out far-fetched sceptical possibilities of error. Accordingly, the contextualist claims that while we have lots of knowledge relative to everyday standards, this claim is entirely compatible with the sceptical claim that we lack knowledge relative to more demanding sceptical standards.

On the face of it, this is a neat resolution of the problem. For one thing, we don't have to deny the closure principle on this view, since provided we stick within a single context – whether everyday or sceptical – we'll either have knowledge of both everyday propositions and the denials of sceptical hypotheses or lack knowledge of both everyday propositions and the denials of sceptical hypotheses (i.e. there will be no context in which one knows the former without also knowing the latter). Moreover, we can respond to the sceptical problem while conceding that there is *something* right about scepticism – the sceptic is, after all, perfectly correct if her argument is understood relative to more exacting sceptical standards.

On closer inspection, however, the contextualist response to scepticism is not nearly so compelling. For one thing, consider again the analogy with terms like 'flat' and 'empty'. Hasn't science shown us that, strictly speaking, *nothing* is ever really flat or empty (because every surface has *some* imperfections, no matter how small, and there are no vacuums in nature)? Of course, we talk as if there are flat surfaces and empty containers, but in fact when we think about it we realise that nothing really corresponds to these ascriptions of flatness and emptiness – we are just talking loosely. Accordingly, if we follow through the analogy with 'knows', then the natural conclusion to draw is that we don't really know anything – because no one could rule out *all* possibilities of error, including sceptical error possibilities – even though we often talk, loosely, as if we do know a great deal.

At the very least, then, it seems that contextualists must be careful what analogy they draw when they say that 'knows' is a highly context-sensitive term. But even if there are context-sensitive terms that better fit the contextualist picture, there will still be other problems outstanding. In particular, perhaps the most pressing difficulty is that it just isn't clear that the sceptical problem does trade on high standards in the first place. After all, the sceptical claim is that *we have no good grounds at all* for thinking that we're not the victims of sceptical hypotheses, not that we have grounds but that these grounds aren't good enough for knowledge. If this is right, then it is hard to see how appealing to different epistemic standards will help since it seems to follow, *relative to any epistemic standards that you care to choose*, that we lack knowledge of the denials of sceptical hypotheses, and this will mean, given the closure principle, that we lack everyday knowledge as well, again relative to any epistemic standards that you care to choose.

Relatedly, if we really can make sense of the idea that we can know the denials of sceptical hypotheses relative to *any* normal epistemic standard, then it is not clear what the motivation for contextualism would be. Why not simply opt for a form of Mooreanism, which maintains that we know the denials of sceptical hypotheses, and leave the matter at that? That is, why not stop with Mooreanism rather than going further and opting for contextualism, which holds *both* that we can know the denials of sceptical hypotheses *and* that knowledge is a highly context-sensitive notion?

So, while superficially appealing, the contextualist response to scepticism, like the other responses that we have looked at, is far from being unproblematic.

• CHAPTER SUMMARY

- Radical scepticism is the view that it is impossible to know very much. We are not interested in the view because anyone positively defends it as a serious position, but rather because examining the sorts of considerations that can be put forward in favour of radical scepticism helps us to think about what knowledge is.
- One dominant type of sceptical argument appeals to what is known as a sceptical hypothesis. This is a scenario which is indistinguishable from normal life but in

which one is radically deceived (e.g. the possibility that one is a disembodied brain floating in a vat of nutrients being 'fed' one's experiences by supercomputers).

- Using sceptical hypotheses, the sceptic can reason in the following way. I'm unable to know that I'm not the victim of a sceptical hypothesis (since such a scenario is indistinguishable from normal life), and thus it follows that I can't know any of the propositions that I think I know but which are inconsistent with sceptical hypotheses (e.g. that I'm presently writing this chapter).

- We noted that this argument seems to rest on the closure principle, which roughly holds that if you know one proposition (e.g. that you are sitting at a computer typing), and know that it entails a second proposition (e.g. that you are not a brain in a vat), then you also know that second proposition. One way of responding to the sceptical argument is thus to deny this principle, and therefore hold that one can know 'everyday' propositions (e.g. that you are sitting at a computer) even while being unable to know anti-sceptical propositions (e.g. that you are not a brain in a vat).

- Given the plausibility of the closure principle, we saw that denying it is easier said than done. One way in which epistemologists have tried to motivate this claim is by arguing that knowledge is essentially concerned with having *sensitive* true beliefs (i.e. true beliefs which, had what is believed been false, the agent would not have held). This is known as the sensitivity principle. Most of our 'everyday' beliefs are sensitive, but our anti-sceptical beliefs are not.

- If one wishes to retain the principle of closure, then one possibility is to opt for Mooreanism and hold that we can know the denials of sceptical hypotheses. One way of doing this is by appealing to the idea that knowledge is essentially concerned with having *safe* true beliefs (i.e. true beliefs which could not have easily been false). This is known as the safety principle. It is possible for our anti-sceptical beliefs to be safe; thus, if knowledge is essentially concerned with safety, we might be able to know such propositions.

- Finally, we looked at the contextualist response to the sceptical problem, which held that 'knows' is a radically context-sensitive term. On this view, while the sceptic is right to contend, relative to her very demanding epistemic standards, that we are unable to know very much, this claim is consistent with our possessing lots of knowledge relative to the more relaxed standards in operation in normal contexts. One problem that we noted for this proposal is that it is not obvious that the sceptical argument does trade on high epistemic standards in this way. Indeed, it seems that the sceptical argument goes through relative to all epistemic standards, not just very austere ones.

• STUDY QUESTIONS

1 What is a sceptical hypothesis, and what role does it play in sceptical arguments? Try to formulate a sceptical hypothesis of your own and use it as part of a radical sceptical argument.

2 What is the closure principle, and what role does it play in sceptical arguments? Give an example of your own of an inference that is an instance of this principle.
3 What is the sensitivity principle? Why do proponents of this principle hold that we need to reject the closure principle?
4 What is the safety principle, and what role does it play as part of a Moorean anti-sceptical argument? In light of this principle, critically assess the Moorean claim that we are able to know the denials of sceptical hypotheses.
5 What is the contextualist response to scepticism? Do you find it persuasive? If so, try to think of some reasons why others might not be persuaded. If not, then try to state clearly why you think the view is problematic.

• INTRODUCTORY FURTHER READING

Greco, John (2007) 'External World Skepticism', *Philosophy Compass* (Oxford: Blackwell). [A sophisticated, yet still accessible, survey of the main issues as regards scepticism of the variety that concerns us in this chapter. Very up to date.]

Luper, Steven (2010) 'Cartesian Skepticism', in S. Bernecker and D. H. Pritchard (eds) *The Routledge Companion to Epistemology* (London: Routledge). [An authoritative and completely up-to-date survey of the kind of scepticism that is of interest to us in this chapter.]

Pritchard, Duncan (2013) *What is this Thing Called Knowledge?*, 3rd edn (London: Routledge). [See part three for a fuller, but still accessible, discussion of the problem of radical scepticism.]

Steup, Matthias, Turri, John and Sosa, Ernest (eds) (2013) *Contemporary Debates in Epistemology*, 2nd edn (Oxford: Blackwell). [This volume contains a number of sections that would be relevant to the topics covered in this chapter. See especially the exchange between Fred Dretske and John Hawthorne on the closure principle (§2); the exchange between Earl Conee and Stewart Cohen on contextualism (§3); and the exchange between Jonathan Vogel and Richard Fumerton on scepticism (§5).]

• ADVANCED FURTHER READING

Pritchard, Duncan (2015) *Epistemology* (Basingstoke: Palgrave Macmillan). [This is an advanced textbook in epistemology. Chapter 6 offers a detailed discussion of the problem of radical scepticism and some of the main responses to this problem in the contemporary literature.]

• INTERNET RESOURCES

Baldwin, Tom (2004) 'G. E. Moore', *Stanford Encyclopedia of Philosophy*, http://plato.stanford.edu/entries/moore/. [An excellent introduction to Moore's philosophy, this page also contains some useful links to further internet resources devoted to Moore.]

Black, Tim (2006) 'Contextualism in Epistemology', *Internet Encyclopaedia of Philosophy*, http://www.iep.utm.edu/c/contextu.htm. [An excellent overview of the issues relating to contextualism, by one of the main figures in the contemporary debate.]

Brueckner, Tony (2004) 'Brains in a Vat', *Stanford Encyclopedia of Philosophy*, http://plato.stanford.edu/entries/brain-vat/. [A useful account of the 'brains-in-a-vat' sceptical hypothesis and its implications for epistemology.]

IMDb Internet Movie Database, http://www.imdb.com/title/tt0133093/. [More information about the movie *The Matrix*.]

Klein, Peter (2005) 'Skepticism', *Stanford Encyclopedia of Philosophy*, http://plato.stanford.edu/entries/skepticism/. [A superb overview of the literature on scepticism, written by one of the world's foremost epistemologists.]

Pritchard, Duncan (2002) 'Skepticism, Contemporary', *Internet Encyclopaedia of Philosophy*, http://www.iep.utm.edu/s/skepcont.htm. [An accessible introduction to the literature on scepticism.]

Part V

philosophy of mind

Berit Brogaard

Philosophy of mind is an area of philosophy dating back to the Ancient Greeks that is devoted to questions about the nature of the mind and mental occurrences and their relation to the external world, the brain and the physical body. The area used to subsume the discipline of psychology. In the 1870s, however, psychology became its own scientific discipline with a greater focus on experimental research and clinical approaches. Though psychology and contemporary philosophy of mind tend to use different methodologies, there is still a considerable overlap among the questions studied in the two disciplines.

Philosophers of mind have been particularly interested in questions such as "What is consciousness?", "What is perceptual experience?" and "What are emotions?". However, the area includes questions about almost anything pertaining to the mind, including questions that lie at the core of psychology, such as, "What is mental illness?", "How can we best analyze personality?" and "What is attention?", as well as questions that are also examined in other areas of philosophy, such as "What are beliefs?", "Are mental states internal to the skull?" and "How do beliefs and desires guide our actions?". In this section we will focus on the first three questions, as those are high on the list of issues that have generated a significant amount of philosophical literature, but we will encounter many other topics along the way.

In chapter 14 we will consider the question of what consciousness is. We will look at why some philosophers have thought that this is a particularly hard question to answer and why empirical answers may not seem to get to the bottom of the issue. In chapter 15 we will address questions about the nature of perception. Most of the perception literature has focused on vision. But we will also look at some of the other sensory modalities. Finally, in chapter 16 we will examine questions pertaining to the nature of emotions. Among other proposals we will consider the question whether emotions should be treated as perceptual experiences.

14

what is consciousness?

- The variety of conscious experience
- The hard problem
- Approaches to the nature of consciousness
- The Mary argument
- The zombie argument

• THE VARIETY OF CONSCIOUS EXPERIENCE

At each moment at which you are aware and alert you are conscious of a wide range of things through your sensory modalities, your inner bodily senses and your cognitive streams. Imagine that you are sitting in a garden on a sunny day. You are visually aware of trees, bushes, grass, water fountains and insects. You are auditorily aware of the sounds of the bees, the voices from your next door neighbors and your tummy that is growling. As you sip your ice tea you can taste the citrus and the coarse-grained tannins while the strawberries on the table and the roses fill your nostrils with a sweet scent. Through the sense of touch you feel your shoes, clothes and the chair you are sitting on. You feel the warmth of the sun on your skin and a slight itch on the inside of your pinky toe. You feel relaxed and content until you remember that your term paper is due tomorrow. Then you start to worry.

All of these perceptual, bodily and emotional experiences are mental occurrences that involve your being conscious of something in the outside world or inside your body. Philosophers call each of these occurrences a "conscious mental state." There are many different ways of dividing up your stream of experience into conscious mental states. If you are visually conscious of a dog and you are also at the same time conscious of a bird chirping through your sense of hearing, then there is a composite conscious mental state that has both experiences as constituents. The largest conscious mental state at a given time is the totality of all your conscious mental occurrences, that is, everything you are aware of at the time in question.

• THE HARD PROBLEM

So, what is consciousness? Philosophers say that it is what it is like to have an experience. When they say that, they treat "experience" in a broad sense that includes sensory and bodily experience, imagination, memories, dreams, and so on, basically everything that may lead you to have an inner mental life. But this "what it is like" talk is not to be understood as a final answer to the question of what consciousness is; it's just a way of characterizing the phenomenon that we are interested in examining. As a way of emphasizing what we are talking about when we ask questions about this type of consciousness we can also use the expression "**phenomenal consciousness.**" "**Phenomenal**" refers to the "what it is like-ness" of experience.

When philosophers ask "What is consciousness?", they are looking for a theory that is true not just of the people who live on earth right now, but of all conscious human beings in the past and the future and also of non-human animals that have conscious experiences, for example, pain and pleasure experiences. The theory that philosophers are interested in must be true also of conscious human beings that don't actually exist but could have existed.

Most researchers agree that it is very difficult to come up with a theory of this kind. In psychology and other empirical sciences researchers have studied the brains of conscious individuals in order to discover some facts about consciousness. A number of studies have focused on people with brain damage. Brain damage can lead to a lack of particular conscious experiences. For example, people with damage to the visual system may lack conscious sight, whereas people with damages to the somatosensory cortex may lack a sense of touch. By looking at how brain lesions affect certain kinds of consciousness, researchers have been able to form hypotheses about which areas of the brain are involved in generating the type of consciousness in question. There are many other ways that we can study consciousness scientifically. One way is through brain imaging. In functional brain imaging scientists look at increased brain activity in particular brain regions in response to particular stimuli. For example, when participants consciously perceive motion, we can observe increased activity in a region of the visual cortex known as area V5. This gives us good reason to think that area V5 is involved in generating visual consciousness of moving objects.

Answering scientific questions about consciousness is a hard thing to do. But many philosophers and scientists think that answering these questions will not help us answer questions about the nature of phenomenal consciousness. The main reason for this is that the neural mechanisms that appear to generate consciousness are neither necessary nor sufficient for consciousness to occur. Particular neural mechanisms are not necessary for particular experiences, because different neural mechanisms can generate the same type of experience. For example, some people who acquire damages to crucial areas of the visual cortex can still generate conscious experiences through alternative pathways that bypass the normal visual pathway. There are also many theoreticians who think that consciousness could arise in material that is not neurological. It has not been ruled out, for instance, that future generations of computers could be conscious.

The neural mechanisms that appear to generate consciousness do not suffice for consciousness to occur either. First of all, many other parts of the brain and body than the so-called **neural correlates of consciousness** must be working properly for particular types of consciousness to occur. Second, it seems difficult to identify a particular causal role that consciousness plays that could not have been played equally well by a neurological system lacking consciousness. This suggests that simply identifying the neural mechanisms underlying a particular form of consciousness does not fully explain what consciousness is.

A further reason to think that answering the current scientific questions about consciousness will not fully answer our questions about the nature of consciousness is that consciousness is essentially subjective. We are conscious of things only from a first-person perspective. Science, on the other hand, is in the business of collecting third-person data. We can take the case of the brain scan as an example. In principle, at least, we all have equal access to the data from brain imaging showing increased activity in area V5 in response to motion. But the only person who can speak to the *experience* of the moving stimuli is the participant in the scanner. Only the participant knows what it is like to have that particular experience.

The problem of discovering what consciousness is, is also sometimes referred to as "the **hard problem**." The problem is so-called because while it is difficult to produce good answers to scientific questions, simply answering the current menu of scientific questions is unlikely to give us the full answer to questions pertaining to the nature of consciousness. Not everyone agrees that answering the question about the nature of consciousness is not simply a matter of answering enough scientific questions, and many philosophers and scientists have come up with theories of what consciousness is. But there is not yet a theory of consciousness that is widely agreed to be true.

● APPROACHES TO THE NATURE OF CONSCIOUSNESS

There are various different ways that philosophers envisage that the hard problem will be resolved. Here we will look at four major groups: Reductionist physicalism, non-reductionist physicalism, **dualism** and panpsychism. **Physicalism**, which is also sometimes called "materialism," holds that the fundamental entities of reality are physical entities, usually microphysical. The fundamental entities of reality might include, for example, quarks, electrons, neutrinos, gravity, electromagnetism, spin and charm, but not consciousness, visual experience, pain, itchiness, fear or irritation. The latter type of entities, and everything else outside of the microphysical realm, are not fundamental but stand in some well-defined relation to the physical realm.

Reductionist physicalists hold that all truths about the microphysical realm logically entail all truths about consciousness. Truths about the microphysical realm thus fully explain truths about consciousness. Reductionists may still agree that there is a hard problem about consciousness but they would say that the difficulty of the problem has to do with our limited knowledge and logical abilities; it does not reflect what the world is like or what can, in principle, be known about it. These people are also said to deny that there is an **explanatory gap** between the mental and the physical.

A special version of reductionist physicalism known as "**functionalism**" also resists the idea of a particularly hard problem of consciousness. Functionalism about consciousness is the view that what makes something a conscious mental state depends on the way it functions in a cognitive or behavioral system. A classical example in the literature is that of pain. A functionalist may treat pain as, for instance, any state which produces the belief that something is wrong with the body and a desire for the state to disappear and which tends to give rise to anxiety, moaning, whining or screaming. If this functional role is played by C-fiber stimulation, then a person is in pain when she undergoes C-fiber stimulation. Role functionalists would identify the pain property with the **functional role property** itself, not the C-fiber stimulation. Realizer functionalists, on the other hand, identify the property with C-fiber stimulation. Either type of functionalism lends itself to a type of reductionist physicalism but it does so at a cost. It reduces consciousness to facts about behavior or other third-person observable traits and thus denies that the subjective "inner" aspect of consciousness is essential to being conscious.

Non-reductionist physicalists believe that there is an explanatory gap between the mental and the physical. That is, they believe that the very nature of consciousness is such that truths about it could not be deduced from truths about the microphysical realm, even in principle. But qua physicalists they nonetheless think that consciousness is grounded in, or **supervenes** on, the physical. If Mother Nature had to create a world like ours, all she had to do would be to fix the microphysical entities and the laws of nature. She would not need to add any mental entities to get all of the varied experiences that conscious beings have. Non-reductionists thus hold that while there is an explanatory gap between the physical and the mental, there is no **ontological gap**: there is no gap in terms of what fundamentally exists.

Philosophers who reject physicalism fall into two main camps. Dualists hold that there are two types of substances or properties. The best-known traditional dualist was the French philosopher and mathematician René Descartes, who held that the mind and the body are distinct substances. Most contemporary dualists hold that consciousness is a **fundamental property** together with the fundamental microphysical properties. On this view, if Mother Nature were to create a world like ours, she would need to start not just with microphysical properties but also with consciousness and psychophysical laws stating how the physical and mental properties relate to each other. Because there are two kinds of fundamental properties, according to the dualist, truths about consciousness could not be deduced from truths about the microphysical realm, even in principle. Dualists thus hold that that there is both an explanatory and an ontological gap between the physical and the mental.

A view related to dualism that also rejects physicalism is **panpsychism**. Panpsychists hold that every entity in the universe is conscious, at least in some minimal way. So, the rock, your tennis shoe and my armchair all have some minimal form of consciousness. Traditionally, many panpsychists have held that consciousness is more fundamental than physical properties. As this view implies that there is only one fundamental entity, it is not a kind of dualism but rather a kind of monism. **Russellian monism** is a variation on panpsychism that holds that the bearers of physical properties have an intrinsic nature that may be psychic in nature. Panpsychism can also take the form of dualism. On this view, although there is consciousness everywhere, mental and physical properties are equally fundamental.

One major problem for panpsychism and related views is to account for how many conscious micro-subjects can add up to a single conscious person. For example, if atoms are conscious micro-subjects in some minimal sense, and atoms compose human beings, how do large numbers of micro-subjects combine to form a single macro-subject with a unified stream of consciousness? This problem is also known as "**the combination problem**," and was first formulated by the American philosopher, psychologist and medical researcher William James.

BOX 14.1 CARTESIAN DUALISM

Cartesian dualism is a position named after the French philosopher and mathematician René Descartes (1596–1650). Descartes held that the mind and the body are fundamentally distinct substances. In his *Discourse on the Method* and *Principles of Philosophy* Descartes presented a first version of a now famous argument for this type of dualism. He argued there that he could imagine, or conceive of, a case in which he had no physical body and no location in space but could not, however much he tried, imagine a case where he himself did not exist as the subject having thoughts and being able to imagine things. The argument was further developed in the second of his *Meditations*, where he argued that he could doubt the existence of matter but not his own existence as a thinker. This has come to be known as *cogito ergo sum* ("I think, therefore I am"). In the sixth of the *Meditations* Descartes argued further that clear and distinct thoughts about the essences of mind and matter reveal that mind and matter are distinct substances.

• THE MARY ARGUMENT

One of the two most-discussed challenges to physicalism is the knowledge argument, also known as the "**Mary argument**." The argument runs as follows. Mary is an excellent neuroscientist confined to a black-and-white room with black-and-white television screens hooked up to external cameras and access to everything that has ever been written about colors and color perception. After years of studying in her cell Mary comes to know every physical fact about colors and color perception. Yet when Mary finally leaves the black-and-white room and sees the colored world for the first time, she learns something new: what it is like to perceive in colors.

The story about Mary was originally meant to undermine physicalism of any kind. If Mary knows every physical fact about colors and color perception but is still able to learn something new about conscious color vision upon her release, then not all truths about consciousness are physical. So, physicalism is false.

As it stands, there is an obvious worry about the argument. If Mary already knows every physical fact about the colors and color perception prior to her release, and facts about conscious color perception are physical, then she already knows every fact about conscious color perception. So, for it to be true that Mary learns something new upon her release, it must be implicitly assumed that some truths about conscious color perception are not physical. But this begs the question against the physicalist. To avoid begging the question it is better to say that, prior to her release, Mary knows all the lower-level physical truths.

Even if modified in this way, however, the Mary argument does not threaten to undermine just any kind of physicalism. If it is true that Mary cannot come to know all truths about conscious color perception in her black-and-white cell, that only shows that these truths cannot be inferred from the lower-level physical truths and therefore are not deducible from the lower-level physical truths. It doesn't undermine the claim that the mental supervenes on the physical. As non-reductionist physicalism does not require that truths about consciousness are deducible from the microphysical truths, the knowledge argument is thus best construed as an argument against reductionist physicalism.

The success of the Mary argument as an argument against reductionist physicalism stands and falls with the learning claim, the claim that upon her release Mary learns a new fact about conscious color perception, a fact which she would have known prior to her release had reductionist physicalism been true. To refute the knowledge argument reductionist physicalists must explain away the appeal of the learning claim.

The Mary argument has generated a large number of articles detailing ways to refute the learning claim. The two main strategies have been to say either that Mary doesn't learn a fact about conscious color perception upon her release but instead acquires an ability that she didn't have before, or that she acquires a phenomenal concept the possession of which requires a kind of direct acquaintance with colors through experience. On either approach, Mary would indeed have known all truths about conscious color perception in her black-and-white room but would have acquired something else (an ability or a concept) upon her release. Whether these replies are successful in refuting the Mary argument is still subject to lively debate.

BOX 14.2 MENTAL CAUSATION

Ordinary speech and thought seem to suggest that the mind can causally influence the physical world. For example, when you remove your hand from the hot plate in response to the pain you feel, it seems that a conscious state causes the body to react. This type of causation is also known as "mental causation." The existence of mental causation formed the basis for one of the main objections to Descartes' dualism, the view that the mind and the body are fundamentally distinct substances. The objection is that the view cannot explain how an unextended, immaterial mind interacts with extended physical matter. The same problem arises for dualists who think that mental and physical properties are equally fundamental. If mental properties are ontologically distinct from physical properties, how do we explain how mental properties can causally influence the physical world? To think that they can goes against one widely accepted doctrine to the effect that the physical realm is causally closed, which means that only physical entities can be causally efficacious. One way of resolving this dilemma is to deny that mental properties can play a causal role. This view is also known as "**epiphenomenalism.**" Whether epiphenomenalism has any unacceptable consequences is still being debated.

• THE ZOMBIE ARGUMENT

The **zombie argument**, also known as "the conceivability argument," is another widely discussed argument against physicalism. The argument can be summarized as follows:

Zombie argument

1 Philosophical **zombies** are **conceivable**.
2 If philosophical zombies are conceivable, then they are **metaphysically possible**.

Intermediate Conclusion: Philosophical zombies are metaphysically possible.
Conclusion: Physicalism (a necessary thesis) is false.

Despite its apparent simplicity, the zombie argument is quite complex once we unpack the premises and the philosophical concepts they contain. Two concepts that are crucial to the argument are *philosophical zombies* and *conceivable*. Unlike movie zombies, philosophical zombies are physically and functionally indistinguishable from us but have no inner mental life. There is nothing it is like to be them. But they nonetheless do all the things we do and say all the things we say. If you were to ask a zombie whether it is a zombie, it would say "no." Likewise, it would *say* that there is something it's like for it to perceive the world. But its claims about its own consciousness would be largely false, as zombies by definition do not have inner subjective experiences.

"Conceivability" is also a technical term. One way to understand it is in terms of what you can know without engaging in empirical discovery. Things you can come to know without having to explore the external world are said to be **a priori**, or logically necessary. It is a priori that $2 + 2 = 4$ and that Venus is Venus but it is not a priori, but **a posteriori**, that water is made of H_2O and that Venus is visible in the evening sky, because we can only discover these things by exploring the external world. Something is conceivable when it is compatible with what we can know a priori, that is, when we cannot rule it out on the basis of claims that are a priori. For example, it is conceivable that water, the clear, odorless liquid that flows in rivers, lakes and oceans and comes out of the drinking faucet in your kitchen, is not made of H_2O but is instead made of another molecule XYZ. There are also ways to understand "conceivability" in terms of what you can imagine to be the case in certain ideal circumstances.

On the first way of understanding conceivability, the first premise thus says that we cannot rule out on the basis of what can be known a priori that there are creatures like us but without inner subjective experiences. On the second way, the premise can be taken to state that we can imagine creatures like us without inner subjective experiences.

The second premise in the zombie argument is that if zombies are conceivable, then they are metaphysically possible. It is not true in general that if something is conceivable, then it is metaphysically possible. There is a long tradition in philosophy of language of taking proper names, such as "Barack Obama," and natural kind terms, such as "water," to refer to a particular entity or kind of entity as a matter of **metaphysical necessity**. The proper name "Barack Obama," for example, refers to the actual man who is currently president as a matter of metaphysical necessity. If we imagine the ways the world might have been but is not as different possible worlds, then we can say that "Barack Obama" refers to the actual man who happens to be president here in all the possible worlds in which the actual man exists. In the majority of these possible worlds Barack Obama is not president but is nonetheless still the same person as the actual man. Likewise, "water" refers to H_2O in all possible worlds in which there is H_2O. "Water is H_2O" is thus metaphysically necessary. However, it was a scientific discovery that water is made of H_2O rather than some other molecule XYZ. So, "water is H_2O" is not a priori, but a posteriori. The claim is a so-called a posteriori necessity. So, it is conceivable that water is not H_2O, even though this is not metaphysically possible. This shows that we cannot infer possibility from conceivability as a general rule.

A posteriori necessities like "water is H_2O" are thus counterexamples to the general claim that if something is conceivable, then it is metaphysically possible. In the zombie argument, however, the claim that zombies exist does not involve proper names or natural kind terms like "water." So, the zombie claim can be formulated in terms that do not give rise to any a posteriori necessities. When there are no a posteriori necessities among a set of claims, and these claims are conceivable, it follows that they are metaphysically possible. This is the main argument for the second premise that if zombies are conceivable, then they are metaphysically possible.

If zombies are metaphysically possible, then the main versions of reductionist and non-reductionist physicalism are false. This is because these positions imply that truths about consciousness supervene on truths about the microphysical. That is, the views imply that in all possible worlds in which the microphysical facts are just like they are in the actual world, creatures that are physically and functionally like us have subjective inner experiences. So, physicalism does not allow for the metaphysical possibility of zombies.

The zombie argument does not refute functionalism that defines consciousness in terms of behavior or third-person observable traits. This is because zombies are stipulated to be functionally identical to us. So, if we are conscious, then that kind of functionalism implies that zombies are conscious, too. However, as noted above, this type of functionalism has the unfortunate consequence that the inner and subjective aspect of consciousness is not essential to the nature of consciousness.

There have been many replies to the zombie argument, and it continues to be at the center of the debate about the nature of consciousness. Some physicalists deny the conceivability of zombies, whereas others argue that they are conceivable but not metaphysically possible. The first reply may hold more promise than the second, as it is difficult to find good reason for thinking that the claim that zombies exist, when spelled out, involves an a posteriori necessity.

Showing that zombies are not conceivable, however, may not be sufficient to refute a more generalized version of the conceivability argument that is formulated without any mention of zombies. Let P be a stand-in for the claim that all the microphysical facts are as they actually are, and let Q be a stand-in for the claim that the facts about consciousness are as they actually are. The generalized conceivability argument can then be summarized as follows:

Generalized Conceivability Argument

1 It is conceivable that P but not Q.
2 If it is conceivable that P but not Q, then it is possible that P but not Q.

Intermediate conclusion: It is possible that P but not Q.
Conclusion: Physicalism (a necessary thesis) is false.

The zombie scenario is obviously a case in which P obtains but in which Q does not obtain. So, an argument to the effect that zombies are conceivable establishes the first premise. However, there are other arguments for the first premise. In fact, we have already encountered one such argument, namely the Mary argument. In the black-and-white room Mary is allegedly unable to infer all truths about consciousness, even though she knows all the micro-physical truths (and has sufficient logic skills). If that is true, then it is also true that all the truths about the micro-physical realm do not logically, or a priori, entail all truths about consciousness. So, it is compatible with what can be known a priori that the microphysical facts are the way they actually are but that the facts about consciousness are different. This is the first premise of the generalized conceivability argument. So, the Mary argument can also be used to establish the first premise of the conceivability argument and hence, via the second premise, the possibility that the microphysical facts are as they actually are but that the facts about consciousness are different from what they actually are, which gives us the conclusion that physicalism is false. So, to refute the first premise of the generalized conceivability argument, it is necessary to rule out the conceivability of a number of other scenarios in which the microphysical facts are as they actually are but in which the facts about consciousness are different from the way they actually are.

• CHAPTER SUMMARY

- Phenomenal consciousness can be characterized as the subjective, inner life we are subject to when we have sensory, bodily and emotional experiences, including desires, fantasies, dreams, and so on. It is what it is like to undergo those mental occurrences.
- While science can offer answers to many questions about consciousness, it is less clear how it can tell us about the nature of consciousness. Finding the answer to the question "What is the nature of consciousness?" is also known as "the hard problem."
- There are different ways of approaching the question of what consciousness is. Reductionist physicalists argue that if only we knew all the microphysical facts and had perfect logic skills, we would be able to deduce all facts about consciousness. Non-reductionists argue that truths about consciousness do not follow logically from truths about the microphysical realm but that they are nonetheless still meta-physically grounded in microphysical truths. So, Mother Nature could create a world like ours by fixing the microphysical truths. She would not need to add anything else to get a world with consciousness in it.
- Functionalism about consciousness is also a kind of physicalism. In its extreme behaviorist form, it takes consciousness to be defined in terms of how conscious creatures behave. A major drawback for this view is that it is unable to capture the subjective, inner aspect of consciousness.
- The main contemporary non-physicalist views about consciousness are dualism and panpsychism. Dualists holds that there are two types of fundamental prop-erties in the universe: physical and phenomenal properties (that is, properties of conscious states). To generate a universe like ours Mother Nature would need to start out with both of these properties. Panpsychists normally maintain that phenomenal properties are the only fundamental, or non-derived, properties and that they are present in everything around us, even in objects like rocks, bicycles, and television sets. However, panpsychists could also take mental and physical properties to be equally fundamental.

- The Mary argument and the zombie argument, two arguments against physicalism, are among the most-discussed arguments in the philosophical literature on the nature of consciousness. They continue to be at the center of the debate in this area.

• SAMPLE QUESTIONS

1 Give examples of your own of the following types of conscious mental occurrences:

- Sensory experiences
- Bodily experiences
- Emotions
- Imaginations
- Desires

2 Why can't we solve the question of the nature of consciousness by finding all the neural mechanisms underlying the different types of consciousness?
3 Explain, in your own words, what the difference is between physicalism and dualism.
4 What is the Mary argument, and how does this argument, if it succeeds, refute reductionist physicalism?
5 State the main premises in the zombie argument. Why does the possibility of zombies imply that physicalism is false?
6 Are there any forms of physicalism that naturally escape the zombie argument?

• INTRODUCTORY FURTHER READINGS

Brogaard, Berit (2013) 'The Status of Consciousness in Nature', in S. Miller (ed.) *The Constitution of Phenomenal Consciousness: Toward a Science and Theory* (Amsterdam: John Benjamins Publishing Company), pp. 330–47. [An evaluative overview of the different forms of physicalism and non-physicalism and the standard arguments for and against these views.]

Gertler, Brie and Shapiro, Lawrence (2007) *Arguing about the Mind* (New York: Routledge). [A succinct and very readable introduction to philosophy of mind, with a focus on consciousness.]

• ADVANCED FURTHER READINGS

Chalmers, David (1995) 'Facing Up to the Problem of Consciousness', *Journal of Consciousness Studies* 2: 200–19. [David Chalmers introduced the idea of a hard problem in this article.]

——(1996) *The Conscious Mind* (New York: Oxford University Press). [A book-length defense of dualism. This is where the zombie argument first appeared.]

Gertler, Brie (1999) 'A Defense of the Knowledge Argument', *Philosophical Studies* 93: 317–36. [A reply to two standard objections to the Mary argument.]

Jackson, Frank (1986) 'What Mary Didn't Know', *Journal of Philosophy* 83: 291–95. [Though Frank Jackson had presented the argument previously, this is the article most people refer to when they write about the Mary argument.]

Levine, Joseph (1983) 'Materialism and Qualia: The Explanatory Gap',. *Pacific Philosophical Quarterly* 64: 354–61. [Joseph Levine introduced the notion of an explanatory gap in this article.]

Nagel, Thomas (1974) 'What Is It Like to Be a Bat?', *The Philosophical Review* 83(4): 435–50. [A classic text arguing that there is a special subjective aspect of consciousness that is not discoverable by standard science.]

• FREE INTERNET RESOURCES

Kirk, Robert, 'Zombies', *The Stanford Encyclopedia of Philosophy* (Summer 2012 Edition), http://plato.stanford.edu/archives/sum2012/entries/zombies/. [An excellent overview of the roles philosophical zombies have played in philosophical arguments.]

Nida-Rümelin, Martine, 'Qualia: The Knowledge Argument', *The Stanford Encyclopedia of Philosophy* (Summer 2010 Edition), http://plato.stanford.edu/archives/sum2010/entries/qualia-knowledge/. [An excellent overview of the debate that has surrounded Jackson's Mary argument.]

Van Gulick, Robert, 'Consciousness', *The Stanford Encyclopedia of Philosophy* (Summer 2011 Edition), http://plato.stanford.edu/archives/sum2011/entries/consciousness/. [An excellent overview of the issues that have arisen in the philosophical literature on the nature of consciousness.]

15
what is perception?

- The varieties of sensory experience
- Direct realism vs indirect realism
- The arguments from illusions and hallucinations
- Phenomenal looks and experience
- The transparency of experience
- Unconscious perception

THE VARIETIES OF SENSORY EXPERIENCE

We gain knowledge of the external world primarily through our perceptual interaction with our surroundings. For example, when I look out of the window in my office and see water come down from the sky, I instinctively form the belief that it is raining. I might cease to believe this if I suddenly get a glimpse of a water system that has been installed on the roof to keep the rooftop plants moist. Both my initial belief and the revision of my belief are based on my experiences of the world. Questions about the nature of perceptual experience have been central to philosophy of mind since antiquity.

Most of the philosophical literature on perception has focused on visual experience, that is, conscious vision. There are, however, many other types of sensory experience. **Auditory experience** is experience of the kind that arises as a result of hearing the sounds made by objects. **Tactile experience** is experience of the kind that results when you press a part of your body against an object. **Olfactory experience** is experience of the kind that can result from using your nose to sniff chemicals emitted by objects. **Gustatory experience** is experience of the kind that can happen from exposing your tongue to the chemicals in, for example, food and drinks. In addition to these five types of sensory experience, there is also experience of the external temperature. This type of experience takes place through skin pain receptors that serve a dual purpose. Because pain receptors are involved in experiencing the external temperature, some forms of pain experience could also be classified as sensory experience, though pain experience is typically dealt with in a separate category of bodily experiences.

Though we talk of experiences in relation to particular sensory modalities (e.g. sight, hearing, touch, smell and taste), we rarely have experiences that are related only to one sensory modality. Most of our experiences are multisensory. They originate in many different sensory modalities and form a single unified experience of the external world. For example, when I am sitting in a café drinking coffee, my total experience involves seeing the coffee mug and the people around me, the sounds of people talking and the espresso maker working its magic, the feeling of my fingers on the keyboard, the smell of coffee and toasted bagels and the taste of the coffee in my mouth.

When sensory experience accurately tracks objects or their properties in the external world, and it does not involve any misperception, it is said to be veridical. **Veridical experience**, however, is not the only type of experience. If a white table is illuminated by red light, it may look red. In that case your visual experience of the table being red is said to be an **illusion**. An illusory experience is an experience that fails to be properly causally related to some of the properties of objects in the external world. Illusory experience may result from abnormal perceptual conditions or from atypical brain processing. Experience can also fail to be properly causally related to the external world altogether, for example, as a result of exposure to drugs, mental illness, brain damage or unusual external circumstances. When experience is not an immediate result of processing external stimuli, it is said to be an **hallucination**.

There are also examples of atypical perceptual experience that consists in attributing properties that belong to one sensory modality to objects that are typically perceived through a different sensory modality. For example, some people experience sounds as colored or people's names as having a taste. This phenomenon is also known as "**synesthesia**." The mixed experiences that occur in synesthesia as a result of sensory blending can also occur within the same sensory modality. In fact, one of the most common forms of the condition is grapheme-color synesthesia, in which letters or numbers printed in black are experienced as having their own special color. Synesthesia can also occur as a kind of automatic mental association, where two features are bound together in imagination or thought. In that case, the experience is not sensory but more like visual memory or thought.

● DIRECT REALISM VS INDIRECT REALISM

One of the classic questions about the nature of perception is that of whether it is direct or indirect. **Direct realism** holds that, at least in veridical cases, perceptual experience involves direct awareness of an external object and some of its properties. For example, a perceptual experience of a ripe tomato involves direct awareness of a tomato and its color, shape, texture, and so on. The view is sometimes expressed in terms of the **phenomenal character**, the "what it's like," of experience. Direct realism normally maintains that, at least in veridical cases, the phenomenal character of the experience is exhausted by the object of the experience and its perceptible properties.

The two main forms of direct realism are **naive realism** and direct **representationalism**. Naive realists hold that perception just is a perceptual relation to an external object and some of its perceptible property instances. For example, a visual experience of a ripe tomato is fundamentally a matter of being related to a real tomato and its shape, color, texture, and so on. In the case of illusions, the object is said to have an appearance that it does not in fact have. According to naive realism, hallucinations are not real perceptions but different types of mental states that can appear introspectively indistinguishable from veridical experiences.

Representationalism comes in varying strengths. The strong version holds that for an experience to have a certain phenomenal character, the conscious "what it's like," of experience, just is for it to have a certain **representational content**. For example, a visual experience of a ripe tomato is a mental state with a content, or proposition, that is made up of a real tomato and its shape, color, texture, and so on. Representationalism, however, need not be of the strong form. On a view sometimes called the "**mental paint view**," two experiences might have the same representational content and yet have different phenomenal characters. For example, if you attend to a tomato at one time and attend to something next to it at a different time, then the two experiences could have the same representational content, according to some advocates, and yet have different phenomenal characters.

There are many views that stand in opposition to direct realism. Philosophers such as Bertrand Russell and G. E. Moore, and more recently Frank Jackson, have taken perceptual experience to be a relation to sense data. This view is also known as the "**sense-datum theory**." Sense data are mind-dependent objects that we are directly related to and directly aware of in perception. They can allegedly have the same properties as external objects (e.g. they can be red and round).

In more recent times the main type of **indirect realism** is indirect representationalism. According to this umbrella of views, the content of experience represents external objects and properties but it need not have the external object that triggered the experience and its perceptible properties as constituents in order for the experience to be veridical.

• THE ARGUMENTS FROM ILLUSIONS AND HALLUCINATIONS

One consideration that has been taken to favor indirect realism is the case of illusions and hallucinations. The argument from illusions in favor of indirect realism runs as follows. Illusions and veridical perceptions can be **introspectively indistinguishable**. For example, you may have an illusory experience of an unripe tomato as red without being able to tell that it is illusory. Yet in the case of illusions, the perceiver is not related to property instances of the external object. As illusions and veridical experiences are of the same basic kind, the perceiver is not related to property instances of the external object in the case of veridical perceptions either. The argument from hallucinations is similar. Hallucinations and veridical perceptions can be introspectively indistinguishable, that is, when you have a hallucination it may be impossible for you to tell that it is not a normal experience when you reflect on its internal features. Yet in the case of hallucinations, the perceiver is not directly related to an external object. As hallucinations and veridical experiences are of the same basic kind, the perceiver is not directly related to an external object in the case of veridical experiences either.

The replies to these types of arguments are multiple and varied. A standard way of refuting the arguments has been to deny that veridical and non-veridical experiences are of the same basic kind. Some naive realists have argued that illusions are mixed mental states that involve a perceptual relation to an external object as well as an appearance of the object having properties it does not have. On this view, an illusion of an unripe tomato as being red involves a perceptual relation to a tomato and an appearance of the tomato being red rather than green. Naive realists normally treat hallucination as a different kind of mental state that perceivers cannot tell apart from veridical perceptions. Because this view classifies veridical experiences as different in kind from hallucinations and perhaps also illusions, the view is also known as "**disjunctivism**." This type of reply to the problems of illusion and hallucination implies that conscious mental states are not divided into basic kinds on the basis of how things introspectively appear to the perceiver. This implication may seem odd, but other considerations may put some pressure on us to accept it.

BOX 15.1 THE EPISTEMOLOGY OF PERCEPTION

Many naive realists hold that the epistemology of perception supports naive realism. A misperception of one's environment does not support knowledge. For example, if I have an illusory experience of the color of a tomato, then I cannot come to know the color of the tomato on the basis of my experience. Veridical perceptions therefore are cases of good perception that support knowledge, whereas misperceptions are cases of bad perception that do not support knowledge. But what makes the good cases good? It's not their internal appearance, as it may be impossible to tell them apart on the basis of how they appear. So, naive realists argue that it must be something external to them. Yet, some naive realists argue, if the good cases were good because of purely external factors, then the fact that the good cases support knowledge may appear to be a matter of luck. So, the good cases must be good because they are perceptual relations to an external object and its perceptible properties. In response to this type of argument, an opponent could say that what make good cases of perception good is not that they *are identical to* perceptual relations to the external world but that they are relevantly causally related to the external world.

• PHENOMENAL LOOKS AND EXPERIENCE

Another consideration that historically has seemed to favor indirect realism turns on a difference in how things look and how things are (the so-called appearance–reality distinction). Frank Jackson has argued that when we see things in the environment, we see them in virtue of perceiving something else. On Jackson's view, the things that we perceive without having to perceive something else are sense-data. Jackson thought that sense-data are something we literally perceive and the only things we are directly perceptually aware of. Jackson's main argument can be articulated as follows:

Jackson's argument from phenomenal looks

1 When our perceptual perspective changes, the thing we are directly perceptually aware of looks like it is changing.
2 If something looks F, then there is an F of which one is directly perceptually aware.
3 The external object does not change when our perceptual perspective changes.

Conclusion: the thing we are directly perceptually aware of is not the external object.

Your perceptual perspective changes, for example, when you turn a coin in your hand. When it is tilted, it looks elliptical; when it's not tilted, it looks circular-shaped. But the coin itself does not change. So, the thing we are directly aware of is not the external coin. Jackson's argument does not establish the sense-datum theory but only the broader view of indirect realism. At the time in question, however, the sense-datum theory was the main form of indirect realism. So, it was natural to take the argument to be an argument for the sense-datum theory.

The argument's second premise is not true in general. For example, if you see a person park a 1963 Ferrari 250 GTO racer in a driveway, he may look filthy rich to you. But this use of "look" does not reveal anything about what you are directly aware of in perception. This use of "look" is what Roderick Chisholm called "the comparative use." "The driver of the Ferrari looks filthy rich" is equivalent to a statement to the effect that the driver has certain perceptible properties in common with someone who is filthy rich. Jackson argues, however, that even though premise 2 is not true in general, it is true for a highly restricted range of predicates and for a special sense of "look," which he calls the "phenomenal sense."

One way for the direct realist to respond to Jackson's argument is to say that perspectival properties (e.g. the apparently elliptical shape of a tilted coin) are relational properties, whereas objective properties (e.g. the circular shape of the coin) are non-relational. One can then argue that we are directly aware of both perspectival relational properties and objective non-relational properties in perceptual experience. This would block the inference to the conclusion that we are not directly aware of the external object that triggered the experience.

BOX 15.2 CHISHOLM'S ADVERBIALISM

On the basis of his account of "look" statements, the American philosopher Roderick Chisholm (1916–99) argued for a distinctive form of indirect realism known as "adverbialism." On this view, perceptual experience is to be understood in terms of relations of perceptual appearance that hold between an external object and a perceiver. For example, if a red tomato perceptually appears red to Bob, then the red tomato and Bob stand in the relation of perceptually appearing to. Chisholm treats the difference between the appearance relations that obtain when the external scene varies as a difference in the ways that the scene perceptually appears. In ordinary language, we use abverbs, such as "quickly" and "slowly," to express the different ways an act can be performed. For example, Mary may be making a sandwich on two different occasions but do it slowly the first time and quickly the second. Basing his approach on how ordinary language works, Chisholm argued that when an object appears red or like a tomato to a subject, then "red" and "like a tomato" should be understood as adverbs, which is why the view is called "adverbialism." So, on this view, when Bob has an experience of a ripe tomato, he is being appeared to redly and tomato-wise. One of the main objections to adverbialism is that it cannot account for the difference between a case in which someone has an experience of a blue circle and a red square and one in which someone has an experience of a red circle and a blue square, as both experience would amount to being appeared to redly, blue-ly, circle-ly and squarely.

• THE TRANSPARENCY OF EXPERIENCE

One feature of experience that has been taken to support direct realism is its **transparency**. Experience is said to be transparent, because when you attempt to reflect on the features of experience itself, all you seem to see is the external object and its perceptible properties. For example, if you were asked to describe your visual experience as you are sitting in your garden, you would most likely describe the trees, bushes and flowers you are seeing, as no other features need to be revealed in the experience.

The claim that experience is transparent has received its fair share of criticism. If you have a blurry experience, then the blurriness could be taken to be a feature of the experience rather than a feature of what is experienced. Arguably, it's not the tree that is blurry but the experience itself. So, a blurry experience does not seem completely transparent. The same goes for things you don't attend to. Things in the periphery of your visual field do not seem sharp and in focus. And if you are deeply emerged in thought, the things right in front of you may not seem sharp and in focus either. So, unattended visual experience does not seem completely transparent.

Transparency is also much more plausible for visual and tactile experience than for experience in the other sensory modalities. Most people don't have perfect pitch. Perfect pitch is the ability to identify or generate a musical note without a reference frame. For example, if a person with perfect pitch hears a church bell, she can tell whether it's a D or an E-flat without any reference frame. People who don't have perfect pitch can't identify notes that way, even after many years of musical training. This may suggest that auditory experience is not as transparent as visual experience. Smell and taste, too, do not seem quite as transparent as visual and tactile experience. The tastes and odors of wine, for example, may not stand out clearly and distinctly.

Moreover, whereas tactile and visual experiences typically reveal the external object in the experience, auditory, olfactory, and gustatory experiences do not do that. Though we say that we hear the church bell, smell the garbage and taste the apple, we often have access only to sounds, smells and tastes without having a clue as to what produced them. Philosophers sometimes argue that the real objects of those experiences are not the external material bodies that produced them but sounds, odors and tastes. Sounds can be treated as disturbance events involving the objects that produced them, and odors and tastes may be taken to be the chemicals that gave rise to the experienced properties. But saying this does not make the experiences seem more transparent. Chemicals and sound events do not seem to be directly revealed in our experiences of them. So, if transparency is an indicator of how direct perception is, then the many cases of experience that are not very transparent provide evidence against direct realism.

• UNCONSCIOUS PERCEPTION

Though most of the philosophical literature on perception has focused on perceptual experience, which by definition is conscious, there has been some interest in unconscious perception among philosophers in recent years. Neuropsychologists David Milner and Melvyn Goodale have argued that there are two functionally and anatomically separate visual pathways in the brain: vision for perception and vision for action. The perception pathway, the ventral stream, starts in the brain's visual cortex and ends in working memory in the prefrontal cortex, whereas the action pathway, the dorsal stream, starts in the brain's visual cortex but ends in the motor cortex in the frontal lobe. The perception pathway is involved in processing perceptual experience, whereas the action pathway generates unconscious maps of the visual scene that guide our ongoing actions. The main pieces of evidence in favor of the two visual pathways come from lesion studies.

Milner and Goodale found that people with visual agnosia, which involves damages to the ventral stream, could not consciously recognize objects in visual experience but could nonetheless manipulate them in action. They also encountered people with damages to the dorsal stream who could not reach to and grasp objects but who had no trouble consciously recognizing the objects they could not grasp. This sort of evidence is also known as "double dissociation." Double dissociation between two brain regions is still one of the best kinds of evidence for hypotheses that posit a difference in function between the brain regions.

If there is vision for action in addition to vision for perception, then the question arises what the nature of vision for action is. Should we understand vision for action as a direct perceptual relation to an external object and some of its properties? Or should we understand it as a representational state without a phenomenal character? There are visual illusions, such as the Ebbinghaus illusion, in which we misperceive the size of a central circle surrounded by larger circles, even though the illusion only marginally affects grasping behavior directed at the central circle. Such cases might appear to suggest that if vision for action is a direct perceptual relation to an external object, then it cannot be the same kind of relation as the one that obtains in vision for perception cases. One way for the direct realist to reply here, however, may be to maintain that it is the same perceptual relation that obtains in the two cases but that the illusory experience also involves an appearance of something that does not obtain. The question of how to account for the nature of vision for action, however, remains largely unsettled.

• CHAPTER SUMMARY

- Though most of the philosophical literature on perception has been devoted to visual experience, there are many other types of perception. Auditory, tactile, olfactory and gustatory experience remain relatively unexplored by philosophers.
- Direct realism holds that perceptual experience is a direct perceptual relation to an object and some of the object's perceptible property instances. The opposing view, indirect realism, maintains that perceivers perceive the world through some intermediaries.
- Indirect realism has been taken to be supported by the perspectival looks of objects, for example, the apparent elliptical shape of a tilted coin. The case of illusory and hallucinatory experience have also been taken to support indirect realism. There are, however, some fairly strong responses that the direct realist can offer in reply.
- One consideration often treated as favoring direct realism is the transparency of experience. When we visually experience the outside world, we normally are only aware of external objects and their visually perceptible property instances and not of any internal features of the experience. This may suggest that there is nothing more to the phenomenology of experience than what is given by the external objects and their properties. However, not all cases of visual experience seem quite as transparent. Nor do auditory, olfactory or gustatory experiences. This non-transparency of many forms of perceptual experience may turn out to be a consideration in favor of indirect realism.
- While most of the philosophy of perception literature has focused on conscious perception, philosophers have started to show an interest in unconscious

perception. There are not yet any major philosophical views about what the nature of unconscious perception is.

• SAMPLE QUESTIONS

1 Give examples of your own of the visual, auditory, tactile, olfactory and gustatory experience.
2 Formulate the problems of illusion and hallucination in your own words, and explain how disjunctivism avoids these problems.
3 Provide some examples of uses of "look" that clearly do *not* reflect what we are directly aware of in visual experience.
4 How might the direct realist reply to Jackson's argument?
5 Give some examples of your own of perceptual experience that may not be transparent.
6 Does the transparency of normal visual experience support direct realism?
7 Can you think of any other potential forms of unconscious perception besides vision for action?

• INTRODUCTORY FURTHER READINGS

Brogaard, Berit (2014) 'The Phenomenal Use of "Look" and Perceptual Representation', *Philosophy Compass* 9: 455–68. [An evaluation of the success of Jackson's argument from phenomenal looks and similar arguments.]
Fish, William (2010) *Philosophy of Perception: A Contemporary Introduction* (London: Routledge). [A very thorough overview of some of the main debates in philosophy of perception.]
Tye, Michael (1997) *Ten Problems of Consciousness* (Cambridge, MA.: MIT Press). [A fairly accessible defense of strong representationalism, a view that has triggered a lot of heated debate.]

• ADVANCED FURTHER READINGS

Block, N. (2010) 'Attention and Mental Paint', *Philosophical Issues* 20 (1), 23–63. [Block here lays out and defends the mental paint view.]
Brogaard, Berit (2012) 'Vision for Action and the Contents of Perception', *Journal of Philosophy* 109(10): 569–87. [A philosophical account of vision for action.]
——(ed.) (2014) *Does Perception Have Content?* Oxford: Oxford University Press. [An edited collection devoted to the question of whether perception has content and related questions. This is a question that is typically answered in the negative by naive realists.]
Chalmers, David (2004) 'The Representational Character of Experience', in B. Leiter (ed.) *The Future for Philosophy* (Oxford: Oxford University Press), pp.

153–81. [An advanced evaluative account of the various possible forms of representationalism.]

Jackson, Frank (1977) *Perception: A Representative Theory* (Cambridge: Cambridge University Press). [A fairly accessible book-length defense of the sense-datum theory that covers the argument from phenomenal looks.]

Siegel, Susanna (2010) *The Contents of Visual Experience* (New York: Oxford University Press). [An advanced book-length defense of the view that visual experience has content of a particular kind.]

• FREE INTERNET RESOURCES

Crane, Tim, 'The Problem of Perception', *The Stanford Encyclopedia of Philosophy* (Spring 2011 Edition), http://plato.stanford.edu/archives/spr2011/entries/perception-problem/. [An excellent evaluative overview of the arguments from illusion and hallucination.]

Huemer, Michael, 'Sense-Data', *The Stanford Encyclopedia of Philosophy* (Spring 2011 Edition), http://plato.stanford.edu/archives/spr2011/entries/sense-data/. [An excellent overview of the sense-datum theory and the various arguments for and against it.]

Siegel, Susanna, 'The Contents of Perception', *The Stanford Encyclopedia of Philosophy* (Fall 2013 Edition), http://plato.stanford.edu/archives/fall2013/entries/perception-contents/. [An excellent overview of the nature of perceptual content and what it means to say that perception has content in the first place.]

Soteriou, Matthew, 'The Disjunctive Theory of Perception', *The Stanford Encyclopedia of Philosophy* (Winter 2010 Edition), http://plato.stanford.edu/archives/win2010/entries/perception-disjunctive/. [An excellent overview of disjunctivism and the arguments for and against the position.]

16

what are emotions?

- Emotions: adaptations or social constructs?
- Feeling theories of emotions
- Cognitive theories of emotions
- Paradox of Fiction
- Emotions and rationality

EMOTIONS: ADAPTATIONS OR SOCIAL CONSTRUCTS?

Joy, anger, sadness, jealousy, guilt, grief and pride are all examples of emotions. Following the work of American psychologist Paul Ekman, it is common to divide emotions into simple, or basic, and complex emotions. The basic emotions are joy, surprise, anger, sadness, fear and disgust. Jealousy, love, guilt, grief, and pride are examples of complex emotions. **Basic emotions** are so-called because they are associated with distinct and universally recognizable facial expressions. The basic emotions can combine to form the complex emotions. For example, contempt is a mixture of anger and disgust. Some of the complex emotions may involve further elements in addition to the basic emotions. For example, grief may involve the basic emotions surprise, sadness and anger but usually also involves cognitive denial.

Whether the six simple emotions really are simple and basic is still up for debate. Paul Griffiths (1997) has argued that they are the only ones among the emotions that form natural kinds and hence can be investigated scientifically. Other emotions do not form a homogeneous class and hence cannot easily be studied scientifically. Jesse Prinz (2004) has argued against the idea that Ekman's six emotions are really simple and basic. Some of them seem divisible into more fine-grained emotional responses. Surprise, for example, may be divided into a positive sense of interest and wonder and a negative low level of panic, or fear. Anger may emerge as a mix of goal frustration and aggression.

The distinction between basic and complex emotions originates in **evolutionary psychology**. Evolutionary psychologists argue that emotions are innate adaptations. They argue, for example, that women tend to experience more jealousy if their male partner is emotionally involved with another woman than if he is sexually involved, whereas men tend to experience more jealousy if their female partner is sexually involved with another man than if she is emotionally involved. They explain this difference as an evolutionary adaptation. For example, they argue that it would be a great risk for ancient women if their man became emotionally attached to another woman, because that would increase the risk of her children dying. The woman's genes then would not be passed on. By contrast, it would be a great survival risk for ancient men if their women had sex with others because that might result in pregnancy and hence in the man having to use scarce resources to raise another man's child. This would limit the passing on of the man's own genes, as he would have fewer resources to keep his own children alive.

In psychology the main opponents of the evolutionary theory hold that emotions are socially constructed. One piece of evidence for **social constructionism** is that people from different cultures seem to recognize different bodily feelings as emotions. Japanese, for example, also has a term 'oime,' which stands for a feeling of indebtedness, and 'fureai,' which stands for a feeling of connectedness. If the social constructionists are right, then the feelings corresponding to oime and fureai are specific to individuals who grew up in Japanese culture and are not felt in the same way by people from other cultures.

Prinz and other philosophers have argued that both of these approaches are too extreme. The view that the emotions are innate adaptations ignores the fact that learning and culture can influence which emotions we have, whereas social constructionism cannot explain why similar emotions are associated with basic bodily responses. The evidence cited by the evolutionary psychologists also does not seem to hold up to scrutiny. The claim that women are more emotionally jealous than men, and that men are more sexually jealous than women, is based on subjective reports from relatively small groups of people who do not represent the general population. Furthermore, the explanation provided for the asymmetry between men and women focuses on ancient cultures where men were in charge of providing for the women and the children but in some cultures women fended for themselves. Women in Ancient Egypt, for example, worked alongside the men they married.

• FEELING THEORIES OF EMOTIONS

One of the most influential theories of the nature of emotions is the **James–Lange theory**, due to the American psychologist, philosopher and medical researcher William James and Danish doctor Carl Lange. According to this theory, emotions are feelings of bodily changes. In a famous quote James stated that you are not crying because you are sad. You are sad because you are crying. Though this is not strictly speaking his view, James put it in these terms in order to emphasize that you don't need to have an emotion first and then a bodily reaction; rather, the emotion is a feeling of a reaction in your body. For example, if you are afraid, that very emotion may consist in a feeling of your heart racing and your palms getting sweaty. The feeling itself should be understood as a kind of bodily experience of changes in the body's physiology.

One of the main critiques of this theory is that it does not capture an important feature of emotions, which may distinguish them from moods such as free-floating gloominess. Emotions tend to be directed toward objects and events in the external environment. For example, Bob's anger may be directed at Lisa or her actions. On many occasions, we can give reasons for why we have the emotions we do. If you are angry, you might cite how a person wronged you. If you experience joy, you might mention a new job, a promotion or a new addition to the family. In some cases, the cited reasons are also the actual causes of the emotion, but they need not be. For example, when asked why he is angry, Bob might say that it's because Lisa jumped him in line. But perhaps the real cause of his anger is something that has been brewing in his subconscious for years and is only now emerging. In contrast to emotions, moods are often free-floating without being directed toward specific people or events. If they are directed at anything, they tend to be directed in a very general way. While a specific reason for a mood can sometimes be provided, there need not be any reasons to cite.

A further problem for the original version of the **feeling theory** is that many emotions cannot be distinguished on the basis of how the body reacts, because emotions often involve very similar physiological changes. Of course, advocates of the original feeling theories could argue that even if two distinct emotions involve similar physiological changes, these changes may not be perceived as identical. This, however, suggests that emotions involve something other than bodily experiences, namely experiences that are directed toward the external world.

So, for the feeling theory to work it seems that it ought to treat emotions as involving both bodily sensations and experiences, or thoughts, of the subject's environment. Moreover, the experiences would need to be properly connected. Experiences of a dog and a bodily fear response need not add up to fear of a dog. For example, you might see a dog without being afraid of it while suffering from an anxiety disorder that has nothing to do with dogs. In that case there is no fear of a dog. For these mental states to add up to fear of the dog, the perceptions or thoughts of the dog must be perceived as triggering the bodily fear response. Contemporary defenders of the feeling theory tend to hold that emotions manifest this more complex kind of dual directedness.

BOX 16.1 SCHACHTER AND SINGER'S ADRENALINE EXPERIMENT

In the 1960s American psychologist Stanley Schachter and his student Jerome Singer gave 184 male college students one of two types of injections: a mild stimulant (adrenaline) or a placebo injection (a saline solution). The students were told that they were given an injection of a new vitamin compound "suproxin" to test their vision. One group of subjects was told about the injection's potential side effects (shaky hands, pounding heart, short breathing). A second group was told that the injection would produce side effects such as itching, numb feet, and headaches. A third group was told that there would be no side effects. After the injections the participants were left alone for twenty minutes with a stooge (who didn't know about the subject's condition). The stooge was either told to behave joyfully, for instance, play with paper, or behave rudely and angrily. The subjects' emotional states were measured relative to the stooge by observation and self-report. Subjects who were misled or naive about the injection's effects behaved similarly to the stooge, either joyfully or angrily. Those who were informed of the expected effects of the stimulant and were given the placebo had little emotional response to the stooge. The informed students were thus able to correctly attribute their feelings to the stimulant, whereas the uninformed or misinformed students were affected by the behavior of the stooge. This led Schachter to suggest that what emotional experience you have depends on how you interpret the situation you are in. The very same body state may be interpreted as frustration in one context but joy in another. Emotional experience, he concluded, thus requires interpretation in addition to an experience of a change in the body state.

• COGNITIVE THEORIES OF EMOTIONS

One of the main alternatives to the feeling theories defended by philosophers are the **cognitive theories**. On the cognitive theories, emotions are cognitive judgments about, or assessments of, the external environment that involve a negative or positive valence. For example, fear may be a negative cognitive assessment of a particular event (e.g. a person threatening you with a knife) as presenting a danger to oneself or close family members.

As evidence for their theory, cognitive theorists cite the existence of emotions that do not involve a bodily element. For example, intellectual emotions, such as pride and justice, need not involve a feeling of any physiological changes in the body. Martha Nussbaum (2001), who is an advocate of the cognitive theory, argues that even an emotion like grief that can be very physical need not be felt as a physiological change in the body. If, however, there are cases of emotions that do not involve feelings of bodily changes, then bodily feelings are not essential to emotions.

In response to this sort of argument, a feeling theorist may argue that even intellectual emotions involve some bodily sensations, they may just be less pronounced than emotions with a strong physiological response, such as rage or ecstasis. Another possible reply is to allow for the possibility that some emotions are fully or partially unconscious. It certainly seems that we can have emotions for long periods of time without feeling anything or without judging that anything is the case. We might carry a grudge for many years but only feel it or think about it occasionally. This suggests that emotions are not always consciously felt. But if emotions are not always consciously felt, then some emotions may only be partially available to conscious awareness. Even when the bodily sensations of an emotion are unavailable, the emotion could involve actual or dispositional changes in the body's physiology. Yet another reply is to allow that different emotions are structured in different ways. Some emotions may involve only bodily sensations, other emotions may involve only a perception of one's environment, and yet other emotions may involve both types of experiences.

It is also worth pointing out that one can reject the theory that emotions involve bodily experiences and still accept that emotions are kinds of perceptions of the external environment. Insisting that the relevant state is cognitive is unnecessary if the goal is to reject the feeling theories, which hold that emotions involve bodily experiences.

Cognitive theories of emotions have been subject to much criticism. One line of attack has to do with the vagueness of the term "cognitive." There are many different types of cognitive acts, and it is not always clear which kind of act emotions are supposed to belong to. Another criticism is that if the theory implies that emotions require special high-level cognitive abilities, then it cannot account for how infants and non-human animals can have emotions, which they clearly seem to have.

● PARADOX OF FICTION

We experience fear in response to scary movies, we feel sad when literary characters go through tragic events, and we experience joy when the heroine defeats great obstacles (see also Part III, chapter 9). A good theory of emotions should be able to accommodate or explain away these kinds of emotional reactions in response to fiction. Emotions in response to fiction, however, can be tricky to account for, as we don't believe fictional characters are real. In other circumstances in which we experience emotions in response to false stories, it seems that our emotions cease the moment we learn that the story was made up. Suppose your friend tells you about her sister's breast cancer. As she goes into the details about how the chemotherapy makes her sick and how her hair is slowly falling out, you are starting to feel really sad. If your friend then tells you that she made it all up and that she has no sister, you immediately cease to be sad. Anger replaces your sadness. So, in other circumstances, when we believe an event is unreal, our emotions cease. How then can we have them in response to fiction when we do not believe the events are real? The problem of accounting for our emotions in response to fictional characters and events is also known as the "Paradox of Fiction."

One type of response to the problem of fiction is to deny that we really have emotions in response to fiction. Perhaps the fear or the sadness or the joy is not real. This type of response, however, is unintuitive. We certainly seem to experience emotions in response to fiction. We may feel them very intensely. A defender of the cognitive theory, however, may say that the fact that we feel reactions in our bodies in response to fiction does not show that we really have the emotions that normally are associated with these bodily responses. In fact, they may say, the fact that we do not evaluate, say, the serial killer in the movie as presenting a real threat to ourselves or our loved ones shows that we do not have the emotion in question but only a physiological response that we mistake for an emotion.

A second type of response to the problem of fiction is to allow that emotions, like perceptual experiences, can be directed at objects that do not exist or at properties that are not instantiated by external objects. Illusory experiences are directed at external objects but not all the properties presented in an illusory experience are properties of the external object. Hallucinatory experiences are directed at objects and properties in the sense that objects and properties are presented in the experience but these objects and properties did not trigger the experience and may not even exist. Emotions may work in a similar way. Emotions might be directed at things in the external environment that do not exist. Grief certainly seems to work that way. Grief can be directed toward someone who died or left, a job that was lost, or a body part that was removed. So, grief is at least sometimes directed at people or things that do not exist and are known not to exist. Emotions may also be directed at things that exist but attribute properties to them that they do not have. You might admire someone for qualities that he does not have or fear a person or thing that isn't dangerous. If emotions can be directed at things that do not exist and even at things that we know do not exist, then there is no reason to think that they could not also be directed at fictional characters, even though they aren't real.

This sort of response does not explain why you would cease to feel sad when your friend tells you that her story about her sick sister is made up but you continue to feel sad when you watch a movie about a person with cancer, even though you know it's fiction. However, it is not clear that there is a real difference here. You cease to feel sad when your friend tells you that she made up her story, but this also coincides with her ceasing to tell the story and your surprise and anger. When a sad movie ends and we are distracted by something else, our sadness ceases in that case as well.

• EMOTIONS AND RATIONALITY

A recurrent theme in the philosophical literature on the philosophy of emotions is that of whether emotions can be rational, or justified (see also Part I, chapter 2). Historically, emotions were taken to be the irrational aspect of human psychology. Notions like rationality and justification were reserved for cognitive states like beliefs. The main reason for this was not that we cannot directly control which emotions we experience. We cannot directly control which beliefs we have either. Rather, the main reason was that it seems that emotions are not sensitive to evidence the way that beliefs are. Evidence about the safety of flying makes people believe that flying is safe, but it does not seem to help people get over their fear of flying.

BOX 16.2 LOVE AS AN IRRATIONAL EMOTION

It has been debated since antiquity whether love is an emotion. Aristotle argued that love is a union between two people. Many contemporary philosophers argue that love is an emotion, or perhaps more precisely, a range of different emotions. One of the topics that recurs most frequently is that of whether love-qua-emotion can be rational or irrational. Some think that love differs from other emotions in resisting rational assessment. They say that it makes no sense to talk about love as rational or irrational. The main reason philosophers tend to give for thinking that love cannot be justified is that there is no irrationality involved in ceasing to love a wonderful person. But if it's irrational to stop loving a person who is still lovable, then it seems that we ought to continue our love. That piece of advice does, indeed, ring false. One could respond, however, that the argument is confusing when it's irrational to cease to love someone and when it's irrational to continue to love someone. Evidence for loving someone might only render it permissible to love them, it may not require that we begin or continue to love them. Love may be irrational, and hence impermissible, if the loved one is misperceived or there is not a proper fit between the loving response and the loved one. But when the loved one is not misperceived and there is a proper fit between the loving response and the loved one, then continuing to love is in all likelihood optional, just as it is optional whether or not you want to perform actions that are not wrong.

There are, however, good reasons to think that emotions can be properly said to be rational and irrational, or justified and unjustified. In ordinary speech we often talk about emotions as justified or unjustified, or rational and irrational. For example, fear of flying is indeed considered irrational, as flying is safe. Moreover, it is not generally true that beliefs are sensitive to evidence, whereas emotions are not. While we may change our beliefs in light of new evidence, we don't always do that. The same goes for emotions. Once I learn that you didn't step on my toe on purpose, I may cease to be angry at you. But sometimes my emotional state may not be sensitive to new evidence. I may continue to be angry in spite of having reasons not to be. Beliefs and emotions thus do not seem radically different in these respects.

Whether a belief is rational or irrational turns on whether it represents the external world incorrectly, or perhaps, whether it is known to represent the external world correctly. The same applies to emotions. We might consider emotions irrational when they do not fit the object or event they are directed at. Being afraid of something that is not dangerous or being angry at someone who hasn't wronged you may be considered irrational. Emotions might also be considered irrational when they involve a misperception of an object despite proper fit. For example, if a child misperceives a piece of furniture as a monster and is struck by panic, the emotion fits the perceived object but we could say that it is nonetheless still irrational because the object is misperceived. As in the case of belief, one could also hold that an emotion is irrational only if the subject *knows* that the emotion misrepresents and yet cannot shake the emotion.

Emotions can also themselves be reasons for acting a certain way and hence can be what makes an action rational or irrational. For example, if you don't pick up the calls from a friend for two days, your reason might be that you were angry at her. Whether this is a good reason depends in part on whether the emotion itself is rational or irrational. If you were angry at her because she received a better grade than you did, then your anger is not a good reason because it doesn't fit the situation. For the emotion to be a good reason there must furthermore be an appropriate fit between the emotion and the action that it is supposed to justify. For example, being angry is never a good reason for killing someone, because anger is not one of the things that can justify killings.

There are other reasons to doubt the traditional view of emotions as the irrational aspect of human psychology. Many scientific studies show that we cannot make long-term rational decisions if we are incapable of having proper emotional responses. Patients with damage to a part of the brain involved in processing emotions, called "vmPFC (ventromedial prefrontal cortex) damage," can perform to a high level on most language and intelligence tests, but they are unable to make appropriate judgments in their planning strategies. People with vmPFC damage do not learn from their mistakes. They keep making the same mistakes over and over again, as long as there is some short-term benefit to this oversight. For example, in the Iowa Gambling test, subjects choose from four decks of cards that provide different levels of reward and punishment. Two decks provide low reward, but also a low level of punishment. Choosing consistently from these decks eventually leads to a net gain of money. The other two decks give you a high reward, but also a high punishment. Choosing consistently from these decks eventually leads to a net loss of money. Neuroscientist Antonio Damasio found that normal individuals initially sampled the advantageous and disadvantageous decks equally, but they learned from their mistakes. After experiencing the high punishments from the disadvantageous decks, they started sampling from the advantageous decks. People with vmPFC damage, on the other hand, continued to sample from the disadvantageous decks, indicating that intact emotional memory is necessary for making good decisions.

People who are incapable of behaving in morally appropriate ways also sometimes have damage to parts of the brain that process emotions. Psychopathy, for example, may involve defects to the vmPFC and other areas required to interpret emotional processing or to process it in the first place. So, rather than being simply the irrational aspect of our psychology, emotions in fact seem to be required to make rational decisions and behave in morally appropriate ways.

• CHAPTER SUMMARY

- Evolutionary psychologists and social constructionists disagree about whether emotions are the result of cultural influences or are evolutionary adaptations. It is likely that emotions are the result of both types of influences.
- On the James–Lange theory of emotions, emotions are feelings of changes in the body's physiology. Contemporary defenders of the feeling theory tend to argue that emotions also involve perceptions or thoughts of objects and events in the external environment.
- Cognitive theories of emotions deny that bodily experiences are constitutive of emotions.
- Emotions in fiction present a problem that theories of emotion must address. One way to explain how we can have emotions in response to people and events that aren't real is to allow for emotions that are directed at objects or events that do not exist.
- Historically, emotions have been considered the irrational aspect of our psychology. However, it seems that some emotions are more suitable than others and hence can be seen as more rational than other emotions. There is another reason why emotions should not be dismissed as irrational: they appear to be required in order for us to make rational and morally acceptable decisions and plan for the long term.

• SAMPLE QUESTIONS

1 Give examples of your own of complex emotions, and state which (if any) of the basic emotions may be involved in forming the complex state.
2 Give examples of your own of emotions that appear to be mostly culturally based and emotions that seem to have a strong evolutionary component.
3 Use a search engine to find additional examples of ancient cultures where women were in charge or where men and women were equal. Determine to what extent these types of cultures provide a challenge to the argument for the claim that women are more emotionally jealous than men.
4 What are the two components of emotions, according to contemporary feeling theories?
5 What sort of evidence is there for cognitive theories of emotions?
6 What is the problem of fiction?
7 Give examples of your own of cases in which emotions are good reasons for action and cases in which they are bad reasons for action.
8 What do people with damages to ventromedial prefrontal cortex tell us about emotions?

• INTRODUCTORY FURTHER READINGS

Brogaard, Berit (2015) *On Romantic Love* (Oxford: Oxford University Press). [This is a mainstream book discussing the philosophy of emotions, with a particular focus on love.]

Deonna, Julien, and Teroni, Fabrice (2012) *The Emotions: A Philosophical Introduction* (London: Routledge). [This is a succinct and very readable introduction to the philosophy of emotions.]

• ADVANCED FURTHER READINGS

Goldie, Peter (ed.) (2010) *The Oxford Handbook of Philosophy of Emotions* (Oxford: Oxford University Press). [A comprehensive treatment of the different issues that have arisen in the philosophy of emotions.]

Greenspan, Patricia (1988) *Emotions and Reasons: an Inquiry into Emotional Justification* (New York: Routledge, Chapman and Hall). [An accessible account of how emotions can serve as reasons for our actions.]

Griffiths, Paul (1997) *What Emotions Really Are: The Problem of Psychological Categories* (Chicago: University of Chicago Press). [A book-length criticism of philosophers working on philosophy of emotions for failing to take data from evolutionary biology into account.]

Nussbaum, Martha (2001) *Upheavals of Thought: The Intelligence of Emotions* (Cambridge: Cambridge University Press). [A book-length defense of a cognitive theory of emotions.]

Prinz, Jesse (2004) *Gut Reactions: A Perceptual Theory of Emotions* (New York: Oxford University Press). [An accessible defense of a contemporary version of the feeling theory, with lots of evidence from the sciences.]

Solomon, R. C. (ed.) (2004) *Thinking about Feeling: Contemporary Philosophers on Emotions* (Oxford: Oxford University Press). [A comprehensive edited collection discussing the set of issues pertaining to emotions covered in this chapter.]

• FREE INTERNET RESOURCES

de Sousa, Ronald, 'Emotion', *The Stanford Encyclopedia of Philosophy* (Spring 2013 Edition), http://plato.stanford.edu/archives/spr2013/entries/emotion/. [An excellent overview of the set of issues raised in this chapter.]

Johnson, Gregory (2009) 'Theories of Emotion', *Internet Encyclopedia of Philosophy*, http://www.iep.utm.edu/emotion/. [An excellent overview of the different theories of emotions, including those presented by psychologists.]

Part VI

metaphysics

Kristie Miller

What is metaphysics? Not only is there a lot of disagreement over particular issues in metaphysics, there is also disagreement about what metaphysics is. Those who engage in metaphysics are typically pretty confident that they can spot it when they see it, but they may not agree about what makes something metaphysics. Some are inclined to think that metaphysics is characterised by its subject matter. If so, metaphysics is defined by the sorts of questions it asks. Others are inclined to think that metaphysics is characterised by its methodology: what makes something metaphysics is not the issues it addresses, but how it goes about investigating those issues. Finally, one might think that what makes something metaphysics is some complex combination of its subject matter and its methodology. Rather than trying to take a stand on whether it is subject matter or methodology that best defines what counts as metaphysics, the best way to get a grasp on what metaphysics *is*, is to see how metaphysics *works*. So we will start off by thinking about some of the sorts of questions metaphysics asks, and what sorts of answers it provides. Then we will think about how it comes by those answers. Is there something distinctive about the methodology of metaphysics? Even if we cannot, in the end, specify exactly what it is for something to be metaphysics, we should at least be in a position to spot metaphysics when we see it.

17

What is metaphysics?

- What is there?
- Are there abstract objects?
- What are properties?
- What sorts of properties and relations are there?
- Wholes and parts
- What could have been?

WHAT IS THERE?

Those who think that metaphysics is characterised by the issues it investigates think that at its heart metaphysics is the philosophical study of what there is, and how those things are related to one another. Even those who think that metaphysics is characterised by how it investigates questions rather than what it investigates typically still agree that we can provide a rough characterisation of the sorts of questions that metaphysicians do, in fact, investigate. Both parties agree that metaphysics is a very broad discipline of philosophy in which many different sorts of questions are asked, and, hopefully, sometimes answered. To give a sense of just how broad metaphysics is in this chapter we are going to think about just a few of the key issues it raises and outline just a few of the positions that philosophers take on these key issues. This should provide us with a good grasp of the scope of metaphysics and an understanding of the kinds of questions it investigates.

ARE THERE ABSTRACT OBJECTS?

Metaphysicians ask the question: what exists? It is natural to think of that question as asking, very roughly, what sorts of material objects exist. Are there quarks? Toasters? Persons? Is our universe infinite? What is space-time? Certainly these are all questions asked in metaphysics. But metaphysics does not limit itself to asking only about material objects. It also aims to investigate whether certain sorts of phenomena exist.

For instance, metaphysicians want to know not just which sorts of material objects exist in our world and where these are located, but, in addition, whether, given that those objects are located where they are, behaving as they do, this is consistent with each of us being agents, or having **agency**, and with each of us acting from **free will**. To determine the answer to the question 'do we have free will?', for instance, it seems that merely noting what sorts of material objects there are, and where these are located, is unlikely, in and of itself, to furnish us with answers. For we first need to know what it would take for there to exist free will – how would the world need to be in order for there to be free will? – and only then can we look at the way the world is and ascertain whether there is any free will. The point is that if metaphysics were simply in the business of listing which material objects exist there would be a range of questions which it would not be well placed to answer, but which are typically thought to fall under its purview.

It is not merely the task of determining whether certain phenomena, such as free will or agency, exist that takes metaphysics beyond the investigation of material objects. Metaphysics is also interested in immaterial or, as they are usually called, **abstract objects**. Abstract objects are objects that are not made of matter, and are thus not located in space-time. Metaphysicians ask whether, when we list the objects that exist in our world, we should include objects such as numbers, stories, functions, sets, shapes, and so on. Those who think there are no abstract objects are typically called **nominalists**, while those who think there are such objects are called **Platonists** (after Plato). Platonists think that we need to appeal to abstract objects if many of our ordinary claims are to come out as true. By analogy, consider the sentence 'a dog sat on another dog'. The sentence might be false because there are two dogs but neither sat on the other. But the sentence will also be false if there are no dogs. For what it takes for that sentence to be true is that there are at least two dogs, and that one of them sits on the other. Platonists think that mathematical language works just like this. They think that the sentence '2 + 2 = 4' is true, and that it could only be true if there exist the numbers 2 and 4 and the function of addition. Moreover, they think it is pretty clear that just as what it is to be a dog is to be (among other things) a material object, what it is to be 2, or to be 4, is to be an abstract object. For while we can have two kettles, or two cats, and these are material objects, it is hard to see how 2 itself could be a material object. After all, you can add 2 to itself to get 4 but you cannot add a cat to itself to get something. Moreover, where would you expect to find 2 if it were a material object? Thus Platonists conclude that the sentence '2 + 2 = 4' could only be true if there exists the number 2 (an abstract object) and there exists an addition function (an abstract entity of some kind), and performing the function of adding 2 to 2 yields yet another abstract object: 4. Since the sentence is manifestly true (just ask any mathematician), they conclude that there exist abstract objects.

Nominalism, on the other hand, is the view that abstract objects do not exist. Some nominalists reason as follows: we do know that the sentence '2 + 2 = 4' is true. But if what made that sentence true was the existence of abstract objects, how could we come to know that it is true? After all, abstract objects are not in space-time and therefore cannot be seen, measured, or otherwise interacted with. So we could not come to know anything about them. So we could not know that adding 2 to 2 equalled 4. So we have good reason to think that it is not the existence of abstract objects that makes true sentences such as '2 + 2 = 4'. If that is right then we have no reason at all to suppose that such objects exist.

The problem for this kind of nominalist lies in saying what it is that makes true sentences such as '2 + 2 = 4' if it is not the existence of abstract objects. It is because of this difficulty that many nominalists take what might seem to be a surprising route. Such nominalists agree with the Platonist that what *would* make the sentence '2 + 2 = 4' true is the existence of certain abstract objects and the relations between them. But, they say, there are no such objects, so the sentence is, really, false. That might seem like a radical conclusion, and it is. Nominalists of this stripe clearly need to explain why the sentence seems to us to be true, why mathematical language is so useful if it is false, and what difference there is between '2 + 2 = 4' and 'Darwin was a fairy'. According to the nominalist both these latter sentences are false. But they want to make sense of the idea that there is some important difference between the two sentences. One popular version of nominalism of this kind is called **fictionalism**.

According to fictionalists mathematics is a little bit like a story or a narrative. Think about the story of Jack and the beanstalk. There are not actually giants, or beanstalks so large you can climb them. So strictly speaking 'Jack climbed a beanstalk and slew a giant' is false. For no one climbed a beanstalk and slew a giant. But that sentence seems to be false in a different way from the following sentence: 'Jack was a Yeti in disguise and the giant was a malformed dwarf'. The reason the latter sentence seems perhaps more false, or at least false in a different way, is that it is clearly not true in the story of Jack and the beanstalk that Jack is a Yeti in disguise or that the giant is a malformed dwarf. Fictionalists about mathematics think that '2 + 2 = 4' is like 'Jack climbed a beanstalk and slew a giant' while 2 + 2 = 5 is like 'Jack was a Yeti in disguise and the giant was a malformed dwarf'. The idea is that there is a long, complex story of mathematics and within that story certain claims are true and others false. Though we are all tempted to say that '2 + 2 = 4' this is because we tacitly assume that we are evaluating that claim within the story of maths. And within that story it is indeed true. But it is strictly speaking false because, just as there is no Jack and no beanstalk, likewise there are no numbers.

To recap then: fictionalists and Platonists agree about what our world would need to be like for claims such as '2 + 2 = 4' to be true. They agree that abstract objects would need to exist. But they disagree about whether they do exist. Since fictionalists think they do not, they need to offer an account of why some mathematical claims intuitively seem to be true, and others false. On the other hand, Platonists need to offer an account of how we manage to attain mathematical knowledge if such knowledge is knowledge of abstract objects.

• WHAT ARE PROPERTIES?

In metaphysics we ask the question: are there properties and if so, what sorts of things are they? Asking what properties are is one of the foundational questions asked by metaphysicians. The issue is foundational because lots of other disciplines in philosophy assume that there are properties and build their accounts on that assumption. For instance, as we see in 'What is Art?' (Part III) philosophers of aesthetics try to define what counts as art in terms of different kinds of properties. In metaethics one of the biggest issues is whether moral properties, like the properties of rightness and wrongness, are really just natural properties, such as the properties of being in pain or experiencing happiness, or whether they are something more than natural properties (see 'What is Metaethics?', chapter 2 of Part II). A nice way of imagining what is being asked here is to imagine there is an all-powerful being that created our world. Suppose that being created all of the natural properties and then distributed them across the world. Did the being thereby also create all the moral properties, or does the being now need to do some additional work to create the moral properties? If the being needs to do some more work then the moral properties are something more than the natural properties. Consider, for instance, cars. We can ask whether, once a robot puts together a bunch of car-parts, it needs to do something more to create a car, or whether putting the parts together in a certain way is enough to create a car. In the case of cars we typically think that just putting the parts together in the right way is enough: nothing else is required. Intuitions differ in the moral case and also in the case of philosophy of mind. In the case of philosophy of mind, philosophers find themselves wondering whether mental properties are really just complex arrangements of physical properties (like brain states) or whether they are something more. As we see later, this is known as the hard problem of consciousness. Notice that all these important debates assume that there are properties, and then try and figure out how different sorts of properties relate to one another. In metaphysics we ask whether there are any properties and if there are, what sorts of things they are.

According to one view properties are abstract objects called **universals**. Universals do not exist in space or time; but objects in space and time get to have the properties they do by instantiating the relevant universals. On this view my dog and my jumper are black because both instantiate the very same universal – blackness – and so share the very same property. According to this view the very same thing – blackness – can exist at different locations when it is instantiated by different objects.

According to this view properties are very different from objects as we typically conceive of them. We typically suppose that objects are not repeatable: they exist at just one place at any one time. If I am in Sydney then I cannot also be in Melbourne unless, perchance, I am very large indeed and I have parts in Sydney and parts in Melbourne. But I cannot be such that all of me is in Sydney, and all of me is in Melbourne. By contrast, properties are repeatable. A property like blackness can be such that the very same thing is both in Sydney and in Melbourne.

Those who think that properties are universals point out that their view can explain why my dog and my jumper are similar in certain respects: they both instantiate the very same property. This sets this particular view about the nature of properties apart from some of its rivals. According to an alternative view there is nothing that my dog and my jumper share: there is no blackness that is located where my dog is and where my jumper is. Instead, on this view, there are entities known as **tropes**. Tropes are individuals, that is, one-off things that exist at just one place and time the way objects exist at just one place at any time. My dog has one trope. My jumper has a different trope. When we say that my jumper and my dog share the same property that is really just to say that each one has a trope, and that those tropes are similar. Defenders of trope theory argue that their view is superior to the view that properties are universals. They note that appealing to abstract entities really offers us no explanation for why my dog and my jumper are similar unless we have a good understanding of what it means for two objects to 'share in' or instantiate a universal, which we do not. Defenders of the view that properties are universals point out that the trope theorist owes us an explanation of what it means to say that the trope had by my dog and the trope had by my jumper are similar; but this is an explanation the trope theorist simply cannot provide because (on pain of circularity) she cannot say that the similarity between the two tropes is a matter of them sharing properties. So both parties to this dispute think there is something important that the opposing view fails to explain.

• WHAT SORTS OF PROPERTIES AND RELATIONS ARE THERE?

Setting aside the more general issue of what properties and relations are, in themselves, there are many important issues in metaphysics about the nature of particular properties or relations. For instance, in the philosophy of time we are interested in determining what sort of structure our world needs to have if it is to have **temporal relations**. Temporal relations are relations that hold between different times.

Some metaphysicians think that temporal relations are characterised entirely by certain static relations: the relations of being earlier-than, later-than and simultaneous-with. These relations order events into an unchanging temporal order. If the event of my birthday is later-than the event of Tim the dinosaur stepping on a flower, then it is, at all times, true that my birthday is later-than Tim stepping on the flower, and true, at all times, that the event of Tim stepping on the flower is earlier-than the event of my birthday. On this view of temporal relations talk about events being future, or being past, is just shorthand for talk of events being later-than, or earlier-than, some other event. So what makes it true that the event of Tim stepping on the flower is *past* relative to the event of my birthday is just that my birthday is later-than the event of Tim's flower stepping. Those who accept this kind of picture of temporal relations are called B-theorists because the relations of earlier-than, later-than and simultaneous-with are said to order events into a **B-series**. On this view, an event's being past, present, or future is nothing more than that event's location in the unchanging B-series. Since an event's location in the B-series never changes, B-theorists reject the idea that time flows.

Opponents of the B-theory are known as A-theorists. According to the A-theory our world is essentially dynamical. Every event has the property of being either past, present, or future, and there is some metaphysical fact of the matter as to which events really are present, which past, and which future. An event's location with respect to these properties (pastness, presentness, futurity) is said to be its location in the **A-series**. The A-theory of time is the view that properties of pastness, presentness and futurity do not depend on an event's location in the B-series. Instead, an event's being at a particular location in the B-series depends on its location in the A-series. Thus if the event of Tim stepping on the flower is in the true, or objective, present, then the event of my birthday is in the objective future. If the event of my birthday is the objective present, then the event of Tim stepping on the flower is in the objective past.

According to **A-theorists** which events have the property of being present changes as time flows. At one time it was the case that Tim's stepping on a flower had the property of presentness – when it was in the objective present – and the time of my writing this paragraph had the property of futurity – since it was in the objective future. But right now the time of my writing this paragraph has the property of presentness, and the event of Tim stepping on a flower has the property of pastness. According to the A-theorist distant future events become ever less distantly future, eventually become present, and then become past, and then recede ever further into the past. So at every moment different events are future, present and past. According to A-theorists this is what it is for time to flow: for our world to change constantly with respect to which events are genuinely present; to change with respect to which events have which A-properties. A-theorists think that their account is a better explanation of the way the world seems to us: it seems as though time flows, and that future events are getting progressively closer to us. Their view vindicates this picture of the world. Yet it is the flow of time and the attendant change in A-properties that many **B-theorists** think generates logical inconsistencies. This is one of the reasons why people are attracted to the B-theory. The worry is that A-theorists are committed to saying that every event has all three properties of pastness, presentness and futurity, since every event is future, present and past. But since the very same event cannot be both past and future, if the A-theorist is committed to saying so she is committed to an inconsistency. B-theorists, of course, face no such problem since they suppose that the only sense in which events are past, present, or future is relative to other events. But since the event of my writing this paragraph can be both future (relative to Tim the dinosaur) and past (relative to future terminator robots) the B-theorist does not face any potential inconsistency. Her only difficulty lies in explaining why the world seems to us the way that it does, if the B-theory is true.

Temporal relations are just one sort of relation that is especially interesting to those working in metaphysics. **Causation** is another example of an important relation. Metaphysicians are, of course, interested in which events are causally related: in what causes what. But they are also interested in what causation is.

There are many different theories of causation – theories about what it is for one event to cause another. Some think that causation is, very roughly, something that happens when one object or event 'biffs', that is, runs into or imparts a mark on, some other object or event. This is often how we think about causation: I cause the damage to your car by hitting your car with my car. These theories are known as **process theories**. A very different view of causation holds that causation is to be understood in terms of one event, the effect, being dependent in the right kind of way on another event, the cause. The idea is that what makes it the case that one event is the cause of another is that had one event not occurred, the other would not have occurred either. Theories of this kind are known as **counterfactual theories of causation** because they analyse causation in terms of counterfactual conditionals. Suppose that event x happened. For illustrative purposes suppose that x is the event of me putting poison in the soup. Suppose, also, that Bert drank the soup and subsequently died. We want to know whether I caused Bert to die. According to the counterfactual theory of causation we ask what would have happened to Bert had I not poisoned the soup. If Bert would not have died if I had not poisoned the soup then, according to this theory of causation, my poisoning the soup caused Bert's death. This view of causation posits no direct link between x and y. It just tells us that x causes y if, had x not occurred, y would not have occurred either. For suppose that x was, instead, the event of me failing to water your plants and y was the event of the death of your plants. I never come near your plants. Yet we can conclude that my failing to water them killed them, since if I had watered them they would have lived.

Each view of causation boasts that it accommodates many of our intuitions about what causation is like, and about which events are caused by which others. On the one hand, counterfactual theories are flexible. They can make sense of the idea that my failing to water your plants caused them to die. Process theorists will say that this is not a case of causation for there is no sense at all in which the supposed cause (my failing to water the plants) 'biffed' the plants and brought about their death. On the other hand, the flexibility of counterfactual accounts of causation is also one of their major drawbacks. My failing to water your plants caused them to die; but then so too did the Prime Minister's failing to water them, and the Queen's failing to water them. In these latter two cases this seems much less plausible and so we might be inclined to say that if neither of these was a cause of your plants dying, then neither was I.

BOX 17.1 TIME AND MCTAGGART

One of the most famous articles in the philosophy of time was written by John McTaggart in 1908 in his 'The Unreality of Time'. Indeed, it was McTaggart who first described and named the A-series and the B-series. He went on to argue for the very controversial claim that time is unreal. In essence, the argument went like this. First, he argued that the A-series is essential to there being time. If there is no A-series there is no time, or so he thought. That was because, roughly, he thought that in the absence of an A-series there isn't really any change because the world as a whole is a static unchanging block. But without change there can be no time. So a world without an A-series is a world without time. He then went on to argue that there is something incoherent in the idea of the A-series. His idea was that if a world contains an A-series then every event in that world must be past, present and future. But that is contradictory: no event is past, present and future. So the A-series itself is contradictory. Nothing contradictory is possible; so no world has an A-series. That means that no world has time, including our own. In fact not only is there no time, but time turns out to be impossible.

McTaggart's paper was a landmark. First, because it distinguished the A-series from the B-series and, second, because it tried to show that the A-series is incoherent. Though almost nobody believed the conclusion to the paper – that there is no time – many thought that McTaggart's argument succeeded in showing that the A-series is incoherent. These people went on to become B-theorists. They rejected the idea that you need to have an A-series to have time, and instead developed the view that time consists in the having of a B-series.

• WHOLES AND PARTS

Mereology is the study of parts and wholes. We typically assume that there are composite objects (wholes) – objects that have parts. We assume that you and I have legs, arms and a head and that these are parts of us. We assume that it is possible to put together Lego blocks in myriad different ways to create different composite objects. Metaphysicians refer to the relation that holds between a whole and its parts as **composition** because the whole is composed of the parts and they want to know under what conditions composition occurs. That is, under what conditions is there an object composed of some parts? There are three possible answers to that question. Contrary to what you and I might typically suppose, **mereological nihilists** think that there are no composite objects: they hold that composition never occurs. Instead, according to most nihilists there just exists a multitude of small simple objects. These objects are simple because they have no parts. Nihilists must, then, explain why it seems to us as though they are composite objects. In particular, they need to tell some story that makes sense of the fact that when I say 'there is a chair in this room' that seems to be true, but when I say 'there is a tiger in this room' that seems to be false. But if there are no chairs and no tigers because there are no composite objects, then neither sentence is true. This problem should look a little familiar: it is reminiscent of the problem faced by fictionalists about mathematical objects. The nihilist has two options. She can say that ordinary sentences such as 'there is a chair in this room' are true even though there is no composite object in the room that is a chair. Then she needs to say what makes such a claim true. Since the nihilist thinks there are lots of simples in the room, she could suggest that what makes the sentence true is the existence of a whole lot of simples in a particular configuration – what is sometimes called simples arranged chair-wise (arranged in such a way that we are inclined to say there is a chair). Most nihilists, however, are inclined to say that our ordinary claims are strictly speaking false. In this, she is like the fictionalist. She thinks that what it would take for our ordinary claims to be true is for there to exist composite objects, but such objects do not exist. Like the mathematical fictionalist, however, the nihilist can explain why some claims seem to us to be true while others seem to be false. For she can suggest that when I say 'there is a chair in there' that claim, though strictly speaking false, is quite close by to a claim that is true: namely that there are simples arranged chair-wise in there. My claim 'there is a tiger in there' is also false, but there is no nearby claim that is true, at least on the supposition that there are not simples arranged tiger-wise in there. The fact that there are simples arranged chair-wise explains why we are inclined to say that there is a chair, and why we are not inclined to say that there is a tiger, in the room, and it vindicates the former claim, and not the latter, as being close-to-true.

Mereological universalists are at the other end of the spectrum from nihilists. They hold that composition occurs under any and every circumstance: every way of arranging objects is one in which there exists a composite object with those objects as its parts. Unlike the nihilist, then, the universalist can say that ordinary claims such as 'there is a chair in there' are made true by the existence of a composite object that is a chair. The nihilist is faced with the opposite problem to the universalist. For she holds that there is something that has my dog today, your cat yesterday, and a balloon tomorrow, as its parts. We could call it a doatoon. We typically do not suppose that there exist doatoons. Universalists try to explain away this oddity by noting that although there is such an object, it is not an object that we are very interested in, and not one we are inclined to talk about in the way we talk about dogs or cats. But it exists nonetheless.

Finally **mereological restrictivists** think that composition sometimes occurs: whether there exists a composite object depends on how some bunch of objects is arranged. If they are arranged one way they compose a dog, if they are arranged another way they compose nothing. Pretty clearly restrictivism is the more intuitive view and this is what motivates its adherents. Nihilists and universalists are typically motivated by the thought that there is no good account that tells us when composition occurs (and does not) which accords with out intuitions about which composites exist, and which does not result in us having to say that it is sometimes a vague matter whether any composite exists at all. The worry that nihilists and universalists have regarding restrictivism is that it seems very difficult to come up with perfectly general, non-arbitrary, conditions under which composition occurs from which it will follow that there exist dogs and cats and toasters but not doatoons.

Nihilists and universalists think that in the end restrictivism is untenable and therefore we have to choose the least bad view of those remaining: nihilism or universalism. Nihilists choose nihilism because they think that universalists unnecessarily posit objects that are not needed to explain the world around us. Universalists choose universalism because they think that nihilists are unable straightforwardly to make sense of ordinary claims such as 'the dog is on the mat' since according to nihilists there are neither dogs nor mats.

BOX 17.2 MEREOLOGICAL RESTRICTIVISM

Mereological restrictivism is, on the face of it, by far the more plausible view. It is easy to think of it as the view that there exist toasters, dogs, cars, houses, people, trees, and so on, but there do not exist any weird amalgams of these things. It has, however, been notoriously difficult to specify any non-arbitrary set of conditions under which composition occurs that yields this result. For instance, one might have been inclined to say that composition occurs just in case a bunch of objects are all in contact with one another. Why is there nothing composed of my dog and the Eiffel tower – because my dog is in Australia and the Eiffel tower is in Paris. But that clearly will not do. First, there are lots of things that we think of as composite objects whose parts are not in contact. My tent is in the garage; but its poles are all separate from one another, as is its fly and the internal tent compartment. I'm still inclined to think that all those things compose something: a tent. Equally, we can see that this account of composition will have us include in our ontology many odd things we do not currently suppose to exist. For suppose I go to Paris and grab a dog and bring it into contact with the Eiffel tower. Does there, then, exist an object composed of the dog and the tower (albeit an object that only exists while the two are in contact)?

This kind of problem arises for pretty much every way you can think of to spell out the composition relation. We are left with a restrictivist ontology, but we rule out as existing some things we typically suppose do exist, and we include some things we typically suppose do not exist. In an effort to find a non-arbitrary way to spell out the composition relation Peter van Inwagen famously ended up defending the view that only those simples arranged in such a way that their joint activity constitutes a life, compose anything. According to this view you, persons, dogs, and trees exist (simples arranged person-wise and dog-wise and tree-wise compose something), but toasters and cars and houses do not (simples arranged toaster-wise, car-wise and house-wise compose nothing). What is notable about this view is that although it is a version of restrictivism it is very revisionary about our ontology. This tells you something about how hard it is to come up with a set of conditions under which composition occurs which yields the sort of everyday ontology to which most of us are intuitively committed.

• WHAT COULD HAVE BEEN?

So far the suggestion has been that the subject matter of metaphysics involves figuring out which objects exist, what properties they have and which relations they bear to other objects. That is certainly part of the story. In addition, though, we want to know not just what our world is like, but also how it could have been different. Part of this requires thinking about the **laws of nature** that govern our world. For notice that we do not merely want to know that this particular salt dissolves in this particular sample of water. We do not even just want to know, for all salt samples that have been, are, or will be, put in water, whether those samples dissolve. For suppose that every sample of salt that is placed in water of a certain temperature does, in fact, dissolve. Then a certain regularity holds: a regularity between salt and dissolution in water (of a certain temperature). But we want to know not just that there is such a regularity, we want to know whether this regularity is lawlike. Consider the fact (suppose it is a fact) that all red-haired women wearing yellow t-shirts that read 'hell yes' are in my living room. No red-haired woman wearing such a t-shirt is ever anywhere but my living room. Then there is a regularity between the location of such women and my living room. But we do not think there is a lawlike connection between the two since we think there could easily be a woman with red hair wearing such a t-shirt who is somewhere outside my living room. This is a *mere* regularity and not a law. In the case of salt and water we want to know whether there is a lawlike relation between placing salt in water that is a certain temperature, and that salt dissolving. So we want to know what would have happened to other samples of salt if they had been placed in water of the relevant temperature. Again, it is worth noting that while both scientists and philosophers want to know whether there is a lawlike relation between, for example, placing salt in water and that salt dissolving, philosophers also want to know what it means to say that a regularity is a mere regularity as opposed to being lawlike. So they are interested in different theories about what it is to be a law of nature. We will not discuss these different views here.

What we can say is that in metaphysics when we ask questions about how our world could have been different there is really a cluster of different questions we might be asking. For instance, we might want to know how our world could have been different if the laws of nature had remained the same. Could I, for instance, have worn a differently coloured jumper today if the laws of nature had been the same as they actually are? Could there have been giant flying spiders if the laws of nature had been the same? The answers to these questions are interesting because they tell us how different our world could have been, had things gone just slightly differently from the way things did go. Equally, though, we might be interested in how the laws of nature themselves could have been different. We might wonder whether it could have been that electrons attracted one another instead of repelling one another. We might wonder whether it could have been that our world had no weak electromagnetic force. These sorts of questions are interesting not so much because it is of interest whether our world could have been one with different laws of nature, but rather, because we are often interested in what else our world would have been like if the laws had been different. We might want to know, for instance, what our world would have been like if there had been no weak electromagnetic force. To answer that question we would need to know what the laws of our world would have been, if that law had been absent.

When we ask questions like this we are interested in what in metaphysics we call **modality**. We are interested in what is possible (what could be the case), what is impossible (what could not be the case), and what is necessary (what must be the case). When we ask whether something is possible, that question is really ambiguous. Suppose I ask whether it is possible that blue whales fly. I might be asking whether it is **nomically possible** that blue whales fly: that is, whether it is consistent with the laws of nature that blue whales fly. The answer to that question is probably that it is not nomically possible that blue whales fly (they are too big and heavy to be supported by wings). We might, however, be asking whether it is **logically possible** that blue whales fly. Logical possibility is a much broader notion than nomic possibility. When we ask whether it is logically possible that blue whales fly, we are asking whether there is any way *at all* that our world could have been, such that there would be flying whales. In effect we are asking whether there is something logically contradictory about the idea of a flying whale. There are certainly some ways our world could not be. For instance, it couldn't be a way such that 2 + 2 equals something other than 4. That's why we say that it is **necessary** that 2 + 2 = 4. Of all the ways our world could be, none of those ways is one in which 2 + 2 equals other than 4. But there is a way our world could be in which there are flying whales; for there is nothing contradictory about the idea that whales fly. So while it is (most likely) nomically impossible that there are flying whales, it is logically possible that there are flying whales. In one sense flying whales are possible, and in another sense they are not.

The answers to modal questions are important and often foundational to other disciplines in philosophy. We noted earlier that metaethics and philosophy of mind aim to investigate the relationship between moral properties and natural properties (metaethics), and between mental properties and physical properties (philosophy of mind). Earlier I told a story about a powerful being. In that story we wondered whether that powerful being would need to do more to create moral properties than just to create and distribute the natural properties. We can ponder a similar question in philosophy of mind: would an all powerful being need to do more to create mental properties than just create and distribute physical properties? Such stories are nice ways to begin thinking about the relationship between certain kinds of properties. If we want to make progress with these questions, however, we want to make them more precise. To do that we need to appeal to modality; for we are really asking whether the distribution of, say, natural properties *necessitates* the existence of moral properties. We are asking whether any *possible* time the all-powerful being creates a world that is exactly like ours in terms of its natural properties, that world is also like ours in terms of its moral properties. So even though in these debates we care about how things are, it is helpful to appeal to modality to help us express the questions we want to ask about why things are the way they are.

We should also care about modality because we care not just about how our world is, we also care how our world could have been different. But questions such as these go well beyond anything that an empirical scientist will ask, or attempt to answer. That nicely brings us to the next chapter of this section. For throughout this chapter it has been clear that while the subject matter of metaphysics includes some of the same subject matter of the empirical sciences, it typically goes well beyond that subject matter. In the next chapter we ask how the methodology of metaphysics differs from that of the empirical sciences.

• CHAPTER SUMMARY

- Metaphysics is the study of what exists and how the things that exist are related.
- Metaphysics asks questions about the nature of abstract objects, properties, laws, causation, time, and modality.
- Metaphysicians attempt to determine whether we need to posit the existence of abstract objects to make sense of our ordinary talk. For instance, they ask whether we need to posit the existence of abstract mathematical objects if ordinary claims such as '2 + 2 = 4' are to come out as true.
- Platonism is the view that we need to posit the existence of abstract objects to make sense of our world; nominalism is the view that we do not.
- Metaphysics asks whether there are properties, and what sorts of things properties are. Some metaphysicians think properties are abstract objects – universals – while others think they are concrete individuals – tropes.
- Metaphysicians want to know about the nature of certain important relations such as temporal relations, causal relations and laws of nature.
- Some metaphysicians think that temporal relations are static: these are known as B-theorists. Others think that temporal relations are dynamic: these are known as A-theorists.
- In metaphysics, disputes about causation are typically disputes about what causation is, not about what causes what. Two leading views about the nature of causation are the counterfactual theory of causation, on the one hand, and process theories, on the other hand.

- Mereology is the study of the relationship between wholes and their parts.
- In metaphysics we want to ascertain under what conditions, if any, some objects compose a further object. There are three main views: nihilism, universalism and restrictivism.
- Metaphysics asks what it is to be a law of nature, and how it is that our world could have differed from the way it in fact is.

• STUDY QUESTIONS

1 Come up with some new examples of things that exist according to the universalist about composition.
2 On what view is it true that if there are tables, then they are not composite objects?
3 According to which view are properties abstract objects?
4 In your own words explain the difference between the A-theory and the B-theory of time.
5 On which theory of causation might it be true that you caused the child to drown by failing to jump in and rescue the child?
6 Do you think it is nomically possible that there be no gravity?
7 Do you think it is a law of nature or a mere regularity that milk in a carton often spills to the floor, but that milk on the floor does not return to the carton?

• INTRODUCTORY FURTHER READING

Armstrong, D. M. (1989) *Universals, An Opinionated Introduction* (Boulder, CO: Westview Press).
Dyke, Heather (2005) 'The Metaphysics and Epistemology of Time Travel', *Think* 9(9): 43–52.
Hoerl, Christoph, Teresa McCormack and Sarah R. Beck (2011) 'Introduction: Understanding Counterfactuals and Causation', in Christoph Hoerl, Teresa McCormack and Sarah R. Beck (eds) *Understanding Counterfactuals, Understanding Causation* (Oxford: Oxford University Press), pp. 1–15.
McDaniel, Kris (2010) 'Parts and Wholes', *Philosophy Compass* 5(5): 412–25.
Mumford, Stephen (2012) *Metaphysics: A Very Short Introduction* (Oxford: Oxford University Press).
Mumford, Stephen and Anjum, Rani Lill (2013) *Causation: A Very Short Introduction* (Oxford: Oxford University Press).
Phillips, Ian (2014) 'Experience of and in Time', *Philosophy Compass* 9(2): 131–44.
Roca-Royes, Sonia (2011) 'Essential Properties and Individual Essences', *Philosophy Compass* 6(1): 65–77.
Sider, Ted and Earl Conee (2005) *Riddles of Existence: A Guided Tour of Metaphysics* (Oxford: Oxford University Press).
Tallant, J. (2011) *Metaphysics: An Introduction* (London: Continuum).

Thomasson, Amie L. (2010) 'The Controversy Over the Existence of Ordinary Objects', *Philosophy Compass* 5(7): 591–601.
Wasserman, Ryan (2010) 'Teaching & Learning Guide For: The Problem of Change', *Philosophy Compass* 5(3): 283–6.

• ADVANCED FURTHER READING

Lewis, David K. (1986/2001) *On the Plurality of Worlds* (Oxford: Blackwell).
van Inwagen, Peter (1990) *Material Beings* (Ithaca, NY: Cornell University Press).

• FREE INTERNET RESOURCES

Balaguer, Mark, 'Platonism in Metaphysics', *The Stanford Encyclopedia of Philosophy* (Spring 2014 Edition), http://plato.stanford.edu/archives/spr2014/entries/platonism/.
Carroll, John W., 'Laws of Nature', *The Stanford Encyclopedia of Philosophy* (Spring 2012 Edition), http://plato.stanford.edu/archives/spr2012/entries/laws-of-nature/.
Korman, Daniel Z., 'Ordinary Objects', *The Stanford Encyclopedia of Philosophy* (Spring 2014 Edition), http://plato.stanford.edu/archives/spr2014/entries/ordinary-objects/.
Markosian, Ned, 'Time', *The Stanford Encyclopedia of Philosophy* (Spring 2014 Edition), http://plato.stanford.edu/archives/spr2014/entries/time/.
Modal Metaphysics http://www.iep.utm.edu/mod-meta/ Ted Parent. Internet encyclopedia of philosophy
Rodriguez-Pereyra, Gonzalo, 'Nominalism in Metaphysics', *The Stanford Encyclopedia of Philosophy* (Fall 2011 Edition), http://plato.stanford.edu/archives/fall2011/entries/nominalism-metaphysics/.
Schaffer, Jonathan, 'The Metaphysics of Causation', *The Stanford Encyclopedia of Philosophy* (Summer 2014 Edition), ed. Edward N. Zalta, http://plato.stanford.edu/archives/sum2014/entries/causation-metaphysics/.
Varzi, Achille, 'Mereology', *The Stanford Encyclopedia of Philosophy* (Spring 2014 Edition), http://plato.stanford.edu/archives/spr2014/entries/mereology/.

18

how do we do metaphysics?

- Metaphysics versus empirical science
- Conceptual analysis
- Indispensability arguments
- *A priori* arguments

• METAPHYSICS VERSUS EMPIRICAL SCIENCE

In the previous chapter we considered a number of different questions that are pondered in metaphysics. What you will have noticed is that many of the questions that we ask in metaphysics are also asked in the empirical sciences, and that many other questions asked in metaphysics are closely connected to questions asked in the empirical sciences. So it seems reasonable to wonder what the relationship is between metaphysics and empirical science. Do they ask the same questions but answer them differently? Are they really one and the same enterprise? How can metaphysics hope to answer empirical questions without using the experimental method? Can metaphysics furnish us with conclusions about our world that go beyond those furnished by the empirical sciences? These are all excellent questions.

The first thing to say is that despite the considerable overlap between metaphysics and empirical science, the questions considered in metaphysics clearly go beyond the questions asked in empirical science. Consider the debate, outlined in the previous chapter, between nominalists and Platonists. Despite the fact that the empirical sciences are deeply interconnected with mathematics – they use mathematics to measure the outcomes of experiments, to present empirical data, and to present theories and models of the world – they are typically not interested in whether there are numbers or sets. Instead, the sciences assume that we can use mathematical language to represent features of our world, but they remain silent on whether this commits us to the existence of numbers, and whether, in doing so, it commits us to the existence of abstract objects. Scientists use maths without really wondering too much what maths is, why (assuming they are) mathematical claims are true, or what makes them true.

Another area in which empirical science and metaphysics overlap lies in their mutual interest in causation. Scientists, like metaphysicians, are interested in what causes what. The difference is that scientists are not principally interested in what causation is: they assume that they know what causation is and are then interested in determining, through experimental method, which sorts of events are causally connected. What is important in the scientific context is often distinguishing causation from mere correlation. Metaphysicians, on the other hand, are interested not only in which events are causally connected, but also in what causation is. In particular, they ask, what makes a relation a causation relation as opposed to some other kind of relation?

Finally metaphysics is like empirical science in that neither is concerned simply with providing a list of the kinds of (or particular individual) objects that exist. Scientists want to know not just that atoms, electrons and protons exist; they also want to know how these three things are related. Those working in metaphysics also suppose that one of the key questions to be addressed is how the things that exist in our world are related to one another. Nevertheless, the questions asked by metaphysicians outstrip those asked by the empirical scientist. Both the scientist and the metaphysician want to know whether electrons are positively or negatively charged. And they want to know how it is that their being negatively charged explains certain phenomena in the world (such as the way in which atoms interact). But those working in metaphysics want to know what it means to say that electrons are negatively charged. Does it mean, for instance, that there is something, a property, and that all electrons share a particular property, namely the property of being negatively charged? Or does it mean that each individual electron has an individual trope in virtue of which it is charged? Further, metaphysicians also want to know whether electrons could, for instance, have been positively charged. That is, they want to know something about the space of possibilities: about modal space. Typically (though not always) empirical science is uninterested in such questions. Scientists want to know about the way actual electrons behave and why they do so; they need not be concerned with whether electrons could have behaved radically differently if our world had been very different.

It should be clear why empirical science and metaphysics are interested in many of the same issues. For both are interested in making sense of our world. It should also be clear why metaphysicians are also typically interested in questions that go beyond those addressed in empirical science. For the empirical sciences take themselves to investigate the world through empirical means: by observing, measuring, and interacting with the environment. But everyone agrees that if there are abstract objects they are not in space-time. So they cannot be the subject of experimentation or observation, and so their existence, or not, is not fodder for the empirical scientist. Likewise, everyone can agree that whether or not there are properties, such that the very selfsame property can be instantiated at different locations, as opposed to there being tropes each of which exists at a particular time and place, is not something that can be adjudicated by empirical science. For both views make the very same empirical predictions. Similarly, it is difficult to see how the empirical sciences could adjudicate the issue of what it is for there to exist causal relations. For the sciences are in the business of running experiments that aim to determine which kinds of events cause which other kinds of events. These experiments are trying to determine whether, for instance, smoking causes cancer, or cancer causes smoking, or something else causes both smoking and cancer, or none of the above. These experiments proceed, in large part, by the experimenter trying to 'wiggle' one variable and seeing what else in the world changes. But such experiments are not well placed to tell us in what causation consists. They are not well placed to tell us whether causation is a matter of counterfactual dependence (as the counterfactual theory tells us) or a matter or some physical process obtaining between cause and effect (as the process theory tells us).

So if metaphysics is to investigate the issues it wishes to investigate, it must avail itself of a methodology that allows it to investigate issues that are not within the purview of the natural sciences. We will turn to consider just what that methodology could be in a moment. First, however, it is worth clarifying that none of this is to suggest that there are not complicated and important relations between metaphysics and science. Consider the case of causation. Scientists are very good at determining when relations are causal. If scientists are very sure that x causes y, and if a metaphysical account of causation is one that it is inconsistent with x being the cause of y, then this might give us reason to prefer a different account of causation that can accommodate its being true that x causes y. That is to say that the outputs of scientific investigation can, and often are, taken to be important constraints when formulating a metaphysical theory of some notion. Or consider temporal relations. We assume that our world is one in which there is time, and where events can be ordered into those that are earlier, and those that are later, than other events. But recently some scientists have suggested that there are no temporal relations: at most there is just a bunch of disconnected moments that are not temporally ordered. Quite apart from the fact that it is fascinating to try to get one's head around the claim that the events in our world are not temporally ordered – that there is no fact of the matter about what just happened, or what will happen henceforth – we learn something interesting about metaphysics by attending to this issue. Metaphysics is sensitive to the outputs of the empirical sciences. It is still empirical speculation that our world has no temporal ordering, but metaphysicians are interested in figuring out what that might mean for developing a picture of our world and us in it. They are interested in trying to make sense of what it means to say that there is no time. They are also interested in figuring out how, if at all, we could make sense of the fact that you and I seem to be the kinds of things that reason and deliberate about what we ought to do in the future, on the assumption that there is no time and hence no future, as such, to deliberate about.

So while metaphysicians are interested in some questions that scientists are not, this does not mean that they do not take science seriously, or that science has no implications for metaphysics; quite the contrary. One important role of metaphysics lies in trying to bring together, on the one hand, the outputs of science, and on the other hand, our first-person experience of the world, to create a consistent picture.

Sometimes it seems as though the picture of our world that we get from science leaves out the **subjective perspective**: the way things seem to us as deliberating, feeling, agents. Metaphysics takes seriously the picture of the world we get from science; but it also takes seriously the way the world seems to us, and it strives to make sense of us as deliberating, feeling, agents, within that world. Trying to make sense of agency if our world lacks time is just one example of the kind of issue that metaphysics tackles when it tries to bring together the scientific picture with the first person agential picture.

So we might say that metaphysics is constrained by empirical science – what metaphysicians say must be consistent with good, well-tested, empirical science. But that leaves a lot of scope for metaphysics since there are many questions that empirical science does not attempt to ask or answer.

• CONCEPTUAL ANALYSIS

While metaphysics is by no means blind to the findings of empirical science, if it is to answer questions that science does not, then it needs a methodology that goes beyond the empirical. But what methodology is that? There is by no means complete agreement between metaphysicians regarding exactly how we ought to try to settle metaphysical questions. One tool in the metaphysical arsenal is what is known as **conceptual analysis**.

In the previous chapter we noted that simply knowing where all of the objects are located in our universe and how those objects interact is not enough to tell us whether or not there is free will. The same will be true for a range of other phenomena that are important in our everyday experience of the world including justice, agency, action, goodness, art, value. That is because these notions do not come into play in physics, chemistry, or biology, or indeed in economics or psychology. Thus we could in principle have a complete scientific picture of our world and yet not know whether or not it contains free will, justice, agency, action or goodness. That is one place in which conceptual analysis comes into play.

There is a good deal of dispute regarding exactly what conceptual analysis is, and what role it ought to play in philosophy in general and in metaphysics in particular. Conceptual analysis of any kind has come under fire during the last few decades. Nevertheless, it seems clear that one role of metaphysics is to try to locate the phenomena that correspond to certain important, ordinary notions, within the description of the world offered by science: a description that typically leaves out such ordinary notions. Equally, it seems clear that if we are to attempt to locate the phenomena that correspond to these ordinary notions we need to have some idea of what we are looking for. Suppose, for instance, that in ordinary discourse we find ourselves frequently talking about fairies. The notion of a fairy is not one that we find in any empirical science (let us suppose). The metaphysician wants to know whether we can, as it were, find room for fairies in the world given the description of the world offered by empirical science. That is, she wants to know whether or not there are fairies. In order to answer that question we will need to have some idea of what the world would need to be like if it were to contain fairies. That is, we need to have some grasp of what the ordinary notion of fairy, as it is used in typical discourse, is meant to be. Only if we have some idea of what it would be for it to be true that there are fairies can we have a hope of working out whether, given the description of our world given by empirical science, we should conclude that there are fairies. The same is true for phenomena like free will and agency.

The project of engaging in conceptual analysis is the project of figuring out what the world would need to be like in order for there to be, for instance, free will, art or agency. Though there may be disagreement about exactly how to go about the project of conceptual analysis there ought not be disagreement that engaging in such analysis is one important component of the methodology of metaphysics which allows it to go beyond the empirical sciences.

We can see how engaging in conceptual analysis will be an important aspect of the project that brings together empirical and metaphysical research on the nature of time. We noted previously that according to some scientists there are no temporal relations, and thus no temporal ordering of moments. These scientists often say that on their view there is no time. One way we might look at this from the perspective of metaphysics, is to say that if these scientists are right about the way the world is, then time does not feature in the best scientific description of the world. Does that mean that these scientists are right that there is no time? It seems that this might depend on what we mean when we talk about time. In order to know whether we should conclude that if these scientists are right there is no time, we first need to know what the world would need to be like in order for us to conclude that there *is* time. We need to engage in some kind of conceptual analysis of our concept of time. Only then can we begin to determine what sorts of conclusions we should draw about the status of time if the world is as these scientists say it is. That is where metaphysics comes in.

BOX 18.1 ARMCHAIR PHILOSOPHY

The role of conceptual analysis and so-called 'armchair philosophy' was at a very low ebb towards the end of the twentieth century. Quine had written a landmark paper 'Two Dogmas of Empiricism' in which he argued that there are no analytic truths. Some took this to amount to the claim that there are no truths that can be known by reason alone. From there began a general scepticism about the prospects of answering philosophical questions by reasoning from the armchair.

It was not until 1998 when Frank Jackson wrote *From Metaphysics to Ethics: A Defence of Conceptual Analysis* that there was a resurgence in interest in what Jackson called 'armchair philosophy'. Jackson saw philosophy as a bridge between empirical science, on the one hand, and folk views of the world, on the other. He argued that the role of conceptual analysis is to tell us about our folk concepts. That does not tell us about the world. We cannot, from sitting in the armchair, find out whether determinism is true: we need science to tell us that. But we can find out whether our concept of free will is one that requires determinism to be false. If our concept of free will is one according to which there is free will only if determinism is false, then we can know, from the armchair, the following: if determinism is true, there is no free will. We can find out whether determinism is true by asking scientists about the nature of our world. From there we can come to know whether or not there is free will. Jackson thought that this is mostly how philosophy progresses, and that it leaves plenty of room for philosophy from the armchair.

• INDISPENSABILITY ARGUMENTS

Another tool in the methodological arsenal of metaphysics consists of what are sometimes known as **indispensability arguments**. These are arguments that aim to provide us with reasons to think that certain objects or properties that do not directly feature in the description of the world offered by empirical science exist. If we return to consider Platonism about mathematics we can see how an appeal to this kind of argument can be used to secure what we could call metaphysical conclusions – conclusions that go beyond those we get from the empirical sciences.

Recall that the Platonist thinks that mathematical objects exist and that these are abstract objects. One argument that Platonists offer for their view goes as follows. Not only are (some) mathematical sentences true, but the use of mathematics in our best science is indispensable. Not only do our scientists in fact express their theories using mathematical language, but there is no way to express those theories without using mathematical language. Just as we should accept that the world is the way our best science says it is – if our best science says that there are black holes then we should believe that there are black holes – likewise if our best science requires the use of mathematics and if mathematical claims are true only if there exist abstract objects, we should believe that there are abstract mathematical objects. Here is the form of the argument:

1 We should be committed to all the entities that are indispensable to our best scientific theories.
2 Mathematical objects are indispensable to our best scientific theories.
3 Mathematical objects are abstract objects.
4 Therefore we should be committed to the existence of abstract mathematical objects.

Indispensability arguments try to show that some entity (object, property or relation) is indispensable to some enterprise or other, and we therefore have good reason to think that the entity exists. The most common sorts of indispensability arguments try to show that the relevant entity is indispensable to our best scientific theory of the world, and on that basis they conclude that we should be committed to the existence of that entity.

Indispensability arguments, such as the one above, have the capacity to take us beyond the objects and properties posited by empirical science. Still, one might be sceptical about the use of indispensability arguments. Consider the following argument:

1 We should be committed to all the entities (and phenomena) that are indispensable to our best theory of the world.
2 Free will is indispensable to our best theory of the world.
3 Therefore we should be committed to the existence of free will.

The idea here is that our best theory of the world is one in which there are freely acting agents since only that theory makes sense of our experience of ourselves in the world.

Free will is indispensable to that best theory. So we should conclude that there is free will. This argument looks dubious: it seems too easy to secure the conclusion that there is free will. We seem somehow to have moved from the fact that it seems to us as though we act freely to the conclusion that we do act freely. Moreover, arguments such as the one above can be, and sometimes are, conjoined with further conceptual claims about what it would take for there to be free will, to come to further conclusions. For instance, one might argue, in part on the basis of conceptual analysis, that what it takes for the action of some agent, A, to be free is for it not to be determined by prior causes over which A has no control. If we combine the conclusion we garner from the indispensability argument, to wit that there are free actions, with the claim that for an action to be free it has to be caused by an agent but not determined by any prior causes outside the agent, then we get the conclusion that there are actions that are caused in this manner. Perhaps there are actions that have this feature, but we seem to have reached this conclusion rather too easily.

There are a few things that can be said at this point. One might suggest that the right way forward is to limit appeals to best theory to best scientific theory. We have fairly good ways of testing scientific theories and of determining which of the competitor theories is the better. Moreover, scientific realists, at least, think we have good reason to think that our best scientific theory tells us about the way the world is. So if some entity is indispensable to our best scientific theory, arguably this gives us reason to think that that entity exists.

A second suggestion is that there is something illicit in conjoining conceptual analysis with the output of an indispensability argument in the manner previously offered. Suppose we accept the indispensability argument. It follows that there is free will. But what, exactly, does that conclusion secure us? Not a lot. It is consistent with the argument that what it takes for there to be free will is nothing more than for there to be some actions for which we hold people responsible and other actions for which we do not hold people responsible. The former are the ones we call free, the latter unfree. Yet it might be that there is no special, metaphysical, feature that the free actions have: they might not be caused in any special way. Perhaps they do not always even issue from the will of the person whose actions they are. It just turns out that, as a society, we have a well-entrenched practice of holding people responsible for some kinds of actions and not for other kinds of actions. Our best theory of the world must take that into account, and as such, our best theory of the world says that there are free actions. And indeed there are: it is just that an action's being a free action doesn't amount to very much (metaphysically speaking). If this is the kind of free action posited by our best theory then we cannot conjoin the conclusion that there is such free action, with an analysis of our concept of free will, to come to the conclusion that there are free actions that are not caused by anything outside the agent herself.

What all of this points to is that we have to be very careful when we bring together the outputs of conceptual analysis of some concept, on the one hand, with the conclusion of, say, an indispensability argument, on the other hand. Different methodological tools in metaphysics can each be useful. But we need to take care in combining them and extracting conclusions. That being said, so far we have seen how the methodology of metaphysics can take us beyond what is given to us by the empirical sciences. In the next section I consider some more ways that the metaphysician can reach conclusions that go beyond the empirical.

• *A PRIORI* ARGUMENTS

The empirical sciences are in the business of investigating our world through empirical methods. They take samples, look at things through microscopes, make measurements, cut things open, perform experiments and so on. Metaphysics is not in the business of doing any of these things. Metaphysics can, by and large, be done from the armchair. The methodology of metaphysics is by and large *a priori*. **A priori knowledge** is to be contrasted with **a posteriori knowledge**. The former is knowledge achieved by reason alone. For instance, we can know that $2 + 2 = 4$ by reason alone: we do not need to go out into the world and count pairs of objects and see that in each case when we add two objects to two objects we get four objects. Likewise, we can know that there are no married bachelors without going into the world and checking, for each bachelor, that he is not married. *A posteriori* knowledge, by contrast, is achieved by interacting in the world. The empirical sciences yield *a posteriori* knowledge. We could not, for instance, come to know that water is H_2O by reasoning alone: we need to be able to look at the microstructure of water to find that out.

Let us call an argument an *a priori argument* if each of its premises can be known *a priori*. Let us call an argument a mixed argument if some of its premises can be known *a priori* and some of its premises can only be known *a posteriori*. Metaphysics trades in both kinds of arguments. It shouldn't be surprising that some arguments in metaphysics are *a priori* arguments. It is hard to see how empirical investigation could issue answers to some of the questions we ask in metaphysics: it couldn't furnish us with answers to questions about whether or not there are abstract objects, whether there are properties or tropes, or what modal space looks like. We also shouldn't be surprised that metaphysicians appeal to mixed arguments. After all, metaphysics is interested in what our world is like. While some ways our world is might be ways that we can come to know through entirely *a priori* means, most of the ways our world is will be ways we can only discover by, at least in part, appealing to empirical features of the world. Thus we might think of mixed arguments as a kind of metaphysical springboard from which we jump from a premise that includes an empirical description of the world, or some aspect of the world, to a conclusion about the metaphysical nature of our world.

To see this, consider the indispensability argument for mathematical objects that was outlined in the previous section. The argument can be mounted, as it were, from the armchair. It does not require the metaphysician to go out into the world and engage in experimentation. On the other hand, it includes an empirical premise: premise 2 says that mathematical entities are indispensable to our best science. We cannot know that to be true *a priori*. If it is true, then it is because it is, in fact, not possible to state our best theories without the aid of mathematics. So this argument is a mixed argument.

Another very common argument form in metaphysics is what you might think of as a sort of complicated cost–benefit analysis of competing metaphysical theories. One thing that typically sets competing metaphysical theories apart from competing scientific theories is that usually the former are **empirically equivalent** while the latter are not. Two theories are empirically equivalent if not only do they make all the same predictions about our world, but they make all the same predictions about every way our world could be. For instance, notice that Newtonian mechanics and the theories of general and special relativity agree about a bunch of actual predictions. But they make different predictions once we start, for instance, to consider objects that are accelerating relative to one another. So it is possible to use empirical data to determine which theory is true. The two theories are not empirically equivalent. Many competitor scientific theories are like this. But not all are. It is typically accepted that different interpretations of quantum mechanics are empirically equivalent even though they posit very different sorts of ontology. So it is worth bearing in mind that it is not only competing metaphysical theories that are empirically equivalent. Nevertheless, it is much more common for competitor theories in metaphysics to be empirically equivalent, than for competitor theories in science to be empirically equivalent. For consider any number of areas of metaphysics. Consider the dispute about whether there are abstract objects or not, or about whether there exist multiply realisable properties as opposed to individual non-repeatable tropes, or about whether there exist composite objects or mere simples arranged in certain ways. Each of these pairs of competitor metaphysical theories make the same empirical predictions. No piece of empirical data could provide evidence that one theory is true and the other false. This is important because it means that an assessment of competitor metaphysical theories can largely be done from the armchair without an appeal to empirical data, or, at the very least, by appealing only to the kind of data to which one has access from the armchair.

Thus metaphysicians will typically evaluate competitor theories in terms of how they do along a range of measures that are usually known as **theoretical virtues**. Theoretical virtues are features of a theory that make it virtuous in some way. The typical virtues include **simplicity**, elegance, **explanatory power** and **parsimony**. Thus it is typically held that, other things being equal, a theory is more virtuous if it is simpler, if it has greater explanatory power (if it explains a range of phenomena), if it is elegant and aesthetically pleasing, and if it posits fewer, rather more, objects, properties and relations. One might also add to this list of virtues the thought that theories are more virtuous to the extent that they preserve more of our pre-philosophical intuitions and are more virtuous the better they mesh with metaphysical theories in other areas. The first of these is especially controversial since if there are metaphysical facts to be discovered why should our intuitions be any guide to what these facts are? By analogy we typically do not suppose that it is a virtue of a scientific theory if it better accords with our pre-scientific intuitions than does some competitor theory, for we see no reason why our pre-scientific intuitions should be any sort of guide to the way the world is. So there is some disagreement about just what sorts of features of a theory make it virtuous. Nevertheless, there is sufficient agreement about the core virtues that it is possible to evaluate competing metaphysical theories relative to those core virtues. Moreover, it is possible for different metaphysicians to evaluate competing theories relative to somewhat different packages of virtues and then to argue about which package of virtues is the better one.

What matters, for our purposes, is that even empirically equivalent metaphysical theories can differ in their theoretical virtues, and so even pairs of empirically equivalent metaphysical theories can be evaluated in terms of their theoretical virtues. Thus a good deal of debate in metaphysics involves arguing about the relative virtues of competing theories. For instance, Platonists argue that their theory is the more simple, elegant and (in some cases) explanatory theory. It is simple and elegant because it says that the reason sentences like '2 + 2 = 4' are true, is because there are numbers and functions like addition, such that performing the addition function on 2 by adding 2 to it yields 4. There is also a sense in which Platonists can argue that their view is explanatory. Platonists can explain why it is that maths is so very useful to us. For they can explain why mathematical claims are true. Fictionalists, on the other hand, will appeal to quite different virtues. According to fictionalists, strictly speaking mathematical claims are false. So fictionalists cannot explain the usefulness of maths in the way that Platonists can: by noting that mathematical claims are often true. Platonists can, and do, suggest that fictionalism is not very explanatory at all in that, they argue, it is hard to see why maths is so useful in science if all of its claims are false! Fictionalists argue that their view is more virtuous because, first, it is more parsimonious. It does not posit an enormous ontology of abstract objects. Fictionalists might also suggest that their view is epistemically more explanatory. It is straightforward to see how one could come to know the content of a fiction. But, as fictionalists point out, it is hard to see how one could come to know about an abstract realm. Thus, in this respect at least, fictionalism better explains our mathematical knowledge.

So even though fictionalism and Platonism are empirically equivalent theories, they have quite different theoretical virtues. This allows the metaphysician to evaluate these theories in terms of which is overall more virtuous. Thus one important way of evaluating competing metaphysical theories involves, first, determining the extent to which each theory has the various different virtues. Sometimes one theory might be better on all the virtues; it is the outright winner. That will give us one, strong, reason to prefer that theory. But more usually one theory does better on some virtues and its competitors do better on other virtues. It is then a difficult task to determine which theory is overall more virtuous. Metaphysicians will argue about how much better a particular theory does with respect to one virtue, rather than another; and they might also argue about which virtues matter most. These are difficult issues to adjudicate, and this goes some way to explaining why some metaphysical disputes are so difficult to resolve.

Nevertheless, this shows that progress can be made in resolving disputes that science cannot adjudicate. It may not always be straightforward, but there is a methodology to which metaphysicians can appeal which can, in principle, allow us to determine which of a range of metaphysical views we should accept. This methodology can do this even where the metaphysical views in question go well beyond anything we can empirically test.

• CHAPTER SUMMARY

- Metaphysicians ask many of the same questions that are asked by empirical scientists, but they also ask questions that go beyond those asked in the empirical sciences.
- Metaphysicians are often interested in questions that cannot be answered by empirical science because they cannot be answered by appealing to experimental method.
- Metaphysics is constrained by our best science: it should be consistent with our best science.
- Metaphysics is in part about locating the important, everyday, things that we care about, within the picture of the world that science gives us.
- Metaphysicians use conceptual analysis as a tool to help them figure out what it would take for us to locate some ordinary notion in the description of the world given to us in science.

- Metaphysicians use indispensability arguments to argue for the existence of objects or properties that we cannot investigate empirically.
- *A priori* arguments are those each of whose premises can be known by reason alone.
- We can evaluate different metaphysical theories by determining which theories are more virtuous.

• STUDY QUESTIONS

1 Give examples of some questions that both empirical scientists and metaphysicians ask, and explain how their approach to answering these questions differs.
2 What is conceptual analysis?
3 What sorts of questions does metaphysics ask that science does not?
4 What is an indispensability argument? Come up with a new example of such an argument.
5 What is an example of something that you know *a priori*?
6 Why is *a priori* reasoning important in metaphysics?

• INTRODUCTORY FURTHER READING

Ney, Alyssa (2014) *Metaphysics: An Introduction*. London: Routledge.
Russell, Gillian (2007) 'Teaching & Learning Guide For: The Analytic/Synthetic Distinction', *Philosophy Compass* 3(1):273–6.

• ADVANCED FURTHER READING

Braddon-Mitchell, David and Robert Nola (eds) (2009) *Conceptual Analysis and Philosophical Naturalism* (Cambridge, MA: MIT Press).
Jackson, Frank (1998) *From Metaphysics to Ethics: A Defence of Conceptual Analysis* (Oxford: Oxford University Press).
Ladyman, James and Don Ross (2007) *Every Thing Must Go: Metaphysics Naturalized* (Oxford: Oxford University Press).

• FREE INTERNET RESOURCES

Baehr, Jason S., 'A Priori and A Posteriori', http://www.iep.utm.edu/apriori/.
Colyvan, Mark, 'Indispensability Arguments in the Philosophy of Mathematics', *The Stanford Encyclopedia of Philosophy* (Spring 2014 Edition), http://plato.stanford.edu/archives/spr2014/entries/mathphil-indis/.
Douven, Igor, 'Abduction', *The Stanford Encyclopedia of Philosophy* (Spring 2011 Edition), http://plato.stanford.edu/archives/spr2011/entries/abduction/.

Russell, Bruce, '*A Priori* Justification and Knowledge', *The Stanford Encyclopedia of Philosophy* (Summer 2014 Edition), http://plato.stanford.edu/archives/sum2014/entries/apriori/.

van Inwagen, Peter, 'Metaphysics', *The Stanford Encyclopedia of Philosophy* (Winter 2013 Edition), http://plato.stanford.edu/archives/win2013/entries/metaphysics/.

19
is our world structured?

- Flat versus mountainous
- Fundamentality and grounding

FLAT VERSUS MOUNTAINOUS

Metaphysics is sometimes characterised as a discipline primarily interested in the question: what is there? That, of course, makes the scope of metaphysics huge. Put like that, though, one might get the impression that those engaging in metaphysics are mostly interested in coming up with a (very long) list of everything that exists, from toasters to quarks. But metaphysics is not best viewed as an attempt simply to provide a list of objects, or even a list of *kinds* of objects, that exist. To be sure, it is part of the task of metaphysics to catalogue the kinds of objects we find in our world. In addition, though, we want to know how the things in the world are related to one another: we want to know how our world is structured.

Recently there has arisen a substantial debate in metaphysics about whether our world is flat as opposed to being what we might call mountainous. Those who think the world is mountainous think that some bits of the world depend on other bits of the world. They think that some bits of the world are **fundamental**, or at least, more fundamental than other bits, and that less fundamental bits of the world depend on more fundamental bits of the world. Thus we have a picture of our world as layered, with the less fundamental being supported by the more fundamental. Those who think that the world is mountainous thus suppose that it is an important part of metaphysics to figure out the structure of our world.

Those who think our world is mountainous want to introduce some new notions into metaphysics. First, they want to introduce the notion of fundamentality. Something is said to be fundamental if it does not depend on anything else. By contrast, something is **derivative** if it does depend on something else. Finally they want to introduce the notion of dependence, or, as it is often known, the notion of **grounding**. It is a matter of some dispute how to understand the notion of grounding, but perhaps the easiest way to think of it is as a relation: something that holds between objects in the world. Then grounding is a relation that holds between things in the world. If one thing, x, is grounded by another, y, then x is less fundamental than y. If y is not grounded by anything then y is fundamental. If our world is mountainous then the right picture of our world is of there being chains of dependence. Objects that are most derivative sit at the top of a chain, and objects become progressively more fundamental (and less derivative) as we move down the chain. The things at the top depend on the things further down, which in turn depend on things further down, and so on. The classic image that might spring to mind here is that of a world being supported by four elephants which are in turn supported by a giant turtle which is in turn supported by another giant turtle and so on. If our world really is structured into chains of dependence then an important question is whether or not those chains end somewhere. That is, it is turtles all the way down so that beneath each turtle is a further turtle, or is there some final, bottom, turtle that supports all of the others: a fundamental turtle upon which all else rests? If chains of dependence are infinite – if there is no bottom layer to the chain – then nothing is fundamental; all we can say is that some things are more fundamental than others, but there is no fundamental level that grounds everything else. If chains of dependence have a bottom layer, then whatever is at the bottom of each chain is fundamental, and these jointly ground everything else.

We could call those who think that our world is mountainous and that the project of metaphysics is to figure out what grounds what, and what, if anything, is fundamental, mountaineers. But not everyone thinks that it is useful to think about metaphysics in this way. We could call the opponents of mountaineers flatlanders. Flatlanders reject the idea that there are grounding relations or that some objects are more fundamental than others. Yet although flatlanders reject the idea that there exist chains of dependence and in this sense think that our world is flat, it is not fair to say that they thereby reject the idea that our world has structure. Nor is it fair to say that they think the task of metaphysics involves no more than listing the objects and properties that exist into a long laundry list of ontology. For it is consistent with thinking that our world is flat, in this sense, that one thinks that there are many important relations that obtain between different bits of our world and that understanding our world crucially involves grasping those relations. Thus, somewhat paradoxically, we might say that flatlanders think our world is flat, but they also think it has structure: they just don't think that having structure is the same thing as having chains of dependence.

Rather, those who think that our world is flat typically think that to talk about the structure of our world is really to talk about some complicated mix of **supervenience**, reduction and entailment (and perhaps also some other relations). So those who defend the view that our world is flat think that we can say all we need to say about the structure of our world without positing some further relation, such as grounding, or some further property, such as being fundamental. Crucially, this is what mountaineers deny: they think that explicating the structure of our world without appealing to notions such as grounding and fundamentality leaves out something very important about the structure of our world.

To appreciate fully what is at stake in this debate we would need to understand, first, what supervenience, reduction and entailment are, and, second, why flatlanders and mountaineers disagree about whether, with these notions (and perhaps some others) in hand, we have all the notions that we need to describe the structure of the world. That is a big task, and not one that we will attempt here. Instead, we will look at just one of these notions – supervenience – and try to see what it is that flatlanders and mountaineers disagree upon.

Supervenience is like jam: it comes in many different varieties. But the key idea is that supervenience is a relation that obtains (or fails to) between two sets of properties. Consider two sets of properties. Call one of these the As and the other the Bs. To say that the As supervene on the Bs is to say that if we want to change the As, we can only do that by changing the Bs. Another way to say the same thing is to say that if the As supervene on the Bs, then if we duplicate the Bs, we thereby duplicate the As. Or, perhaps better still, when we fix the B-properties we thereby fix the A-properties.

Think about the relationship between your mass, on the one hand, and all of the matter that makes you up, on the other hand. Call the property of you having a certain mass your M property. Call the property of being composed of a certain set of matter your C property. M supervenes on C. To see that, notice that once we fix C – we fix exactly of what matter you are composed – we thereby fix M, your mass. If we duplicate all of the matter of which you are composed we thereby duplicate your mass. To put the point the other way around, it is clear that you could not change M without changing C. If you want to change your mass, you have to change the amount of matter of which you are composed. If this were not so, then weight loss (which is really mass loss) would not be the trial that it is.

With this notion of supervenience in mind, we can now make even more precise the questions we asked earlier about the relationship between moral and natural properties, and the relationship between mental and natural properties. In both those cases when we asked whether a powerful being needed to do something extra to make mental or moral properties, other than just distribute the natural and physical properties, we were asking about supervenience. We were asking whether moral properties supervene on natural properties, and whether mental properties supervene on physical properties. If you think that mental states supervene on physical states then you think that once you fix the relevant physical states, you thereby fix the mental states that supervene on those physical states. Put somewhat less abstractly, if the mental state of desiring chocolate (or the property of having that mental state) supervenes on brain state B1 (or the property of having that brain state) then if I bring about B1 (I 'fix' that B1 is the case) I thereby bring about (fix) that the desire for chocolate is the case. There's nothing more that I need to do to bring about the desire for chocolate other than, as it were, bringing about B1. Moreover, if I find that someone has a desire for chocolate, then the only way I change that desire is to mess with their brain states and make it the case that B1 does not obtain. There's no way to keep the B1 brain state, but remove the desire for chocolate.

It's easy to see that supervenience is an interesting and important relation because it tells us about the way that sets of properties travel around together. If mental properties supervene on physical properties (or, more specifically, on brain states) then that is an important discovery. Supervenience is what is known as a **nonsymmetric** relation. That means that if the As supervene on the Bs, then it may be that the Bs supervene on the As, or it may be that the Bs do not supervene on the As. Mountaineers think that this is what makes the supervenience relation a poor one by which to understand the structure of our world. Remember that according to mountaineers we want to understand how some bits of our world are grounded by (or more generally, depend on) other bits of our world. But it is pretty plausible to think that if A depends on B, the B does not depend on A. That just seems to be part of what we mean when we talk about dependence. So mountaineers think that whatever relation we are looking for to understand the structure of our world, it had better be an **asymmetric** relation. Roughly, a relation, R, is asymmetric if it follows that if A Rs B, then it is not the case that B Rs A. So the relation of 'being the mother of' is asymmetric, because if Pru is the mother of Denise, then Denise is not the mother of Pru (and likewise for any other pair of objects). Symmetric relations are relations such that if A Rs B, then B Rs A. The relation 'is next to' is like that. If Todd is next to Bill, then Bill is next to Todd, and likewise for any two objects that are such that one is next to the other. Finally, a relation is nonsymmetric if on some occasions when it holds it holds asymmetrically, and on other occasions it holds symmetrically. Supervenience is a nonsymmetric relation. For in some cases where the As supervene on the Bs it is also the case that the Bs supervene on the As (so the relation on that occasion holds symmetrically) and sometimes where the As supervene on the Bs it is not the case that the Bs supervene on the As (on that occasion the relation holds asymmetrically). The zombie argument is articulated in Part V (chapter 14, 'What is Consciousness?'). It attempts to show that the mental does not supervene on the physical because it could be that there exists the very same arrangement of physical properties in some world, but in that world some mental properties are absent.

If mental states do supervene on physical states this looks like a case in which the supervenience relation holds asymmetrically. For it is plausible that even if our mental states supervene on our brain states, the reverse is not the case. Consider the mental state of being in pain. Suppose that my mental state of being in pain supervenes on my brain states. There might, however, be lots of different brain states I can be in, each of which realises in me the mental state of being in pain. Then it will be true that when you fix the properties of my brain you thereby fix which mental state I am in. When you fix that my brain is in state B2, you thereby fix that I am in pain. But now suppose instead you fix that I am in pain. It does not follow that you have thereby fixed that I am in brain state B2. For there is any number of other brain states that I could be in, and it still be true that I am in pain. If that is so, then the property of being in a mental state of being in pain supervenes on the property of having brain state B2. But the property of having brain state B2 does not supervene on the property of being in the mental state of being in pain. If so, then mental states supervene on brain states, but not the other way around, and we have a case of asymmetric supervenience.

Supervenience relations tell us how properties co-vary: they tell us which properties we find together and which properties we need to wiggle, as it were, to make changes to other properties. Those who think our world is flat think that we can partly understand the structure of our world in terms of supervenience relations. Our world is structured in such a way that mental properties supervene on physical properties, but the reverse is not the case. That tells us something interesting about the relationship between those two sets of properties, and what it tells us is something about the structure of our world. We can understand that structure perfectly well without introducing some new relation, such as grounding, and we can understand it without thinking that some things in our world are fundamental, and that other things depend on those fundamental things.

Mountaineers, however, think flatlanders are wrong about this. Mountaineers want to say not merely that mental properties supervene on physical properties while physical properties do not supervene on mental properties, but, in addition, that this is because physical properties ground mental properties. It is because mental properties depend on physical properties. Mountaineers point out that the fact that mental properties supervene on physical properties does not tell us that the former are dependent on the latter: it just tells us how the two sets of properties co-vary. Of course, making such a point will not convince the flatlander since she thinks there is nothing more to say except that these properties co-vary in certain ways.

Is there something more that can be said? Mountaineers think there is. It is not so easy to see by looking at the examples we have just seen. But consider the following, known as the Euthyphro problem. Euthyphro wondered whether good things are good because God loves them, or whether God loves them because they are good. We don't need to think that there is a God to think that, at the very least, we can make sense of this question. But now suppose that if there is a God, then God exists of necessity: that is, there is no possible world in which God fails to exist. Then it follows that in every possible world God loves the good.

In light of that, consider two properties: the property of being loved by God, and the property of being good. Call the former LOVED, and the latter GOOD. In every possible world LOVED supervenes on GOOD: for once we fix the property of what is loved by God, we thereby fix the property of what is good. To put it another way, the only way to change what is good, is to change what God loves. But notice that the reverse is also true. GOOD supervenes on LOVED. For once we fix the property of being good, we thereby fix the property of what God loves. So in this case the supervenience relationship is symmetric. Yet despite that, the mountaineer argues, it seems perfectly sensible to ask whether something's being loved by God depends on its being good, or whether something's being good depends on its being loved by God. So appealing to supervenience is of no help at all in resolving the Euthyphro question, or, indeed, in posing the question in the first place. Even to make sense of what is being asked we need to introduce some new relation of dependence – what mountaineers call grounding. We can then ask whether God's loving something is what grounds its being good, or whether something's being good is what grounds its being loved by God. And if there are grounding relations there will be an answer to that question.

It won't really do for the flatlander to reply to the mountaineer that she doesn't think there is any God, for there are other examples that work in much the same way. Consider Socrates the man. Now consider what is known as the **singleton set** of Socrates. That is the set that has just Socrates as a member and nothing else. Let's not worry too much about what sets are. That is a big dispute in itself. But the existence of sets (whatever they might be) is certainly less controversial than the existence of a deity. Indeed, most philosophers and mathematicians think that sets exist. But now notice that in any world in which there is Socrates there is also his singleton set. And in any world in which there is a singleton set of Socrates, there is Socrates. The two go around together just as, in our previous example, God's loving something went around with that thing's being good. This means that the property of Socrates' existing supervenes on the property of the Socrates' singleton set existing and the property of Socrates' singleton set existing supervenes on the property of Socrates existing. The supervenience relation between the two is perfectly symmetric. But, mountaineers point out, it seems intuitive to think that the set depends on Socrates but that Socrates does not depend on the set. That is, it's pretty tempting to think that the set exists because Socrates does, rather than that Socrates exists because the set does. Yet because the supervenience relationship between the two is symmetrical on this occasion, we cannot capture that intuitive idea by appealing to supervenience. Hence, mountaineers argue, we need some additional relation to help us make sense of the structure of our world.

Flatlanders could respond to mountaineers by trying to find some other relation that will do the job on these occasions. And while entailment clearly will not do, perhaps reduction might. We will not consider this issue here. To be clear, though, mountaineers think that no other relation will do the job and some flatlanders are inclined to agree. These flatlanders typically want to say that sometimes what appear to be sensible questions to ask really aren't sensible at all. The thought, here, is that it seems to us as though it is sensible to ask whether God loves things because they are good or they are good because he loves them, because we are tacitly, without realising it, imagining that there are worlds in which either God loves things, but those things are not good, or worlds in which things are good but God does not love them. We are imagining that God's love, and goodness, can come apart in some world, and thus imagining that it makes sense to ask, in worlds where they do not come apart, which depends on which. But of course, if there were such worlds then the supervenience relation between God's loving something and its being good would not be symmetrical. It would either be the case that wherever God loves something, it is good (goodness supervenes on God's love) but in some worlds there is goodness that God does not love and so it is not true that God's love supervenes on goodness. Or it would be that whenever something is good, God loves it (God's love supervenes on the goodness) but there are worlds in which God loves things that are not good and so it is not the case that goodness supervenes on God's love. If things were this way then we could sensibly ask questions about the relationship between God's love and goodness. But we are being asked to entertain the idea that they are not this way: that the two never, under any circumstances, come apart. Here, the flatlander thinks, it simply makes no sense to ask which one depends on the other. So the fact that the relations to which the flatlander can appeal in understanding the structure of our world will not allow us to answer the Euthyphro question is not, to the mind of the flatlander, any sort of drawback since for her there is no sensible question to be asked or answered.

Flatlanders and mountaineers agree that doing metaphysics is about explicating a range of important relations that obtain between objections and properties in our world. Neither thinks that metaphysics is primarily about making a list of things that exist. They do, however, disagree about what resources we need if we are to understand the structure of our world. Mountaineers think that we need to posit additional primitive relations to our ontology: relations of grounding. Flatlanders think we do not.

BOX 19.1 MONISM AND PLURALISM

In this chapter 'monism' and 'pluralism' refer to two views that are better known as 'priority monism' and 'priority pluralism'. Indeed, there are many views that can be called 'monism' and many that can be called 'pluralism'. For monism really just refers to the idea that there is only one kind of thing. Pluralism refers to the view that there are multiple kinds of things. Thus, for instance, substance monism is the view that there is just one kind of substance, and substance pluralism is the view that there are many different kinds of substance. So, for instance, substance dualists are almost certainly substance pluralists since they think there are at least two kinds of substance: mental substance and physical substance.

Within mereology and the metaphysics of composition, monism and pluralism are views about objects and their parts. In fact, the views described in this chapter as monism and pluralism are really better described as priority monism and priority pluralism. According to this pair of views there exist composite objects, and the debate is about which is more fundamental – the composite whole or its parts. Priority pluralists think that the parts are more fundamental than the whole, and priority monists think the whole is more fundamental than the parts. This pair of views should be distinguished from what is now sometimes known as existence monism. Existence monism is the view that only the whole exists, and the whole has no parts. This view, also known in some quarters as 'blobjectivism', is the thesis that our world exists, but our world lacks proper parts. So in fact there are dogs, toasters, or houses which are themselves objects and which are parts of the world. This is a radical view. Like mereological nihilism, this view has to try to make sense of what we say in ordinary language. Typically it does so by suggesting that although there is no object that is a dog, there is a region of the world that has certain doggish properties, and this region is what makes true (or approximately true) claims such as 'there is a dog' and 'the dog is black'. So most of what we ordinarily say will come out as true, even though the whole has no parts at all.

• FUNDAMENTALITY AND GROUNDING

Suppose we agree with the mountaineer that we need to posit a new dependence relation and that we will call that relation grounding. Then there is a range of further questions we can investigate. On a case-by-case basis, of course, we can ask for any two things whether or not one depends on the other. Indeed, with the notion of grounding under our belts we can distinguish positions that it would otherwise be difficult to distinguish.

For instance, a debate has begun between two views now called **monism** and **pluralism**. In this context, monism is the view that the whole is more fundamental than its parts. In particular, then, on the assumption that our world is a whole, this is the view that that whole, the world, is more fundamental than any of its parts. Monism is, in fact, usually the view that the whole is not just more fundamental than the parts, but that the whole is ungrounded – it is the fundamental thing – and its parts are grounded in that whole. This is to be contrasted with pluralism, according to which the parts are more fundamental than the whole. Thus this is the view that if the world is one whole, then the world is less fundamental than any of its parts. Indeed, pluralists are typically committed to the view that of the many parts, there is some set of parts that are fundamental (ungrounded) and that these parts are simples. These are the parts of the whole that have no further parts (hence they are simple). These simple objects are the fundamentals upon which the rest of the world rests.

It is noteworthy that in the absence of an appeal to a grounding relation it is hard to see how we would distinguish monism from pluralism. For the monist and the pluralist each believes in the same objects and properties. They just disagree about what grounds what.

This is just one area in which we can see how a new debate can play out between mountaineers. These new debates are ones in which participants agree that there is a grounding relation and agree that the purpose of metaphysics is, in part, to determine what grounds what, but in which they disagree about what does, in fact, do the grounding.

BOX 19.2 TURTLES ALL THE WAY DOWN

We have seen that mountaineers puzzle over the question of whether it is turtles all the way down: that is, whether there is something (or many things) that are fundamental, and upon which everything else is grounded, or whether the chains of dependence go on to infinity, never terminating in something that is fundamental. That makes it seem as though there are just two options. The first is one in which there are chains and these terminate in something fundamental. The second is one in which there are chains that go on to infinity and have no final member. But these aren't the only options. There are really lots of options. Suppose that instead of there being linear chains there are instead circular chains of dependence. Then the chain itself can have a finite number of members, and each member of the chain depends on some other member, but no member is fundamental. Here there is no unique best way of saying which things are more fundamental and which less fundamental. Indeed, for any member of the chain it is both the case that every other member in the chain depends on it, and the case that it depends on every other member in the chain.

Another set of options suggests itself once we realise that just because we are inclined to think that such chains go from the very large to the very small, it does not follow that one of these (the very large) or the other (the very small) is the fundamental level. It could be that the most fundamental things are the macro-sized things that we think of as being in the middle of a chain of dependence. It could be that medium-sized macro objects ground all of the bigger objects (planets, mountains, solar systems) and that they also ground all of the smaller objects (atoms, quarks, etc.) and that there are no grounding relations between the smaller and the bigger. On this view there is a fundamental level (the macro-sized objects) which give rise to two distinct chains of dependence, one of which includes all the small-sized objects and the other of which includes all the large-sized objects.

There are, then, all sorts of ways that our world could be, in terms of its grounding relations. Some of these are much less plausible than others, but it is the job of the mountaineer to consider these options.

Amongst mountaineers there is also scope for disagreements of a somewhat different kind. For we can expect mountaineers to ask some more general questions about the way grounding works and about the structure of our world. For instance, we can expect mountaineers to ask whether the grounding relation itself is fundamental. What does that mean? Well suppose that Bert is grounded by Ernie. So there is a grounding relation that holds between Bert and Ernie. Now we can wonder whether the fact that Ernie grounds Bert is itself grounded by something else. Indeed, one can imagine asking: what grounds the fact that Ernie grounds Bert? It seems that there are only two possible kinds of answer we can give. One is to say that something grounds the grounding. Ernie grounds Bert, and something grounds the grounding of Bert by Ernie. The other possible answer is that nothing grounds Ernie's grounding of Bert. If nothing grounds Ernie's grounding of Bert, then that Ernie grounds Bert must be fundamental. For what it is to be fundamental to be ungrounded (to not be grounded by something else).

On the face of it, both of these responses look perplexing. Indeed, one can imagine a flatlander arguing against the existence of the grounding relation by arguing that both options are hopeless. Since the two options are the only two possible options, if they are both hopeless then we have reason to be sceptical of the idea that there are grounding relations. Why do these two options look unappealing?

Consider the first option: something grounds Ernie's grounding Bert. Call the grounds of Ernie's grounding Bert, Doug. So Doug grounds Ernie's grounding Bert. But what ground Doug's grounding Ernie's grounding Bert? Presumably something does. Call that thing Bob. Then Bob grounds Doug's grounding Ernie's grounding Bert. You can probably see the worry. We are going to be led into an infinite regress of grounding of grounds. For each grounding relation that holds between two objects, like Bert and Ernie, there will be an infinite number of further grounds that ground that grounding relation. This yields an explosion of grounding relations. There are really two different worries with this proposal. The first is that it yields so many grounding relations: if we were considering the theoretical virtue of parsimony, this view would not look very good. But not only are there so very many grounding relations, but, in addition, the grounds go on ad infinitum. We wanted to know what grounds Ernie's grounding Bert. But there is no final answer to that question. There is an infinite chain of grounds that ground Ernie's grounding Bert. One might feel, however, that this is hardly satisfactory. Indeed, one might think that if the chain goes on to infinity then really nothing grounds the fact that Ernie grounds Bert. After all, whichever grounding fact we appeal to in order to explain the relation between Ernie and Bert, that will be grounded in something further, which will be grounded in something further, and so on.

The second option is to say that nothing grounds Ernie's grounding Bert. The grounding fact, as it were, is itself fundamental. So grounding itself is ungrounded. Yet that also seems unsatisfactory. Flatlanders think that there is no call to appeal to grounding at all. But if you are a mountaineer you have the intuition that some things really do ground other things and that this is where the important metaphysical action is at. But if grounding itself is ungrounded, then whenever there are objects such that one grounds the other, there will never be any explanation for the fact that the one grounds the other: there will never be any grounds for the grounding. But if grounding can be ungrounded, one might wonder, why can't Bert himself be ungrounded? Why can't we simply be flatlanders?

In a way, then, this first question, 'is grounding grounded?', presents something of a dilemma for the mountaineer. She needs to answer that question in a way that is plausible, and neither of the options looks all that great. That is not to say that there are not possible responses. The mountaineer might adopt the first option but suggest that the regress in question is not a bad one. Or she might adopt the second option and explain why it is fine to think that grounding is ungrounded. In each case, though, she has some work to do.

The second question that naturally faces the mountaineer is the question of whether or not the chains of dependence in our world terminate. A chain of dependence terminates, in this sense, if it has a first member of the chain that is not itself dependent on any other member in the chain. Assuming that that first member (if there is one) is not dependent on the member of any other chain, then that first member is fundamental. It is, as it were, one of the turtles at the bottom that is supporting the rest of the world. This question, unlike the first, does not really present any sort of problem for mountaineers. Rather, it is a question about what sort of structure they think our world is most likely to have. This is a fascinating question. Some mountaineers think that our world will have chains that terminate. These mountaineers think that it is not turtles all the way down. They are motivated to this thought because it seems as though if the chains do not terminate then nothing is really grounded in anything. For, the worry proceeds, this would be a case in which grounding relations go on ad infinitum, never bottoming out in any fundamental way. This is a somewhat different worry from the one we just encountered. There, we were concerned that grounding relations themselves might have grounds, and that *those* grounds might not terminate. But here the worry is that grounding relations themselves might not terminate. Suppose you ask me what grounds Bert, and I tell you Ernie does. That is all well and good. And perhaps I can then tell you that Phil grounds Ernie, and than Helen grounds Phil. But if there is no end to this, if for any object I choose something grounds that object, and so on forever, then it is very much as though the whole edifice of grounding is floating in space. For there is no base upon which the chain of dependence sits. Some mountaineers find this prospect worrisome; they think that in such an event we would not really have any good explanation for why things are as they are. For although I can explain why Bert is as he is, by explaining why Ernie is as he is, that explanation goes on ad infinitum, since in order to explain why Ernie is as he is we need to appeal to Phil, and then to Helen, and so on with no end. Thus some mountaineers think that every world in which some things ground others will be a world in which chains of dependence terminate in fundamental things. Others think that there is no reason why there couldn't be worlds in which dependence chains fail to terminate, but they think that our world is not like that. We, as it were, got a nice, well-behaved world in which all derivative things are, ultimately, grounded in something fundamental. Finally, there are those mountaineers who think it is an open question whether our world is one in which the chains of dependence terminate.

Regardless of what we think about some of these particular issues, it is clear that appealing to grounding relations gives the metaphysician an extra tool by which she can make distinctions she could not otherwise make, and hence by which she can construct views and ask questions that she could not otherwise. Whether that is a good thing depends on whether or not one finds those questions sensible, and the views useful. Flatlanders think they are not; mountaineers think they are.

• CHAPTER SUMMARY

- Metaphysics is not just interested in listing the kinds of objects that there are; it is also interested in figuring out the structure of our world.
- Flatlanders think that our world is flat. They think that it does not have any relations of dependence that cannot be captured by the sorts of relations we already have in our metaphysical tool box.
- Mountaineers think our world is mountainous. They think we need to introduce new notions into our tool box to understand the structure of our world because they think our world is structured by chains of dependence.
- Mountaineers think that there exist grounding relations which hold between things so that if one thing grounds another, then that thing is more fundamental than the thing it grounds.
- Supervenience is a relation that obtains between sets of properties; it tells us how properties co-vary with one another.
- Flatlanders think that supervenience relations tell us about the structure of our world; mountaineers disagree.
- Mountaineers must decide whether they think grounding relations are themselves grounded in something further, or are instead fundamental.
- Some mountaineers think that chains of dependence must terminate, others think that they do terminate in our world, and still others think it an open question whether or not they terminate in our world.

• STUDY QUESTIONS

1 Explain, in your own words, what the difference is between simply making a list of what exists, and explaining how the world is structured.
2 Why do mountaineers think that appealing to supervenience is not a good way to understand the structure of our world?
3 Give an example where the As supervene on the Bs in an asymmetric way.
4 Can you find an example that is like the Euthyphro problem, in which two sets of properties supervene in a symmetric way across all possible worlds?
5 Do you think that mountaineers are right and we need to posit a grounding relation? Explain why.
6 Explain why some mountaineers think that chains of dependence must terminate.

• INTRODUCTORY FURTHER READING

Correia, F. (2008) 'Ontological Dependence', *Philosophy Compass* 3(5): 1013–32.
Leuenberger, S. (2008) 'Supervenience in Metaphysics', *Philosophy Compass* 3(4): 749–62.
Schaffer, J. (2009) 'On What Grounds What', in David Manley, David J. Chalmers and Ryan Wasserman (eds) *Metametaphysics: New Essays on the Foundations of Ontology* (Oxford: Oxford University Press), pp. 347–83.
Trogdon, K. (2013) 'An Introduction to Grounding', in M. Hoeltje, B. Schnieder and A. Steinberg (eds) *Varieties of Dependence: Ontological Dependence, Grounding, Supervenience, Response-Dependence* (Munich: Philosophia Verlag), pp. 97–122.

• ADVANCED FURTHER READING

Bennett, Karen (2011) 'Construction Area (No Hard Hat Required)', *Philosophical Studies* 154(1): 79–104.
de Rosset, Louis (2013) 'Grounding Explanations', *Philosophers' Imprint* 13(7).
Wilson, Jessica M. (2014) 'No Work for a Theory of Grounding', *Inquiry* 57(5–6): 535–79.

• FREE INTERNET RESOURCES

Lowe, E. Jonathan, 'Ontological Dependence', *The Stanford Encyclopedia of Philosophy* (Spring 2010 Edition), http://plato.stanford.edu/archives/spr2010/entries/dependence-ontological/.
McLaughlin, Brian and Bennett, Karen, 'Supervenience', *The Stanford Encyclopedia of Philosophy* (Spring 2014 Edition), http://plato.stanford.edu/archives/spr2014/entries/supervenience/.
Rickles, D., 'Supervenience and Determination', http://www.iep.utm.edu/superven/ Internet encyclopaedia of philosophy.

Part VII

philosophy of science

Axel Gelfert

What is science? A somewhat flippant answer would be: science is what scientists do for a living. But who is a scientist? And how do we tell properly trained scientists from those who merely arrogate to themselves the authority in matters of knowledge that is commonly associated with science? The term 'scientist' did not come into existence until the early nineteenth century, when it was coined by the English physicist, philosopher, and polymath William Whewell (1794–1866). It indicated the gradual emergence of science as a profession – that is, as something people can pursue for a living. Until then, science had been mainly the preserve of private individuals (often with significant independent wealth to support their endeavours).

In this Part, we will be looking at some of the major philosophical questions that emerge from the rise of science as a major factor in modern life. Throughout, we will be looking at science in its various capacities: as a field of knowledge and a source of understanding, as an ambitious account of the most fundamental structure of the world, as a set of theoretical tenets and a collective endeavour with a varied history that comprises successes, failures, and dead-ends.

Chapter 20 will explore the general question of what science is, and whether there is anything we can say, in general, about the various scientific disciplines and their underlying methodologies. We will begin with a discussion of public perceptions and the self-image of scientists, before exploring how science poses a challenge to our commonsense understanding of the world. While science is often said to be the study of the natural world around us, based on careful and systematic observation, we will find that central concepts such as observation, explanation, and prediction are not at all obvious, but instead require careful analysis.

In chapter 21, we will consider the nature of scientific theories and the often under-appreciated role that scientific models play in making sense of the world around us. Scientific models are needed whenever we are dealing with situations or systems that are too complex to be studied directly on the basis of theoretical 'first principles'. As an example, we will discuss the role of models in explaining the Earth's changing climate. While our understanding of the Earth's climate has improved vastly over the decades, there inevitably remain uncertainties, and this will prompt us to also consider the question of how much certainty it is reasonable to demand from science.

In the final chapter of this Part, we will ask the question 'Is science getting closer to the truth?'. This question, which is usually discussed under the label of 'scientific realism', requires us to delve deep into the history of science. It also requires us to consider the question of whether scientific theories and claims play merely an instrumental role in the prediction and explanation of phenomena, or whether we should take them literally and commit ourselves to their truth (or approximate truth). As we will find, historical considerations of *scientific theory change* pose a serious challenge to such realist commitments – yet, at the same time, scientific progress over the course of history has also been regarded as a powerful argument in support of scientific realism.

20
what is science?

- Public perceptions and the self-image of science
- The scientific and the manifest image
- Observation and experience
- Explanation and prediction
- Pseudo-science and the demarcation problem

PUBLIC PERCEPTIONS AND THE SELF-IMAGE OF SCIENCE

The word 'science' probably conjures up different images for different people: a white-coated figure, silently toiling away at the lab bench; a radio telescope on a mountain top, peering into the majestic depths of the universe; a set of equations scribbled on a blackboard, perhaps confounding – as in one of those Gary Larson cartoons – a group of wild-haired (and probably male) scientists. Carry out a Google Images search for the term 'science', and the first few pages are filled precisely with such cartoonish images of science. Most of us are, of course, aware that these are distorted representations of the sciences and of those who practise them: no one truly thinks that the typical biologist, chemist, computer scientist, geologist, or mathematical physicist fits the 'lonely genius', 'mad scientist' or 'Dr. Strangelove' mould. But the persistence of such stereotypes speaks to the presence of conflicting popular perceptions of what science is, what it does, and how we ought to relate to it.

Some of these tensions are due to a conflict between how we think science *actually is* and how it *should be*. In philosophical parlance, setting out to characterise what is actually the case is called a *descriptive* project, whereas developing a framework for how things ought to be is a *normative* endeavour. This distinction is familiar from moral philosophy. We all know that human beings do not always act as they ought to, yet describing how they fall short of normative demands may nonetheless be a philosophically insightful project. After all, it may turn out that we are simply demanding too much! In this sense, the descriptive side of a philosophical project – that is, looking at how science (or morality, for that matter) *actually* works – may well tell us something about its normative limits. For example, we might demand that scientists, in the interest of objectivity, should *never* let their other (non-scientific) beliefs and values influence their research. But scientists are only human, and if it turns out that nobody actually succeeds in separating out their scientific 'persona' from the rest of their personality, perhaps we need to rethink what we mean when we regard scientific **objectivity** as a worthwhile goal.

Let us look at a few of these perceptions and expectations in a bit more detail. From early on – which, in the present context, means the period of the Scientific Revolution (a somewhat problematic term, usually taken to refer to the time from the mid-sixteenth to early eighteenth century) – science has been associated with *utility*. Of course people have always pursued useful knowledge about the natural world, but the systematic and organised pursuit of such knowledge *in general* was, arguably, a novel feature of science as it gradually emerged from the early-modern period onwards. The prospects of science were perhaps most clearly articulated by some of the major philosophers of the day. As the philosopher and statesman Francis Bacon (1561–1626) put it in 1597: 'Knowledge itself is power.' Bacon envisioned science as an institutionalised, state-funded endeavour devoted to 'the enlarging of the bounds of human empire', arguing that the dignity of science 'is maintained by works of utility and power'. Thomas Hobbes (1588–1679), best known for his political philosophy, likewise made it clear that 'increase of Science [is] the way; and the benefit of mankind, the end'.

However, the immediate utility of *pure* science – that is, science whose primary aim is ascertaining the *truth* about a particular subject matter, rather than finding solutions to practical challenges – is often far from obvious. This is why, in recent years, scientists have come under increasing pressure to demonstrate (for example, in their funding applications) the 'relevance' of their research and its potential for applications. Yet many would argue that the pursuit of truth and an increased understanding of the workings of nature are valuable in their own right, even when they are not of immediate (or even potential) usefulness. Indeed, if practical utility were all there is to science, it would not be clear why we should value truth in science so much. After all, many falsehoods might be just as useful as the corresponding truths – either because, within relevant contexts of application, they would be practically indistinguishable from truth (think of using Newtonian physics instead of relativity theory in everyday situations), or because they might even be more useful in some way (for example, when widely believed falsehoods would make a population more easily governed).

But inaccurate portrayals of science are not limited to the general public. Many scientists, too, cultivate a self-image of themselves and of science which is far from accurate and which – even in those rare instances where individual scientists act according to this self-image – certainly does not generalise to all of their colleagues. One might find this surprising. Surely, if one wants to know what science is, should one not simply ask those who practise it for a living? But, if what I just said is true, then scientists might not be the best source to turn to for information *about science*. On reflection, however, this should not seem too paradoxical. After all, scientists are good at *doing* science, just as goalkeepers are good at stopping the ball. But in much the same way as a successful goalkeeper may not be able to tell us *exactly how* he manages to usually catch the ball – let alone explain to us what makes for a good football match – a good scientist may be unable to tell us how she arrives at her hypotheses or what makes for a fruitful research programme. When pressed on what constitutes the '**scientific method**' – which they often take to be a single, unified methodology – many scientists will claim that science proceeds by positing explanatory hypotheses for observable phenomena, which are then ruthlessly subjected to **testing**. Hypotheses and results that cannot be replicated are discarded, and only those theories and hypotheses that survive severe testing are retained – at least for the time being.

This self-image of science as primarily concerned with conjecturing hypotheses, followed by severe testing and attempted **replication** of results, is loosely inspired by the twentieth-century philosopher Karl Popper (1902–94). It casts the scientist in the almost heroic dual role of both creator and destroyer of scientific hypotheses: someone who 'sticks his neck out' when proposing scientific theories, but is at the same time willing to retract his views once contravening evidence is observed. This, however, is not how science works. Scientists are often strongly committed to theories and hypotheses they have developed, and they do not admit defeat easily. Furthermore, scientists do not devote nearly as much time to replicating and testing the results of others as this picture suggests. Self-correction in science does occur, but in a much less explicit way that is guided by many other goals of inquiry.

The 'heroic' self-image of science as a process of conjecturing, testing, and refuting hypotheses coincides with popular perceptions of science on an important point: science, we are told, is based on facts, which in turn are derived from careful observation of the world around us, in a way that is not prejudiced by personal opinions or value commitments. Anyone with the right training, sufficient patience, and access to the relevant evidence must, in principle, be able to come to the same conclusions – hence, the oft-repeated sentiment that, as the nineteenth-century biologist T. H. Huxley (1825–95) put it, 'science is common sense at its best; that is, rigidly accurate in observation, and merciless to fallacy in logic'. The rest of this chapter will analyse whether this is a viable characterisation of science.

• THE SCIENTIFIC AND THE MANIFEST IMAGE

Is science really just 'common sense writ large'? Let us consider what a commonsensical conception of the world might look like. According to such a conception, things in the world *seem* to me the way they do because that is simply the way they *are*. A ripe apple tastes sweet because it contains sweetness, the heavy wooden table in front of me is a solid object, time moves from the past to the present to the future. Some of this knowledge (if indeed it is knowledge) is known to me directly: I can taste the sweetness of the apple when I bite into it. Other commonsense claims require some **inductive inference**; that is, generalising from past instances to future instances.

Thus, I know that dark clouds are a good (though not perfect) indicator that it will rain, and after having lived in a particular place for a long time, I may even know *which* kinds of dark clouds are especially likely to result in rain.

But such commonsense reasoning is often unreliable. For one, it privileges anecdotal evidence: we tend to give greater weight to events and occurrences that have happened *to us* than to those that have happened to others. Anyone above a certain age also knows that sometimes our senses play tricks on us, for example in the case of optical illusions. This means that we cannot always assume that the way things *seem* to us is the way they actually *are*. Science, too, calls into question many of the beliefs we would form if we were to rely on appearances and common sense alone. Thus, although it seems to us that, over the course of a day, the sun moves across the sky and around the Earth, we know that it is really the Earth revolving around its own axis which causes this appearance.

A distinction drawn by the American philosopher Wilfrid Sellars (1912–89) is useful here. Sellars distinguishes between the *manifest image* and the *scientific image* of the world. The term 'manifest image' refers to the way things are given to us in everyday experience – not in the naïve sense of taking every appearance at face value, but in the form of a collectively shared, coherent worldview. In short, the manifest image is how we think of the world when we are untutored by (or simply not concerned with) science. In the world according to the manifest image, dark clouds are a good sign of rain, tables are solid objects, ripe apples have sweetness, other people have beliefs and desires, time moves from the past to the present to the future, and so on. The manifest image need not be a naïve view of the world – indeed, it can contain sophisticated beliefs and assumptions about, say, how people act, which materials are fit for which purpose, or concerning correlations between different kinds of observable phenomena (think of weather sayings such as 'a sunny shower won't last an hour' etc.).

While the manifest image of the world is a refined version of our shared commonsense picture of the observable world around us, it remains at odds with the world according to science – that is, with the *scientific image* of the world. Science tells us that the world is chock-full of unobservable entities, hidden causal relationships and – think of the weird world of quantum physics – events and processes that defy commonsense understanding.

BOX 20.1 PHILOSOPHICAL ATOMISM

An early precursor to the later conflict between the scientific image and the manifest image may be found in philosophical atomism. The ancient Greek pre-Socratic philosopher Democritus (*c.* 460–370 BCE) put this in stark terms when he pointed to the gap between what we conventionally think the world is like and what it is really like: 'By convention sweet and by convention bitter, by convention hot, by convention cold, by convention colour; in reality atoms and void.' Though Democritus's atomic hypothesis was entirely speculative at the time, modern physics seems to vindicate its underlying intuition: that, at the most fundamental level of physical reality, all there really is, is fundamental particles and fields. Hence, at least according to one interpretation of the scientific image of the world, the wooden table in front of me is not solid throughout, but is composed mostly of empty space, interspersed with tiny elementary particles.

And science's assault on the manifest image of the world that guides us in our everyday activities is not limited to fundamental physics. For example, psychologists tell us that people's behaviour is not usually well explained by deep-rooted character traits – such as being 'courageous', 'generous', or 'greedy' – but is to an astonishing degree determined by accident and circumstance. (For example, people are much more helpful and generous if they have just encountered a positive surprise – such as finding a coin on the ground.) And on at least some accounts of biological evolution – such as Richard Dawkins's controversial 'selfish gene' hypothesis – the bewildering diversity of life on Earth is best explained not by adaptation at the level of organisms and species (though these are clearly the most salient biological features in our manifest image of the world), but by competition between genes for resources, so as to make more copies of themselves. Whether it concerns the material constitution of the world around us, our place in the natural world, or the very facts of human psychology, the scientific image of the world often leads to – sometimes painful – challenges to conventional wisdom.

• OBSERVATION AND EXPERIENCE

In our discussion of public perceptions and the self-image of science, we encountered the influential view that science is based on facts, which are themselves derived from careful observation of the world around us, in a way that is not biased by subjective factors. Science, it would appear, is primarily a matter of closely observing nature and of subsequently organising our observations in systematic and insightful ways. Yet, as we have seen in the previous section, one major contrast between the manifest image of the world and the scientific image is that the latter makes reference to unobservables. According to the manifest image, the table in front of me is made from solid beechwood and has a yellow shimmer; according to the scientific image, it is made from complex organic molecules, which themselves are constituted by invisible atoms, separated by empty space, reflecting light at a wavelength of around 570–90 nanometres. How, one might ask, do we get from a commitment to the primacy of observation to such scientific claims involving unobservables?

The question of how science can claim to be based on observation can be approached from two angles. The first concerns the nature of observation and how scientists go about generating and recording observational data. The second concerns the question of how scientists arrive at theories, generalisations, and laws of nature – many of which involve claims about unobservables – on the basis of such observational data. Let us discuss each of these aspects in turn.

What is an **observation**? Being visual animals, most of us would tend to identify observation with the visual inspection of a state of affairs and our recognition of it as such. Thus, I can claim to have observed a parrot sitting on a branch in a tree if I have seen it with my own eyes and was able to identify the bird as a parrot. (Of course, I could still be said to have observed the parrot if I had only heard its distinctive call and had recognised it as such, even though the bird was hidden in the foliage.) Understood in this way, observation is a more complex notion than what may be called '*simple seeing*', in that it requires '*seeing-as*' – that is, the ability to subsume visual evidence under certain concepts. Someone who lacked the concept of 'parrot' could still have the same sensory impression as, say, an expert ornithologist – that is, he could experience the same visual image ('simple seeing') – but would not recognise the bird *as* a parrot. So, even though both observers saw – literally – the same object, only the trained ornithologist could be credited with a proper observation.

Not everyone would agree with this characterisation of observation as contrasting with simple seeing. Indeed, in the first half of the twentieth century there were influential attempts to develop theoretical frameworks that would make it possible to 'build up' justified belief in complex statements from extremely simple observation reports (or '**protocol sentences**'). So, an empirical claim such as 'there is a parrot in a tree' (or a statement of a scientific law, such as Newton's laws of motion) was thought to be reducible to simple perceptual reports such as 'there is a red patch at a 45 degree angle in my visual field' (or, more succinctly, 'red here now'). The motivation for this ambitious project was derived from the thought that some perceptions were so simple that there could be no disagreement about them: anyone occupying the same spatiotemporal location and equipped with the same biologically hardwired perceptual apparatus would come to the same judgment.

From such perceptual reports it would then be possible to build up – through careful definitions that allow for the aggregation of individual experiences, in combination with the use of inductive logic – a more complex vocabulary, in which the *meaning of scientific concepts* could be stated. This philosophical project found its most radical expression in the work of the **logical empiricists**, who tried hard to eliminate any theoretical (= non-observational) scientific terms – in particular, any talk about unobservables or hidden structures – reducing them instead to observational facts. Following in the tradition of **empiricism** – that is, the school of thought according to which all knowledge is derived from sensory experience – the meaning of all scientific terms must ultimately reduce to simple observational statements.

Despite immense theoretical efforts, logical empiricism ultimately did not succeed in its positivist goal of reconstructing science in a 'neutral', purely observational language. Partly this was due to the complexity of the task: developing logical tools for aggregating experience to account for theoretical terms in science proved to be simply too formidable. Furthermore, the very thought that there could be such a thing as a neutral observation language came under attack, since, as Norwood Russell Hanson put it, 'there is more to seeing than meets the eyeball'. In the opening paragraph of his *Patterns of Discovery* (1958), Hanson considers the following example:

> Imagine Johannes Kepler on a hill watching the dawn. With him is Tycho Brahe. Kepler regarded the sun as fixed: it was the earth that moved. But Tycho followed Ptolemy and Aristotle in this much at least: the earth was fixed and all other celestial bodies moved around it. Do Kepler and Tycho see the same thing in the east at dawn?
>
> (Hanson 1958: 5)

Hanson's answer is 'no'. Assuming that there is nothing wrong with either Kepler's or Brahe's eyes, both will, of course, have the same physical image projected onto their retinas. But this does not mean that their perceptual *experiences* will be the same: we do not have direct access to what is projected onto our retina – only to what our complete visual and cognitive system generates on its basis. Nor, according to Hanson, would it be appropriate to attribute any difference in perceptual judgments to different *interpretations* of the same visual experience: 'One does not first soak up an optical pattern and then clamp an interpretation on it' (Hanson 1958: 9). Visual experiences, on this view, are not solely determined by the object, together with our biologically hardwired perceptual apparatus, but are also shaped by background knowledge, expectations, and the theoretical and conceptual framework with which we approach the world.

But if observation is *theory-laden* in this way, then the very idea of reducing scientific terms to a neutral observation language might seem ill-conceived. Whether **theory-ladenness** really does preclude the possibility of observation functioning as a 'neutral arbiter' of scientific claims has been the subject of much debate. What it suggests, though, is that scientific facts and theories cannot simply be pieced together from observed phenomena, but are themselves required for making sense of what we observe in the world.

• EXPLANATION AND PREDICTION

Science not only records observations and collects factual knowledge about the world, it also aims to identify recurring patterns and regularities, and tries to account for them in ways that further our understanding. Indeed, it is often regarded as the sign of a mature science that it does not content itself with giving a 'laundry list' of empirical findings, but is able to state principles, laws and regularities, along with their conditions of application, which explain observed phenomena as well as predict new ones.

What is an explanation? In ordinary usage, an explanation is simply an answer to a 'why' question. Asking questions about why things are the way they are and offering explanations – sometimes speculative ones – is part and parcel of human nature: we explain how others behave by making assumptions about their character, infer causes that would explain why the car broke down, and give historical explanations of war and conflict. When we are able to relate the event or phenomenon to be explained (the **explanandum**) to things we already know or assume to be true, in a way that makes the explanandum seem inevitable or predictable, we typically enjoy a sense of greater *understanding*. At a psychological level, then, explanation is intimately associated with a sense of familiarity: a successful explanation gives us understanding by rendering the explanandum familiar.

But we expect more from scientific explanations than merely a psychological feeling of familiarity – not least since we know how often our ordinary expectations, and our subjective sense of familiarity, turn out to be wrong or misplaced. Around the middle of the twentieth century, philosophical theories of scientific explanation coalesced around the project of accounting for explanations in logically grounded, non-psychological terms. This project was spelled out most clearly by the German-American philosopher Carl Gustav Hempel (1905–97) in a series of papers. Hempel's model of scientific explanation is known variously as the '**covering-law model**', '**deductive-nomological model**', or simply '**D-N model**'.

The basic idea of Hempel's model is that explanations typically take the logical form of an argument from premises that do the explanatory work (that is, from the **explanans**) to the **explanandum** as the conclusion that follows from the premises. Not just any set of premises and conclusions, however, will qualify as a *scientific explanation*, and much of the philosophical literature concerning the covering law model is devoted to characterising which conditions the premises and conclusions must satisfy, and what relations must hold between them.

Hempel sets out three main conditions. First, the premises should logically *entail* the conclusion: if the premises are true, then so is the conclusion. The connection between the explanans and the explanandum is thus characterised by deductive logic. Second, the premises must contain at least one statement of a *general law* of nature, where this nomological ('law-like') statement does some work in establishing the link between the explanandum and the explanans. In other words, the premises must *subsume* the explanandum under a *lawlike regularity* that covers the case at hand. (Exactly what constitutes a 'law of nature' is something we will discuss in the next chapter.)

These first two conditions make clear why the covering law model is also called the 'deductive-nomological' model: it combines the virtues of deductive logic – in particular, its indisputable truth-preserving nature – with the scientific impetus to explain particular phenomena as instances of general laws of nature. The third and final condition demands that *all* the premises be actually true: that is, the argument should not only be a *possible* explanation, but should, in fact, be an *actual* explanation of the explanandum. In short, Hempel's model of explanation portrays the phenomenon to be explained as the logically necessary outcome of general laws of nature as they apply to specific circumstances.

What the covering law model aims to give us is an account of the general structure of answers to 'explanation-seeking why questions': we are first confronted with a puzzling or surprising phenomenon and subsequently account for it in terms of general laws applied to specific circumstances. For example, when Henri Becquerel, in 1896, discovered that photographic plates in his laboratory had turned dark although they had not been exposed to light, he subsequently explained this by the presence of uranium salts near the plates and by the effects that radioactivity has on photosensitive materials. The circumstances that led him to this new discovery were simply an instance of a general law of nature, according to which radioactivity affects photographic plates in much the same way as exposure to light would.

However, there is nothing in the logical structure of covering law explanations that requires that the explanandum must be known first and that the explanatory premises are only filled in later. If the relevant general laws of nature are known, one should be able to apply them also to, for example, circumstances that one has newly brought about in order to predict what will happen then. Indeed, this is how Becquerel immediately proceeded, by testing the effect of shielding the photographic plates from the uranium salts using different materials (such as a sheet of glass, aluminium foil, paper, etc.). Whether one is dealing with an already existing phenomenon standing in need of explanation, or one is making a prediction about what will happen under new circumstances, in both cases the deductive-nomological structure of the covering law model remains untouched. Explanation (of already known phenomena) and prediction (of new phenomena), according to Hempel, are two sides of the same coin. This **structural identity thesis** may be put as follows: 'Every prediction is a potential explanation, and vice versa.'

The very features that made the covering law model attractive to Hempel and other mid-twentieth-century philosophers of science – its reliance on 'timeless' logical deduction and laws of nature – give rise to some counterintuitive consequences and counterexamples. The most famous case is the so-called *flagpole example*. Imagine measuring the shadow cast by a flagpole one morning, when the sun is at a 45-degree angle, and finding it to be 10m long. Why is the shadow 10m long? The answer is clear: because the flagpole itself is 10m in height and light travels in a straight line, given the sun's location at the time of measurement, the length of the flagpole's shadow must match its height. According to the covering law model, this is a perfectly acceptable scientific explanation since it explains a specific phenomenon (the length of the shadow) in terms of a general law ('light travels in a straight line') and specific conditions that accurately describe the case at hand (the location of the sun and the height of the flagpole).

However, a problem arises from the fact that the specifics of the case at hand – the lengths of the shadow and of the flagpole, respectively – are perfectly interchangeable: given how the case is described, we can equally deduce the height of the flagpole from the length of its shadow, in conjunction with the same laws of nature and other background conditions (e.g. the sun's being at a 45-degree angle). That is, by the lights of the covering law model, it would appear that we can *explain* the height of the flagpole by the length of its shadow. But what explains the height of the flagpole has nothing to do with the length of its shadow. Whatever height the flagpole has is explained by other factors – perhaps 10m is the standard height of flagpoles, or someone specifically ordered a 10m flagpole (as opposed to a more expensive 12m flagpole) – but not by the length of the shadow it happens to cast at a particular time of the day. By contrast, the length of the shadow is clearly explained by the height of the flagpole – not least because the shadow is *caused by* the flagpole (which blocks out the sunlight, thereby casting a shadow on the ground).

Incidentally, the flagpole example not only shows that more may be required for scientific explanation than merely subsuming a specific situation under a general covering law, but it also drives a wedge between explanation and prediction, thereby casting doubt on the structural identity thesis. For, even though one cannot use the length of the shadow to explain the height of the flagpole, in the case as described one can very well *predict* the height of the flagpole reliably. That is, not every prediction needs to be founded on genuinely explanatory relationships.

• PSEUDO-SCIENCE AND THE DEMARCATION PROBLEM

No exploration of the question 'What is science?' would be complete without a discussion of how one might distinguish between science and pseudo-science. This demarcation problem has enjoyed a mixed career in the philosophy of science and, every so often, surfaces in the public arena as well, for example in disputes about whether homeopathy should be treated on a par with evidence-based medicine or whether 'intelligent design' theory should be taught in schools alongside the synthetic theory of evolution.

Karl Popper, whom we encountered in the first section of this chapter, proposed **falsifiability** as a **demarcation criterion** for what constitutes a proper scientific claim. If a claim cannot, in principle, be refuted by empirical findings, it should not be deemed scientific. Indeed, the degree to which a theory is 'scientific' roughly corresponds to the extent to which it makes testable predictions: the more specific and unambiguous a theory's claims and predictions are, the more empirical content it has. A theory that was so vague that no imaginable sequence of events or observations could ever decisively refute it would not be a good theory: precisely because such a theory would be unable to discriminate between different courses of events, it would lack empirical content.

Popper's emphasis on prediction and testing goes against the grain of much of science's traditional emphasis on explanation and confirmation. Traditionally, the more instances and observations cohered with a scientific theory, the more trustworthy it was thought to be. Confirmation of a theory would gradually accrue over time, edging it ever closer to the goal of subjective certainty. Yet, as Popper realised, confirming evidence too often is merely in the eye of the beholder: if you are looking for evidence, you will always find it. This is especially true of theories that are so vague that they allow for the flexible reinterpretation of empirical findings.

In this regard, Popper singled out Freudian psychoanalytical theory, among others, as an example of a **pseudo-science**. Put crudely, when a Freudian psychoanalyst diagnoses a patient as suffering from an Oedipus complex, such a diagnosis would simply be unfalsifiable: if the patient agrees with his psychoanalyst's assessment, this would constitute obvious confirmation of the diagnosis, yet if he disagrees, it would be open to the psychoanalyst to interpret this denial as evidence of just how deep the patient's repression of his Oedipus complex runs. A good scientist, according to Popper, should not seek to 'immunise' his claims against empirical challenges in this way, but should focus on deriving testable predictions and should willingly give up his theory if it does not fit with empirical reality.

Just as Hempel tried to harness the 'truth-preserving' power of logical deduction to give an objective, 'non-psychological' model of explanation, Popper likewise emphasised the power of logical deduction. For Popper, however, the true significance of deductive reasoning lay in our ability to decisively refute premises if the conclusion of an otherwise valid deductive argument is found to be false. As long as a theory's testable predictions are supported by our observations, we have no reason to reject it; yet it only takes one conclusive counterexample to, once and for all, refute a theory – or so the falsifiability criterion would have us believe.

Challenges to falsifiability as a demarcation criterion between science and pseudo-science arise from the history of science as well as from actual scientific practice. History of science is replete with examples of apparent mismatches between theory and empirical data that later turned out to be entirely benign. For example, for much of the nineteenth century astronomers were puzzled by the orbit of Uranus, which consistently differed from the predictions of Newton's gravitational theory as applied to the planets. Yet, rather than considering Newton's theory falsified by the observed mismatch with the empirical data, in 1845 the astronomers Urbain Le Verrier in Paris and John Couch Adams in Cambridge independently posited the existence of an – as yet undiscovered – planet that was thought to be responsible for the deviations in the orbit of Uranus. Shortly afterwards, the planet Neptune was discovered. (Interestingly, the deviations in the orbit of another planet – Mercury – proved to be resistant to explanation in Newtonian terms and could only be explained later by Einstein's general relativity theory.)

In actual scientific practice, scientists often devote considerable time to defending their favourite theories, rather than hastily giving them up at the first sign of an empirical mismatch. This need not be unscientific. Whether or not continued adherence to a theory is rational or irrational, scientific or unscientific, is less a matter of a 'one-size-fits-all' demarcation criterion, and more a matter of the spirit and manner in which the defence of any given theory is mounted.

• CHAPTER SUMMARY

- Philosophers of science tend to ask general questions about science, understood both as a set of scientific theories and as a collective human endeavour. Such general questions include, but are not limited to: *What is science? What characterises a scientific explanation? How can we distinguish between science and pseudo-science?*

- Philosophy of science has both a descriptive and a normative dimension. A descriptive approach seeks to characterise the way science is actually being done and to explain how it has developed historically. A normative approach aims to improve science, for example by developing suggestions about how scientists *ought to* conduct themselves in their investigations of nature.

- The scientific image of the world – that is, the most accurate description of the world science provides us with – may come into conflict with the manifest image of our shared everyday experience. For example, science often explains phenomena in terms of unobservables and hidden mechanisms, which are not part of our everyday experience.

- The gap between what science tells us about the world and what is directly given to us in sensory experience raises the important question of how science is to be grounded in observation.

- Logical positivists argued that scientific terms and concepts had meaning only insofar as they could be reduced to observational facts.

- There is more to observation than meets the eyeball. In particular, it has been suggested that observation is *theory-laden*: what we observe is itself a function of our background knowledge and the acquired concepts we bring to bear on the world.

- One of the central goals of science is to provide explanations of various phenomena. According to the covering law (or deductive-nomological) model, for a scientific explanation to be successful, it must be able to subsume the phenomenon to be explained (the explanandum) under an overarching ('covering') law of nature, by spelling out the specific circumstances in which the law deductively entails the explanandum.

- In a number of cases (including the famous 'flagpole example'), the covering law model is unable to account for important asymmetries that characterise scientific explanations. Thus, while the height of the flagpole (in conjunction with relevant circumstances, such as the position of the sun) explains the length of its shadow, the converse is not true. Alternative models, such as causal accounts of explanation, have been proposed in response to the shortcomings of the covering law model.

- Philosophers of science have repeatedly attempted to find ways of demarcating science from pseudo-science. Karl Popper proposed falsifiability as a demarcation criterion: in order for a theory to count as scientific it must at least be potentially falsifiable by empirical results. According to falsificationism, a theory or hypothesis that cannot, as a matter of principle, be refuted by empirical findings should be deemed unscientific.

• STUDY QUESTIONS

1 Should philosophers of science aim to give an accurate description of actual scientific practice, or should they make normative recommendations on how to improve science?
2 Can conflicts between the manifest image and the scientific image be resolved? If so, how?
3 Is the covering law model of scientific explanation more appropriate for some scientific disciplines than for others?
4 Can explanation and prediction come apart in other ways than the ones discussed above?
5 Are there questions that science cannot, as a matter of principle, answer? Are such questions necessarily pseudo-questions?

• INTRODUCTORY FURTHER READING

Barker, Gillian and Philip Kitcher (2014) *Philosophy of Science: A New Introduction* (New York: Oxford University Press). [This is a readable and engaging survey of the philosophical discussion about the sciences and their place in society.]

Hacking, Ian (1983) *Representing and Intervening: Introductory Topics in the Philosophy of Natural Science* (Cambridge: Cambridge University Press). [A stylishly written and very readable introduction to selected topics in the philosophy of science, written by one of the most influential contemporary philosophers of science.]

Rosenberg, Alex (2012) *Philosophy of Science: A Contemporary Introduction* (London: Routledge). [This is a comprehensive and systematic introduction, which covers all the major issues in contemporary philosophy of science.]

• ADVANCED FURTHER READING

Hanson, Norwood Russell (1958) *Patterns of Discovery: An Inquiry into the Conceptual Foundations of Science* (Cambridge: Cambridge University Press). [A classic discussion of the problem of theory-ladenness of observation.]

Hempel, Carl (1970) *Aspects of Scientific Explanation (And Other Essays in the Philosophy of Science)* (New York: Free Press). [Contains Hempel's papers on the deductive-nomological model of explanation, and other classic papers that give a flavour of mid-twentieth-century philosophy of science in the logical empiricist tradition.]

Longino, Helen (2001) *The Fate of Knowledge* (Princeton: Princeton University Press). [This book attempts to bridge the gap between descriptive science studies and more traditional philosophy of science, and seeks to overcome many of the dichotomies that arise from the perceived antagonism between rational and social factors in science.]

Popper, Karl (1963) *Conjectures and Refutations: The Growth of Scientific Knowledge* (London: Routledge). [A collection of papers that summarises Popper's views on such issues as the demarcation between science and non-science, the role of falsifiability, and the growth of knowledge.]

Strevens, Michael (2011) *Depth: An Account of Scientific Explanation* (Cambridge, MA: Harvard University Press). [At 536 pages and 1.8 pounds, this book does not lend itself to bed-time reading; however, it provides a thorough and original up-to-date discussion of scientific explanation in all its facets.]

• FREE INTERNET RESOURCES

Hansson, Sven Ove (2014) 'Science and Pseudo-Science', *Stanford Encyclopedia of Philosophy*, http://plato.stanford.edu/entries/pseudo-science/. [An up-to-date overview of the debate about how to distinguish between science and pseudo-science, including comments on the unity and/or disunity of science.]

Research Topics and Readings in History and Philosophy of Science (University of Cambridge), http://www.hps.cam.ac.uk/research/. [Intended as a research guide for advanced undergraduates, this website contains useful annotated bibliographies on many issues in the history and philosophy of science.]

21

can we trust scientific models?

- Theories and laws of nature
- Abstraction, idealisation, and laws
- What is a scientific model?
- Complexity and convergence: the case of climate models
- Science and certainty

THEORIES AND LAWS OF NATURE

It is one of the oddities of how the public views science that the term 'theory', in ordinary usage, is often taken to refer to speculative hypotheses, for which there is as yet little evidence. This usage is starkly at odds with how scientists understand the term 'theory'. In science, to call something a 'theory' is essentially to elevate it to the status of an *integrated body of explanatory hypotheses*, which are capable of unifying disparate phenomena and which typically enjoy considerable empirical support. Whole subdisciplines, consisting of successful and cohesive research programmes, are thus designated 'theories' – think of 'quantum theory' in physics, 'game theory' in behavioural economics, or the 'synthetic theory of evolution' in biology. (This is why the epithet 'That's just a theory!' – as applied to, say, the systematic study of the fact of biological evolution – is usually a dead give-away of the lack of understanding on the part of those who utter it.)

What exactly do we mean when we say that a theory is an 'integrated' body of explanatory hypotheses? 'Integration' obviously requires more than merely giving a 'laundry list' of hypotheses, but we need to be more specific about what level of integration is required and how it is to be achieved. One prominent position has been that science should take a leaf out of the book of mathematics (no doubt inspired by the historically influential view that the 'Book of Nature' is itself written in mathematics!). More specifically, scientific theories should aim for **axiomatisation** – in the same way that the whole of Euclidean geometry can be derived from a small set of foundational axioms that are simply stipulated to be true. On this account, scientific theories are integrated systems of explanatory hypotheses, with logical deduction as their central organising principle.

There is a direct parallel between this way of thinking about scientific theories and the **deductive-nomological** (or *covering law*) model of explanation we encountered in the previous chapter. Recall that, according to the **D-N** model, a scientific explanation is successful if it derives the phenomenon to be explained (the explanandum) from premises that describe the case at hand and include at least one general statement of a law of nature. It is only natural, then, to generalise this overall picture of explanatory inferences to scientific theories as well. According to what has come to be called **hypothetico-deductivism**, scientific theories consist of sets of hypotheses, from which testable predictions are derived through logical deduction, which are then checked by comparison with observable facts. Relevant observations may either be gathered through data collection in a natural setting (as an ecologist might when he documents occurrences of different populations in their natural habitat) or may be brought about through active experimentation (e.g. when a team of physicists fires up a particle accelerator to bring into existence short-lived elementary particles, which are then recorded by various measurement instruments).

However, whereas in mathematics we are free to explore seemingly arbitrary systems (e.g. various different geometries, topologies, or higher-dimensional spaces), in science we cannot simply stipulate a set of axioms and see which consequences we can logically derive from them. This raises the question of which sort of statements should take the place of axioms in science. Again, the parallel between hypothetico-deductivism and the deductive-nomological model of explanation offers some guidance. Given the important role that laws of nature appear to play in (many) scientific explanations, it seems reasonable to also assign them a central place in any axiomatisation of scientific theories.

But what is a law of nature? There is considerable philosophical agreement about *some* features of laws of nature. For example, as far as their logical form is concerned, laws are universal statements of the sort 'All As are Bs' or 'Whenever conditions of type C obtain, an event of type D occurs'. A good example of this logical form would be Newton's *law of gravitation*: 'All massive objects attract each other with a force that is proportional to the objects' masses and inversely proportional to the square of the distance between them.' Furthermore, laws of nature do not refer to particular objects; that is, they refer to *all* objects of a particular *kind*, not to selected individuals. (A question, however, arises for laws in such disciplines as biology: such laws – if indeed they exist – would arguably apply only to life *as it has evolved on Earth*; that is, they might not be truly universal – evolution of life on other planets might have 'locked in' laws of biological inheritance or population dynamics different from ours.)

But not all true universal statements are laws of nature. Consider the statement 'All bachelors are unmarried'. Although true, this does not tell us anything lawlike about a particular sort of object in the world – that is, *bachelors* – but simply reports the conventional meaning of the term 'bachelor'. Thus, more is required to render a universal statement a law of nature. This requirement is often framed in terms of *necessity*. Contrast, for example, the following true statements:

1 All solid spheres of pure gold have a diameter of less than a thousand miles.
2 All solid spheres of pure plutonium have a diameter of less than a thousand miles.

There is every reason to believe that both statements are true; that is, nowhere in the universe do we find a perfect sphere with a diameter of a thousand miles or more, made entirely of pure gold or plutonium. But whereas (1) is true by accident – simply because nothing in the actual history of the universe led to the formation of a gigantic sphere made entirely of gold – (2) is true as a matter of necessity: long before one could assemble a sphere of plutonium that size, a chain reaction would be triggered, making it impossible to complete one's project. (No such restriction would apply to assembling a gigantic sphere of gold.) In this sense, the laws of physics *prevent* the assembly of a gigantic sphere of plutonium: they are what makes it true that, nowhere in the universe, at any point in time, could there exist a gigantic sphere of plutonium. Whereas (1) is true by cosmic coincidence, (2) is true as a matter of **nomic necessity**: in this universe, given the laws of physics, *it could not have been different*.

• ABSTRACTION, IDEALISATION, AND LAWS

As an example of a scientific theory, let us consider Newtonian mechanics, which – although now known to be at best an approximation of the truth about physics – marks one of the most significant historical steps forward in Western science's understanding of nature. In line with our discussion above, Newtonian mechanics conforms well to the goal of providing an integrated set of explanatory hypotheses, with proposed laws of nature taking the place of axioms. The laws in question are, of course, Newton's three *laws of motion* and the already mentioned law of gravitation.

Newton's *first law* restates Galileo's principle of inertia and, in the English translation of the Latin original of Newton's *Principia*, reads as follows: 'Law I. Every body persists in its state of being at rest or of moving uniformly straight forward, except insofar as it is compelled to change its state by force impressed.' The *second law* amounts to the definition of a force F acting on a body, which it defines as the product of the body's mass and its acceleration: $F = ma$. The *third law* of motion is the famous statement that 'for every action, there is an equal and opposite reaction'; or, as Newton explains by way of example: 'If you press a stone with your finger, the finger is also pressed by the stone.' The idea is not that forces acting on the same body always cancel out, but rather that action and reaction forces come in pairs.

Whereas Newton used the third law of motion to derive the principle of *conservation of momentum*, modern formulations of mechanics take the conservation of momentum to be the more fundamental idea (since it can be seen as the flip side of the fact that physical processes are symmetric under continuous translations in space). This goes to show that there is some leeway in the axiomatisation of one's scientific theories, such as classical mechanics.

At the same time, Newton's laws of motion nicely illustrate that science is not just, as we discussed in the previous chapter, 'common sense writ large'. After all, common sense seems to tell us that, if we wish to keep an object moving at constant speed in a straight line, we need to apply a constant force: we know from everyday experience that, once we cease to apply a force, any moving object will soon come to a halt. (Indeed, *Aristotelian physics* had assumed that objects would return to their 'natural place', once they ceased to be under the influence of external forces.) Yet Newton tells us that this is a mistaken conception of force and motion. If, in everyday experience, a force is necessary to sustain an object's linear movement, then this is only because of the presence of friction, which must be compensated for. Without the presence of friction, the continuous application of force would gradually *accelerate* the object more and more.

So far we have focused on Newton's three laws of motion which were thought to govern all mechanical motion. Let us now add the (already mentioned) law of gravitation to the discussion and look at how this changes our overall conception of Newtonian physics. Recall that the law of gravitation states that any two massive objects attract each other with a force that is proportional to each object's mass and inversely proportional to the square of the distance between them. If this is so, one might very well wonder whether Newton's first law – which describes what happens if an object is not subject to any force – applies *anywhere* in the world. But even if Newton's first law was found to have no 'pure' instances anywhere in the world, it can still be regarded as expressing an important *counterfactual* about the world: namely that, *if* an object was not subject to any external forces, *then*, with nomic necessity, it would remain in its state of being at rest or of uniformly moving in a straight line.

The presence of various massive objects, all interacting with each other, raises other problems for the practical application of Newton's laws to real systems. As an example, consider the project of calculating the orbit of a particular planet in the solar system, say the orbit of the Earth around the Sun. Calculating the Earth's orbit would be unproblematic if only the Earth and the Sun existed. But, of course, the Earth is accompanied by the Moon, which exerts an additional gravitational force, and there are many other celestial objects, such as the other planets, different comets, asteroids and clouds of dust – not to mention the rest of the galaxy and, indeed, the universe. A full **representation** of the solar system – that is, a complete description of every object in it, along with the forces each exerts and is subject to, according to Newtonian physics – would involve an enormous number of equations, which it would be impossible to solve, whether analytically ('with pencil and paper', so to speak) or numerically (e.g. with a supercomputer).

And yet, we do not seem to run into any major problems when it comes to calculating the Earth's orbit around the sun – or that of any other planet – to a high degree of accuracy. Indeed, as mentioned earlier, calculations of the orbits of planets were so accurate that, by the middle of the nineteenth century, it was possible to predict new planets on the basis of slight deviations in the orbits of other planets. How is that possible? The key strategy is one of *simplifying* our mathematical representation of the system we are dealing with, in this case the solar system. Clearly, not all objects in the solar system are equally important. The gravitational influence of distant planets on the Earth's orbit, let alone that of small comets and meteorites, is simply negligible. And in the centre of the solar system sits a massive object, the Sun, whose gravitational force on any one planet dwarfs that of all the other objects in the solar system combined.

Recognising that not all elements of a physical system need to be considered, and that the interactions between the remaining elements can be simplified – for example because some forces are negligible as compared with others (as in the case of gravitational forces *between* planets versus the gravitational pull exerted by the Sun on *each* planet) – is an important step in constructing a manageable representation, which may then be considered in place of the full description of the real system. Scientists routinely use *abstraction* and *idealisation* to achieve just the right level of simplification. While there is some debate about whether abstraction and idealisation are methodologically different, or whether they are essentially two sides of the same coin, on a first approximation one may think of abstraction as leaving out detail – that is, dropping certain elements (e.g. meteorites, comets, and other smaller physical objects) from our representation of the real system – while idealisation injects some (hopefully negligible) distortion into the relations between what remains in our representation of the real system. For example, we might idealise gravitational interactions in the solar system by assuming that, even if we include the sun and all the planets, what really needs to be considered is only the gravitational force exerted by the sun on each planet. This greatly simplifies the applications of the laws of motion, which are now applied in a more restricted way, not to a full representation of the solar system with all its ingredients, but to a *model* of it that was generated by stripping away unnecessary detail and distorting (within limits) some of the relations that hold between the remaining elements.

• WHAT IS A SCIENTIFIC MODEL?

Our account of theories over the past two sections was heavily indebted to what we called hypothetico-deductivism: the idea that theories are sets of explanatory hypotheses, some of which are *assumed* to be true – much like axioms would be in other formalised deductive systems – and from which *observable consequences* must be derived, which are then compared with empirical data. Axiomatisation is a powerful guiding principle for making sense of how scientific theories achieve the degree of integration and unification that they exhibit; at the same time, however, axiomatisation is not something many scientists care about when they devise new scientific theories.

This mismatch – between what philosophers have thought scientific theories are like, and what scientists care about when they engage in theorising – need not be a problem *per se*. We've already seen in the previous chapter that, in order to get a better understanding of science, it may sometimes be necessary to give a *philosophically informed reconstruction* of science, rather than take at face value the self-image of scientists. However, to the extent that we do not want philosophy of science to 'operate in a vacuum', so to speak, but instead want it to map on to actual scientific practice, the mismatch forces us to recognise that not all scientific activity can be described in the terms outlined in the previous discussion of scientific theories.

Much scientific activity is devoted not to creating cleaned-up axiomatised scientific theories – though where this is possible, as in Newtonian mechanics, it is often considered a great scientific success! – but to gaining understanding of a limited segment of reality through the use of **scientific models**. In science education, we often gradually introduce more complex material, such as the quantum physics of the atom, via simpler models, such as Rutherford's and Bohr's models of the atom. But these were themselves at the time important advances in our understanding of nature, and many scientific disciplines – especially those which, like biology or psychology, deal with complex systems that do not lend themselves to 'cleaned-up' theories with universal laws of nature at their heart – continue to deal with models and modelling as their *primary* objects of study.

What, in general, is a 'scientific model'? This is not an easy question to answer. At the time when hypothetico-deductivism and the deductive-nomological account of scientific explanation reigned supreme, philosophers of science understood the term 'model' in the way logicians and mathematicians did: as an interpretation of an axiomatic system, such that all the theorems of the system automatically turn out true. But this is not how scientists typically use the term 'model'. An alternative picture is suggested by our discussion above. There we saw how one can construct a Newtonian model of the solar system by simply positing that the only relevant objects – that is, the only ones that exert gravitational forces on each other – are the planets and the Sun (or, even more simplistically, *each* planet and the Sun).

In reality, of course, there is no such thing as a solar system consisting only of the planets and the Sun – as we saw, this deliberate simplification is only achieved by ignoring smaller bodies like comets, moons, and other factors such as friction or electromagnetic fields. But, by resolving to treat the simplified system as a (fictional) 'stand-in' for the real system, we have nonetheless arrived at a model of the solar system. This model is no longer an 'interpretation' of the full theoretical description, but exhibits an eliminably *constructive* element – that is, certain choices about what is, and isn't, important, which are not imposed on us by any intratheoretical concerns.

This picture of scientific models becomes even more complex (or, as detractors might put it, even murkier) if one considers that scientific models not only include theoretical representations – e.g. sets of equations or fictional objects such as Newtonian 'point masses' – but also include material models (such as ball-and-stick models of chemical molecules), scale models (which are commonly used in engineering), substitute models (in areas where there is no developed theory available), and many others. This has led many recent philosophers of science to favour an account of scientific models that acknowledges their partial independence from both theory and data, as well as their heterogeneous nature, which may encompass elements from various domains; thus understood, models are whatever it takes to 'mediate between' the realm of fundamental theory and the phenomena we encounter in the world.

• COMPLEXITY AND CONVERGENCE: THE CASE OF CLIMATE MODELS

In early 2010, volcanic ash from the eruption of the Icelandic volcano Eyjafjallajökull paralysed air traffic across much of Europe. In response, an angry airline CEO, in an interview with the BBC, blamed civil aviation authorities for relying on 'mere models' in making their decision to close airspace. While the CEO's frustration may have been understandable from a business point of view (and may have even been rhetorically effective), from a scientific point this was a rather disingenuous thing to say. After all, modern aircraft, too, are engineered and designed on the basis of models, and the underlying scientific theories of air flow and turbulence are not all that different, whether one wants to predict the distribution of volcanic ash or its effects on jet engines.

The fact of the matter is that, when dealing with complex scientific problems, we are ineliminably dependent on the use of scientific models. The question is how to assess scientific models and their predictions in the absence of complete knowledge of what a solution to the 'full' (that is, non-simplified) problem would look like.

Consider a complex scientific problem such as global climate change. As most people are aware, the Earth's atmosphere, because of the presence of greenhouse gases such as carbon dioxide, stores energy and heat. While this is what makes life on Earth possible in the first place, the accumulation of greenhouse gases through the burning of fossil fuels means that gradually more and more energy is being retained – which, according to basic physics, must manifest itself in changes to the Earth's climate system. Different manifestations of this phenomenon are possible: added energy might lead to a (not necessarily evenly distributed) rise in surface or ocean temperatures, to changes in the air and water currents, to 'kinetic' events such as storms and hurricanes, or to a host of other irreversible effects (such as melting of ice sheets, glaciers, etc.), or any combination of the aforementioned effects. One thing that will not happen, however, is that, as more energy accumulates in the Earth's climate system, everything will stay as it was.

This much can be known simply on the basis of elementary thermodynamics.But while the basic mechanism of the anthropogenic contribution to the greenhouse effect has been well understood for some time (see text box 'History of the greenhouse effect'), the devil is in the details. The Earth is a complex system, and while predictions of *average* temperature rises are scientifically interesting, specific consequences – such as heat waves or droughts – are often *local* and cannot simply be deduced from the basic laws of the thermodynamics of the Earth's atmosphere. This is where the use of numerical climate models is not only important, but ineliminable. If one is interested in specific predictions about what will happen in different parts of a complex system, there is simply no other way than by using models and computer simulations.

BOX 21.1 HISTORY OF THE GREENHOUSE EFFECT

The basic mechanism of the Earth's greenhouse effect has been known since at least the second half of the nineteenth century. The Swedish scientist Svante Arrhenius (1859–1927) already calculated that a doubling of the CO_2 concentration would lead to an average temperature rise of around 5 degrees Celsius – which is not very different from contemporary predictions of global average temperature rises. By the middle of the twentieth century, awareness of the prospect of anthropogenic (i.e. man-made) climate change was spreading and was widely reported in popular science magazines. Indeed, in 1965, U.S. President Lyndon B. Johnson deemed it necessary to make a Special Address to the United States Congress, in which he declared: 'This generation has altered the composition of the atmosphere on a global scale through […] a steady increase in carbon dioxide from the burning of fossil fuels.' (It might seem ironic, given the ongoing political stalemate on how to deal with climate change, that fifty years ago a U.S. President correctly reported the nascent scientific consensus on the reality of global climate change!)

What makes modelling the climate so difficult is the coexistence of competing processes, which operate at different scales and which trade off against each other. For example, rising temperatures increase evaporation, which increases the presence of water vapour, which in turn is itself a potent greenhouse gas. But once water vapour condenses to form clouds, this increases the albedo of the planet: clouds reflect sunlight back into space before it can heat up the planet. These two processes pull in different directions, simultaneously increasing and reducing the greenhouse effect. Clouds, of course, are highly localised phenomena, and modelling the exact distribution of clouds under changing conditions is a nigh-impossible task.

And yet, climate models have shown vast improvements over the last couple of decades, not least because of the massive increase in computing power. Generally speaking, climate models consist of a set of equations that are discretised on a grid (which represents the atmosphere) and are evaluated numerically on supercomputers.

While some equations are derived from first principles (such as the laws governing fluid dynamics, similar to Newton's laws of motion), other processes – such as changes in global forest cover and other environmental responses – need to be parameterised. What one finds, as a result, is a spectrum of different coexisting models, ranging from simple energy-balance models (how much sunlight goes in, how much energy is reflected back into space?) to general circulation models (GCMs), which take into account the coupling between the atmosphere and the oceans and, in some cases, geochemical processes.

One might worry that this diversity of factors – each of which introduces uncertainties and error margins into one's model – precludes the possibility of successfully modelling something as complex as the Earth's climate and renders any meaningful comparison between the various models impossible. But this overlooks the fact that there are numerous ways in which climate models can be confirmed. For example, models can be tested with different data sets: if a model is able to reproduce past observed climate phenomena and to track current developments, this should boost our trust in the model's explanatory and predictive value. Furthermore, if different types of models – each with its own, independent methodological starting point (e.g. energy-balance models versus GCMs) – converge on the same answers (e.g., regarding the increase in mean surface temperature that would be expected from a doubling of carbon dioxide concentrations), such convergence is good evidence that the models are capturing a real underlying phenomenon. Finally, independent empirical evidence may support individual aspects of specific models. For example, reconstructions of past temperatures, based on observations of biological data (such as ancient tree rings, pollen or coral samples), cohere well with ice core records extracted from glaciers, and such data may be used to independently test and calibrate climate models.

• SCIENCE AND CERTAINTY

When dealing with complex systems, there is a temptation to demand higher standards of evidence and proof than in simpler situations of which we – often wrongly – think we have a better intuitive grasp. Nobody wants to jump to conclusions when circumstances are murky. But what may sound like a sensible strategy for reasoning under conditions of uncertainty, may turn out to be irresponsible if one's demands for certainty exceed what is reasonable, all things considered.

When it comes to the predictions of climate science, one sometimes hears dismissive voices saying that 'As long as scientists cannot accurately predict the weather, we cannot trust their claims concerning climate change'. But this confuses apples and oranges. Climate is an *aggregate* phenomenon, which represents long-term averages of temperature and precipitation across a region in space; weather, by comparison, is a highly localised phenomenon and, more often than not, is experienced differently by different people. (Consider what different people might consider 'a fine day'!)

Saying that we should not trust climate models until the day when scientists can accurately predict whether there will be a shower in my neighbourhood tomorrow is like saying that we should not trust forecasts of economic growth until economists can accurately predict which type of car I will buy next.

Unreasonable expectations of certainty in an uncertain world may be naïve, but they become outright irresponsible when individuals begin to value their fallible and anecdotal first-hand experience more highly than the cumulative expertise of the scientific community. Who hasn't come across mocking remarks to the effect that 'If there is global warming, how come it snowed so much last December?'. (Never mind that increased snowfall at higher latitudes may well be the result of increased evaporation, caused by higher temperatures, at lower latitudes.) What such remarks convey is a mistaken – indeed arrogant – misconception of the role of first-hand experience in coming to conclusions about the world. While science must ultimately be grounded in careful observation of nature, this does not license privileging one's own subjective (and often biased) first-hand experience over the aggregate data collected using properly calibrated measurement instruments and subsequently analysed using models and theories which, though fallible, are based on a sophisticated understanding of the fundamental causal processes that govern the world around us.

• CHAPTER SUMMARY

- The term 'theory', in science, is used to refer to an integrated body of explanatory hypotheses, which are capable of unifying disparate phenomena and which typically enjoy considerable empirical support.
- Hypothetico-deductivism conceives of scientific theories as sets of hypotheses, from which testable predictions are derived through logical deduction, which are then tested by comparison with observable facts.
- Laws of nature typically occupy a central place in scientific theories and may even be accorded a status similar to that of axioms in mathematical theories.
- Laws of nature are often thought to differ from mere universal generalisations in that they have nomic necessity. Thus, while it may well be true that nowhere in the universe do we find a solid sphere of pure gold with a diameter of a thousand miles or more, this is purely a matter of cosmic coincidence and could have been otherwise. By contrast, the claim that nowhere in the universe is there a solid sphere of pure plutonium with a diameter of a thousand miles or more is true as a matter of lawlike necessity: long before we could have assembled such a sphere it would have triggered a nuclear chain reaction, preventing us from completing our project.
- Many scientific problems are too complex to be solved directly using our best available scientific theories. In such cases, it is necessary to simplify the problem by using abstraction and idealisation in order to construct more manageable representations of the 'full' system.

- Scientific models include mathematical models, toy models, scale models, material models, substitute models, and representations using other formats and media. On a narrower definition – which, however, is at odds with how the term is used in science – a model is an interpretation of an axiomatic system, such that all the theorems of the system automatically turn out to be true.
- When it comes to the study of complex systems such as the Earth's climate, the use of scientific models and computer simulations is unavoidable. Such models may be assessed in terms of empirical fit, predictive and explanatory value, and utility for specific (e.g. policy-relevant) purposes.
- Beyond the predictive and explanatory successes of individual models, convergence between different models can be a good indicator that we are capturing a real underlying phenomenon.

• STUDY QUESTIONS

1 Why do you think there is a mismatch between the way the term 'theory' is used in everyday language and the (much more positive) meaning it has in science?
2 Is axiomatisation an important or legitimate goal in scientific theorising?
3 Do all scientific theories need to contain statements of laws of nature?
4 Could the laws of nature have been different?
5 Can we think of scientific models as applications, or limiting cases, of scientific theories?
6 What is more important in assessing scientific models: empirical fit or convergence between different models of the same phenomenon?

• INTRODUCTORY FURTHER READING

Hesse, Mary (1966) *Models and Analogies in Science* (Notre Dame: Notre Dame University Press). [This is a widely cited and accessible introduction to the role of models in physics. Although the philosophical debate has since moved on, the book still rewards the reader with insight and much food for thought.]

Klee, Robert (1996) *Introduction to the Philosophy of Science: Cutting Nature at Its Seams* (New York: Oxford University Press). [This is an introductory textbook which devotes significant space to the discussion of scientific theories; unlike most textbooks in the philosophy of science, it focuses on examples from outside physics, in particular biology.]

• ADVANCED FURTHER READING

Bailer-Jones, Daniela (2013) *Scientific Models in Philosophy of Science* (Pittsburgh: University of Pittsburgh Press). [A comprehensive discussion of how models have been used and interpreted in both historical and contemporary contexts.]

Cartwright, Nancy (1983) *How the Laws of Physics Lie* (Oxford: Oxford University Press). [The author argues that the allegedly 'deepest' fundamental laws of modern physics do not, in fact, describe the very real regularities that exist in nature.]

Edwards, Paul N. (2010) *A Vast Machine: Computer Models, Climate Data, and the Politics of Global Warming* (Cambridge, MA: The MIT Press). [A thorough account of the science behind climate models, written by a historian of science and technology.]

Lange, Marc (2007) *Natural Laws in Scientific Practice* (New York: Oxford University Press). [A thorough investigation of the character and place of natural laws in the sciences.]

Morgan, Mary S. and Margaret Morrison (1999) *Models as Mediators: Perspectives on Natural and Social Science* (Cambridge: Cambridge University Press). [An influential collection of case studies which significantly broadened the philosophical understanding of scientific models.]

Nagel, Ernest (1979) *The Structure of Science: Problems in the Logic of Scientific Explanation* (Indianapolis: Hackett). [First published in 1961, this magisterial work conveys a flavour of mid-twentieth-century philosophy of science, with its unabashedly ahistorical, prescriptive outlook.]

• FREE INTERNET RESOURCES

Frigg, Roman (2012) 'Models in Science', *Stanford Encyclopedia of Philosophy*, http://plato.stanford.edu/entries/pseudo-science/. [An introductory survey of the philosophical debate about scientific models, which points out various connections with other areas in philosophy.]

PhilSci Archive: Models and Idealization (University of Pittsburgh), http://philsci-archive.pitt.edu/view/subjects/models-and-idealization.html. [Lists numerous freely downloadable papers on the philosophy of scientific models, thereby conveying a good sense of the diversity of scientific models and philosophical approaches.]

22

is science getting closer to the truth?

- Realism, instrumentalism, and the question of truth
- Underdetermination and the no-miracles argument
- The challenge from scientific revolutions
- What scientific progress might be

● REALISM, INSTRUMENTALISM, AND THE QUESTION OF TRUTH

A central metaphysical debate among the scholastic philosophers of the Middle Ages concerned the question of whether *universals* exist: general characteristics or qualities that were instantiated by particular things. While *realists* held that universals had an independent existence over and above their particular instantiations, *nominalists* argued that universals were nothing more than 'names' that we give a group of similar things. William of Ockham (*c.* 1287–1347), the originator of the principle of *Occam's razor* – that 'entities must not be multiplied beyond necessity' (in other words, that we should, all else being equal, prefer the simplest hypothesis in our explanations) – expressed the nominalist position forcefully when he argued that 'no universal, unless perhaps it is universal by a voluntary agreement, is something existing outside the soul in any way'.

The realist question of what exists independent of the human mind and social convention also arises in the context of science. The question of **scientific realism**, however, no longer concerns the existence of universals per se, but instead asks whether the world, as studied by science, really exists and whether it has its properties independently of our beliefs about it. Scientific realists answer this question affirmatively: there is a world out there, beyond what is given to us in sensory experience, and this world contains many properties and entities – including unobservables – which science is in a position to tell us about. Scientific realists, of course, do not claim that everything science tells us is always true. They acknowledge that scientific knowledge is fallible and that, historically, there have been many scientific theories that were once believed to be true, but later found to be false. Yet, in addition to the thought that scientific claims are about the world as it is independently of us, scientific realists typically also endorse a *historical thesis* about science: namely, that science is gradually moving closer to a true account of what the world around us is really like.

Scientific realism contrasts with **instrumentalism**, which holds that science is an instrument for the prediction and explanation of phenomena *rather than* a way of approximating objective reality. Thus understood, instrumentalism expresses less a commitment to the usefulness of science in practical contexts, than an anti-realist sentiment. Science, according to the instrumentalist, is something we help ourselves to, in a purely auxiliary way, when trying to make sense of the world around us; however, in doing so, we need not endorse as true the various claims science makes about unobservable entities, hidden mechanisms, and causal processes. Instrumentalism, thus, is a more intellectually cautious – or, as realist critics might say: timid – position than scientific realism, given that it withholds belief in many instances where the realist would take the claims of science 'at face value'.

Scientific realism is usually seen as entailing a thesis about the convergence of science upon a true account of the world. According to such *convergent realism*, scientific theories are offered as approximations to the truth and – in the long run, in successful cases – will converge upon correspondence with the facts. On this account, science is making progress if a new scientific theory is closer to the truth than its predecessor. But this immediately raises a puzzle: given that truth is an 'all or nothing' affair, how can a false scientific theory be 'closer' to the truth than another? Can there be such a thing as 'approximate truth', and what does it take for a (false) scientific theory – such as Newtonian mechanics, which has been superseded by Einstein's relativity theory – to nonetheless count as 'approximately true' (for example at low energies and low velocities)?

One of the first philosophers to systematically explore the notion of 'approximate truth' was Popper, whom we encountered earlier (see chapter 20) as a proponent of falsifiability as a criterion for demarcating science from pseudo-science. In his early work, in line with the idea of falsificationism, Popper held that the only kind of progress scientific inquiry can hope for is the falsification of a theory or hypothesis. However, in his later work Popper acknowledged that some false theories may nonetheless realise the goal of truth more effectively than other (also false) theories. To be clear: even if neither of two theories A and B is true *as a whole*, it may be the case that one theory exhibits greater *verisimilitude* (truth-likeness) than the other. Verisimilitude was defined by Popper as follows:

Theory A has greater verisimilitude than theory B if and only if

(1) all the true consequences of B are true consequences of A,
(2) all the false consequences of A are consequences of B,
and (3) either some consequences of A are true that are not consequences of B,
or some consequences of B are false that are not consequences of A.

Crudely speaking, verisimilitude requires us to 'count', and compare, the various true and false consequences of two theories: that theory which has more true (and fewer false) consequences than its competitor is then deemed more 'truth-like'. Unfortunately, it turns out to be exceedingly difficult to develop a workable framework for comparing degrees of verisimilitude. Critics of Popper were quick to point out that it is simply impossible – given the infinite number of logical consequences that would need to be considered – to give a conclusive criterion for determining which of two theories has greater verisimilitude. Indeed, it was shown that, for *any* false theories A and B, *neither* is closer to the truth than any other – a result that, for obvious reasons, proved fatal to Popper's definition.

• UNDERDETERMINATION AND THE NO-MIRACLES ARGUMENT

One argument against scientific realism takes as its starting point the thought that, for any finite set of observations, we can always come up with different, incompatible theories which would nonetheless be equally able to account for what we have observed. In order to see that this is possible, one need only imagine that the differences that render the competing theories incompatible only concern situations or phenomena that we did not, and perhaps never will, encounter. Philosophers of science refer to this worry as the argument from **underdetermination of theory by data**.

If one agrees with the argument from underdetermination, it is clear that this should have repercussions for one's stance on the issue of scientific realism. For, if it is indeed the case that observational data are always accounted for by a multiplicity of scientific theories, what reason could we ever have to prefer one theory over another? And if there is no way to choose between competing scientific theories, how can we ever hope to decide which of those that are compatible with the data is the true one?

Many people have argued, however, that this way of framing the underdetermination worry overstates the extent of the problem. In actual cases of scientific controversy, the challenge is rarely that scientists cannot agree to choose among competing theories that account equally well for the same data. Rather, scientists differ in their views on which phenomena are significant and on how a good theory should account for them. Though there will often be significant overlap in what the various competing theories explain, each will have particular strengths and weaknesses – phenomena it can, and cannot, explain – and scientists disagree on the relative significance of each of these. In addition, theories will differ in other respects as well. For example, one theory might be simpler, in that it posits fewer entities and distinct processes, and might therefore be judged preferable (by the lights of Occam's razor; see previous section) to another, more complicated theory – even though the latter may make more accurate predictions.

In other words, cases where underdetermination prevents choosing between two competing theories may be quite rare. However, a possible exception concerns theories that are formulated using different mathematical frameworks. The Hungarian physicist Eugene P. Wigner, in an influential text titled 'The Unreasonable Effectiveness of Mathematics in the Natural Sciences' (1960), voiced the worry that, because we do not fully understand the reasons behind the usefulness of mathematics in describing nature, 'we cannot know whether a theory formulated in terms of mathematical concepts is uniquely appropriate': for any mathematically formulated scientific theory, it is conceivable that an equally successful competitor – perhaps based on a new, as yet undiscovered branch of mathematics – could exist. Had we inherited a different set of mathematical frameworks, our scientific theories concerning the very same phenomena, though equally successful, might have looked very different. And since, *ex hypothesi*, any evidence for our current scientific theories would also lend support to such hypothetical competitors based on competing mathematical frameworks, there is little reason to believe that our scientific theories are the 'correct' ones.

Yet even this argument for underdetermination may not be as conclusive as it looks. While it points to a logical possibility, there are few examples in the history of science where the possible existence of (a multiplicity of) equally adequate mathematical frameworks has caused problems. In the early stages of the quantum revolution in physics, there existed two alternative formulations of the newly emerging quantum theory: Werner Heisenberg's *matrix mechanics* and Erwin Schrödinger's *wave mechanics*. But these were later subsumed under a unified formulation (in terms of Hilbert spaces), and physicists nowadays would have no trouble translating the results of matrix mechanics into the language of wave mechanics, and vice versa. Worrying about which of the two formulations is correct would be rather like worrying about which of the two sentences 'il pleut' (in French) and 'es regnet' (in German) is the *true* representation of the fact that it is raining.

Defenders of scientific realism have turned to a number of arguments in order to rebut anti-realist worries about our alleged inability to single out successful theories. One such influential argument is the so-called '**no-miracles argument**'. As realists are wont to point out, scientific theories not only allow us to describe observed phenomena in nature, but also enable us to manipulate the world around us, realising hitherto unknown technological possibilities and bringing about new states of matter and entirely new phenomena.

The no-miracles argument draws on a large array of theory-driven scientific and technological successes (see text box 22.1, 'Laser technology'), in order to make a forceful case that success of this sort would have to be a *miracle*, if it weren't for the truth (or approximate truth) of the underlying scientific theories. The fact that we are able to reliably bring about, in routine fashion, novel phenomena such as laser light, and succeed in exploiting and manipulating nature in a controlled way, makes it exceedingly likely that we are basing our manipulations and interventions on

> **BOX 22.1** LASER TECHNOLOGY
>
> Laser technology – the term is an acronym that stands for 'light amplification by stimulated emission of radiation' – has become ubiquitous; lasers are used in science and manufacturing, as well as in medicine ('lasik' eye surgery), entertainment, and even as keychain laser pointers in the office context. Lasers produce light that differs from natural light in terms of its coherence, intensity, and narrow spectrum. The terms 'stimulated emission' and 'light amplification' refer to the fact that, in a laser, an external electromagnetic field is applied, at a frequency associated with a particular light-emitting quantum transition of electrons in a gain medium, which then gives rise to a rapid emission of photons at a particular wavelength. Unlike natural light, which is the result of thermal emission, the stimulated emission of photons in a laser is a highly correlated, non-random process – made possible by the laws of quantum physics, but requiring highly specific, planned technological conditions.

theories that are, in fact, truthfully representing the world around us. While the no-miracles argument does not prove that our scientific theories are true, or approximately true, it asserts that there is simply no other explanation that could satisfactorily account for the technological and predictive successes of science.

• THE CHALLENGE FROM SCIENTIFIC REVOLUTIONS

Without doubt the most serious challenge to arguments in favour of scientific realism arises from the history of science. At the very least, historical considerations put significant pressure on naïve versions of scientific realism, according to which science inevitably, and in unilinear fashion, approaches a true account of objective reality. In this section, we shall focus on two different arguments that can be taken to have anti-realist implications. The first invites us to acknowledge the vast number of scientific theories that, although once widely accepted, later turned out to be false. The second argument reflects on the consequences of theory change in science and on how radical shifts may lead to **incommensurability** between two theories.

The first argument takes as its starting point the long list of theories that were once considered successful, and were widely accepted, yet were given up in favour of new theories (many of which would themselves later turn out to be false). In an influential paper titled 'A Confutation of Convergent Realism' (1981), Larry Laudan lists more than a dozen formerly accepted scientific theories – including the humoral theory of medicine, the phlogiston theory of combustion, the caloric theory of heat, different aether theories in physics, the theory of spontaneous generation in biology, and many more – all of which were once successful and well confirmed, yet which contained central concepts (such as the aether or phlogiston) that do not refer to anything in the world.

Given that past successful scientific theories so often turned to be false, Laudan argues that we should not be optimistic about the fate of our current best scientific theories. Laudan's **pessimistic meta-induction**, as this argument has become known, asserts that, on the contrary, we should operate on the assumption that scientific theories we now take to be true will themselves, over time, turn out to be false. That is, not only is technological and predictive success not a sign of the likely truth of our current scientific theories – contrary to what the no-miracles argument would have us believe – but the historical evidence suggests that, given enough time, even our best successful theories will be refuted by the evidence.

In response to the pessimistic meta-induction, scientific realists have sometimes argued that we cannot draw inductive conclusions about current scientific theories on the basis of those predecessor theories that have been refuted. Inductive reasoning – that is, reasoning from past to future instances – only works if we are dealing with instances of the same kind. But in the case of the pessimistic meta-induction, we are being asked to draw conclusions about theories that, unlike their predecessors, so far have withstood the test of time. The reason for the relative persistence of our current scientific theories may very well be that they, unlike those (past) theories on which we perform our inductive generalisation, are true or approximately true. Dismissing current successful theories because their predecessors were shown to be false would be rather like counting the participants in an Olympic 100 m race and, having counted seven losers so far, inferring that, therefore, the eighth runner, too, must have lost the race. In other words, it would overlook the fact that, in the race towards truth, there may well be winners among our current scientific theories.

Another line of response to Laudan's argument reverts to the notion of approximate truth (which, as we have already seen, is itself far from unproblematic). Past scientific theories that, strictly speaking, have been refuted, may nonetheless contain more truths than their predecessors. Furthermore, even when central ideas of a theory are refuted, and the theory is replaced by a new one, parts of the old theory may nonetheless carry over to the new one. This, one might argue, vindicates the scientific realist idea that science gradually converges upon a true account of objective reality.

However, as the historian and philosopher of science Thomas Kuhn has argued in his famous book *The Structure of Scientific Revolutions* (1962), comparing past and present theories may not be as easy as one might think. This is because theories that are separated by what Kuhn calls 'paradigm shifts' may be *incommensurable*; that is, it may be impossible to conclusively determine the extent to which two theories overlap in respect of their content and truth. Kuhn arrived at this controversial suggestion on the basis of careful case studies from the history of science. Close inspection of the track record of science, Kuhn argued, reveals a historical pattern of periods of so-called '**normal science**' – characterised by widespread (tacit) agreement about scientific theories, methodologies, and goals – punctuated by '**scientific**

revolutions' that lead to radical shifts in the theoretical understanding and scientific practice within a particular discipline. (It is important to note that, according to Kuhn, scientific revolutions can be found throughout the history of science; that is, he is using the term not to refer to 'the' Scientific Revolution that marked the emergence of science in early-modern Europe.)

Periods of normal science are marked by adherence to what Kuhn calls a **paradigm** – that is, a shared set of practices, methods, theoretical principles, scientific theories, and judgments concerning what constitutes a valid scientific problem. Agreement on this wide range of factors need not be explicit, but is acquired by scientists during their training and education, and is spread and reinforced through what goes on at scientific conferences, in laboratories and research institutes, at universities, and via practices such as peer review and scientific publishing. Normal science is productive and cumulative, in that it tackles manageable problems within a shared paradigm and theoretical framework.

However, during any period of normal science one usually finds '**anomalies**': problems that appear to resist successful resolution within the dominant paradigm. Examples would be the anomalous precession of the perihelion of the planet Mercury, which could not be accounted for by Newtonian physics and was only explained by Einstein's theory of general relativity, or the problem of black-body radiation – that is, the spectrum of electromagnetic radiation emitted by a body at thermal equilibrium – which could not be calculated using classical physics, but was later explained by the hypothesis that radiation can only be emitted in 'quantised' form.

Scientific revolutions occur when anomalies that had previously been disregarded, or 'quarantined', by normal science are suddenly recognised as significant. Usually this requires that a scientific paradigm has weakened and has lost its grip on a sizeable minority of researchers, who are now beginning to explore other theoretical alternatives. If a viable alternative theory emerges, large parts of the scientific community may shift allegiance to the new theory (and its attendant experimental practices and methodological assumptions), and a new paradigm may begin to form. Examples of such **paradigm shifts** are found in all scientific disciplines, ranging from the quantum revolution in physics to the rise of DNA-based molecular biology to the theory of continental drift in geology.

Because a paradigm shift affects not only the explicit theoretical content of science, but also tacit assumptions, the meanings of scientific terms, and experimental practices and conventions, scientists working from within a new paradigm may no longer be able to appreciate what their predecessors, who worked under a different paradigm, cared about, or even what their theories meant. This, Kuhn argues, is the source of incommensurability between past and present scientific theories. For example, phlogiston theory, which postulated the existence of a fire-like element – phlogiston – that would be released during combustion (thus explaining the observable phenomenon of fire), is not something of which contemporary chemists can make much sense. However, this lack of intelligibility from our present-day viewpoint is not an intrinsic feature of phlogiston theory, which at the time was widely accepted and enjoyed a number of explanatory successes; instead, it is the result of a number of paradigm shifts that separate contemporary chemistry from its eighteenth-century precursor. Searching for truth, or 'partial truth', in those predecessor theories, it has been argued, risks projecting contemporary scientific assumptions onto obsolete theoretical frameworks, thereby rendering claims about the preservation of theoretical content across scientific theory change dubious at best.

• WHAT SCIENTIFIC PROGRESS MIGHT BE

Over the course of the past three chapters we have encountered very different views of science. On one side, we find positions such as Popper's falsificationism, which issues strongly normative prescriptions about how scientists *ought to* conduct themselves when investigating the world around us. On the other side, we have philosophers such as Kuhn, who see their task as primarily a descriptive one and who emphasise that the history of science is not one of unilinear progress. At the same time, it seems undeniable that we know a great deal more about the world today, thanks to science, than at any point in the past.

This raises the question of how we should think about the notion of scientific progress, and whether it is possible to increase the prospects of science, without falling back into dubious patterns of thought such as naïve faith in science or a frivolous 'anything goes' relativism. (In the interest of fairness, it should be mentioned that Paul Feyerabend (2010: vii), the philosopher of science most often taken to task for advocating a form of 'methodological anarchism', made it very clear that '"anything goes" is not a "principle" I hold [...] but the terrified exclamation of a rationalist who takes a closer look at history'!)

One idea has been to adopt a conciliatory position that accepts that the history of science is varied and is marked by successes and failures, as well as dead-ends, while nonetheless insisting that it is possible to identify criteria that allow us to tell 'good' from 'bad' science. This, roughly, has been the position of Imre Lakatos's *methodology of scientific research programmes*. Like Kuhn, Lakatos argues that scientific theories are parts of larger units of analysis, which he calls **research programmes**. Unlike Kuhn's all-encompassing notion of 'paradigm', which includes not only theoretical statements and methodological assumptions, but also non-propositional ingredients such as experimental practices, scientific apparatuses, and elements of the social organisation of science, Lakatos's notion of a 'research programme' focuses squarely on the theoretical content, auxiliary hypotheses, propositions, and mathematical frameworks that are being used in a given (sub)discipline.

Within a given research programme, we can distinguish between a core theory and sets of auxiliary hypotheses. The 'hard' theoretical core is central to the research programme, and is protected from falsification by the 'protective belt' of auxiliary hypotheses. This way, the core elements of a research programme are given sufficient opportunity to be developed and gradually modified, rather than being hastily rejected as soon as contravening empirical data is found. When scientists come across potentially falsifying data, they first modify the auxiliary hypotheses that form the protective belt; only if the empirical challenges cannot be resolved this way will they begin to call into question the hard theoretical core of a research programme. (This is meant to address worries arising from Popper's falsificationism, which risked rejecting scientific hypotheses too soon, before scientists have had a chance to assess whether a theory can survive an attempted falsification.)

The distinction between a hard theoretical 'core' and a 'protective belt' of auxiliary hypotheses allows Lakatos to identify a number of criteria for when a research programme should be considered progressive or degenerating. The most important criterion is whether a research programme is successful in making *novel predictions* of as yet unobserved phenomena, at least some of which are subsequently corroborated through experiments or further observations. By contrast, a *degenerating research programme* is one in which auxiliary hypotheses are introduced purely defensively, in an ad hoc way, solely in order to protect the theoretical core; this gives rise to a proliferation of theoretical ingredients which, over time, will be unable to keep up with new empirical challenges.

While Lakatos's methodology of scientific research programmes is hardly the last word when it comes to making sense of scientific theory change, one of its merits consists in making judgements of scientific progress a case-by-case affair. Science in its entirety may simply be too vast and diverse to allow for wholesale generalisations about whether or not science is getting closer to the truth. But this does not preclude assessing individual scientific research programmes – or similar intermediate units of analysis – in terms of whether they exhibit signs of progress or signs of degeneration. Perhaps, then, we need to acknowledge that we cannot arrive at philosophical conclusions about science unless we are willing to engage deeply, and in a sustained way, with scientific research programmes themselves.

• CHAPTER SUMMARY

- Scientific realism is the position that the world as described by science exists independently of us and contains properties and entitities – including unobservables – which science is in a position to tell us about. The claims of science are to be taken 'at face value'; for example, claims about unobservable entities are really about objects in the world, and are not merely a shorthand way of reporting complexes of sensory experience.
- Instrumentalism holds that science is something we help ourselves to, in a purely auxiliary way, for the purposes of predicting phenomena and manipulating the world around us; however, we need not endorse as true the various claims science makes about unobservable entities, hidden mechanisms, and causal processes.

- Scientific realism is usually associated with a historical thesis about how science develops. According to convergent scientific realism, some scientific theories are true (or at least approximately true) and genuinely refer to objective features of the world. As science progresses, scientific theories gradually move closer to the truth and give an ever more complete account of objective reality.
- The no-miracles argument asserts that the truth, or approximate truth, of our current scientific theories is the best explanation of their explanatory, predictive, and technological successes.
- Anti-realists object to the no-miracles argument by insisting that success – whether explanatory, predictive, or technological – can always be accounted for by multiple scientific theories (including potential competitors we have not yet considered).
- According to the underdetermination thesis, there is always the possibility of different, incompatible theories that account equally well for the same data.
- Historians of science have pointed out that, as they sometimes put it, 'history is a graveyard of scientific theories'. According to the pessimistic meta-induction, the failure of past scientific theories gives us inductive grounds for expecting that our current scientific theories, too, will turn out to be false.
- Scientific realists argue that, even if past scientific theories were strictly speaking false, many elements of old theories survive and carry over to the new ones. This suggests that science is gradually moving closer to the truth.
- The incommensurability thesis holds that comparisons between past and present scientific theories, in respect of their content and truth, are often inconclusive or even impossible. This, according to Kuhn, is because past and present scientific theories are separated by scientific revolutions and their attendant paradigm shifts, which affect explicit as well as tacit assumptions about the significance and meanings of scientific terms and theories.
- As an alternative to Kuhn's notion of paradigms, which Kuhn thought governed periods of normal science, Lakatos proposed scientific research programmes as an intermediate unit of analysis. A research programme consists of a hard theoretical 'core' and a 'protective belt' of auxiliary hypotheses; only the latter can be readily revised in the light of contravening evidence.
- Scientific research programmes are deemed progressive if they are successful in making novel predictions; by contrast, degenerating research programmes are marked by a tendency to resort to ad hoc modifications as a purely defensive move in order to protect themselves from falsification. Whereas degenerating research programmes struggle to maintain their tenability, progressive research programmes suggest new questions and lines of research.

• STUDY QUESTIONS

1 Scientific realists argue that we should take scientific claims about unobservables 'at face value'. Are there limits to which unobservables we should consider real,

and if so where should we draw the line? Are electrons real? What about virtual particles, chemical orbitals, or selection pressures in evolutionary biology?

2 Does underdetermination pose a serious threat to scientific realism?

3 Does the failure of past scientific theories count against the truth of our current best scientific theories?

4 What would it take to overcome the problem of incommensurability between past and present scientific theories?

5 Which is a better unit of analysis for making sense of scientific theory change: Kuhn's notion of 'paradigm' or Lakatos's notion of 'research programme'?

• INTRODUCTORY FURTHER READING

Kuhn, Thomas (1962) *The Structure of Scientific Revolutions* (Chicago: University of Chicago Press). [Kuhn's book is a modern classic and an easy and exciting read.]

Nola, Robert and Howard Sankey (2007) *Theories of Scientific Method: An Introduction* (Durham: Acumen). [An excellent survey of the philosophical debate about scientific methodology, which devotes a lot of space to the distinctive theories of method proposed by Popper, Kuhn, Lakatos, Feyerabend and others.]

• ADVANCED FURTHER READING

Chakravartty, Anjan (2010) *A Metaphysics for Scientific Realism: Knowing the Unobservable* (Cambridge: Cambridge University Press). [An up-to-date discussion of recent positions in the scientific realism debate, including its connections with the metaphysics of science.]

Feyerabend, Paul (2010) *Against Method* (London: Verso). [First published in 1975, this book argues for the anarchic character of science and against a belief in a single, monist 'scientific method'.]

Hoyningen-Huene, Paul (1993) *Reconstructing Scientific Revolutions: Thomas S. Kuhn's Philosophy of Science* (Chicago: University of Chicago Press). [An exceptionally clear and thorough introduction to Kuhn's philosophy of science.]

Lakatos, Imre (1980) *The Methodology of Scientific Research Programmes* (*Philosophical Papers*, vol. 1) (Cambridge: Cambridge University Press). [Contains a detailed exposition of Lakatos's methodology of scientific research programmes.]

Laudan, Larry (1981) 'A Confutation of Convergent Realism', *Philosophy of Science* 48(1): 19–49. [This article contains the classic statement of Laudan's pessimistic meta-induction.]

Psillos, Stathis (1999) *Scientific Realism: How Science Tracks Truth* (London: Routledge). [A sophisticated and thorough defence of scientific realism.]

van Fraassen, Bas (1980) *The Scientific Image* (Oxford: Oxford University Press). [A hugely influential and hard-hitting critique of scientific realism, which develops van Fraassen's distinctive anti-realist alternative, which he calls 'constructive empiricism'.]

Wigner, Eugene P. (1960) 'The Unreasonable Effectiveness of Mathematics in the Natural Sciences', *Communications on Pure and Applied Mathematics* 13(1): 1–14. [This is an influential paper which reflects on the puzzling question of why mathematics is so useful in the sciences.]

Wylie, Alison (1986) 'Arguments for Scientific Realism: The Ascending Spiral', *American Philosophical Quarterly* 23(3): 287–97. [An excellent article that traces the dialectic of the debate between scientific realists and anti-realists in a clear and readable manner.]

• FREE INTERNET RESOURCES

Bird, Alexander (2011) 'Thomas Kuhn', *Stanford Encyclopedia of Philosophy*, http://plato.stanford.edu/entries/thomas-kuhn/. [A summary of Kuhn's life, work, and philosophical influence, along with a thorough discussion of the arguments put forward by Kuhn's critics, especially against his controversial incommensurability thesis.]

Chakravartty, Anjan (2011) 'Scientific Realism', *Stanford Encyclopedia of Philosophy*, http://plato.stanford.edu/entries/scientific-realism/. [A comprehensive survey article which outlines and contrasts the main variants of scientific realism and anti-realism, and goes on to consider their relative philosophical merits.]

Part VIII

philosophy of
religion

Tim Mawson

In the analytic tradition, 'the **philosophy of religion**' means philosophical reflection on the claim that God exists; in particular then what, if anything, the claim means and, if it means something, whether or not we have reasons for believing it true or believing it false. In this Part therefore we shall look at the following three questions: (1) What are God's properties? (2) Is belief that God exists reasonable? And then, finally, (3) Is faith in God reasonable?

Before starting on that substantively, I shall say a little bit more about the rationale behind posing each of these three questions.

First, then, question 1: What are God's properties? The intention in asking this question is not, as its phrasing may perhaps suggest, to suppose that there is certainly something that we may properly refer to by the name 'God' and that we only need concern ourselves with working out what properties this thing has. Rather, it is to ask what God's properties are *if* He exists; if you think God doesn't exist, you might thus be happier phrasing the issue as one of what God's properties would be were He to exist.

In the several millennia in which philosophers have reflected on the issues, an answer to this question has emerged which – it may come as a surprise to those outside the discipline to learn – has achieved consensus. It's called the classical theistic concept of God. There are, as the need for a prefix 'classical' may suggest, dissenters from this consensus within what one might think of as still broadly theistic world-views, but they are very much the minority. The fact of consensus is a point worth stressing at the outset, because a common view outside the discipline is that the term 'God' is a very vague one or that it means a variety of things to a variety of people. This may be true of the term 'God' as it finds itself used in the wider population, but it is definitely not true of the term as it finds itself used within the discipline of the philosophy of religion. The term 'God' has a more agreed-upon definition than 'knowledge', 'consciousness', 'physicality', 'science', or indeed almost any of the other things that we philosophers inquire about. At least at the definitional end of the subject of the philosophy of religion, what I have to say then is less controversial than what other contributors to this volume have had to say about their objects of study. It is perhaps worth noting that theologians in the last few hundred years – really since Kant – have used the word 'God' in a largely 'deregulated' way; in theology, 'God' does mean a variety of different things to different people (and only vague things to lots of people); my point is that in the philosophy of religion, it doesn't.

So, answering the first question is, in the first instance, simply a matter of unpacking the classical theistic concept of God. We might leave answering the first question there were it not for the fact that the classical theistic concept is one the consistency of which has been attacked. So, we do well in thinking about the answer to question 1 if we introduce some of the most prominent lines of attack on the consistency of that answer. When I talk of lines of attack on the consistency of the classical theistic concept of God, I have in mind arguments to the effect that some of the properties of God – either in isolation or when combined – are ones which we have reason to believe it is logically impossible that it be instantiated or co-instantiated. So, to give an indication: if, as the classical theist maintains, God is all-powerful, then He must be able to do evil things. But if, as the classical theist also maintains, God is of necessity perfectly good, then He must be unable to do evil things. But no being can both be able and unable to do evil things. Therefore God – as the classical theist conceives Him – cannot exist. That's the sort of argument I have in mind when I speak of attacks on the consistency of classical theism and we'll look, as I say, at some of these in answering the first question. What about the second question?

You'll recall that the second question we'll be looking at is this: Is belief that God exists reasonable? Philosophers are – more or less by definition – people who care about the reasonableness of a belief, so it need come as no surprise that the Philosophy of Religion concerns itself primarily with arguments for and against the reasonableness of belief in God. And thus, in answering this question, we'll need to look at the arguments on both sides, arguments for the thesis that there is a God (**theism**) and arguments for the thesis that there's not (**atheism**). By the time we get to address this second question directly, it will already have been addressed somewhat indirectly by what we've said in response to question 1. If there's a convincing argument to the effect that the classical theistic concept of God is inconsistent, then we know from that alone that it cannot be any more reasonable to believe that God exists than it is to believe that, say, a square circle exists. But in fact only a small proportion of people *are* convinced by arguments to the effect that it's logically impossible that God exists. Thus for most people the second question is a 'live' one.

Like any other thesis in metaphysics, the thesis that there is a God is one that has attracted many arguments, both for and against, and some of these arguments are very complicated. Indeed, as people have generally cared more about whether or not there's a God than they have about any other issue in metaphysics, philosophers have developed more and more complicated arguments concerning this issue than they have any other. We shall have to be selective and we shall have to simplify. Nevertheless, my hope and realistic expectation is that we'll be able to give at least a flavour of the most prominent arguments on each side of the theism/atheism debate. (A terminological 'n.b.' is in order at this point. Here and from now on I'm using the term 'theism' to refer to the view that there is a God in the classical theistic sense and 'atheism' to refer to the view that there's not. There are alternative uses of these terms in the literature, e.g. sometimes 'theism' is used to refer to the view that we *know* that there is a God in the classical theistic sense and 'atheism' to refer to the view that we *know* that there's not.) So, those are the sorts of things we'll be looking at in addressing the second question.

Our third and final question, it will be recalled, is this: is faith in God reasonable? My intention in asking this question is to allow us to think about the relationship between faith and belief and between faith and reason. Is it permissible to believe by faith what it remains unreasonable to believe on evidence? Is it permissible if the evidence is equally balanced, so that it is neither reasonable nor unreasonable to believe on it? Is it reasonable to allow pragmatic considerations – the potential 'pay offs' of beliefs or failures of belief – to influence what beliefs one has? Addressing these sorts of questions will provide us with occasion to step back from the arguments we've been looking at in addressing question 2 and consider the reasonableness (or otherwise) of demanding arguments before one believes that there's a God or believes in God. Pending arguments either way, should the 'default' be atheism, theism, or suspension of belief on the issue altogether?

So, between them, these three questions stake out the territory of the philosophy of religion and thus the territory we'll be doing our best to map – and, to stress, it will only be a 'sketch map' – in the rest of this Part.

A final point now, before we get on with addressing these three questions substantively, this point addressed to a concern that will have arisen for some readers. I expect that, having read what I've said so far, some of my readers will be very suspicious of the discipline of the philosophy of religion *per se*.

From what I've said so far, it will be obvious that the Philosophy of Religion is methodologically premised on the assumption that human reason is up to the task of discovering at least some truth about God. Some people are sceptical about this assumption: they hold that, rather than placing faith in our reason, we should humbly bow before the fact that if we are to come to know anything about God at all, it can only be because He reaches down and makes it known to us with a revelation; it cannot be to any extent because we reach up towards Him with our reason. The discipline of the Philosophy of Religion does indeed proceed on the anti-sceptical assumption that our reason is not, as one might put it, 'totally depraved'; it proceeds on the assumption that our reasoning powers, though no doubt fallible, are not *hopelessly* fallible. And it then just adds to this assumption the undeniable thought that a fallible guide *is still a guide* and, when a fallible guide is the only guide we have, it's thus the guide we should follow. But, such sceptics sometimes push back, we *do* have another guide – a divine revelation. Significantly, quite what these sceptics about human reason then go on to cite as the genuine divine revelation varies between them. And so to such sceptics we may insist that we obviously need a guide to tell us which of the putative-revelation guides is the genuine one and this ultimate guide, this 'guide to the guides' as it were, can only be – fallible though it is – our reason. It is an old point, no doubt as old as the discipline itself, but John Locke well put it in his *Essay* (book IV, ch. XVIII. sec. 10): 'Whatever God hath revealed is certainly true; no doubt can be made of it. This is the proper object of faith. But whether it be a divine revelation or no, reason must judge.' And so we move on in this area of philosophy as we do in all others, following the path picked out for us by our fallible but ultimate guide, reason. Our determination to follow this path, hard though it may be and leading us, as it may do, in directions that we wish we did not have to travel is what makes us philosophers above all else.

23

what are God's properties?

As mentioned in the introduction, the several millennia that philosophers have taken thus far to consider this question have resulted in an answer that has won a widespread if not universal consensus. The result is the classical theistic concept of God. The classical theistic concept of God is the concept of God as a being who has the following nine properties: He is personal; incorporeal/transcendent; omnipresent/immanent; omnipotent; omniscient; eternal; perfectly free; perfectly good; and necessary. To understand the classical theistic concept of God, we thus need to understand these properties and the conceptual difficulties and philosophical puzzles that they may raise. Before turning to this task, it is worth noting that my dividing these properties into nine, rather than dividing them into some other number, is at least somewhat arbitrary. As we shall see, at least some of these properties are conceptually entailed by others. Indeed, I shall later argue for a version of what is sometimes called the **Doctrine of Divine Simplicity**. As I think this is best interpreted, this is the theory that *all* the nine essential properties on my list are best seen as differing aspects of the single and simple property that constitutes the divine essence – the property of being the most perfect person possible. Be that as it may, the point I am making here is a more modest one, *viz.* that whilst I've divided the divine nature into nine properties, some other classical theists might sensibly divide it into a different number or indeed not divide it at all.

The same point arguably goes for some properties of God that I haven't yet listed at all and won't in fact have time to talk about. I won't have time to talk about them even though they are universally supposed by classical theists to be properties of God. These are properties that I have not listed because, whilst they are universally ascribed to God by classical theists, they are held not to be essential to God; God could have still been God yet not have had them. This cluster of properties springs from God's having created something other than Himself, and most specifically from His having created us. Personally, I endorse arguments to the effect that given that God's created a universe with people in it, then He must (of necessity) create value for them; reveal Himself to them; and offer them everlasting life. But those are controversial arguments. What is not controversial amongst classical theists is that even though these properties are not essential to God – for that He create anything other than Himself is not essential to Him (but rather a result of His free choice) – they are in fact properties that God has. And thus philosophical reflection on them is generally taken to be a proper part of the philosophy of religion, though – as I say – I won't have time to talk about these issues here. Philosophical reflection on properties that are *not* universally ascribed to God by classical theists – e.g. that He is triune; that He atoned for the sins of humanity at the Cross – is usually taken to be a part of the adjacent discipline of philosophical theology. So, that having been said, back to my list of God's 'nine' properties.

• THE CLASSICAL THEISTIC CONCEPT OF GOD

Personhood

The first of the nine properties on my list is that of **personhood**. It is obvious from the way that theists interact with (or at least take themselves to be interacting with) God in their religious lives – most obviously in worship and prayer – that they regard God not as an impersonal supernatural force, but as a person. They praise and thank Him for things in the past and they ask Him to do things in the future; they ask Him questions and they listen for answers. All of this is to suppose that God is a person, a someone not something – a someone who has beliefs about certain things; who cares about certain things; whom one can thus reason with and please or displease by certain actions that one can choose to perform; and it is to suppose that God Himself performs actions in turn in order to affect the world as He sees fit. I would incline to say that being that sort of thing just *is* what it is to be a person, but even if I'm wrong in my understanding of what it is to be a person, some understanding of what it is to be a person must be coherent and substantial if it's coherent and substantial to say that there are any persons (which it obviously is), and thus the theistic claim that God is a person must be coherent and substantial. At this stage, then, discussion of the divine property of personhood seems to me to turn into discussion of the property of personhood as such and thus it relocates itself outside the discipline of the philosophy of religion (probably into the discipline of the philosophy of mind); or at least it relocates itself for the time being. It may be that it returns to us; if, e.g., we were to be led to a concept of personhood whereby it was impossible for there to be an incorporeal person, it might return pretty quickly. This brings me to the second property on my list.

Incorporeality (transcendence)

God is supposed by theists to differ from persons such as you and me: He is supposed not to have a body, but rather to be incorporeal. This is the second property on my list. Even if theists may hold – though most don't – that we human persons *have to have* bodies, theists are thus committed to holding that it is not a truth about persons *per se* that they cannot be incorporeal. Thus, as mentioned at the end of the previous paragraph, certain 'findings' in the philosophy of mind may have implications for the coherence of theism; alternatively, one's commitment to theism might make one sceptical of certain 'findings' in the philosophy of mind. It seems to me that the best way for the theist to proceed here is to claim that by describing God as incorporeal, they simply mean that there is no section of matter distinct from others that is especially privileged as that which God knows about more directly than He knows about others or over which He has more direct control than others. In other words, when theists describe God as incorporeal, they are best construed as simply saying that there is no particular place where God is in the sense that by being there He is absent from being somewhere else. What about when they describe Him as omnipresent?

Omnipresence (immanence)

When theists describe God as omnipresent, the third property on my list, they are, I suggest, best construed as saying that there is no section of matter that is not one He knows about directly or that is not under His direct control. When they describe God as omnipresent, they are saying that there is no place where God is to any extent absent. God's incorporeality is His not being present anywhere in particular; His **omnipresence** is His not being absent from anywhere in particular. Personally, I prefer the term 'transcendence' to refer to the divine property that is more usually called 'incorporeality' by theists. (I prefer it because it seems to me that the theist may – indeed should – say that the universe is God's body, but that's an unusual view.) To pair with 'transcendence', one might prefer the word 'immanence', rather than 'omnipresence'. God is immanent in the physical world as He is not in any way ignorant of it or unable to control it by direct acts of His will.

Omnipotence

Not only is God supposed to be a supernatural – transcendent yet immanent – person, God is supposed by theists to be the most powerful person there could be: He is all-powerful or (the same thing in Latin) omnipotent, the fourth property on my list. The more powerful one is the more one can do, so one might suggest that we define an omnipotent being as a being who can do anything. This is a good starting point, but in fact there are certain well-known problems with this definition as there are certain things which the word 'anything' might be taken to include that, on reflection, the philosophical consensus is that we should not require an omnipotent being to be able to do.

First, let's make the point that it's usually taken to be no restriction on God's **omnipotence** that He cannot do the logically impossible; for example, He cannot make someone remain a bachelor whilst they get married. If one asks, 'Can an omnipotent being do X?' and substitutes for X things that don't make sense, the answer to the question is 'No'. But it's 'No', not because one's described something that an omnipotent being can't do, but because one's failed to describe anything at all. So, even if God can do anything, He can't do the logically impossible because the logically impossible isn't anything – it isn't even a possibility. That's why we call it the logically impossible.

What about this? Can an omnipotent being make mistakes? There's no logical impossibility about making mistakes. We do it every day. So, if the concept of omnipotence doesn't entail that God could make mistakes, that must be for a reason other than one that I've just sketched. Again, there's a usual answer, which, in short, is that some abilities, which one might – if one was not thinking carefully enough or did not know enough – call powers, are really more correctly labelled liabilities and the more powerful one is, the less of these abilities one will have, not the more. Our ability to believe a false answer to some question is a liability, not a power. So, if you imagine a situation in which you become rationally convinced of the true answer to a particular question and thus have removed from yourself the ability to believe any of the various false answers to that question, you are thereby imagining a situation in which you are increasing your power even though you are losing some abilities. Given that the ability to make mistakes is a liability not a power, so we can see that the answer to the question, 'Can an omnipotent being make mistakes?' is 'No'. Omnipotence implies no liabilities whatsoever.

We can make mistakes and an omnipotent being – should one exist – cannot, so there is something that we can do that an omnipotent being – should one exist – cannot do. This is why our first stab at a definition of omnipotence – a being is omnipotent if He can do anything – isn't quite right. Can we adapt it? A being is omnipotent if He has all powers that it is logically possible to have (and no liabilities) perhaps? To cut a long story short, it seems to me that this isn't quite right either, because of the complicating factor that what abilities are liabilities and what are powers can depend on what other abilities one has. So – at the end of all this – I would suggest we define an omnipotent being as a being with the most power-granting set of abilities that it is logically possible anyone might have. How are we to understand what being omnipotent in this sense entails, which abilities are in this set and which aren't? Here we must acknowledge that we will soon run up against limits imposed by our own finitude. But we must equally acknowledge that we can make some progress.

Whenever one is considering an ability to do something which – of logical necessity – disables one from doing something else, one will have to use one's intuition to decide which of these abilities is most power-granting, the answer thus leading one to decide which to ascribe to an omnipotent being and which to deny of Him. Is it more power-granting for one to be able to create a stone so heavy that one could not oneself lift it or is it more power-granting to be able to lift any stone? Plausibly, our intuition tells

BOX 23.1 THE PARADOX OF THE STONE

There are a number of alleged 'paradoxes' of omnipotence, that is attempts to show that the concept of omnipotence is, in and of itself, logically contradictory and hence that we can know that no omnipotent being exists from the armchair, as it were. One of the most famous goes back to the Middle Ages and is called 'The Paradox of the Stone'. It can be put in a number of ways, one being this:

1 Either God cannot create a stone so heavy that He Himself cannot then lift it or He can create a stone so heavy that He Himself cannot then lift it.
2 If God cannot create a stone so heavy that He Himself cannot then lift it, then He is not omnipotent since there is something He cannot do, viz. create the stone in question.
3 If God can create a stone so heavy that He Himself cannot then lift it, then He is not omnipotent, since there is something He cannot do, viz. lift the stone in question.
4 Therefore, God (if defined as omnipotent) cannot exist.

I sketch my solution to this paradox in the main text, but there is no consensus that mine (or indeed anyone else's) is the correct solution; there is no consensus that a solution is possible at all; this and related paradoxes of omnipotence thus continue to attract discussion.

us, it is the latter. If so, then an omnipotent being would have the power of being able to lift any stone and not have the liability of being able to create a stone so heavy that He Himself could not lift it.

Obviously, in using one's intuition in this way to understand what is entailed by omnipotence, one is making what is at least in part an evaluative judgement – Which of these is it better to be able to do? And evaluative judgements vary to some extent between people. Perhaps you think it would be better to be able to create a stone so heavy that one could not oneself lift it than it would be to be able to lift any stone. If so, you'll have a different understanding of what abilities are entailed by omnipotence from me. But this worry can be over-emphasised in two ways.

First, it is not a worry about the meaning of omnipotence, just a worry about how much agreement we are likely to be able to reach about what abilities are entailed by omnipotence. Second, evaluative judgements aren't completely different from person to person. We've already seen that we value true beliefs over false and thus we think that being able to make mistakes is an ability which in itself one would always be better off without. Thus an omnipotent being could never make mistakes. And even on questions such as the stone 'paradox' (the usual name given to the question I raised in the previous paragraph), almost everyone's intuition is that it's better to be able to lift anything than to be able to create something one cannot oneself lift. Thus we may reasonably hope to be able to make at least some progress in understanding what is entailed by omnipotence in this *ad hoc* fashion. So, it seems to me, the traditional philosophical puzzles about the divine property of 'omnipotence' may be resolved. But it is only fair to point out before moving on that they are still a lively topic of debate within the discipline.

Omniscience

As well as being omnipotent, God is supposed to be omniscient, to know everything. One need only look elsewhere in this volume to discover that there is no consensus over what knowledge is, but luckily we do not need to find out exactly what knowledge is in order to go some way in characterising **omniscience**, for we may say that a being is omniscient just if it is the case that for all truths, that being knows that truth. The usual worry with this property is not with anything intrinsic to it, but rather that, in having it, future free action becomes impossible. In light of this worry, some theists actually say that God does *not* know the future, or at least infallibly know it. And these theists' reasons for thinking this are usually not that they think they need this *ad hoc* restriction on omniscience to preserve freedom, but stem from their viewing God's **eternality** as His being everlasting inside time. So, let's leave omniscience and look at the next divine property on my list, eternality.

Eternality

All theists are agreed that God is eternal in the sense that He has no beginning and no end within time, but they divide over whether this is because He is inside time but everlasting or outside time. Let's call the view that He is inside time the 'temporal' view and the view that He's outside, the 'atemporal' view. Is God eternal in the way that some people used to think the universe was – it's something the various stages in the history of which are related by being before or after one another, but it has no first or last stage; it stretches back infinitely into the past and infinitely into the future? Or is God eternal in the way that some people have thought numbers are – the number seven is not in any temporal way before or after the number eight; it exists outside time altogether? The traditional and majority view amongst those theists who have considered the alternatives is certainly the atemporal view. On this view, God atemporally knows infallibly everything that will happen at times that are – from our point of view now – future, but He cannot be said to know now what will happen at times that are from our point of view and His future, because His point of view in contrast to ours is not a point of view within time.

However, many have felt some dissatisfaction with the atemporal view as such. Why? It seems to me that the main reason is understanding prayer (and, more generally, God's interrelations with His creatures). On the atemporal view, God's not affected in any way by His creatures; and this seems – to many, but not all – religiously unsatisfactory. Given the temporal view of God's eternality, it's seemed to many best to say that God doesn't infallibly know the future; He doesn't know it wherever that future depends on the free actions of His creatures (as it often does) or Himself (as it always does). Why? Because future free actions are ones that are undetermined by the present (otherwise they wouldn't be free) and thus unknowable (with infallibility) from the present; thus, not even an omnipotent temporal God should be expected to know them.

This view sometimes goes by the name 'open theism'; for God, as for us, the future is open. Open theism is not the traditional view and it is still, it seems fair to say, something of a niche product, but it is also fair to say that it is gaining 'market share'. (Alert readers who already know a bit of philosophy may have noticed that a certain view of freedom – libertarianism – has been in the background here, setting up the problem. Not to worry if you didn't; there's no need to know what libertarianism means to understand this chapter. But if you do happen to know what it means, you may be helped to know that libertarianism has not been universally held by theists, but it is the view held by most contemporary theistic philosophers of religion – it seems to them needed to solve the **Problem of Evil**. Thus it does in fact tend to set parameters on the responses to 'the Problem of Divine Foreknowledge' as it's usually called.)

Perfect freedom

The next property on my list is **perfect freedom**; as with knowledge, philosophers are not at all agreed about what freedom involves. Fortunately, as with knowledge, we do not need to know exactly what it involves to make some progress in understanding the traditional theistic claim that God is perfectly free. Even though, as already mentioned, most contemporary theistic philosophers of religion are libertarians about freedom, there's a view that spans the various theories of the essence of freedom and which we can use here. This is the view that freedom requires (on some views it simply is) the power to bring about what one wishes to bring about. So God's being perfectly free then must entail Him not being in any way constrained in His bringing about what He wishes. God, as we have seen, is omnipotent, so He could never be less than perfectly free in what He chose to do as a result of not having enough power to do anything closer to what He wished to do. And God is omniscient, so He could never be less than perfectly free in what He chose to do as a result of not knowing exactly what it was He was doing. (I report that, personally, it seems to me that this wouldn't be the case were He not omniscient about the future, which then gives us a reason to prefer the atemporal understanding of eternality.) There are then none of the limitations on God's freedom that there are on ours and it is in virtue of this that we describe Him as perfectly free.

Perfect goodness

Theists believe then that God is perfectly free. We are free to do bad things as well as good. Does God have the ability to do bad things? The traditional theistic answer to this has been that He does not have this ability: He cannot do anything that is less than perfect. Doesn't that make Him less powerful than us then? No – the answer is given – for the ability to do less than is perfect would be a liability rather than a power for Him. In fact, not only can God not do anything bad, but also He can only do whatever it is that would be perfect. Various controversial things about value now need to be assumed for me to unpack this, in particular its objectivity and the distinction between obligatory and supererogatory acts. So, with the caveat in mind that what I am about to say is controversial, allow me simply to state the view.

The fact that something would be morally good is an objective reason to do it. If one is morally obliged to do something for someone in a particular situation, then one should do that thing for anyone in the same situation. For example, if I have a debt due to Mr Jones and I can easily pay it without failing in some greater obligation to someone else, I should pay it; if I have a similar debt owed to Mr Smith, I should pay that too. The fact, let us suppose, that I don't like Mr Smith whereas Mr Jones is a good friend of mine does not in any way reduce my obligation to pay Smith relative to my obligation to pay Jones. But as well as the obligations we have to people, there are things which it would be good to do for people yet which we are not obliged to do for them. For example, let us suppose that the birthdays of both Mr Smith and Mr Jones are imminent and that both would equally be (and highly) delighted by receiving from me, as a present, a signed copy of my latest book (it is my example, so I may stipulate various as-a-matter-of-fact unlikely states to obtain). If so, then it would be good for me to give both of them such a gift, but to neither am I obliged to buy a present. If I allow the fact that I don't like Smith but like Jones to sway me into giving a present only to Jones, then whilst I haven't been as good as I could have been, I haven't failed in any obligation. We may call such acts 'supererogatory'.

When one does something good for someone that goes beyond what one is obliged to do for them, it is not true that one should do the same thing for anyone in their situation. In the case of a supererogatory act, one cannot do it from a disinterested sense of duty; one can only do it for the sake of the person for whom one's doing it. In virtue of this necessary 'directedness' towards the good of the particular people for whom one is performing them, it does not seem unnatural therefore to call acts of supererogation acts of love. God's **perfect goodness** then is His perfectly fulfilling His duties towards His creatures and, furthermore, whenever there is a possible best or joint best thing for Him to do for them, His doing that too, which is His perfectly loving them. In virtue of all of this, He is (necessarily) perfectly good.

Necessity

The final property on my list is necessity. There are many sorts of necessity. There's conceptual/logical and mathematical necessity – if he's a bachelor then he can't be married; every number must have a successor. There's what's usually called metaphysical necessity – everything that begins to exist must have a cause. There's physical necessity – if it was a particle, then it couldn't have been travelling faster than the speed of light. There's moral necessity – you must make an effort to pay your debts. There's aesthetic necessity – By Act Four, it's impossible for Macbeth to live happily ever after. There are no doubt other sorts of necessity too. Each of them uses a sense of necessity – a 'must', a 'couldn't' – but each uses a different sense. In what sense of necessary do theists regard God's existence as necessary?

Some have held that God's existence is logically necessary, that one actually contradicts oneself – albeit perhaps in a non-obvious way – if one denies God's existence. As we shall see in the next chapter, this thought forms the basis of the Ontological Argument for God's existence. It's even possible to extract from Kant the view that we must see God's existence as aesthetically necessary. But these have been minority opinions amongst theists. Most theists have understood the necessity of God's existence as some form of metaphysical necessity.

Unfortunately, metaphysical necessity is notoriously difficult to elucidate. Most philosophers are agreed that there is such a thing as metaphysical necessity, but there is no consensus over how to understand it. (It is worth noting that the most prominent philosopher of religion alive today, Richard Swinburne, would not accept that God is metaphysically necessary.) Here, as so often before, we see the Philosophy of Religion butting up against other areas of philosophy, and arguments in these other areas have the potential to affect issues here. Be that as it may, this claim concludes my brief discussion of God's essential properties.

• THE CONSISTENCY AND COHERENCE OF CLASSICAL THEISM

As I have talked about the essential properties of God, you will have noticed that they are very far from being conceptually autonomous. Being omnipotent and omniscient entail God's being perfectly free – these properties entail that there is nothing which constrains God's actions (no external power that can trump His will and no ignorance that can misdirect it). Given His perfect freedom, He cannot but be perfectly good, for goodness is a reason for action. He can never have any countervailing reason to do anything less than perfectly good; His omnipotence entails that He can fulfil His obligations and do the best possible thing for His creatures (whenever there is one) or one of the joint best (whenever two or more are equally good and none better); and His omniscience entails that He knows what this is/these are. I might have argued in the other direction: in order to be perfectly good, God must be omnipotent – so that He will always be able to do what is morally perfect – and omniscient – so that He will always know what to do. This then could have led me back to transcendence and immanence. In order to be omnipotent and omniscient, God cannot depend on anything – including any physical thing – for His knowledge; nor can any physical thing be beyond his direct control. He must be both transcendent and immanent in space and time. God's omnipotence also entails that everything depends on Him for its existence and He depends on nothing for His, so He is in that sense necessary and if He's necessary, then He must be eternal. There cannot be anything that could cause Him to cease to exist so He must either be outside time or inside time but necessarily everlasting, the two different views theists have on the divine property of eternality.

In fact, then, one might say that God only has one essential property – His being the most perfect person possible – and the nine properties that I've been talking about are best seen as merely facets of this property. From a proper understanding of what it would be to be the most perfect person that there could be, one would be able to derive all the *prima-facie*-distinct essential attributes of God. Whatever one makes of this last claim of mine, it seems to me that the classical theistic concept of God is a consistent one (possibly even something stronger, a coherent one – the properties 'hang together') and thus the belief that God exists might be true. It's logically possible that there's a God. 'So what?', one might ask. All sorts of things are logically possible. It's logically possible that there's a teapot orbiting the Sun but, even so, nobody who believed in the existence of such a teapot could be counted as reasonable. The next question to ask in the case of God then is obvious. We'll turn to it in the next chapter.

BOX 23.2 THE IMPORTANCE OF THE SIMPLICITY OF GOD

I've indicated in the main text that I have sympathy with an interpretation of 'the doctrine of simplicity', viz. the thesis that God is (or would be) a relatively simple being. Personally, I might even push the boat out further: He is (or would be) the most simple being possible. But others would of course disagree, thinking that God is (or would be) somewhat or even very complicated. One may wonder how, if at all, the issue of the simplicity/complexity of God relates to the issue of how rational it is to believe in Him. Some, myself included, think that there's a very close connection between the two because theories that posit few and simple entities to explain certain evidence are overall to be preferred on that evidence over theories that posit more and/or more complex entities. There are some general arguments regarding what is known as the *underdetermination of theory by data*, arising from the work of two twentieth-century philosophers in particular, Duhem and Quine. These arguments persuade many, myself included, that when evaluating an hypothesis we should consider not just its evidential basis, but also other factors, such as whether it offers a simpler explanation than rival hypotheses. The issues here are larger than the philosophy of religion. All I can do is flag up: (a) the fact that my approach assumes certain things about them; and (b) the fact that philosophers who share my perspective on these larger issues will, if they judge my endorsement of the claim that God is (would be) very simple to be wrong, then, quite properly from those starting points, rate the evidential support given to theism by any evidence lower than I would incline to rate it.

CHAPTER SUMMARY

In this chapter we've looked at the various properties of the classical theistic God or, perhaps better, various aspects of the single property of being the most perfect person possible. The classical theistic concept of God is the concept of God as a being who has the following characteristics: He is personal; incorporeal/transcendent; omnipresent/immanent; omnipotent; omniscient; eternal; perfectly free; perfectly good; and necessary. I've argued that the classical theistic concept of God, whilst no doubt raising certain interesting philosophical puzzles with these properties, is consistent: it's logically possible that there's a God. But all sorts of things – teapots orbiting the Sun, for example – are logically possible. Only a proper subset of the logically possible are things believing in which is reasonable. The next issue that suggests itself as worthy of our investigation then is whether or not belief in God is reasonable.

STUDY QUESTIONS

1 Which of the traditional divine properties do you think is most problematic for the theist to render consistent when considered in isolation?
2 Which two or more of the traditional divine properties do you think is most problematic for the theist to render consistent when considered together?
3 How is omnipotence best defined?
4 Is the theist best advised to conceive of God's eternality as His being outside time or inside time but everlasting?
5 In what sense(s) of 'could' should theist and atheist agree that at least there could be a God? In what sense(s) should they disagree that there could be a God?

INTRODUCTORY FURTHER READING

Leftow, B. (1997) 'Eternity', in P. L. Quinn and C. Taliaferro, (eds) *A Companion to Philosophy of Religion* (Oxford: Blackwell), pp. 257–63. [This addresses the issue of how best to unpack the notion of God's eternity, i.e. His 'eternality', as I call it.]

Mawson, T. J. (2005) *Belief in God* (Oxford: Oxford University Press), part I. [This is an expanded version of the material of this chapter and addresses some issues surrounding the properties of God which theists do not think of as essential to Him yet which they all agree He has.]

Morris, T. (1991) *Our Idea of God* (Notre Dame, IN: University of Notre Dame Press). [A very good overview.]

Swinburne, Richard (1993) *The Coherence of Theism* (Oxford: Oxford University Press). [This is another engagement with the issues, but one that comes to some different (as well as some similar) conclusions about how best to understand the divine properties. Overall, Swinburne is optimistic, as am I, that the concept of God is consistent and indeed coherent.]

Wierenga, Edward (1991) *The Nature of God* (Cornell). [Another very good overview.]

Zagzebski, L. (2007) *Philosophy of Religion: A Historical Introduction* (Blackwell). ['Does what it says on the tin', which is something slightly different from the ahistorical approaches taken in some of the other works in the list.]

• ADVANCED FURTHER READING

Adams,R. M. (1983) 'Divine Necessity', *Journal of Philosophy* 80: 741–51. [This is reproduced in R. Adams, *The Virtue of Faith* (Oxford: Oxford University Press, 1987) and in Tom Morris (ed.) *The Concept of God* (Oxford: Oxford University Press, 1987). This last is a very good collection to have to hand when thinking about the topics of chapter 23.]

Brower, Jeffrey (2008) 'Making Sense of Divine Simplicity', *Faith and Philosophy* 25: 3–30. [This is a more recent discussion in the doctrine of divine simplicity than Stump's (see below).]

Leftow, B. (1991) 'Timelessness and Foreknowledge', *Philosophical Studies* 63: 309–25. [This is a good treatment of the 'problem of divine foreknowledge' issue.]

Martin, Michael and Monnier, Ricki (2004) *The Impossibility of God* (Amherst, NY: Prometheus Books). [This is an interesting collection of essays that share a more sceptical view about the coherence of theism.]

Morriston, Wes (2001) 'Omnipotence and Necessary Moral Perfection: Are They Compatible?', *Religious Studies* 37: 143–60. [Morriston says 'No'. If you want to follow up the debate, there's a reply by me and a reply-to-a-reply by him in later editions.]

Stump, Eleonore (2003) *Aquinas* (London: Routledge), 92–130. [This talks about the doctrine of divine simplicity as it was articulated by its most famous proponent.]

• INTERNET RESOURCES

http://www.philosophersnet.com/games/god.php. [It's a good test of the consistency of your views about God. It raises the Euthyphro Dilemma, something which we've not had chance to think about in the chapter: is morality created by God?]

The paper by Adams on divine necessity is available at: http://www.jstor.org/stable/2026018.

24

is belief that God exists reasonable?

Arguments are what purport to give us reasons for believing their conclusions and, as mentioned in the introduction, there have been many arguments advanced in the Philosophy of Religion, both for Theism and for Atheism. We shall therefore need to be selective and we shall need to simplify.

There are three broad categories of arguments for Theism: those which proceed from the mere concept of God (the **Ontological Argument** or – really – family of arguments); those which proceed from this plus the mere fact that there is a universe (the Cosmological Argument or again – really – family of arguments); and those which proceed from the concept of God and some particular fact or facts about this universe (e.g. the **Design Argument**). We'll look at the arguments I've just named as examples, one from each category then. In doing so we will leave out many variants of the Ontological and Cosmological Argument and leave out many other arguments that would fall into the last category, for there are many particular facts about the universe that have been supposed to be evidence of God. The most notable omissions of this last sort are the Argument from Religious Experience; the Argument from Reports of Apparent Miracles; and the Moral Argument.

For Atheism, things are simpler: there's only one argument we need to consider – the Problem of Evil. ('The Problem of Evil' is the name that's usually given to the Argument from Evil to the non-Existence of God; it's only even potentially a problem, obviously, if you're a Theist.) We only need consider this because, in effect, we've already covered arguments for atheism that start from the mere concept of God in addressing question 1 (see chapter 23).

Whilst one might argue for the non-existence of God from the concept of God plus the mere fact that there is a universe by relying on the principle that if there were a God, He would have good reason not to create any universe at all, this principle would be very implausible. Indeed, given our analysis of what it would mean to be perfectly good, one may dismiss such arguments very quickly: it does not seem at all plausible to say that God – were He to exist – would have been under an obligation to create no universe whatsoever or that it would have been good for Him to create no universe whatsoever. To whom could He have been under this obligation? For whom could it have been good? *Ex hypothesi*, there would have been nobody else around and He could hardly be said to be obliged to Himself not to create or to harm Himself by bringing others into existence.

Thus, the only sort of argument against the existence of God that's left to consider is an argument that starts from some particular putative fact about the universe, a fact which there is at least *prima facie* reason to suppose the theistic God would not have wanted to create. If, as is traditional within the discipline, we allow the word 'evil' a rather stretched sense, to mean anything that is in any sense bad, we may therefore call all such arguments versions of the Problem of Evil. So, that's the argument against Theism which we'll consider at the end of this section. First, though, the three arguments *for* Theism. And, first amongst these, the Ontological Argument.

• THE ONTOLOGICAL ARGUMENT

The Ontological Argument was first thought of by St Anselm almost a thousand years ago and can be stated very briskly.

1 God, by definition, is perfect.
2 It is better to exist than not to exist.
3 Therefore, God exists.

Were – *per impossibile* – God not to exist, but rather just be an idea in our minds, then He wouldn't be perfect; but God is by definition perfect, so He cannot fail to exist; He cannot fail to exist any more than a bachelor can fail to be unmarried. Now, though this argument and variants of it continue to have defenders, it's been obvious to most that something's gone wrong with it ever since Anselm first propounded it and energy has generally been expended on diagnosing what's gone wrong with it rather than defending it.

It seems to me that one thing that's gone wrong with this argument is that premise 1 is ambiguous. Is this premise using the term 'God' to pick something out and then attributing a property, albeit an essential one, to it? If so, we could not know that the term 'God' had secured reference without already knowing the conclusion of this argument, that there is a God. However, if premise 1 is not using the term 'God' to pick out something and then attribute a property to that thing, then it must mean something like 'If there is a God, then He is by definition perfect', but then, although it can be known to be true without first needing to know that there is a God, it cannot support the conclusion that God exists but only the conclusion that if there is a God, then He exists. And that conclusion is a rather unexciting one.

Premise 2 has also come in for (to my mind, again justified) attack. One can beat around the bush for quite a long time here, but eventually one gets to another point that was first made by Kant: existence is not a predicate. Existence is not in fact a property that things have, so it's not a property that God has even if He does exist. That being so, it's not a property the having of which adds to His perfection. So, for two reasons, it seems to me as it does to most: the Ontological Argument is not a good argument for Theism.

If we think of the essence of the Ontological Argument as its proceeding merely from the concept of God, then there are arguments which are recognisably different from the argument I've just laid out and yet deserve to be considered versions of the Ontological Argument. And some of these variants continue to attract defenders. In the space available, it is hard to say anything useful that is true of all of them, but even I – no fan of any – would concede that some are not vulnerable to the criticisms I've just levelled against the argument just sketched. Nevertheless, my view is that all versions of the Ontological Argument fail to respect adequately the unbridgeable difference between manoeuvring within a concept and discovering whether that concept, however defined, does or does not have an instantiation. And thus I personally conclude none of them work; I conclude that if we're going to find evidence of God's existence, we'll have to consider more than the mere concept of God. Where shall we look? The only place we can: the world which He's supposed to have created. It's seemed to many that the mere fact that a universe exists is evidence enough. This brings me then to the next argument on my list, the Cosmological Argument.

• THE COSMOLOGICAL ARGUMENT

As with my discussion of the Ontological Argument, I don't have time to discuss more than one version of the Cosmological Argument. I shall focus on the variant of the Cosmological Argument that starts from the contingency of the cosmos, from the fact that the universe could have been different from the way that it is – it might not even have existed at all. There are arguments that start from general-enough features of the universe to get to count as cosmological yet which don't focus on its contingency. The one discussed most often nowadays is the Kalam Cosmological Argument; it starts from the fact that the universe had a beginning. Some of the criticisms of the Cosmological Argument I shall look at apply to the Kalam too *mutatis mutandis*, but I shall not myself be pausing to make these connections. Here's the argument I'll be looking at:

1 The universe is contingent: not only might it have not been as it is, but also it might not have been at all.
2 All contingent physical things require sufficient explanation of why they are as they are rather than in some other way or not at all (a restricted version of the Principle of Sufficient Reason).
3 Therefore, the universe must have an explanation of why it is as it is and the best contender for being that explanation is God.

With respect to the first premise, it's hard to believe that this is false. The universe in its details just does seem contingent. To deny that it's contingent in its details runs contrary to our intuitions about every fact that we take to be contingent. You think that you could have failed to read this book; you think you could have failed to exist; and so on. I think these things too and, if the universe were necessary in all its details, then those thoughts and numerous other similar ones would have to be wrong.

One might say that it is the boundary conditions and indeterministic laws of nature that are necessary, everything else – the details – being (due to the indeterminism) contingent. But, whilst not as obviously wrong, this still seems wrong because it seems as if the boundary conditions and laws of nature could have been different too. Just as each of us can coherently think of the possibility of our never having existed, by imagining – for example – a possible world in which our parents chose never to have children, so we can coherently think of the possibility of our never having existed by imagining the boundary conditions and/or laws of nature being such as to mean that life could not form. There does then seem to be quite a bit of pre-reflective intuitive support for the first premise. Of course one might be sceptical about the reliability of intuitions in such cases. In any case, I'll move on to look at the second premise.

It seems to me that the second premise is the most questionable. One can indeed, it seems to me (though not everyone), sensibly ask the question why there is this universe, but it does not follow from the fact that a question can be asked that it must have an answer. If we allow that there's contingency in the world, then ultimately we must reach a brute fact on *any* explanatory account, a contingent fact that itself has no explanation. So, why not stop with the universe? Perhaps there is no explanation of this admittedly contingent and finite universe. To think like this would be to reject the restricted form of the Principle of Sufficient Reason that the proponent of this version of the Cosmological Argument needs, the principle that requires contingency in the finite aggregate of physical stuff that is the universe to have an explanation, 'restricted' because it wouldn't demand the same from the contingency in God's mind that was His decision to create this universe rather than some other. (It's perhaps worth saying that Leibniz – the originator of the name – held the unrestricted version of the Principle of Sufficient Reason.) Is this then the way for the opponent of the argument to go? It seems to me that it is, for, after all, aren't there scientists who would deny that the Principle of Sufficient Reason applies to all physical stuff?

Some – indeed the majority – of those who specialise in quantum mechanics interpret it as telling us that, albeit at the subatomic level and within the parameters imposed by certain laws, certain happenings are genuinely random. A certain atom decays at a certain time. 'Why did it do so then, rather than a couple of seconds earlier or later?', we ask. 'There's no reason', these scientists are happy to say. The mere existence of this opinion amongst obviously cognitively well-functioning scientists is sufficient to show that it can't after all be constitutive of rationality that one thinks that the Principle of Sufficient Reason has universal scope in the realm of finite physical stuff.

It may need to be taken to have universal scope for folk-scientific thinking about the domain of 'medium-sized dry goods' as one might call it, but not elsewhere.

One might hope to go along with the consensus amongst scientists, yet save the Principle of Sufficient Reason 'for later use'. One might say something like, 'Okay, there is genuine randomness in physical stuff at the quantum level, but why is the world in this way random? The various outcomes have probabilities associated with them; why those probabilities rather than some others? Why indeed any form of randomness rather than determinism?'

These are, I suggest, sensible questions. But the point to observe in relation to them is that if one's already relinquished the universal applicability of the Principle of Sufficient Reason to physical stuff by saying that at the subatomic level there are things to which it doesn't apply, then there's no need from consistency anymore to suppose that these sensible questions that one is now raising have answers. If one's asking why the world is such that at the quantum level there are things to which the Principle of Sufficient Reason doesn't apply, one ought to consider the possibility that the fact that the world is such that at the quantum level there are things to which the Principle of Sufficient Reason doesn't apply might itself be a fact of a type that one's already admitted, a fact about physical stuff to which the Principle of Sufficient Reason doesn't apply. The appeal to size – 'But these quantum happenings are so very small and the Universe as a whole is so very big' – need not detain us; the Universe was very small in the past – very, very small at the Big Bang.

And then finally, what of the leap to God as the best contender for explaining the universe? There are a number of debates to be had here around the age-old question, 'Why is there anything at all?' I can only record that, personally, I have sympathy with this stage in the argument – God is the best 'contender' for answering this question.

Personally, then, I am optimistic about the first premise and the viability of concluding that if the contingent universe does have an explanation, it's one in terms of God's decision to create it. But, personally, I think there's no rational compulsion, or even pressure, on us to take the contingency of the universe as one requiring an explanation. The Principle of Sufficient Reason in the form required to take us from collections of physical stuff to an explanatory entity outside such (and then stop), which is the form the argument requires, is one that cannot be plausibly argued to be constitutive of rationality and is one the adoption of which begs the question against **physicalism** (if the contingency of the universe is granted). One can't have a good argument against the view that physical stuff doesn't need any explanation premised on the principle that physical stuff does need an explanation. This it seems to me – more fundamentally than any quibbles one might have with the rest of the argument – dooms the Cosmological Argument.

If we're to find reason to believe that God exists, we'll have to look down into the details of the universe He's supposed to have created to see if we can find evidence of

Him there. There are many such details we might focus on. But we'll look at only a very restricted set of details; we'll focus on just one version of the Design Argument – the fine-tuning version of it.

• THE DESIGN ARGUMENT (FROM FINE-TUNING)

'What is this thing, fine-tuning?' one may ask. Scientists have discovered that various features of the universe and of the laws of nature which dictate how the universe evolves need to have values lying within a very small range if the universe is to be conducive to life in the broad sense that it is. For example, scientific consensus is that the universe began in a Big Bang some 14 billion years ago (approximately). Scientists have discovered that the rate of expansion of the universe from that Big Bang had to fall within a very small range if it was not either to expand so fast that stars, planets and the like never evolved or expand so slowly that the same consequences followed. If stars and planets never formed, then life could never have formed. The exact figures for the ranges within which this and other constants must lie if there is to be the possibility of life are not always agreed, but it is always agreed that they are very narrow; certainly, one in a billion would not overstate the case.

Of course scientists can't re-run the Big Bang or change the values of constants in the laws of nature in their laboratories – that, after all, is why they're called 'constants'. But they can perform computer simulations for differing values and, when they do so, they find that if any of these things had been different, by even a fraction of a fraction of a per cent, the universe would not be – in the broad sense that it is – conducive to life. The fact is then that had the initial or boundary conditions been even ever so slightly different from the way that they are, life could never have formed. In this sense, then, the universe could be described as 'fine-tuned' for life. The fine-tuning version of the Design Argument suggests that this phenomenon needs some explanation and that God is the best explanation.

This argument has – as do all the others – a number of 'ins and outs' and, given the shortage of space available to me, what I want to do is not what I've done with the Ontological Argument and the Cosmological Argument, viz. give a formal presentation of one version of it and discuss the premises of that version in turn. Rather, I want to give an insight into its general structure through an extended thought experiment. Then, having briefly alerted you to what seems to me the most controversial assumption behind the argument in all its variants, I shall simply leave the thought experiment with you as a putative analogy and encourage you to reflect on it and the assumptions behind it at your leisure.

Imagine yourself then, if you will, back in the 1930s. You visit the local electrical shop with a view to buying your first radio. As you enter, you notice that the shop – though large and generally well stocked – is bare of radios, but there is obviously a large storeroom through an open door behind its counter and, immediately behind that counter, stands a man asking if he can help you. You ask the man if he can

BOX 24.1 RELIGIOUS EXPERIENCE AND IRRELIGIOUS EXPERIENCE

The most notable omission in my treatment will be for many 'The Argument from Religious Experience'. After all, if you asked the average believer why it is that he or she believes in God, he or she would almost certainly not talk about any of the arguments I've talked about, but rather about his or her own experience of God. Either in some prolonged way or at some particular moments in his or her life, he or she will have had experiences which seemed to him or her to be of God. What, if any, evidential value do such experiences have, (a) for the person having them and (b) for the rest of us? Needless to say, these issues attract different answers from different philosophers. I myself am relatively optimistic about them having evidential value, but – by the same token – I am optimistic about certain 'atheistic experiences' being evidence in favour of atheism. If you pray to any God out there that He reveal Himself to you and it seems to you that He has done so, then it seems to me that – ceteris paribus – that experience is in itself at least some evidence for you that God is out there. By the same token, if you pray to any God out there that He reveal Himself to you and it seems to you that He hasn't done so, then it seems to me that – ceteris paribus – that's at least some evidence for you that He's not there. It's sometimes said that you can't infer anything from a silence, but I think this is a case where one could. What do you think?

provide you with a good radio and – you not being confident about using this new technology – one that is already tuned-in to a radio station. You tell him you don't have a preference for any particular radio station over any other. 'That'll all be no problem', he says. He disappears into the storeroom for a few moments and returns with a shiny Bakelite radio, a large tuning dial in its centre. You purchase it. When you get home, you set it up in pride of place in your living room and turn it on. You find as it crackles into life that it's already tuned-in to a radio station, the BBC World Service. You sit back in an armchair and listen.

As you sit, you start to reflect on whether or not the man in the shop had himself to tune the radio; presumably, even though you didn't need to tune it, *he* needed to do so. Or perhaps not. Perhaps these radios come from the factory pre-tuned. Well, presumably *someone* must have tuned it – if not the man from the shop, then someone at the factory. Or perhaps not. Perhaps pretty much anywhere the dial is set will result in the radio picking up some radio station or other. As you sit, it occurs to you that there's an experiment you can do to determine whether or not someone had to tune your radio and perhaps, if so, whether or not they had a preference for the BBC World Service over alternative stations: twist the dial and see how quickly it de-tunes from the BBC World Service and how quickly it re-tunes to other stations.

You reason as follows. Were you to turn the dial and find that it stayed tuned-in to the BBC World Service for all of its possible 360 degrees of rotation, there'd be no reason at all to suppose that there had been a tuner; indeed, it would be hard to conceive of what a 'tuner' *could do* in such a case, even in principle. In such a circumstance, the radio couldn't, in a sense, be 'tuned-in' to the BBC World Service because it couldn't be 'tuned-out' of that station. Were you instead to find as you turned the dial that it stayed tuned-in to the BBC World Service for, say, 180 degrees, and the remaining 180 degrees were taken up by static, you could infer that, absent any tuner, there would have been a 50 per cent chance of its being tuned-in to the one and only station that it can pick up, so, whilst its position could have been set by a tuner, you'd have no great reason to think it had in fact been set by a tuner rather than chance; and, even if it had been set by a tuner, given that there's only one radio station available, it couldn't be inferred by you to have a preference for this radio station over alternatives; there *are* no alternatives. As it is, let's suppose you conduct the experiment and you find that, as you turn the dial, the radio detunes instantly; moving the dial by even a fraction of a hair's breadth in either direction detunes it from the BBC World Service and results in the radio pouring out static instead. What can you infer from this?

It seems to me that you can infer that your radio almost certainly does have a tuner. To gain evidence that this tuner had a preference for the BBC World Service over other radio stations, you'd have to turn the dial until you found some other radio stations or had failed to find any others. As already observed, if it's static all the rest of the way around, then you couldn't infer a preference for the BBC World Service over alternatives – there wouldn't be any alternatives. If, conversely, it was, say, static for 10 degrees either way, but then filled with alternative radio stations, you could infer a preference for the BBC World Service over these alternatives; it'd be reasonable for you to infer that the BBC World Service had been aimed at, rather than that the tuner would have been equally happy with any old station and just happened to hit on the BBC World Service. But, as it stands – your merely having turned it the smallest of amounts in either direction and your having found that it went to static so quickly when you did so – you just have evidence of a tuner. Given how quickly it went to static, indeed we may say you have evidence of 'a fine-tuner'.

My suggestion is that this is a good analogy for the state of play with regard to the fine-tuning of the universe. We have reason from this fine-tuning to think that there is almost certainly a fine-tuner. Is the best contender for being such God? Not obviously. If there are enough universes each of which tries out one of the possible values for the fine-tuned constants, then that would explain why they hit the values they do in one universe, which is the phenomenon that needs explaining. So, positing a multiplicity of universes – such views usually therefore go by the name 'multiverse' views – is another contender for best explanation. In terms of our analogy, we might say that if the factory churns out enough radios with the dials set at random, eventually the chances of one of them being fine-tuned by accident become appreciable however fine-tuned a dial needs to be to pick up a station.

Variants of the multiverse hypothesis are therefore, it seems to me, contenders along with the God hypothesis for explaining the fine-tuning of the universe. When I wrote my book, *Belief in God*, I thought they were in the lead; now I've reversed that ranking. I wonder what you will think.

Finally, I should draw attention to what seems to me the most controversial premise of the argument, the premise that I have called elsewhere the assumption of 'trans-universality' of value. For the argument to work, it must be true over all or at least a very wide range of possible worlds that life of our sort is valuable. In the context of the analogy, this assumption was slipped-in rather covertly; it's the equivalent of our assuming that there's something special about being tuned-in to a radio station rather than just picking up static. As indicated earlier, rather than defend my ranking of God as a better explanation than any multiverse view or defend the assumption of the trans-universality of value, I'm now going to leave it all with you, to reflect on at your leisure.

That then concludes my brief sketch of three of the arguments that have been advanced for theism, one from each of the three categories of arguments. Much more could, indeed should, be said about each one and variants of each one; and there are numerous other arguments for the existence of God that I've not even mentioned. Each of the arguments I have discussed and each of my most notable omissions – the arguments from **religious experience**, **miracles**, and **morality** – continue to attract defenders and attackers. All bear further consideration. As does the one argument against the existence of God, to which we'll now turn, the Problem of Evil.

BOX 24.2 BELIEVING IN MIRACLES

There is an argument that finds expression as early as the Gospels themselves, where – at John 3.2 – someone says to Jesus, 'Rabbi, we know that thou art a teacher come from God: for no man can do these miracles that thou doest, except God be with him.' David Hume wrote one of the most famous pieces in the philosophy of religion on the argument that we gain evidence of the truth of theism from reports of apparent miracles, such as those we find in the Gospels. In essence, he argued that it was always more rational to believe in some naturalistic explanation of the reports (the reporters made an honest mistake or were out to deceive) than to believe a supernaturalistic one, that the miracle actually occurred. He concluded his apparently devastating critique with a sarcastic quip to the effect that, notwithstanding what he'd argued hitherto, of course miracles must happen because, given what he'd argued hitherto about how irrational it is to believe in them, the only explanation of the fact that anyone *does* believe in them is that it's a miracle. This quip inspired J. K. Mackie, one of the most influential mid-twentieth-century philosophers of religion, when he was deciding on the title of his most famous book in the area:

he called it *The Miracle of Theism* (1982). Hume's original piece is undoubtedly brilliant – stylistically and philosophically – and his argument has undoubtedly been hugely influential. Whilst it is now widely held to be defective (indeed there is no real controversy over its being defective in at least some respects) polished-up versions of the Humean argument do seem to many to 'put the boot on the other foot' as it were when it comes to reports of miracles. Philosophically informed believers tend now not to use reports of miracles as independent 'stand-alone' evidence of the truth of their religion; they tend to use such reports either only as evidence when appropriately buttressed by other arguments or even as, in themselves, no evidence at all, but rather things which they would indeed have been unreasonable in believing were it not for other arguments.

• THE PROBLEM OF EVIL

The Problem of Evil is the argument against the existence of God on which most attention has been – and continues to be – focused. I think one can best start to engage with this argument by putting it formally. Here's one way of so putting it.

1 God is by definition omnipotent and perfectly good.
2 Evil is by definition that which is to some extent and in some respect bad.
3 God, being omnipotent and perfectly good, could never be compelled or have any reason to bring about or allow to be brought about something that was to any extent and in any respect bad, i.e. evil.
4 So, if there were a God, then there'd be no evil.
5 There is evil.
6 So there's no God.

Presented thus, the Problem of Evil is a deductively valid argument. So the Theist – committed as he or she is to denying 6 – must deny one or more of the premises. Premises 1 and 2 are definitional claims: omnipotence and perfect goodness are constitutive of the theistic conception of God and in an argument one may define one's terms however one wishes, so this – perhaps rather stretched – sense of 'evil' may be allowed to stand. Premise 4 follows from 1, 2 and 3, so the Theist can't deny 4 unless he or she has more basically denied one or more of 1, 2 and 3. Premise 5 is obviously correct and, given 1 to 5, the conclusion that there is no God, 6, drops out deductively. So the theist must deny 3.

Contra 3, then, theists have traditionally thought that God could well – and the evidence of evil suggests does in fact – find Himself with good reason to allow evil to be brought about. The theist expends his or her energy making this plausible. Again, there are a number of 'ins and outs' here and, given the space available, I think that I do best to make a no doubt rather sweeping generalisation about theistic attempts to render plausible the denial of 3; try to render it plausible myself in the light of a few analogies; and then again leave it all for you to reflect on at your leisure.

It seems to me that the theist is committed to saying by way of defending his or her denial of 3 that God is justified in allowing evil if (but presumably only if) it is overall worth it in some larger scheme of things and no individual – even if he or she is a short-term victim of the system, as it were – can ultimately reasonably complain about his or her treatment. Thus the theist will be assisted if he or she can locate plausible higher-order goods which require lower-order evils of metaphysical **necessity** (the best contender here, it seems to me and to many, is *ante-mortem* morally significant free will, understood in a libertarian sense) and if he or she can show that, on his or her preferred view, there is a heavenly afterlife which will adequately compensate short-term victims with long-term goods. The theist needs to maintain that for every creature who suffers this side of the grave, there will come a day – perhaps only on the other side – when they truly say that as individuals their suffering has been more than adequately compensated for and on which they will be able to see how their suffering fitted into a greater whole which was overall worth it, worth it for it allowed for an *ante-mortem* world of significant freedom. That is perhaps rather abstract and leaves the value judgements needed rather unclear; allow me to make it more particular and vivid.

As I recall, Herodotus tells a story of the barbarian despot, Xerxes, talking with a general in his court about his plans to invade Greece. Xerxes asks the general how many men he thinks the Greeks would need to muster before they would dare to oppose him in battle. The general asks Xerxes whether he wants an answer that will please him or the truth. Xerxes, one imagines rather coldly, asks for the truth.

The general tells him that if the Greeks have ten thousand men, then ten thousand will fight him; if they have only a thousand, then a thousand will fight him; if they have only a hundred, then still those hundred will fight him. Xerxes cannot believe this, for he plans to invade with the largest army the world has yet seen. If these Greeks were under the iron control of a tyrant, such as himself, he reasons, then perhaps they might go forward – even against impossible odds – from their fear of that tyrant and his lash. But these Greeks, he has heard, are free men and freedom is the end of discipline.

The general replies that the Greeks are indeed free, but this is only because they have a master whom they respect more than they could fear any tyrant. This master is their duty. This they listen to and this they – freely but uniformly – obey. And what it commands is ever the same: not to retreat in the face of barbarism, however great the odds; rather, where possible, to advance against it; in any case, to stay firm in their ranks; to conquer or die.

A world without evil would be a world where we could turn every sword into a ploughshare; it would be a world where we never needed to fight because it would be a world where there was never anything worth fighting. A world with terrible barbarians is a world where there are people worth fighting; it is a world where we need swords as well as ploughshares; and it is a world where it's open to us to choose either to go forward into battle against the barbarians like free Greeks or meekly yield to them as would the craven slaves of a barbarian despot. We are free to choose to be heroes or villains, to sacrifice ourselves or to save our own skins, to do our duty or to shirk it. And that we are free in this sense – for at least our *ante-mortem* lives – is a good thing. But it's a good thing that, of its nature, requires bad things.

It seems to me then that if Theism is right, God was faced with a choice to create nothing; to create a world with no such freedom but no evil (Heaven straightaway); or to create a world with a finite amount of this freedom and thus evil, a world in which He compensates everyone for their suffering in an afterlife (a world like ours, with Heaven afterwards). That our experience gives us reason to believe that if He exists, He has chosen the latter of these three systems does not – I would suggest – give us any reason to believe that He doesn't exist. Personally, then, I conclude that the occurrence of evil in the world provides us with no reason whatsoever to think that there's not a God. If Theism is right, there will come a time when every sword may safely be turned into a ploughshare, but if Theism is right, that time is not yet. For now, we are called to act as free Greeks.

This then concludes my very brief discussion of a very small number of the arguments that have been advanced for the existence of God and even briefer discussion of the main argument that has been advanced against the existence of God. Of course, on such topics almost everything one says is controversial. I can only plead again considerations of space for not having given other ideas and arguments an airing and tell you that you shouldn't take my word for anything (other than the fact that you shouldn't take my word for anything, of course). Of course you shouldn't; you are after all, philosophers above all else.

• CHAPTER SUMMARY

In this chapter, I suggested three broad categories into which arguments for and against Theism must fall: those that begin from the mere concept of God; those that begin from this plus the mere fact that there is a universe; and then, finally, those that begin from all of that plus some particular fact or set of facts about the universe. We've looked at an argument from each category for the existence of God: a version of the Ontological Argument; a version of the Cosmological Argument; and a version of the Design Argument. I gave my personal view that the last of these – the fine-tuning version of the Design Argument – gives us reason to believe that there is a God. One can group arguments against the existence of God into these three categories too. We have in effect already looked at arguments against the existence of God that proceed merely from the concept of God, in chapter 23; and, in fact, it would be very implausible to suggest that the mere existence of a universe is evidence that there's no God. That being so, we looked solely at the Problem of Evil – the one remaining argument against the existence of God. I gave my personal view that it doesn't give us reason to think that there's not a God. Here, even more so than in my treatment of the material of chapter 23, I feel I should underscore the fact that what I have said is controversial. Many philosophers who are much more clever than me would disagree with it; some rate versions of the Ontological Argument or the Cosmological Argument more highly; some rate the fine-tuning version of the Design Argument less highly; some rate the Problem of Evil more highly. And, as mentioned, there are many arguments that I haven't even been able to discuss, although some of the most prominent omissions did get a mention – the arguments from religious experience, apparent miracles, and morality. Here, as always, you must not take my word for anything.

• STUDY QUESTIONS

1 Can any version of the Ontological Argument be defended?
2 Why is there anything at all?
3 Is the fine-tuning of the universe evidence of God?
4 What facts, could they be established, would count as evidence, either for or against the existence of God?
5 Is there any solution to the Problem of Evil?

• INTRODUCTORY FURTHER READING

Mackie, J. L. (1982) *The Miracle of Theism* (Oxford: Oxford University Press). [This is the classic response, and still one of the best, to the sort of case that Swinburne and I would present for the reasonableness of theism.]

Mawson, T. J. (2005) *Belief in God* (Oxford: Oxford University Press), part II. [This goes into a few more of the ideas and arguments connected with belief in God.]

Swinburne, Richard (2004) *The Existence of God* (Oxford: Oxford University Press). [This is another engagement with the arguments, which makes some similar (as well as some dissimilar) points to my own.]

Taliaferro, C. (1998) *Contemporary Philosophy of Religion* (Oxford: Blackwell). [This is a very good overview of the wider territory.]

• ADVANCED FURTHER READING

Hick, J. H. (ed.) (1964) *The Existence of God* (London: Macmillan): extracts from Anselm, Aquinas, Descartes, Leibniz, Kant. [Here's a collection of the historical sources on the Ontological Argument.]

Manson, N. (ed.) (2003) *God and Design* (London: Routledge). [A good collection of essays on the Design Argument.]

Philipse, Herman (2012) *God in the Age of Science?* (Oxford: Oxford University Press). [This is a more philosophically advanced (sceptical) engagement with the case for Theism. Philipse really pushes hard against Swinburne in particular.]

Plantinga, A. (1975) *God, Freedom and Evil* (London: George Allen & Unwin), pp. 85–112. [Here's a more modern source than Hick.]

Rowe, W. (1975) *The Cosmological Argument* (Princeton: Princeton University Press). [A (generally sceptical) analysis of the prospects for the Cosmological Argument.]

Rowe, W. L. (1979) 'The Problem of Evil and Some Varieties of Atheism', *American Philosophical Quarterly* 16: 335–41. [This is a 'classic' paper and has generated much interest.]

Swinburne, R. (1998) *Providence and the Problem of Evil* (Clarendon). [Swinburne's most comprehensive treatment of the best argument against God.]

• FREE INTERNET RESOURCES

Arguing for and against the existence of God is an activity that has generated more internet chat, blogs, and so forth than arguing for or against any other issue in philosophy. This means that one is somewhat spoilt for choice as one goes online. But it is also the case that the quality of much of the argument one finds online is very low. There is gold out there, but also a lot of dross. William Lane Craig, a defender of the Kalam Cosmological Argument (which I rather bypassed in my chapter), is an excellent presenter of arguments for the existence of God and he regularly debates worthy opponents (but also, sometimes, less worthy ones). This is a good debate at http://www.reasonablefaith.org/media/craig-vs-millican-university-of-birmingham.

As mentioned in the chapter, my views on the Design Argument have changed since I wrote my book. My current view, arguing that the fine-tuning version of the Design Argument makes it as reasonable to believe in God as it is to believe that emeralds won't turn blue tomorrow, may be found in a lecture which I delivered at the Royal Institute of Philosophy and the text of which may be accessed free of charge from my webpage: http://www.philosophy.ox.ac.uk/members/philosophy_panel/tim_mawson.

25
is faith in God reasonable?

● FAITH AS BELIEF IN AS WELL AS BELIEF THAT

One can believe that something is true but not have **faith** in it. I believe that some politicians have a policy of encouraging people to think of university education as simply training for the 'job market' beyond, but I don't believe in this policy; I don't have faith in it. What am I saying about myself when I utter this sentence? Well, I'm saying that although I believe that a certain thing – in this case a policy – exists, I do not believe that it should exist. *Believing that* is an intellectual commitment; *believing in* is a moral or existential commitment, a trusting in one person; course of action; or set of ideals, rather than another. So belief that does not require belief in. Does belief in require belief that? Can one believe in (or disbelieve in) something whilst not believing anything about it? One cannot, for the simple reason that one's belief in (or disbelief in) has to have some sort of belief that associated with it to act as the handle by which it grabs the thing that one's believing in (or disbelieving in) and makes sure it's that thing that one's believing in (or disbelieving in) rather than something else or nothing at all. Beliefs-in require beliefs-that and thus faith as a matter of belief in God, must also be a matter of belief that there's a God. In looking at arguments for and against the truth of theism, we've been looking at how reasonable the belief that element of faith in God might be. But perhaps the reasonableness of the belief in element of faith might exceed the reasonableness of the belief that element and even 'drag it up' somewhat. Let's explore that idea for a moment or two.

Belief in may certainly sustain itself at a particular level whilst the certainty of the relevant belief that vacillates. Take my belief in the cause of opposing the displacement of the concept of education in people's minds by that of training. If a week or so goes by without anyone in power pushing forward the programme of attacking universities which concern themselves with an alternative vision, my belief that this is the policy of certain politicians might wane. But whilst my belief that there's something to oppose here might thus wax and wane, my belief in opposing it – if it does indeed exist – might remain unchanged in its strength. And it seems to me that one might have better – indeed overwhelming – reasons to hold the belief in opposing the displacement of the educational ideal than one has for the belief that element, that there's something there to be opposed. Matters are similar, it seems to me, with the belief in element of faith in God.

It won't be possible to believe in God without believing in at least a vacillating way that there is a God. It may be possible to believe that there's a God yet not believe in Him. If there's a Devil, then he believes that there is a God with much less vacillation than any of us, but he passionately disbelieves in God; he's committed himself to quite another set of ideals and objectives. But of course believing that there's a God – a being who is, amongst other things, omnipotent and perfectly good – whilst not believing in Him, i.e. whilst not making a moral or existential commitment to Him, must be irrational. There cannot be anything more rational as an object of faith than God.

Faith in God then is a combination of believing that there's a God and believing in Him. It is not possible to believe in God whilst not believing that He exists, but it is possible – albeit supremely irrational – to believe that He exists yet not believe in Him. On the truth of Theism, not believing in God will lead inevitably to idolatry, which is making one's ultimate moral or existential commitment to something less worthy than God, putting one's ultimate trust in something less trustworthy than one could have put one's trust in. Faith in God is the opposite of idolatry. It's no surprise then that – from a Theistic point of view – one is commended for having faith. Having faith represents the 'turning' of oneself to God's will that will make the Last Judgement heavenly rather than hellish. So, can the positive pay-offs of the belief in element of faith, as I am calling it, make up for a shortfall in first-order reasons for having the belief that element? And then add to these first-order reasons its own brand of second-order reason? There is a well-known argument, Pascal's Wager, to the effect that it can. Personally, I am somewhat sceptical about Pascal's original argument, but it continues to attract defenders as well as attackers. And there now follows a similar thought that I would endorse.

Don't studies show that people who have faith in God have healthier and happier lives than those who don't? Isn't it very plausible to suggest that these studies show that having faith in God brings much more happiness than is lost by the earthly pleasures that the religious life may discourage one from indulging in? I don't have time to look at these studies here; a thorough investigation of them would belong more properly to the psychology or perhaps sociology of religion. But if the evidence of these studies is that – putting aside for a moment whether or not there's a God – those who have faith in God benefit overall in this world to a certain extent, then as – if there's a God – we may be sure they will not suffer from having had faith in Him in the next world, so we may say that there's overall a Pascal's-Wager-type non-truth-directed reason for us to do what increases our chances of having faith in God.

> **BOX 25.1** FAITH: BELIEVING WHAT YOU KNOW AIN'T SO?
>
> Mark Twain once defined faith as 'believing what you know ain't so', but that can't be right. I'll give one million pounds to anybody reading this who can make themselves believe – even for a moment – that they have three arms. If you believe my offer to be a genuine one, then you'll take yourself to have good reason to believe what you know to be false – that you have three arms. One million pounds would be, I am supposing, a life-changing sum of money for you and a fleeting false belief that you had three arms, whilst no doubt disturbing, wouldn't be too inconvenient for you. So why is it that you cannot make yourself believe that you have three arms? Is it just a quirk of your psychology that you can't do that? In other words, is it logically contingent that beliefs-that are not under the direct control of the will? It is not. Your beliefs-that are your beliefs about what the world is like. If you tried to acquire a particular belief simply because you would get some money as a result of doing so, then you'd know that you were attempting to acquire a belief by a mechanism which wouldn't make it more likely that you would acquire a true belief rather than a false one. But if you knew that that was how you were going to acquire a particular mental state, then you could not think of whatever mental state you got yourself into as a result as a belief that. You couldn't because you'd know that that mental state was not related to how the world is and your beliefs-that have to be mental states which you believe are related to how the world is in a way which makes them more likely to be true than false. You can't regard some mental occurrence of yours as a belief that you have three arms whilst you realise that you have no truth-tracking reason for having that mental occurrence, for you can only take as your beliefs-that mental occurrences which you take to have some truth-tracking relation to the world. That's what makes those mental occurrences beliefs-that, rather than something else. Contra Mark Twain, then, believing by faith cannot be a matter of believing what you know (or even what you believe) ain't so. It seems that faith can only have as its objects things that you don't know (or indeed believe) ain't so.

• THE 'ETHICS' OF BELIEVING IN GOD

The sort of argument we've been looking at in this chapter raises an issue which looks at first glance like it might have a certain methodological priority to all the other issues we've addressed, the issue of what is the right 'ethics of belief' for belief in God or belief that there's a God. (We'll actually talk solely in terms of belief in God in what follows for reasons of simplicity.) Should one believe in God only if one has positive reasons in favour of doing so or is it permissible to believe in Him without such reasons? In what space remains and by way of concluding then, I want to see what can be done to decide which of the various options for an ethics of belief in God is right prior to deciding whether or not God exists. Let's start then by getting these options out onto the table. One of them is as follows:

1 We should believe in God only if we have positive reasons to do so.

Many atheists hold that this is the right ethics of belief for belief in God and, thinking that there are no such reasons, they thus think of themselves as doing as they ought when they remain atheists. But many theists hold that this is the right ethics of belief as well; the difference between many theists and atheists then is just that the theist thinks that there are in fact good reasons for believing that there is a God and the atheist thinks that there are not. But option 1 is not the only option.

There are some who believe in God even though they do not take themselves to have any positive reasons for doing so and who do not consider themselves in any way intellectually irresponsible. Deciding whether or not there's a God, such people say, is a 'leap of faith', rather than a conclusion of reason. The most moderate variant of this ethics of belief we might summarise as follows:

2 We are permitted to believe in God even if we don't have any positive reasons for doing so, as long as we don't have any positive reasons against.

Obviously, on the first view, in order appropriately to believe in God, one has to have both positive reasons for doing so and solutions to arguments which would purport to overwhelm these reasons with reasons against (e.g. the **Problem of Evil**). But on this second view, it is alright to have no positive reasons for believing in God, just so long as one still has those solutions to things like the Problem of Evil. On this second view, the hurdle is lower. As you might expect, then, many atheists object to this ethics of belief. Indeed many seem to find it infuriating and quickly lose patience with people who seem to be espousing it. But if people who espouse 2 set your teeth on edge, the next group we'll consider will make you wish you'd had them taken out.

There are people who hold an even more extreme ethics of belief than 2, one which suggests that we are justified in believing 'by faith' things which are actually contrary to reason. We might summarise that view as follows:

3 We should – or at least are permitted to – believe in God even though, or maybe even because, it is contrary to reason.

On this view, at its most extreme, belief in God becomes appropriate and proportionate to the extent that one has reasons against it. No need now then even for a solution to the Problem of Evil, indeed better not to have one for then one can revel all the more in the glorious absurdity of one's faith. On this understanding, the hurdle isn't just low, it's below ground. Atheists who wish to attack this as the right ethics of belief for belief in God find themselves making common cause with many theists, *viz.* all those who hold either of the first two ethics of belief.

The three options for one's ethics of belief that I've enumerated above seem to be mutually exclusive and exhaustive. One of them must be right. Let's look at these options in a little bit more detail to see whether we can vindicate the hope that we can decide which one is right prior to deciding whether or not there's a God. First one first: we should believe in God only if we have positive reasons to do so.

How might one defend this? One might base a defence of it on something like W. K. Clifford's principle, 'it is wrong always, everywhere and for anyone, to believe anything upon insufficient evidence.' But that principle would cause too much collateral damage: it would undermine the propriety of our believing things we all think it is permissible to believe and yet for which we have no evidence at all, e.g. the future will resemble the past. We weren't all created five minutes ago with a host of false memories. There is an external world and it is more or less as our senses present it to us.

It seems that one can generate sceptical scenarios (we're all disembodied spirits being fooled by a demon; we're all brains in vats; et cetera) that are indistinguishable from the points of view of the people in them from being in the world we take ourselves to be in. In that the differences between these scenarios and what we take to be reality are then 'evidence transcendent', so we cannot have any evidence – let alone sufficient evidence – against these scenarios being false. Yet we all do, nevertheless, think them false and do not think ourselves irresponsible in so thinking. Clifford's principle is too strong.

To avoid this sort of collateral damage, yet successfully hit belief in God, one could seek to narrow the focus of the principle in some non-question-begging way. But, it seems to me, this can't be done. So, for example, one might say that the principle applies only to topics on which there's widespread disagreement amongst sincere, intelligent and well-informed (at least about areas other than the one in question) people. This then would allow back in as entirely proper our common-sense beliefs that there's an external world and so on, but still keep out belief in God.

However, even with this narrowing, the principle still causes too much collateral damage; all our fundamental moral beliefs get hit, one example being our belief in the principle itself. The modified Cliffordian principle is itself something on which there's widespread disagreement amongst sincere, intelligent people. So, if it's true, it cannot be properly believed to be so unless one has sufficient evidence in its favour. It seems one can't provide that. So it looks as if option 1 is one we can't have reasons to believe is true, or at least reasons to believe is true prior to collecting reasons to believe that there is or that there's not a God. It might of course be true anyway. (Something's being something which, if true, is something which one cannot find reasons to suppose is true is not that thing's being false.) Let's leave it on the table then.

What about 2? We are permitted to believe in God even if we don't have any positive reasons for doing so, as long as we don't have any positive reasons against.

How might one defend this? Again, the issue in defending it is avoiding collateral damage, i.e. we don't want to end up 'defending' it whilst inadvertently defending the obviously indefensible (and thus not really defending it at all). But, this time, the danger is not that we might keep out too much, but that we might let in too much.

So – to return to an example of Russell's – we do not think that we are permitted to believe that there's a teapot orbiting the Sun (even though – I take it – we don't have any positive reasons against this hypothesis). Thus we'll need to come up with something special about God relative to teapots and the like, something special that isn't question-begging and which allows us to believe in God but disallows us from believing in Russell's teapot.

William James, responding directly to Clifford, seems to me to have done one of the best jobs here, but – to cut a long story short – it doesn't seem to me to be conclusive. That is to say that even whilst it is no doubt true that there are some things that we are permitted to believe (even should believe) when we don't have any positive reasons for doing so – we might go back to our examples of the beliefs that the future will resemble the past; that we weren't all created five minutes ago with a host of false memories; and that there is an external world and it is more or less as our senses present it to us – the belief that God exists does not seem to me to be able to be categorised amongst these on grounds independent of God's existence.

To expand a little on that last point: it is necessary that there are some things which we are permitted to believe (even should believe) even though we don't have any positive reasons for doing so. If that weren't the case, then, for every one of our beliefs, we'd need another belief (to be the required reason backing it up), but that would generate an infinite regress and we cannot have an infinite number of beliefs. If then believing some things without any positive reasons in their favour is intellectually inescapable for finite minds such as ours, it is intellectually responsible; we are at least permitted to do it, probably should do it. The only real question can be over what beliefs fall into this category of beliefs, which we may call 'properly basic' beliefs.

Whilst there's unlikely to be much controversy over putting things like 'there's an external world' into the category of properly basic beliefs, there is likely to be controversy over putting things like 'God exists' into it. It seems that if there is an external world, then belief that there is such a world is likely to be properly basic and, given that we all do believe that there is an external world, so we can all agree that believing that there is without any reasons is at the least permissible. Similarly, it seems that if there is a God, then belief that there is might well be properly basic too (indeed probably is properly basic for at least some people – God Himself, for example), but, given that we do not all believe that there is a God, so we cannot expect that we'll all agree that believing that there is without any reasons is at the least permissible. (Here we might insert non-truth-directed reasons for belief as pertinent – James himself did so.)

It seems to me that the contemporary philosopher of religion Alvin Plantinga is right when he says – roughly – that if God exists, then we are permitted to believe in Him even if we don't have any positive reasons for doing so; and, if God doesn't exist, then we're not. It looks to me then as if 2 is something we can't have reasons to believe is true either, or at least reasons to believe is true prior to deciding whether or not there is a God. As with 1, it might be true nonetheless. It too needs to stay on the table. What about 3? We should – or at least are permitted to – believe in God even though, or maybe even because, it is contrary to reason.

At last, we've found a view that we have reason to reject: it's impossible to articulate the view without giving oneself a reason to reject it. Premise 3 is saying that we should (i.e. have overall reason to) – or at least are permitted to (i.e. don't have overall reason not to) – do something even though, or maybe even because, it is contrary to reason, i.e. we have overall reason not to do it. But the claim that we have greater or equal reason to do something which we at the same time have greater reason not to do is a straightforward contradiction.

So we may conclude that the right ethics of belief for belief in God cannot be 3. It must be either 1 or 2. And we may conclude that our initial hope that we could decide which of these is right methodologically prior to deciding whether or not there's a God is misguided; we can't. Premise 1 is right if there is no God, but 2 might be right – indeed almost certainly is right for some (God Himself, presumably) – if there is a God. What to do next then? It looks as if it'll need to be a return to the issues we raised under the second of our three questions in this section, a return to looking at arguments for and against Theism. But this brief excursion has not been a waste of time, for what might otherwise have seemed a strange result may now be anticipated as at least possible.

If the line of argument pursued in this chapter is right, we should be open to the possibility that if our studies of the arguments for and against Theism were to end up giving us reasons to believe Theism, then they might end up giving us reasons to believe that these reasons weren't after all necessary. That fact – the fact that we might, by finding reasons to believe that there is a God, be finding reasons to suppose that we don't need these reasons – might explain why some of those who do believe in God are so indifferent to the fact that they can give no reasons for their belief. And realising that might make those of us who are atheists and who, when it comes to articulating our ethics of belief for belief in God, would say something along the lines of option 1 a little bit more patient with those of us who are theists and would subscribe to something along the lines of option 2.

BOX 25.2 THEISMS, ATHEISMS AND AGNOSTICISMS

Naturally, how easy or hard it is to make a case for/against theism, agnosticism, or atheism depends in part on how you define them. In these chapters I've been taking these terms in a certain way, but there is no consensus that this is the best way to take them and thus there is an annoying phenomenon in the discipline, that of 'speaking past' one another in debates that are nominally about the defensibility of the same view. Indeed I type this paragraph on the morning of the first day of the biennial British Society for the Philosophy of Religion Conference, the theme of which this year is 'Atheisms'; we're going to spend a couple of days considering the variety of views that may legitimately be called Atheism. If one inflects one's definition of Theism, Agnosticism, or Atheism with contested notions such as knowledge or reasonableness, then the possibilities multiply; one does not need to venture outside the covers of this very volume to discover that knowledge and reasonableness are themselves things over the best definitions of which there is no consensus. A recent work (S. Bullivant and M. Ruse (eds) *The Oxford Handbook to Atheism* (Oxford: Oxford University Press, 2013)) defines atheism as the view that a failure to believe that there's a God is not unreasonable. In this sense of Atheism, Atheism's being true is compatible with there being a God; it might well be that there is a God and yet that for some (not for God Himself, presumably) the evidence that they have is insufficient to render it positively unreasonable for them to fail to come to the belief that there's a God. Thus many theists in my sense (people who believe that there is a God) have no need in consistency to deny atheism in the Bullivant/Ruse sense, i.e. to deny that at least some other people might well be 'not unreasonable' in failing to join them in their belief in God.

• CONCLUSION

This concludes my answer to the question, 'What is this thing called "The Philosophy of Religion"?' I naturally hope it has been of interest to you and hope indeed that you will be interested enough to look further into the ideas and arguments with which the discipline concerns itself. Theism has been – and still is – the most popular metaphysical system in the history of human thought; the religions which it undergirds – most notably, Judaism, Christianity and Islam – provide world-views which inform and give meaning to the lives of billions, billions who would claim then that the Philosophy of Religion concerns the most important issues towards which we may ever direct ourselves. You would find it hard then, I think, to maintain that it is not a worthy object of your interest.

• CHAPTER SUMMARY

In this chapter, I've given a brief account of what it means to have faith in God; I have suggested that having faith in God is having both a belief in (a moral or existential commitment to Him) and having a belief that (He exists) and I've argued that the belief in element may persist and thus faith persist even if the belief that element vacillates to an extent. I have myself endorsed a version of Pascal's Wager, that the this-worldly benefits of believing in God may give one a non-truth-directed reason to have faith in God and, therefore, indirectly (given that belief that there's a God is necessary for faith), for belief that there's a God. But this is to assume something about the ethics of belief. In the last part of this chapter, we stood back and considered what the ethics of belief for belief in God should be and, in particular, if we could work out an answer to this prior to deciding whether or not there is a God. And I concluded that we could not.

• STUDY QUESTIONS

1 How would you explain the 'belief in/belief that' distinction?
2 Can you come up with some examples from your life of things you believe-in/ disbelieve-in?
3 How is 'faith' best defined?
4 Can any version of Pascal's Wager be defended?
5 Can one say anything general about which of Theism, Atheism, or Agnosticism should be the 'default', absent evidence either way? If not, why not?

• INTRODUCTORY FURTHER READING

Mawson, T. J. (2005) *Belief in God* (Oxford: Oxford University Press), conclusion. [Here I give an expanded account of the nature of faith as I see it and go into a bit more detail about the version of Pascal's Wager that I'd endorse.]
Penelhum, T. (ed.) (1989) *Faith* (Basingstoke: Macmillan). [A nice short overview of the topic.]
Plantinga, Alvin and Wolterstorff, Nicholas (1983) *Faith and Rationality: Reason and Belief in God* (Notre Dame: University of Notre Dame Press) [This is worth reading early on.]
Swinburne, Richard (2005) *Faith and Reason* (Oxford: Oxford University Press).

• ADVANCED FURTHER READING

Adams, R. M. (1987) *The Virtue of Faith* (Oxford: Oxford University Press), part I.
Alston, W. P. (1985) 'Plantinga's Epistemology of Religious Belief', in J. Tomberlin and P. van Inwagen (eds.) *Alvin Plantinga* (Dordrecht: Reidel), 289–311. [This is

an analysis of Plantinga's views of the time; they have changed slightly since. See Free Internet Resources below.]

Bullivant, S. and M. Ruse (eds) (2013) *The Oxford Handbook to Atheism* (Oxford: Oxford University Press).

Kenny, A. (1983) *Faith and Reason* (New York: Columbia University Press), chs 1–3.

——(1992) *What is Faith?* (Oxford: Oxford University Press).

• FREE INTERNET RESOURCES

Plantinga, A. (1999) *Warranted Christian Belief* (Oxford: Oxford University Press), parts 2 and 3. This is Plantinga's fully developed view and is available at: http://www.oxfordscholarship.com/view/10.1093/0195131932.001.0001/acprof-9780195131932

Finally, there are some very good internet encyclopaedias of Philosophy; one of the best to my mind is 'Stanford'. It has excellent entries for all the topics and arguments of all three of my chapters and is easily searchable. After each entry, there is an extensive bibliography if you wish to follow up yet further, many of the items from which will themselves be findable online: http://plato.stanford.edu/.

Happy hunting (and thinking).

Part IX
the meaning of life

Thaddeus Metz

From one perspective, many of the chapters in this book could be viewed as about what makes a life meaningful. If there were no external world, wouldn't our lives be pretty meaningless, akin to living in *The Matrix*? If our actions were not free and we were not responsible for our behavior, wouldn't our lives be trivial, like those of animals? How could our lives be meaningful if there were no objective moral standards, or if we failed to live up to them? Isn't justice something to advance because one's life would be more important for doing so? And, finally, isn't the existence of God central to whether our existence is significant?

While it is not being suggested that philosophy as a whole is ultimately about the meaning of life, that value has implicitly driven a variety of philosophical inquiries to some degree. This Part focuses strictly on that value, seeking to answer the question of what, if anything, confers meaning on our lives.

In addition to this question having tacitly motivated many philosophical investigations, it is also the subject of many of the oldest and most widely read written works in the world, such as the Hebrew Bible in the monotheistic tradition, the *Vedas* and *Upanishads* in Hinduism, and the *Analects* and the *Mencius* in Confucianism. Many of the 'best seller' religious texts are not solely about what fundamentally exists and how to be pleased or to act justly, but in addition usually address issues of meaning in life. That is plausibly the case, even if they do not use those specific words, for instance, the author of the biblical Book of Ecclesiastes writes of life being 'vanity' ('meaningless', in our terms), while those in the Confucian tradition say that one should strive to become 'wise' or 'great'.

Despite the question of life's meaning having an extremely long history in systematic human thought, it is only recently that it has grounded a distinct field among professional philosophers. Philosophical and literary texts devoted to the question of what, if anything, makes life meaningful began to be salient in the nineteenth century, with notable essays and books by Arthur Schopenhauer and Leo Tolstoy. In addition, the writings of the nineteenth-century thinkers Søren Kierkegaard and Friedrich Nietzsche led to the **existentialist** movement of the twentieth century. Existentialism is a branch of philosophy that reflects on the nature of individuals and on how they must take responsibility for living their lives in the face of doubt about the existence (or nature) of God and objective values. This orientation was most clearly exemplified by the works of the French thinkers Albert Camus and Jean-Paul Sartre. Finally, in the twenty-first century, those who have been doing the most work on the topic of life's meaning have tended to be based in the UK, the US and other English-speaking parts of the world. Since the post-war era, Anglo-American philosophers have substantially been the ones to create a field that focuses on '**meaningfulness**', maintaining that it deserves independent inquiry for being a positive value that is largely distinct from other goods such as **happiness**, understood as pleasant experiences, and **morality**, behavior that does not merit guilt or censure.

This Part focuses largely, but not exclusively, on recent Anglo-American philosophical thought about what makes, or at least would make, our lives meaningful. Most now seeking to answer that question are interested in some respect in how an individual's life can be better or worse (although a smaller number are interested in more 'cosmic' questions such as whether humanity as a whole or the universe has a point). When it comes to appraising a given person's life, contemporary philosophers generally maintain that, if it is meaningful, it is so to a certain degree and in virtue of something that is normally higher than mere physical pleasure while on earth, something that it would be sensible for one to be very proud of, or for others to greatly admire about one.

For example, it is fairly uncontroversial to say that the following kinds of actions and attitudes are meaningful: rearing children with love, being a good friend, working for a charity, rescuing someone from an undeserved fate, accomplishing something at sport, creating works of art, making intellectual discoveries, working to overcome problems with one's personality, and participating in a religious community. In contrast, intuitively meaningless behaviors include: urinating in snow, chewing gum, scratching an itch, taking joy in the pain of others, cheating on a test, and stealing from others on the web. (There might be unusual situations in which these could be meaningful, but that would require telling a convoluted story, one that would probably appeal to an additional and entirely different condition, such as one from the meaningful list above.) Now, what is the fundamental difference between the meaningful conditions and those that are meaningless? It would be fascinating if all the meaningful elements had something – indeed, *one* thing – in common.

A theory is a view of what that might be, and this Part considers three theoretical perspectives about life's meaning. The first chapter addresses the principle that meaning in life is just a matter of conforming to God's will. The second engages with the theory that the meaning of this life on earth is merely a function of an afterlife, a state of one's soul after one's body has died. While the first two views are obviously **supernaturalist** or spiritualist, the third one is not, and is instead **naturalist** or materialist, where these words mean neither being in touch with nature nor being an avid consumer. Instead, they are meant to connote the principle that a meaningful life is possible in a purely physical world, one in which there is neither God nor a soul, so long as one behaves in a particular way.

26

must God exist for your life to be meaningful?

- God-based theories of meaning in life
- God as the source of morality
- Meaning without morality?
- Morality without God?
- Objections to God-based theories in general

GOD-BASED THEORIES OF MEANING IN LIFE

In the introduction to this Part, I noted that when speaking of 'meaning in life', most inquirers have in mind something in a person's life that is of higher value than physical pleasure and that merits substantial admiration or pride. One natural suggestion about where such a value could come from is a supernatural realm, one beyond earth or the physical world more generally. In particular, relating to a holy being seems to be a good candidate for how to obtain meaning in one's life; while a purely physical being could feel pleasure, it would arguably take a spiritual and perfect being to ground a qualitatively different and superlative value such as meaningfulness.

This chapter considers the supernaturalist view that a life is meaningful if and only if it is in a certain sort of relationship with God, the holy being as commonly conceived in the monotheistic tradition of Judaism, Christianity and Islam. That is, God is understood to be a person who exists in a spiritual realm, is the source of the physical universe, and is all-powerful, all-knowing and all-good. According to a **God-based theory** of meaning in life, one's life is meaningful only insofar as God, so construed, exists and one relates to God in the right sort of way. Here are two implications of that view: if God does not exist, then everyone's life is meaningless; and if God does exist, but one does not relate to Him in the appropriate way, then one's life is meaningless.

Note that by a God-based theory, merely believing that God exists is *not sufficient* for a meaningful life. God must actually *exist* for our lives to be capable of significance. Faith in a being that is not real is not enough for meaning, according to the present perspective.

In addition, notice that for a God-based theory of meaning in life, it is not true by definition that believing in God is even *necessary* for one's life to meaningful. Of course, many who hold such a theory do contend that at least part of the relevant relationship to have with an existing God is to believe that He exists. However, there is nothing contradictory about a God-based theorist holding the view that atheists and agnostics could have meaningful lives, perhaps by doing works of which God happens to approve.

More generally, there is debate among God-based theorists about what it precisely is about God that alone could make our lives meaningful. Some have suggested that if God had not created us, then our lives would be random, in the sense that it would be sheer luck that we exist. Only God could prevent our lives from being accidental and hence meaningless, so one argument goes. Others have maintained that without God, there would be no one to remember us; in the absence of someone with an eternal mind, we would vanish without a trace, which would make our lives insignificant.

Although these rationales have been proffered by philosophers and theologians, they are not the dominant ones, and probably for good reason. As they stand, they have a difficult time accounting for the intuition that degrees of meaning differ among people, that some have more meaningful lives than others. To say that does not imply that people have an unequal value from a moral perspective. Even supposing that everyone matters equally for the purposes of morality, it still seems true that some people have had very meaningful lives, while others have not. Surely, the lives of Nelson Mandela and Mother Teresa were much more meaningful than the lives of either a serial killer or what Susan Wolf, one of the living philosophers who has written the most on meaning in life, calls 'The Blob', someone who spends as much time as he can drinking beer while watching television sit-coms alone. The problem with the above arguments is that they cannot easily explain what the difference is between the former and the latter lives. Either God intentionally created everyone and everyone's life is meaningful, or God did not and no one's life is. Either God will remember all of us forever and all our lives are meaningful, or God will not and no one's life is.

Another way to put the point is that the above rationales seem poised to explain why the human race as a whole is meaningful or has a point, but are not well designed to explain why an individual person's life is meaningful in comparison to the lives of others. There could be ways of revising the arguments so that they are less 'cosmic' and do not have the implication that the meaningfulness of one's life necessarily stands or falls with that of everyone else's. However, instead of pursuing that strategy, this chapter instead articulates another God-based theory, one that on the face of it easily accounts for the idea that there are different degrees of meaning between people's lives.

• GOD AS THE SOURCE OF MORALITY

According to the most influential reason for thinking that only God could make our lives meaningful, one's life is meaningful to the extent that one does what God wants one to do. Call this view the '**purpose theory**' of meaning in life. If one does the opposite of what God intends for one, or simply fails to do very much of what God intends, then one's life is meaningless. If, in contrast, one does much to fulfill the reason for which God created one, then one's life is meaningful, and it is more meaningful, the more one carries out God's aims. Such a view is prevalent in all three of the monotheistic religions: 'Ye shall observe to do therefore as the Lord your God hath commanded you' (*Deuteronomy* 5.29); 'Our Father which art in heaven, Hallowed be thy name. Thy kingdom come. Thy will be done, as in heaven, so in earth' (*Luke* 11.2); 'I have only created Jinns (spirits) and men, that they may serve Me' (*Qur'an* 51:56).

On some versions of this perspective, God has a separate intention for each of us, a unique path that has been tailor-made to fit our specific conditions and that we must traverse in order to live meaningfully. The more common version, though, is one according to which God ascribes the same goal to all of us. Most God-based philosophers and religious thinkers have contended that one thing God would want all of us to do is to behave morally. More specifically, it has been common to hold what is called the '**divine command theory of morality**', according to which what makes something moral or immoral, right or wrong, permissible or forbidden, is the bare fact that God has told us either to do it or not to do it. From this perspective, if God did not exist, then there would be no moral rules that apply to all of us.

And such a godless world would seem to entail meaningless lives, since it would mean that what the Nazis did was not wrong and that there are no binding standards for all of us to live up to. In contrast, if God exists, then what God has commanded every human being to do is morally right, where the more we do what God commands, the more meaningful our lives.

To bring things together, note how powerful is the present explanation of why a relationship with God is alone what would make our lives meaningful. Where does the higher value of meaning come from, a value that transcends our physical capacity for pleasure? From a holy being who is in a spiritual realm. Why is God necessary for meaning in life? Because without God having commanded us to do some things rather than others, there would be no invariant moral rules by which to abide. What explains the different degrees of meaning in people's lives? Some have lived up to

God's commands better than others. What accounts for the significance of Nelson Mandela's and Mother Teresa's lives in comparison to the relative insignificance of a serial killer's and The Blob's? The former have done much more to fulfill God's moral commands than have the latter.

BOX 26.1 JOHN COTTINGHAM

John Cottingham (1943–), who for many years has been based at the University of Reading, has been the most powerful English-speaking philosophical voice in the twenty-first century to defend a God-based perspective on meaning in life. In this selection from one of his many books, *The Spiritual Dimension* (2005), Cottingham explains and defends the view that life would be meaningless without an objective morality, which could come only from God. He replies both to the concern that God could command intuitively immoral actions and to the worry that God's commands would degradingly treat us merely as a means to His end. Do you find his replies convincing?

Cottingham, 'The Metaphysics of Value' and 'God as the Source of Morality', edited excerpt from *The Spiritual Dimension* (Cambridge: Cambridge University Press, 2005), pp. 46–49 and 49–54

A familiar objection to the religious position is that it is repugnant to say that God's commands create value. If God's will is simply the will of a powerful being who controls our lives, then this cannot of itself give us reason to conform to his will (that is, a moral reason, as opposed to a merely prudential consideration). If God's commands are worthy of our obedience, then this must be because they are good. But this in turn suggests that God's will cannot be the source of value; rather it must reflect value.…This reasoning creates a dilemma for the theist who sees morality as rooted in the will of God (a dilemma whose elements go back to the perplexing 'Euthyphro problem' first articulated by Plato). On the one hand, the mere fact that a supreme being (arbitrarily) wills X cannot provide a moral reason for doing X; on the other hand, if the reason we should obey God's commands are antecedently right or good, then God no longer appears to be the source of morality.…

The standard reply to this dilemma (the line taken by Augustine and Aquinas and by several modern defenders of the idea of divinely based morality) is that goodness is inseparable from God's nature. God neither issues arbitrary commands, nor is he subject to prior moral constraints; rather his commands necessarily reflect his essential nature, as that which is wholly and perfectly good.

[….]

Consider the graphic and somewhat revolting example in the *Hitchhiker's Guide to the Galaxy*, of the cow genetically engineered to be capable of thought and speech, and to enjoy being killed and eaten for the pleasure of the customers in the 'Restaurant at the End of the Universe'....If the theistic view of our human existence were like this, if our lives were merely of instrumental value to some higher being who had shaped our nature simply and entirely to suit his own purposes, then it is hard to see how our actions and choices in pursuit of our deepest inclinations could, in these circumstances, have any genuine moral meaning. But the theistic conception is of a good and loving creator who desires that his creatures lead lives that are of value to themselves (as well as to him). And this makes a crucial difference.

• MEANING WITHOUT MORALITY?

How have philosophers questioned the above rationale for thinking that a relationship of obedience to God is essential for one's life to be meaningful? One strategy has been to contend that meaning is possible despite a lack of morality, or even despite immorality. One case discussed in this context concerns the artist Paul Gauguin, who is reputed to have abandoned his wife and children to go and develop his painting in Tahiti. Although the historical evidence about that is unclear, suppose it were true. Consider someone who leaves his family in the lurch but as a consequence becomes a great artist. It seems this person's life could be fairly meaningful by virtue of having produced masterpieces, which does not seem to be a moral matter, and, furthermore, was made possible only by an immoral deed.

There are a number of replies that one might suggest, here. For one, some maintain that the immorality would have in fact 'polluted' the works of art, so that no real meaning could come from producing them by an immoral means. Suppose that someone killed innocent people in order to use their blood in his paintings; surely, the wrongful production of the art would undercut its significance. Maybe something similar goes for the case of Gauguin.

For another, some contend that creating great artworks can in fact, upon reflection, be seen to be a kind of moral behavior. There are those, especially in the consequentialist tradition of ethics, who contend that right actions are those that improve people's quality of life in the long run. Even though Gauguin's family was not well off as a result of his alleged abandonment, that was arguably outweighed by Gauguin's having made many other (hundreds of thousands of) people live better lives as a result of the influence of his paintings.

Finally, some argue that God's commands would be not merely to be moral, but also to engage in additional kinds of activities. According to some views, God would command us to be as much like God as we can. Since God is normally conceived not merely as all-good (morally perfect), but also as all-knowing and all-powerful, perhaps we are expected not merely to live moral lives, but also ones that develop our knowledge and creativity, where, because of our limited natures, we sometimes have to make trade-offs among these goods. Such a view could explain the meaningfulness not merely of art, but also intellectual achievement, perhaps even when these come at some cost to moral considerations.

• MORALITY WITHOUT GOD?

A second major way to object to the idea that obedience to God is the key to meaning in life is to grant that a moral life is necessary for, perhaps even exhaustive of, a meaningful life, but to deny that God's commands could ground moral rules. One objection along these lines is that if something is right merely because God commands it, then anything at all could conceivably be right, which is counterintuitive. If God commanded you to torture babies for fun, or to kill your son (perhaps named 'Isaac') in order to show your devotion, then it would be right to do so, supposing that moral rules were identical to whatever God tells you to do. However, so the objection goes, it could never be right to torture babies for fun, and so it cannot be true that moral rules are identical to whatever God tells you to do. Moral rules must have some other source.

The immediate inclination is to reply that God would never command anyone to torture babies for fun. But more needs to be said than that. For the point is that if what makes something right is the bare fact that God has commanded it, and if God *could* command one to torture babies for fun, then, *if* God were to do that (regardless of whether God in fact would), then it would be right to do. And the objection is that such an action could never be right.

What needs to be argued is that God *could not* command anyone to torture babies for fun. And what some philosophers of religion and theologians contend is that what God could command would be fixed by God's nature. For example, one influential philosopher of religion, Robert Adams, who has taught at UCLA, Yale University and the University of Oxford, maintains that if God existed, God's nature would be to love, and a being that is essentially loving simply could not command anyone to torture babies for fun. Instead, it could command people only to love God and one's neighbor, as per the Christian tradition.

At this point, other issues arise that cannot be addressed in any depth here. For example, some critics, including the existentialist Jean-Paul Sartre, contend that another major problem with the divine command theory of morality, and the purpose theory it is meant to support, is that it would in fact be immoral for God to issue commands to us, setting aside the content of the commands. Although God would be higher than us, we nonetheless have a dignity, one that would be degraded if we were expected to do slavishly whatever another person told us to do. Even if God, and not merely another human being, were the one to command us, and even if the command were to be loving or otherwise to live morally upright lives, we would thereby be bossed around in an immoral way, undercutting our ability to obtain meaning by doing God's bidding, so goes the objection.

BOX 26.2 RICHARD NORMAN

Richard Norman (1943–) is Emeritus Professor of Moral Philosophy at the University of Kent and is currently Vice-President of the British Humanist Association. The author of several books on ethics, he is especially well known for *On Humanism* (2004), in which he defends a naturalist approach to values and life. In excerpts from a journal article titled 'The Varieties of Non-Religious Experience' (2006), a play on the title of *The Varieties of Religious Experience*, a book by the believer William James, Norman argues that human beings can still live morally, appreciate beauty and experience transcendence if there is no God. Is he correct about these things, or are there important values that would be unavailable to human beings in a godless world?

Norman, 'The Varieties of Non-Religious Experience', *Ratio* 19 (2006): 474–94 (edited excerpts)

(The) suggestion which I want to consider is that we have a distinctive experience of the authoritative character of moral values or moral judgements, and that theism makes best sense of this experience....I accept that there is something to be explained here: the sense that we have of something which we ought or ought not to do, regardless of our own wants and inclinations. A theistic transcendental argument may then take the following form. The authority of morality, it may be said, is explicable only as a personal authority, since only persons can make claims on us of a kind which limit or override our own wants and inclinations. The force of moral demands cannot, however, be explained in terms of the claims which finite persons (such as other human beings) make on us; it can only be explained by the authority of a personal god.

My reply to such an argument would be that the authority of the moral 'ought' can in fact be sufficiently explained in terms of the limits imposed on our actions by the recognition of other finite persons. The wrong that we do, when we do what morally we ought not to do, is always a wrong done to another person (normally another human being, but perhaps also a non-human animal)....The wrong is the wrong done to the person to whom the lie is told.... If I lie to someone, the wrong I do to him is that of deceiving him. If I break my promise to someone, the wrong I do to her is the wrong of letting her down. If I treat someone unjustly or unfairly, the wrong I do to him may be the wrong of exploiting him.

• OBJECTIONS TO GOD-BASED THEORIES IN GENERAL

Turn now to an objection that applies not specifically to the idea that the divine command theory is a promising reason for thinking God is essential for meaning in life. Instead, consider a problem facing the broader principle that God is essential for meaning in life (full-stop), that one's life is meaningful just insofar as one relates to God in a certain way, whether by fulfilling God's (moral) purposes, or by doing so in some other fashion altogether.

It is tempting for critics to contend that there is no evidence that God exists. However, this is not, as it stands, an effective objection to any God-based theory, which is, strictly speaking, the view that one's life *would be* meaningful just to the extent that God existed and one related to Him in a certain way. If God does not exist, this position would not be refuted; instead, it would merely entail that no one's life is meaningful.

However, at this point, a stronger objection can be made, namely, that it seems intuitively possible for at least some meaning in life to obtain in the absence of God. Suppose, for the sake of argument, that God does not exist, that we are the only persons in the world. Would it truly follow that the only good available to us would be pleasure, and that meaning would be unavailable to us? It seems to many that, even if God did not exist, the lives of Mandela and Mother Teresa would be meaningful, or at least more meaningful than the lives of a serial killer and The Blob. It appears to many, including many religiously inclined thinkers, that it would still be worth striving for certain goals, ones that we could be sensibly proud of, even if they were not assigned by, or otherwise grounded on, God.

• CHAPTER SUMMARY

- The meaning of life as a philosophical inquiry is mainly about whether an individual's life has a certain kind of value in it, namely, one that is usually worth more than physical pleasure and merits emotional reactions of substantial pride and admiration.
- When philosophers in the English-speaking world address issues of meaning in life, they often seek to articulate and defend theories about what, if anything, makes a life meaningful, accounts of what all meaningful conditions have in common as opposed to meaningless ones.
- There are two broad kinds of theories, supernaturalist and naturalist, which differ according to whether a spiritual realm is deemed necessary for life to be meaningful.
- One kind of supernaturalist theory is a God-based view, according to which a necessary and sufficient condition for a meaningful life is relating to God in a certain way. The most influential instance of this view is that one must fulfil God's purpose in order to live meaningfully, since a life is meaningful insofar as it

conforms to moral rules and since only God's purpose, as expressed in His commands, could ground moral rules.

- Two major objections to that position are that meaning seems possible without engaging in moral action, and that God's commands could not in fact ground meaning via moral rules, either because God could command us to do something intuitively immoral, or because it would be immoral for God to command us to do anything.

- Although it does not tell against a God-based theory as such merely to argue that God does not exist, it would be a strike against such a theory if meaningful lives seemed possible in the absence of God, which they do to many, including many who are religiously inclined.

• STUDY QUESTIONS

1 Supernaturalism differs from naturalism in that only the former contends that a spiritual realm is necessary for our lives to be meaningful. What do you think makes something spiritual as opposed to physical?

2 What is your judgement of the case of Gauguin, as described above? Was his life meaningful? If so, what difference is there between his case and the one regarding using innocent people's blood as paint?

3 Consider some additional ways, besides being a great painter, by which a person's life could arguably be meaningful apart from being moral, that is, meaningful in virtue of 'non-moral' considerations. (Notice the difference between doing something that is *non-moral*, i.e. neither morally blameworthy nor morally praiseworthy, and *immoral*, morally blameworthy.)

4 Recall the objection that God's commands cannot be what ground morality since God could command anything at all, including intuitively immoral behavior such as torture. One promising reply is that God's commands would be determined by God's unchanging nature as loving. Would an essentially loving God be consistent with other features that God is often thought to exhibit, for example, punishing people for their guilt, perhaps even damning them eternally?

5 Try to develop a plausible reply to the objection that meaning cannot consist in fulfiling God's commands since it would be degrading of the dignity of human persons for God to command them.

• INTRODUCTORY FURTHER READING

Cottingham, John (2003) *On the Meaning of Life* (London: Routledge). [Written for a generally educated audience, this book, which is a pleasure to read, defends the idea that life would be meaningless without God, mainly because we could not achieve worthwhile goals on our own without His help.]

Kurtz, Paul (2012) *Meaning and Value in a Secular Age* (Amherst, NY: Prometheus Books). [Several essays by an influential atheist about how life can be meaningful in the absence of a spiritual realm and belief in it.]

Martin, Michael (2002) *Atheism, Morality, and Meaning* (Amherst, NY: Prometheus Books). [A vigorous defense of a naturalist approach to morality, in the first half of the book, and to meaning, in the second. Very critical of Christian approaches to both.]

Thomson, Garrett (2003) *On the Meaning of Life* (South Melbourne: Wadsworth), esp. pp. 15–67. [In this textbook for undergraduate philosophy majors, the author critically explores not only the purpose theory of meaning in life, but also additional arguments for thinking that God or spirituality is essential.]

Walker, Lois Hope (1989) 'Religion and the Meaning of Life and Death', in L. Pojman (ed.) *Philosophy: The Quest for Truth* (Belmont, CA: Wadsworth Publishing Co.), pp. 167–71. [Contends that concerns about autonomy and degradation are overrated, and that without God there would be nothing to ground a conception of morality according to which humans have an equal standing.]

• ADVANCED FURTHER READING

Adams, Robert (1999) *Finite and Infinite Goods* (New York: Oxford University Press). [An intricate defence of a divine command theory of morality, developed and defended in the context of a comprehensive theistic account of value.]

Baier, Kurt (1957) 'The Meaning of Life', repr. in E. D. Klemke and S. M. Cahn (eds.) *The Meaning of Life: A Reader*, 3rd edn (New York: Oxford University Press, 2008), pp. 82–113. [A lecture that targets Christian accounts of what makes a life meaningful, and voices the concern that God would degrade us, and not help to make our lives meaningful, were He to command us.]

Hartshorne, Charles (1984) 'God and the Meaning of Life', in L. S. Rouner (ed.) *On Nature* (Notre Dame: University of Notre Dame Press), pp. 154–68. [The famous process theologian contends that since we could be part of an everlasting unity only by constituting part of God's mental life, particularly by being remembered by God, God is essential for meaning in our lives.]

Mawson, Timothy (2012) 'Recent Work on the Meaning of Life and Philosophy of Religion', *Philosophy Compass* 8: 1138–46. [A useful overview of the latest professional philosophical literature on God and the meaning of life.]

Metz, Thaddeus (2013) *Meaning in Life: An Analytic Study* (Oxford: Oxford University Press). [Spends several chapters (see esp. pp. 77–160) exploring a wide array of arguments for supernaturalist conceptions of meaning in life, contending that they all ultimately rely on the claim that perfection is necessary for meaning, a claim he contends is implausible.]

Nozick, Robert (1981) 'Philosophy and the Meaning of Life', in his *Philosophical Explanations* (Cambridge, MA: Harvard University Press), pp. 571–619. [Is sympathetic to the idea that God is necessary for 'deep' meaning in life, not because only God could ground moral rules, but rather because only God could be unlimited.]

Quinn, Philip (2000) 'How Christianity Secures Life's Meanings', in J. Runzo and N. Martin (eds.) *The Meaning of Life in the World Religions* (Oxford: Oneworld Publications), pp. 53–68. [Although the author admits that some meaning would be available in a world without God, he advances the idea that obeying a Christian God would greatly enhance meaning in life.]

Wielenberg, Erik (2005) *Value and Virtue in a Godless Universe* (Cambridge: Cambridge University Press). [Defends the possibility of morality and meaning on the supposition that atheism is true.]

• FREE INTERNET RESOURCES

Craig, William Lane (1994) 'The Absurdity of Life without God', http://www.bethinking.org/is-there-meaning-to-life/the-absurdity-of-life-without-god. [An influential 'apologist' for Christianity, the author provides several reasons for thinking that life would be meaningless without God, including the idea that no universally binding moral rules would exist.]

Di Muzio, Gianluca (2006) 'Theism and the Meaning of Life', *Ars Disputandi* 6, http://www.arsdisputandi.org/publish/articles/000241/article.pdf. [Focused on refuting several of William Lane Craig's rationales for thinking that God's existence is necessary for meaning in life.]

27

must your life never end for it to be meaningful?

- Soul-based theories of meaning in life
- Obtaining perfect justice
- Making a permanent difference
- Immortality as sufficient for a meaningless life?
- Immortality as not necessary for a meaningful life?

• SOUL-BASED THEORIES OF MEANING IN LIFE

The previous chapter discussed how God might be necessary for meaning in one's life, but did not mention anything about having a soul. Some supernaturalists might suggest that meaning is not simply a function of a relationship between us on earth and God in a transcendent realm during our eighty or so years there. Instead, or at least in addition, meaning involves the promise of **immortality**.

There are, in principle, a variety of ways that one could be immortal, that is, never face **death**. The dominant view among those sympathetic to the idea that immortality is a necessary condition for meaning in life has been that, for one's existence to be significant, one must possess a soul, a spiritual substance that constitutes one's identity, can exist apart from one's body, and cannot be destroyed (at least not by anything physical). However, that need not be the only way to live forever, which seems metaphysically possible even if one lacks a soul. Imagine vampires who could find enough blood to drink in an ever-expanding physical universe. Or imagine that super-duper technology were able to scan one's brain states and put them into a new body whenever one's old one wore out.

Besides the ontological matter of what it is that might last forever, something spiritual or something merely physical, there is a further matter of precisely what it would mean to live a life that would never end. For many, that would mean remaining in time forever, where there is always a future to come. However, others in the supernaturalist tradition have instead thought of immortality in terms of entering an atemporal realm, where there is no distinction between past, present and future.

Since the prospect of a purely physical immortality seems remote, and since it is hard to understand what it would mean for a finite person to exist atemporally, most religious people think of immortality in terms of one's soul continuing to live on forever in time after one's present body has died. This chapter works with that construal of immortality when exploring **soul-based theory**, the view that a life is meaningful if and only if one has a soul that will exist in a certain state in a maximally desirable afterlife, often called 'Heaven', either by inhabiting a new body, or by entering a purely spiritual realm where there are no bodies.

Notice that just as a God-based theory makes no essential reference to a soul, so a soul-based theory makes no essential reference to God. That is, it is possible for one to think that the key to a meaningful life is living forever in a certain way, where that need not mean that one is in touch with God or even that God exists. Many from Eastern religious traditions think in this way. For example, Hindus believe in an enlightened unity of one's soul with a deity ('Brahman') that is quite unlike what monotheists mean by 'God', and Buddhists typically reject the existence of any deity whatsoever, seeking *nirvana*, a state in which one's soul is no longer reborn in the physical world. There have also been philosophers and religious thinkers in the Western tradition who have held that meaning in this life is a function of an afterlife, without any reference to God, though the dominant view among them has been that meaning is a matter of meeting God in Heaven.

Before turning to the major arguments for a soul-based theory, note that this view does not imply that one in fact has a soul. It is a theory of what would make life meaningful, and it says one's life would be meaningful if and only if one had a soul that were destined to exist in a certain way upon the disintegration of one's current body. If no one has a soul, then this theory entails that no one's life is or can be meaningful. If people generally have souls, but a particular person has not done what will put her soul into a good state, then her life is meaningless, but others' might not be.

• OBTAINING PERFECT JUSTICE

There are two influential arguments in favor of soul-based theory, the first one of which is that an afterlife is necessary in order for perfect justice to be realized, where life in a world without that would be non-sensical.

First, consider **retributive justice**, a state of affairs in which an individual's well-being (or woe) tracks the extent to which she lived a moral life (or an immoral one). A world would be more retributively just, the more the good get the reward they deserve and the bad get the punishment (the 'payback') they deserve.

Second, there is **restitutive justice**, a state of affairs in which individuals who have been wrongfully harmed are compensated for what they have lost, ideally by those responsible for the wrongdoing. A world would be more restitutively just, the more the innocent get the reparation (the 'payment') they deserve for having undergone burdens and the guilty are the ones to supply it.

The present argument for a soul-based theory is that a soul is necessary in order for these two kinds of justice to obtain. It is obvious that during the time people are embodied on earth, neither retributive nor restitutive justice is fully done. The innocent suffer without complete compensation, the guilty do not fully make up for the harm they have caused, the good are not rewarded in proportion to their goodness, and the wicked are not punished in proportion to their wickedness. According to some defenders of a soul-based theory, one must be able to outlive the inevitable death of one's body in order for perfect justice to be done, and, of most urgency, for justice to come to those who have been innocent and good. This position is suggested by Ecclesiastes in the Hebrew Bible, excerpts from which are reprinted below, and it has been particularly influential among those of the Jewish and Islamic faiths (those in the Christian tradition tend to think of Heaven as a matter of grace, i.e. more of a gift than a reward).

Many of course believe that God must exist, too, in order for justice to be meted out. It is common to think of God as an ideal judge who puts the good in Heaven and the bad in Hell. However, note two important points, here. For one, on this approach, God would probably not be what *constitutes* meaning in life, and would be merely a *means* by which justice, the key factor, would come about. For another, in principle, it appears metaphysically possible for an impersonal, i.e. unconscious, force akin to *karma* to divide the good and the bad and to distribute benefits and harms to them accordingly, meaning that it is not so clear that God, understood to be a spiritual person, is even a *necessary* means by which to realize justice.

Setting aside the issue of whether God is necessary for perfect justice, there are serious problems with it as a rationale for soul-based theory; for it is far from clear that a soul is necessary for perfect justice. Granting, for the sake of argument, that perfect justice is necessary for meaning in life (is it truly?), and that perfect justice does not obtain on earth (could it, though?) and hence that some kind of afterlife is necessary for it to obtain, it does not yet follow that one must be able to live *forever* in order for perfect justice to be done. Furthermore, why think that one must be able to live *in a spiritual state* in order for justice to be done?

It seems that humans could deserve an eternity in Heaven only if they could do something infinitely good (or an eternity in Hell only if they did something infinitely bad). One may reasonably doubt that infinite (dis)values are possible in our finite world. And even if they were, it would not follow that both eternality and spirituality are needed to give people what they deserve. The trouble is that, supposing one can do something infinitely (dis)valuable in a finite amount of time here on earth, it would seem that a response proportionate to this deed requires merely a finite amount of time and one in a physical dimension. If infinitely good or bad deeds are possible in a finite timespan in the physical universe, then so are punishments and rewards matching these deeds.

It is worth reflecting more about the relationship between justice and an afterlife. Some philosophers of religion have suggested that a soul is necessary in order to become perfectly upright and hence deserving of Heaven, something one cannot do in the time one has on earth. Others have contended that in order to be able to survive the death of one's current body, one has to have an indestructible spiritual nature, so that even if one does not strictly speaking deserve eternal life, one cannot avoid receiving it upon getting what one does deserve.

BOX 27.1 ECCLESIASTES

In Ecclesiastes, a chapter from the Holy Bible (King James Version), the author does not question the existence of God, but nonetheless proclaims that life is 'vanity' (i.e. in vain, or pointless) because of the injustices facing mortal beings. The wicked appear to prosper in this world, often enough at the expense of the upright, while neither the wicked nor the upright appear to survive the deaths of their bodies. A meaningful life, for the author, appears to be one in which a person is good, does not die and receives some reward in an afterlife. Can there be meaning apart from these conditions, or is the alternative just to 'eat, drink and be merry'?

Ecclesiastes (edited excerpt)

The Holy Bible: King James Version. 2000 (taken from: http://www.bartleby.com/108/21/)

For that which befalleth the sons of men befalleth beasts; even one thing befalleth them: as the one dieth, so dieth the other; yea, they have all one breath; so that a man hath no preeminence above a beast: for all is vanity.

All go unto one place; all are of the dust, and all turn to dust again.

Who knoweth the spirit of man that goeth upward, and the spirit of the beast that goeth downward to the earth?

Wherefore I perceive that there is nothing better, than that a man should rejoice in his own works; for that is his portion: for who shall bring him to see what shall be after him?

* * *

There is a vanity which is done upon the earth; that there be just men, unto whom it happeneth according to the work of the wicked; again, there be wicked men, to whom it happeneth according to the work of the righteous: I said that this also is vanity….

All things come alike to all: there is one event to the righteous, and to the wicked; to the good and to the clean, and to the unclean; to him that sacrificeth, and to him that sacrificeth not: as is the good, so is the sinner; and he that sweareth, as he that feareth an oath.

This is an evil among all things that are done under the sun, that there is one event unto all.

* * *

Whatsoever thy hand findeth to do, do it with thy might; for there is no work, nor device, nor knowledge, nor wisdom, in the grave, whither thou goest.

I returned, and saw under the sun, that the race is not to the swift, nor the battle to the strong, neither yet bread to the wise, nor yet riches to men of understanding, nor yet favor to men of skill; but time and chance happeneth to them all.

For man also knoweth not his time: as the fishes that are taken in an evil net, and as the birds that are caught in the snare; so are the sons of men snared in an evil time, when it falleth suddenly upon them.

• MAKING A PERMANENT DIFFERENCE

Another influential argument for a soul-based theory appeals to the idea that if we lived only eighty or so years, the length of our lives would be minuscule, as would be their impact. No reputable astrophysicist doubts that the universe has been in existence for approximately 14 billion years, and many of them believe that it will continue to expand forever. The typical human lifespan is a puny blip by comparison. In addition, we are stuck on a single rock in an enormous sea of trillions of trillions of rocks in space. Not only is the influence of our lives restricted to this one planet, but an overwhelming majority of us influence only the tiniest space on it. We affect our homes and workplaces, i.e. only a handful of people on earth, who, for all we can tell, also are destined to die.

From this perspective, sometimes called the **_sub specie aeternitatis_**, which is Latin for the point of view of eternity, nothing of one's life appears to matter. Everything about oneself appears trivial and nothing seems worth doing. From such reflections stems the following argument for a soul-based theory: in order for one's life to be meaningful, one must make a permanent difference to the world, something one can do only if one has a soul. This argument has been famously advanced by Leo Tolstoy in the reading below.

Critics have questioned this argument mainly in two ways. First, it seems possible to avoid taking up the *sub specie aeternitatis*. Although we can look at our lives from that standpoint, why should we? It seems reasonable to evaluate our lives from a more local perspective, judging their significance in light of features that are characteristic of, or normal for, human beings. From the point of view of eternity, it does not seem worth saving the life of a person who will die soon anyway, whereas from the point of view of humanity, it seems worth saving the life of a mortal person, and precisely *because* she is so fragile and has nothing else to look forward to beyond her time on earth. Philosophers have yet to sort out the role of standpoints in appraising lives; it is still a live issue.

The second objection to the present rationale for soul-based theory is that, even if making a permanent difference were necessary for one's life to be meaningful, it is not clear that one must be immortal, or have a supernatural essence, in order to do that. Suppose that, upon your death, God fondly and eternally remembered your good deeds, or angels never stopped singing your praises. Philosophical work needs to be done to explain why *you* must live forever and *in a spiritual state* in order for you to make the relevant sort of infinite and positive difference to the world. On this score, some might be tempted to suggest that you must go to Heaven in order to help complete God's life in some way. Might the meaning of your life be to help make God's more meaningful?

BOX 27.2 LEO TOLSTOY

Tolstoy (1828–1910), the famous Russian author of *War and Peace, Anna Karenina* and *The Death of Ivan Ilych*, became severely depressed and underwent an emotional crisis at the height of his fame. In a short book, *A Confession* (1882), he recounts what happened and (in parts not reprinted here) how he resolved the crisis. In the excerpt from this work, which is probably the most widely read text on the meaning of life, Tolstoy contends that life is meaningless if it will end, since nothing would then be worth doing. Can you think of anything to say to Tolstoy that might console him and get him to change his perspective?

Tolstoy, *A Confession* (edited excerpt)

(taken from: http://www.ccel.org/ccel/tolstoy/confession.html)

My life came to a standstill. I could breathe, eat, drink, and sleep, and I could not help doing these things; but there was no life, for there were no wishes the fulfillment of which I could consider reasonable. If I desired anything, I knew in advance that whether I satisfied my desire or not, nothing would come of it.... The truth was that life is meaningless. I had as it were lived, lived, and walked, walked, till I had come to a precipice and saw clearly that there was nothing ahead of me but destruction. It was impossible to stop, impossible to go back, and impossible to close my eyes or avoid seeing that there was nothing ahead but suffering and real death....

And all this befell me at a time when all around me I had what is considered complete good fortune. I was not yet fifty; I had a good wife who loved me and whom I loved, good children, and a large estate which without much effort on my part improved and increased. I was respected by my relations and acquaintances more than at any previous time. I was praised by others and without much self-deception could consider that my name was famous. And far from being insane or mentally diseased, I enjoyed on the contrary a strength of mind and body such as I have seldom met with among men of my kind....

[But] I could give no reasonable meaning to any single action or to my whole life....Today or tomorrow sickness and death will come [they had come already] to those I love or to me; nothing will remain but stench and worms. Sooner or later my affairs, whatever they may be, will be forgotten, and I shall not exist. Then why go on making any effort?...

"Family"...said I to myself. But my family – wife and children – are also human. They are placed just as I am: they must either live in a lie or see the terrible truth. Why should they live? Why should I love them, guard them, bring them up, or watch them? That they may come to the despair that I feel, or else be stupid? Loving them, I cannot hide the truth from them: each step in knowledge leads them to the truth. And the truth is death.

"Art, poetry?"...Under the influence of success and the praise of men, I had long assured myself that this was a thing one could do though death was drawing near – death which destroys all things, including my work and its remembrance; but soon I saw that that too was a fraud. It was plain to me that art is an adornment of life, an allurement to life. But life had lost its attraction for me, so how could I attract others?...

My question – that which at the age of fifty brought me to the verge of suicide – was the simplest of questions, lying in the soul of every man from the foolish child to the wisest elder:..."Why should I live, why wish for anything, or do anything?" It can also be expressed thus: "Is there any meaning in my life that the inevitable death awaiting me does not destroy?"

• IMMORTALITY AS SUFFICIENT FOR A MEANINGLESS LIFE?

There have been two strategies by which naturalists (and sometimes even God-based theorists) have objected to soul-based theories, one much bolder than the other. According to the bolder rationale, explored here, an immortal life could not avoid being meaningless. That is, if one wants a meaningful life, then one had better be mortal, for otherwise it would be impossible to obtain. Defenders of this perspective usually do not deny that one would be reasonable to fear death, but maintain that, all things considered, it would be best for one eventually to die. Why think so?

For one, many philosophers and psychologists contend that life could not avoid becoming boring if one were to live forever. Although humans enjoy eating and making love, and find it worth taking up challenges, just how many times could they do such things and find them interesting, engaging, stimulating?

Others note that in an infinite lifespan, one would have to repeat certain activities over and over again, which would undercut their ability to confer meaning on one's life. Intuitively, a life that is repetitive is not one that is very meaningful; *vide* the movie *Groundhog Day* in which the main character relives the same twenty-four hours over and over again. Although the character's personality does develop during this time, eventually he 'maxes out' the extent to which he can be virtuous and help other people, and he ends up doing the same good deeds repeatedly. Naturally, this character is relieved when the cycle is ended and he is then able to live in a way that includes something different. But some philosophers believe that, if one lived forever, at a certain point there could be nothing new.

Finally, some contend that if we were immortal, then many of our activities would lose their importance, since life and death matters would not be at stake. One could neither risk one's life for the sake of others, nor save anyone else's life. And if upon the disintegration of people's bodies, they would go to Heaven (or alternately go to Hell upon deserving that), then why should one work to keep them alive in physical form? It seems that the meaningfulness of being a doctor, a lifeguard, a firefighter or the like depends precisely on our not being immortal and instead having only this earthly life.

One way to sum up these points is by viewing them as contending that Heaven is ultimately impossible. Supposing that the word 'Heaven' is defined as a maximally desirable existence that lasts forever in a spiritual state, these critics are maintaining in effect that it cannot exist; eternality is incompatible with a maximally desirable existence, perhaps even with a decent one.

More has been written on these considerations by philosophers over the past forty years than ever before, with debate continuing on them. Could one avoid becoming bored over the course of trillions of years? If so, how? If not, would one's life inevitably become pointless? Would one indeed have to repeat one's activities over an eternity, and, if so, would that unavoidably make one's life senseless? If one could not risk or save life, would all of one's activities necessarily be empty? Pleasure or happiness would probably be available, but would meaning?

BOX 27.3 MARTHA NUSSBAUM

Martha Nussbaum (1947–) is the Ernst Freund Distinguished Service Professor of Law and Ethics at the University of Chicago. One of the most prolific philosophers alive, she has written many books on a variety of important topics, including the nature of the emotions, the point of a liberal arts education, the nature of justice, the proper basis for legal decision-making, sexual ethics, patriotism, and animal rights. The following is a short selection from a long and intricate paper about Lucretius' views on death. Lucretius (99 BC–55 BC) was a Roman poet and philosopher, famous for having argued that death should not be viewed as something bad. Nussbaum similarly argues, by reflecting on the lives of the Greek gods, that immortality would be undesirable for human beings, in that we would lose a sense of preciousness and urgency, as well as be unable to display important virtues such as courage in the face of death. Is she right about these things?

Martha Nussbaum, 'Mortal Immortals: Lucretius on Death and the Voice of Nature', *Philosophy and Phenomenological Research* 303 (1989), 303-51, at pp. 336–40 (edited excerpt)

[A] thought experiment has…been performed, by Homer and by Greek culture as a whole: it is the story of the Olympian gods, frozen immortal anthropomorphic adults. The question we want to ask of their story is, how many of the virtues and values we prize would turn up in their unbounded lives?…

The first thing we notice about the gods is that they cannot have the virtue of courage, as we know and honor it. For courage consists in a certain way of acting and reacting in the face of death and the risk of death.…

This means, as well, that the component of friendship, love, and love of country that consists in a willingness to give up one's life for the other must be absent as well – indeed, must be completely mysterious and obscure to people whose experience does not contain the sense of mortality. Thus, as in fact we see in Homer, there is a kind of laxness and lightness in the relationships of the gods, a kind of playful unheroic quality that contrasts sharply with the more intense character of human love and friendship.

[…]

Political justice and private generosity are concerned with the allocation of resources like food, seen as necessary for life itself, and not simply for play or amusement. The profound seriousness and urgency of human thought about justice arises from the awareness that we all really need the things that justice distributes, and need them for life itself. If that need were removed, or made non-absolute, distribution would not matter, or not matter in the same way and to the same extent.

[…]

And, in general, the intensity and dedication with which very many human activities are pursued cannot be explained without reference to the awareness that our opportunities are finite, that we cannot choose these activities indefinitely many times. In raising a child, in cherishing a lover, in performing a demanding task of work or thought or artistic creation, we are aware, at some level, of the thought that each of these efforts is structured and constrained by finite time. And the removal of that awareness would surely change the pursuits and their meaning for us in ways we can scarcely imagine – making them, perhaps, more easy, more optional, with less of striving and effort in them, less of a particular sort of gallantry and courage.

• IMMORTALITY AS NOT NECESSARY FOR A MEANINGFUL LIFE?

The previous criticisms of soul-based theory were bold in contending that an interest in a meaningful life counsels not wishing for a soul, or not drinking an 'immortality elixir', assuming one existed for otherwise mortal beings. The other kind of objection is more modest for not drawing that conclusion and instead maintaining that having a soul is not necessary for meaningfulness.

The rationale for thinking that meaning is at least possible despite mortality is similar to the objection made to God-based theories. Suppose, for the sake of argument, that none of us survives the perishing of our bodies, that we die along with their disintegration. Would it truly be the case that the lives of Albert Einstein, Pablo Picasso and Nelson Mandela were pointless and had nothing going for them beyond that of The Blob?

• CHAPTER SUMMARY

- One kind of supernaturalist theory is a God-based view, while another is a soul-based theory, according to which a necessary and sufficient condition for a meaningful life is putting one's soul into a certain state, which might or might not include relating to God.

- There are two major rationales for a soul-based theory, with one being the idea that eternal, spiritual life after the death of one's body is necessary in order for perfect justice to be realized, and, especially, for the innocent to be compensated and the good to be rewarded.
- The second major argument for soul-based theory is the idea that a life is meaningful only insofar as it makes a permanent difference to the world, something that one can do only if one has a soul.
- Both arguments face the common objection that it appears hard to explain why having a soul is necessary either to realize perfect justice or to make a permanent difference to the world.
- Soul-based theories themselves face two kinds of objections, the bolder of which maintains that immortality could not avoid being meaningless, because of considerations such as boredom and repetition. The more modest objection is that, even if one could have an immortal and meaningful life, the latter does not require the former.

• STUDY QUESTIONS

1 Illustrate the difference between retributive and restitutive justice by coming up with your own examples.
2 It seems true that the natural world, as we know it, does not make perfect justice possible. However, it is not obvious that only a supernatural realm could make it possible. How might someone try to argue that in some other, metaphysically possible physical universe, perfect justice could be realized?
3 Are you tempted to look at your life *sub specie aeternitatis*? Does it best explain why you are striving to get an education, or why you want a family, or why you have been proud of various facets of your life?
4 Which strategies do you use to avoid getting bored? How likely would they be to work over the very long haul, viz., in the course of eternity?
5 This chapter did not really discuss the common religious view that *both* God and a soul are jointly necessary and sufficient for meaning in life. How might an appeal to God help the defender of soul-based theory respond to objections either to her theory or to the arguments for it?

• INTRODUCTORY FURTHER READING

Belshaw, Christopher (2005) *10 Good Questions about Life and Death* (Malden, MA: Blackwell). [Composed for the undergraduate, this text addresses a variety of questions about meaning in life and related topics such as whether it is bad to die and whether one should drink an 'immortality elixir' if one could.]
Ellin, Joseph (1995) *Morality and the Meaning of Life* (Fort Worth, TX: Harcourt Brace College Publishers), esp. pp. 306–22. [In this textbook, the author critically

explores Tolstoy's and others' concerns that our finitude is incompatible with meaningfulness, and also argues that immortality would get boring.]

Heinegg, Peter (ed.) (2003) *Mortalism: Readings on the Meaning of Life* (Amherst, NY: Prometheus Books). [Accessible snippets on the bearing of death on life's meaning from more than fifty thinkers from a variety of different time periods.]

• ADVANCED FURTHER READING

Baier, Kurt (1997) 'A Good Life', in his *Problems of Life and Death: A Humanist Perspective* (Amherst, NY: Prometheus Books), pp. 59–74. [Contends that the proper way to appraise the worth of a human life is in terms of what is normal for, and accessible to, our species, which implies that if none of us is immortal, death cannot make our lives meaningless.]

Bruckner, Donald (2012) 'Against the Tedium of Immortality', *International Journal of Philosophical Studies* 20: 623–44. [Offers several reasons for thinking that an immortal life could avoid boredom, including the ideas that humans tend to forget what they have experienced and are good at finding new things to do.]

Chappell, Timothy (2007) 'Infinity Goes Up on Trial: Must Immortality Be Meaningless?', *European Journal of Philosophy* 17: 30–44. [Defends the idea that a meaningful life is compatible with (but does not require) living forever, responding to a variety of objections to that idea.]

Davis, William (1987) 'The Meaning of Life', *Metaphilosophy* 18: 288–305. [Argues that an afterlife is necessary for a meaningful life, particularly since the injustices of this world would otherwise go uncorrected by God.]

Fischer, John Martin (1994) 'Why Immortality is Not So Bad', *International Journal of Philosophical Studies* 2: 257–70. [In what is probably the most widely read defence of the idea that living forever need not get boring, the author points to a variety of pleasures that human beings welcome experiencing over and over again, at least after a certain amount of time has passed.]

Goetz, Stuart (2012) *The Purpose of Life: A Theistic Perspective* (New York: Continuum). [Unlike a very large majority of those who have reflected on meaningfulness, this author contends that it amounts to being perfectly happy, which entails experiencing pleasure forever.]

Williams, Bernard (1973) 'The Makropulos Case: Reflections on the Tedium of Immortality', in his *Problems of the Self* (Cambridge: Cambridge University Press), pp. 82–100. [A difficult but widely discussed work about whether it would be desirable to live forever; in it the author was one of the first to argue systematically that it would not, since one could not avoid becoming bored.]

• FREE INTERNET RESOURCES

Kass, Leon (2001) '*L'Chaim* and Its Limits: Why Not Immortality?', *First Things* 113: 17–24. http://www.firstthings.com/article/2007/01/lchaim-and-its-limits-why-not-immortality. [Argues that immortality would be sufficient for a meaningless life for many reasons, such as that we would neither appreciate life if we lived forever, nor have the opportunity to perform heroic deeds.]

Metz, Thaddeus (2003) 'The Immortality Requirement for Life's Meaning', *Ratio* 16: 161–77. https://ujdigispace.uj.ac.za/handle/10210/2285. [Contends that the major arguments for thinking that immortality is necessary for meaning in life are weak, and work to reconstruct them so that they are stronger.]

Schopenhauer, Arthur (1851) 'On the Vanity of Existence'. http://en.wikisource. org/wiki/On_the_Vanity_of_Existence. [Maintains that our lives are pointless in part because they are so short and inconsequential.]

Trisel, Brooke Alan (2002) 'Futility and the Meaning of Life Debate', *Sorites* 14: 70–84. http://www.sorites.org/Issue_14/trisel.htm. [Contends that immortality is not necessary for a meaningful life since many values and worthwhile goals could be realized in a finite lifespan.]

28

how might a meaningful life be possible in a purely physical world?

- Naturalist theories of meaning in life
- Subjectivism and its critics
- Objectivism and its critics
- Hybrid theory and its critics
- Objections to naturalism

NATURALIST THEORIES OF MEANING IN LIFE

The previous two chapters critically explored supernaturalist theories of what makes a life meaningful, according to which meaning is constituted by something spiritual, either relating to God or putting one's soul into a certain state (or both). In contrast, this chapter addresses naturalist theories, which are a broad collection of views according to which a meaningful life is possible in the absence of anything spiritual, and merely in the physical world as known particularly well by scientific means.

Defenders of naturalism need not be atheists or agnostics (even if many in fact are). Naturalists can coherently believe that God and a soul exist, either on evidential grounds or merely on faith. What makes them naturalists is the view that meaning in life is not exhausted by engaging with God or one's soul, i.e., that meaning would be possible even if these spiritual conditions did not exist. Just as it is possible to be a God-based theorist about meaning and an atheist about God's existence (the combination of which entails that life is meaningless), so there is no incoherence in being a theist about God's existence, but a naturalist about meaning.

There are three major versions of naturalism, which are discussed in separate sections below. They differ with respect to the degree to which life's meaning is a function of a particular individual's attitudes. According to **subjectivism**, what makes a life meaningful varies substantially, depending on the subject. More carefully, it is the view that what is meaningful for an individual depends entirely on her psychological orientations, that is, her beliefs, desires and choices (which need not be contained in a soul). Such a view is 'relativistic', maintaining that there are no universal standards for a meaningful life, and that meaning instead differs from person to person, roughly in terms of whatever is 'meaningful to' a given person.

On the other side of the spectrum is **objectivism**, the view that an individual's contingent attitudes do nothing to constitute what makes her life meaningful. This kind of perspective is 'absolutist', a matter of contending that there are invariant standards of meaning that apply to all human persons, regardless of what they think, like or decide (while denying that these standards are constituted by the mind of God).

In between these poles is a **hybrid theory**, according to which meaning in life arises when both subjective and objective conditions come together. Hybrid theorists maintain that there are objective standards for meaning in life, but that they confer meaning on a person's life when, and only when, she is subjectively attracted to them. According to this perspective, neither a purely subjective nor a purely objective theory is adequate on its own.

This chapter spells out all three versions of naturalism, considers arguments for and against them, and concludes by considering ways that supernaturalists would question them as a whole.

• SUBJECTIVISM AND ITS CRITICS

Subjectivism, recall, is the view that what makes a life meaningful is relative to the individual, and is constituted by her particular attitudes. For example, if one person finds gardening meaningful, likes doing it and chooses to do it, then it is indeed meaningful for her. Gardening would not, by the present theory, be meaningful for someone who thought it is a waste of time, did not enjoy it and elected to avoid it.

A number of ideas motivate theorists to hold a subjective account of meaning in life. One is the intuition that a variety of different kinds of meaningful lives are possible. A second is the idea that a meaningful life is not boring, and instead is a matter of an individual being passionate about something. A third is the suggestion that a meaningful life is one in which a person is true to herself, where authenticity is something utterly specific to a given individual. A fourth is the argument that since there is no evidence of God or a soul, but there is evidence that some lives are meaningful, meaning in life must simply be a matter of what people happen to find meaningful – for where else could meaning come from?

Although these arguments were compelling to many English- (and French-)speaking philosophers in the twentieth century, fewer accept them in the twenty-first, for two major reasons. First, most of the above arguments support subjectivism no more than they do the hybrid theory, which includes subjective elements (on which see more below).

Second, a purely subjective view, which rejects the relevance of anything mind-independent for determining what is meaningful, has counterintuitive implications. To use an example from the famous American political philosopher John Rawls, imagine that someone's foremost goal in life were to count blades of grass, a goal that she achieved day after day. Or to invoke an example from the influential Canadian philosopher Charles Taylor, consider someone who most wanted to maintain 3,732 hairs on her head, and were careful to do so. Or think about The Blob, who above all wants to see how much beer he can drink while watching sit-coms by himself.

For most contemporary philosophers, such actions could not be meaningful, or at least they would not be meaningful merely in virtue of the fact that someone thought they were important, enjoyed doing them and chose to do them. For many in the field, in order for such actions to be meaningful, there must be more to them than has been described so far – they must lead to relationships, or accomplishments, or virtues, or artworks or the like.

In short, the most serious problem for subjectivism is that it has a difficult time making sense of the two lists from the introduction of this Part, one of intuitively meaningful conditions and one of conditions that uncontroversially lack meaning. In reply, subjectivists usually point out that the counterexamples are merely hypothetical, i.e. that no one in the real world truly wants to do them. Instead, they suggest that what is common to the intuitively meaningful conditions is, roughly, that people typically want to do them the most.

However, it is not hard to fish around and dig up actual cases of people devoting much of their time and other resources towards intuitively inane things. In addition, the deep problem is this: *if* someone were to find such behavior meaningful, to like it and to seek it out, then it *would be* meaningful for her, supposing subjectivism were true. But, so the objection goes, it would not be meaningful; the person has to pursue something else in order to have an existence that matters.

BOX 28.1 WILLIAM JAMES

William James (1842–1910) was an American philosopher and psychologist whose most influential ideas were about emotion, truth, faith, religion and the nature of the self. In the following excerpt from a lecture he gave to his students (1899), James presents a subjectivist account of what makes a life significant. According to James, a significant life is one in which a person passionately and vigorously strives to realize an ideal, where 'ideals are relative to the lives that entertain them'. Do you think there can be meaningless ideals, or is every ideal simply 'meaningful to' the person who champions it?

James, 'What Makes a Life Significant?' (edited excerpt)

(taken from: http://www.uky.edu/~eushe2/Pajares/jsignificant.html)

If there were any such....exceptional individuals, however, what made them different from the rest? It can only have been this – that their souls worked and endured in obedience to some inner ideal, while their comrades were not actuated by anything worthy of that name....

The barrenness and ignobleness of the more usual laborer's life consist in the fact that it is moved by no such ideal inner springs. The backache, the long hours, the danger, are patiently endured – for what? To gain a quid of tobacco, a glass of beer, a cup of coffee, a meal, and a bed, and to begin again the next day and shirk as much as one can. This really is why we raise no monument to the laborers in the subway, even though they be our conscripts, and even though after a fashion our city is indeed based upon their patient hearts and enduring backs and shoulders. And this is why we do raise monuments to our soldiers, whose outward conditions were even brutaller still. The soldiers are supposed to have followed an ideal, and the laborers are supposed to have followed none....

(W)e are led to say that such inner meaning can be complete and valid for us also, only when the inner joy, courage, and endurance are joined with an ideal. But what, exactly, do we mean by an ideal?...An ideal, for instance, must be something intellectually conceived, something of which we are not unconscious, if we have it; and it must carry with it that sort of outlook, uplift, and brightness that go with all intellectual facts. Secondly, there must be novelty in an ideal – novelty at least for him whom the ideal grasps. Sodden routine is incompatible with ideality, although what is sodden routine for one person may be ideal novelty for another. This shows that there is nothing absolutely ideal: ideals are relative to the lives that entertain them....

Now, taken nakedly, abstractly, and immediately, you see that mere ideals are the cheapest things in life. Everybody has them in some shape or other, personal or general, sound or mistaken, low or high; and the most worthless sentimentalists and dreamers, drunkards, shirks and verse-makers, who never show a grain of effort, courage, or endurance, possibly have them on the most copious scale....

But...the more ideals a man has, the more contemptible, on the whole, do you continue to deem him, if the matter ends there for him, and if none of the laboring man's virtues are called into action on his part – no courage shown, no privations undergone, no dirt or scars contracted in the attempt to get them realized. It is quite obvious that something more than the mere possession of ideals is required to make a life significant....

Ideal aspirations are not enough, when uncombined with pluck and will. But neither are pluck and will, dogged endurance and insensibility to danger enough, when taken all alone. There must be some sort of fusion, some chemical combination among these principles, for a life thoroughly significant to result.

• OBJECTIVISM AND ITS CRITICS

Defenders of objectivism have a relatively easy time avoiding counterexamples of the sort that appear to apply to subjectivism. Objectivists maintain that there are certain ways of being and functioning in the physical world that are meaningful 'in themselves', apart from whether a particular person thinks they are meaningful, enjoys them or chooses them. Whereas the subjectivist maintains that meaning is something that is created, the objectivist, in contrast, contends that it is something that is discovered. From the latter perspective, there are mind-independent facts about what is meaningful and what is not, about which individuals and even entire societies can be mistaken.

In this respect, for the objectivist, inquiry into meaningfulness is analogous to science: just as there is an independent fact of the matter that water is H_2O, and someone who thought otherwise would be mistaken, so there is an independent fact of the matter that urinating in snow does not confer meaning on a life, and if someone thought otherwise, he would be incorrect. Just as scientists have learned over time that water has a certain chemical composition, so philosophers and other reflective people have ascertained that meaningfulness has a certain pattern to it.

There are a wide variety of objective theories in the literature. It has been argued that all meaningful conditions are those in which one improves the quality of life of people and animals, or realizes human excellence in oneself, or promotes goods such as knowledge, friendship and autonomy, or makes progress towards certain ends that only humanity as a whole might be able to achieve, or exhibits creativity. In the reading below, Harvard philosopher Robert Nozick contends that meaningfulness is just a matter of a person transcending limits to connect with valuable entities beyond herself such as other persons, artworks, theories and ecosystems.

Subjectivists are quick to point out the multiplicity of objective theories, and that none has been able to proclaim itself a clear winner. In the face of so many differences about what constitutes meaning in life, subjectivists often argue that subjectivism makes the best sense of them; there is no one best answer, because what is meaningful varies from person to person. In addition, subjectivists contend that the objectivist perspective misses out on psychological facets that are clearly relevant to the degree to which a person's life is meaningful. They claim that a person who is utterly bored

BOX 28.2 ROBERT NOZICK

Robert Nozick (1938–2002) had one of the most imaginative and wide-ranging philosophical minds of the twentieth century, and had been based at the Department of Philosophy at Harvard University. In one of his books, *The Examined Life* (1989), he provides more than two dozen 'meditations' on a variety of topics about life, including God, love, sex, creativity, death, happiness and enlightenment. In the meditation titled 'Value and Meaning', from which the following excerpt is taken, Nozick presents an objectivist account of meaning, according to which a life is more meaningful, the more it connects with things beyond it, particularly with objects of intrinsic value, which Nozick contends are characteristically organic unities. Can you think of an intuitively meaningful condition that does not amount to a positive relationship with an organic unity beyond oneself?

Nozick, *The Examined Life* (New York: Simon and Schuster, 1989), pp. 162–8 (edited excerpt)

Let us consider things frequently said to be valuable in themselves. We begin with works of art. Recall what happens in art appreciation classes. You are shown how the different parts and components of a painting are interrelated, how the eye is led from place to place by forms and colors, how it is brought to the thematic center of the painting, how these colors, forms, and textures fit the theme, etc. You are shown how the painting is a unity, how the diverse elements constituting it form an integrated and united whole. A painting has aesthetic value, theorists have held, when it manages to integrate a great diversity of material into a tight unity....Such a 'unity in diversity' was termed an organic unity because organisms in the biological world were thought to exhibit the same unity wherein diverse organs and tissues interrelate to maintain the life of the organism.

[...]

Value is not the only relevant evaluative dimension. We also want our lives and our existence to have meaning. Value involves something's being integrated within its own boundaries, while meaning involves its having some connection beyond these boundaries. The problem of meaning itself is raised by the presence of limits. Thus, typically, people worry about the meaning of their lives when they see their existences as limited, perhaps because death will end them and so mark their final limit. To seek to give life meaning is to seek to transcend the limits of one's individual life....Sometimes this occurs by leaving children behind, sometimes by advancing some larger aim that is beyond oneself, such as the cause of justice or truth or beauty....

Meaning cannot be gained by just any linkage beyond boundaries, for instance, with something that is completely worthless. But that thing linked with to gain meaning need not itself be meaningful....We already have seen that there is another way for something to be worthwhile: it can have value. Value is a matter of the internal unified coherence of a thing....

Meaning can be gained by linking with something of value. However, the nature of the linkage is important. I cannot give meaning to my life by saying I am linked to advancing justice in the world, where this means that I read the newspapers every day or week and thereby notice how justice and injustice fare. That is too trivial and too insubstantial a link.

by, and even hates, helping others cannot acquire any meaning from doing so, *contra* the objectivist perspective.

• HYBRID THEORY AND ITS CRITICS

At this point, one can readily see why the hybrid version of naturalism is the most widely held theory these days. According to this view, a person's life is meaningful if and only if she is subjectively attracted to objectively attractive projects. If a person is engaging in something objectively worthwhile, but does not love doing it, or is not otherwise keen to do it, then she cannot obtain meaning from it. And if a person loves doing something, but it is not objectively worthwhile, e.g. he loves being a serial killer, then, again, no meaning can come from it. According to hybrid theorists, it is the combination of the subjective and the objective that is necessary and sufficient for meaning in life; either one on its own is not enough for an attractive account.

Since the hybrid theory includes an objective component, it can avoid counterintuitive implications about behavior such as urinating in snow or eating ice cream being meaningful if someone is 'into' that activity. And since it also includes a subjective component, it can account for many of the motivations for subjectivism, e.g. the ideas that a meaningful life includes one with passion, varies depending on the person's interests, and involves being true to one's inner nature.

Although the hybrid theory is powerful and commonly believed, it still gets attacked from both sides, as it were. Subjectivists contend that there are no such things as objective conditions of meaning. Perhaps only God could create universal standards for human beings, and it is unlikely that God exists, so many of them say, which means that we must be the ones to create our own meaning in life.

And from the other pole, objectivists maintain that, even if subjective elements do contribute to a meaningful life, they are not necessary for it. A particularly strong example here is volunteering to be bored so that others will not be bored. If boredom or a more general lack of subjective attraction were sufficient for an action to be meaningless, then this kind of sacrifice could never be meaningful, and yet perhaps it could be.

BOX 28.3 SUSAN WOLF

Susan Wolf (1952–), currently based at the University of North Carolina-Chapel Hill, is one of the philosophers who has most driven naturalist inquiry into life's meaning since the mid 1990s. Her book devoted to the topic, *Meaning in Life and Why It Matters* (2010), is based on a prestigious set of talks that she was invited to give, the Tanner Lectures on Human Values. In the book she articulates and defends a hybrid view of what makes a life meaningful, according to which meaning consists of loving things that are objectively worthy of love, and engaging with them in a positive way. It is worth asking which sorts of things are worth loving – is there a pattern to them?

Wolf, *Meaning in Life and Why It Matters* (Princeton: Princeton University Press, 2012), pp. 7–13 (edited excerpt)

According to the conception of meaningfulness I wish to propose, meaning arises from loving objects worthy of love and engaging with them in a positive way….

What is perhaps most distinctive about my conception of meaning, or about the category of value I have in mind, is that it involves subjective and objective elements, suitably and inextricably linked. "Love" is at least partly subjective, involving attitudes and feelings. In insisting that the requisite object must be "worthy of love," however, this conception of meaning invokes an objective standard. It is implicit in suggesting that an object be worthy of love (in order to contribute meaning to the lover's life) that not any object will do. Nor is it guaranteed that the subject's own assessment of worthiness is privileged. One might paraphrase this by saying that, according to my conception, meaning arises when subjective attraction meets objective attractiveness.

Essentially, the idea is that a person's life can be meaningful only if she cares fairly deeply about some thing or things, only if she is gripped, excited, interested, engaged, or as I earlier put it, if she loves something – as opposed to being bored by or alienated from most or all that she does. Even a person who is so engaged, however, will not live a meaningful life if the objects or activities with which she is so occupied are worthless. A person who loves smoking pot all day long, or doing endless crossword puzzles, and has the luxury of being able to indulge in this without restraint does not thereby make her life meaningful. Finally, this conception of meaning specifies that the relationship between the subject and the object of her attraction must be an active one. The condition that says that meaning involves engaging with the (worthy) object of love in a positive way is meant to make clear that mere passive recognition and a positive attitude toward an object's or activity's value is not sufficient for a meaningful life. One must be able to be in some sort of relationship with the valuable object of one's attention – to create it, protect it, promote it, honor it, or more generally, to actively affirm it in some way or other.

OBJECTIONS TO NATURALISM

How do supernaturalists question naturalism? Mainly by advancing the arguments that were critically explored in the previous two chapters, that is, those relating to the divine source of moral rules, the lack of perfect justice on earth, and the *sub specie aeternitatis* according to which the impact of merely physical lives is trivial.

Objections to these arguments, which naturalists tend to offer, were also considered. In addition, it was noted that many philosophers have the intuition that at least some meaning in life would be possible in the absence of a spiritual realm. There are, however, a few supernaturalists who lack that intuition and who in effect maintain that one may as well commit suicide if God does not exist or if one will not live forever. Tolstoy acutely expresses that perspective in the above reading.

Much more common these days, however, is the suggestion that supernaturalist theories should be construed in a different way, not to say that life would be utterly meaningless without God or a soul, but that it would be much more meaningful, or evince a deeper kind of meaning, with them. This is pretty much where the current debate among professional English-speaking philosophers stands, with some of the next stages of inquiry likely to be a matter of considering different quantities and qualities of meaningfulness and what the world and one's life must be like in order to exemplify them.

CHAPTER SUMMARY

- A naturalist theory differs from a supernaturalist one in that the former denies that a spiritual realm is necessary for life to be meaningful; according to naturalism, a significant existence can be had in a purely physical world as known by science.
- There are three major kinds of naturalist theories, namely, subjectivism, objectivism and a combination of the two, hybrid theory.
- According to subjectivism, what is meaningful varies from person to person, depending on her particular beliefs, interests and decisions. Although this view makes good sense of the relevance of passion and authenticity for meaning in life, and why there are many different types of meaningful lives possible, it has counterintuitive implications about which lives can be meaningful.

- According to objectivism, there are mind-independent factors that determine whether something is meaningful or not, about which individuals can be mistaken. Although this view readily avoids the most serious counterintuitive implications about which lives can be meaningful, it fails to make good sense of the relevance of passion and authenticity for meaning in life. In addition, the lack of consensus among rational inquirers with regard to the nature of purportedly objective conditions suggests that there might not be any.

- According to the hybrid theory, meaning in life is a matter of subjective attraction to objective attractiveness, which is the dominant view among contemporary philosophers mainly because it obtains most of the advantages of both subjectivism and objectivism. However, subjectivists and objectivists continue to deny that both elements are essential for the best theory of what makes life meaningful.

- Supernaturalists typically object to naturalism by invoking the arguments for its opposite, supernaturalism, as critically explored in the previous two chapters. In addition, contemporary supernaturalists tend to be sympathetic to the idea that, while some meaning would be possible in a purely physical world, a deeper or greater kind of meaning would not be possible without God and/or a soul.

• STUDY QUESTIONS

1 Must a supernaturalist be a theist, and must a naturalist be an atheist? Explain why or why not in your own words.
2 Try to provide some real-life examples of intuitively meaningless activities that some people have thought were meaningful and/or pursued with great interest.
3 If you had to pick one of the naturalist theories, which one would you favor, and why?
4 Subjectivists and hybrid theorists tend to maintain that only positive attitudes are relevant to meaning, i.e. that one must think well of something, or love it, or want it to engage with it. Can you think of cases in which meaning is constituted at least in part by negative attitudes such as hating?
5 What might it mean to claim that a spiritual realm is necessary for a 'deeper' or 'greater' meaning in life than what naturalism can ground? In addition, is the claim plausible, or might there be some possible way to have such meaning in a world where no spiritual realm exists?

• INTRODUCTORY FURTHER READING

Belliotti, Raymond (2001) *What Is the Meaning of Life?* (Amsterdam: Rodopi). [Favors naturalism and rejects a subjective approach to meaning in the context of critical discussion of a variety of classic thinkers such as Aristotle, Nietzsche and Schopenhauer.]

Eagleton, Terry (2007) *The Meaning of Life: A Very Short Introduction* (Oxford: Oxford University Press). [A light and lively essay on a variety of facets of the question of life's meaning, often addressing linguistic and literary themes. Rejects subjective ('postmodern') approaches to meaning in favor of a need for harmonious or loving relationships.]

Martin, Raymond (1993) 'A Fast Car and a Good Woman', in D. Kolak and R. Martin (eds.) *The Experience of Philosophy*, 2nd edn (Belmont, CA: Wadsworth Publishing Co.), pp. 556–65. [In this chapter from a textbook, the author advances the subjective view that meaningfulness is a matter of getting what you want, but is pessimistic about the extent to which people are able to get much of what they want.]

Singer, Peter (1993) *How Are We to Live?* (Melbourne: Random House Australia). [Composed for the generally educated reader, in this book the author defends an objective, utilitarian approach, according to which the more a person benefits other people and animals, the more meaningful her life.]

Taylor, Richard (1970) *Good and Evil* (New York: Macmillan Publishing Co.), pp. 319–34. [One of the most widely reprinted and read texts on life's meaning, which is based on the thought experiment of Sisyphus, mythically condemned by the Greek gods to roll a stone up and down a hill forever. In this chapter, the author maintains that the most important kind of meaning is subjective, obtaining whatever one most strongly desires.]

• ADVANCED FURTHER READING

Brogaard, Berit and Smith, Barry (2005) 'On Luck, Responsibility, and the Meaning of Life', *Philosophical Papers* 34: 443–58. [The authors defend what is aptly called an 'intersubjective' theory of meaning in life; for them, it is a matter of engaging in activities that rank highly by the standards of success that one's society accepts.]

Dworkin, Ronald (2000) 'Equality and the Good Life', in his *Sovereign Virtue* (Cambridge, MA: Harvard University Press), pp. 237–84. [Distinguishes between two major naturalist theories, one according to which a life that matters produces good results in the long run and another, hybrid view, according to which it exemplifies skillful performances that one endorses, where the author defends the latter.]

Frankfurt, Harry (1982) 'The Importance of What We Care About', *Synthese* 53: 257–72. [The most sophisticated subjectivist writing today, the author defends the view that meaning in life is constituted by caring about something.]

Kauppinen, Antti (2012) 'Meaningfulness and Time', *Philosophy and Phenomenological Research* 82: 345–77. [Unlike most of the other entries here, this one explores the idea that a large part of what makes a life meaningful is the pattern it displays as it develops over time.]

Levy, Neil (2005) 'Downshifting and Meaning in Life', *Ratio* 18: 176–89. [Argues that great meaning in life would come not from working less and spending more time with family, but rather by actively progressing towards highly worthwhile states of affairs that cannot conceivably be realized, such as perfect justice and complete knowledge.]

Mintoff, Joseph (2008) 'Transcending Absurdity', *Ratio* 21: 64–84. [Advances a complex theory of what makes a life meaningful according to which one's life is more meaningful, the more it achieves transcendent ends, roughly, goals that are objectively good, long-lasting in duration, and broad in scope.]

Taylor, Richard (1987) 'Time and Life's Meaning', *The Review of Metaphysics* 40: 675–86. [Although the author is better known for his earlier, subjectivist account of meaning in life, he changed his mind and eventually defended the objectivist view that what makes a life meaningful is solely the extent to which it is creative.]

• FREE INTERNET RESOURCES

Metz, Thaddeus (2011) 'The Good, the True and the Beautiful: Toward a Unified Account of Great Meaning in Life', *Religious Studies* 47: 389–409. https:// ujdigispace.uj.ac.za/handle/10210/8584. [Critically explores a variety of non-subjective theories of what makes a life particularly meaningful, and develops a new one that purportedly avoids and explains their weaknesses.]

Sartre, Jean-Paul (1946) 'Existentialism is a Humanism', Philip Mairet, tr. http:// www.marxists.org/reference/archive/sartre/works/exist/sartre.htm. [The famous French existentialist explains and defends his version of subjectivism, which he summarizes with the phrase 'existence precedes essence', by which he means that what a particular person is or ought to be is determined only by the choices she makes.]

Appendix

how to write a philosophy essay

Duncan Pritchard

I begin with an important caveat. To some extent, what follows is merely my own view about what makes a good philosophy essay, and hence you should treat this advice with a note of caution. In particular, it is always wise to check with whoever is teaching the course regarding what they are looking for in a good philosophy essay, in case it diverges from the advice I'm offering. That said, I think my suggestions are relatively uncontroversial. Although I will be focusing on philosophy essays specifically, this advice will be generally applicable to essay writing in most fields.

First off, you should *pay careful attention to the formulation of the question*, and make sure that your essay is devoted to answering that specific question. In particular, you should resist the temptation to simply start describing everything you know about the topic in hand, which I find is a common mistake in essays. (Relatedly, you should make sure that your essay doesn't start out as an answer to the question in hand but gradually drift into being an essay about something else entirely.) There is an art to setting good essay questions, and often a lot of thought goes into their formulation in order to ensure that the person answering the question is being assessed on how much they have really understood the topic in hand. The point is that simply reading someone list everything they know about a topic doesn't really give you much of an idea of how much they have understood, and for that you really need to see how they engage with a very specific question on that topic.

Second, make sure that you *write clearly and stick to the point*. Good philosophical writing is usually very precise and clear, with little by way of extraneous information.

So, for example, in an essay on Wittgenstein's epistemology, don't bother listing biographical details about the man himself, and certainly don't get into a discussion of what his views were in other areas of philosophy unrelated to the question in hand. You won't get any marks for such superfluous information, and it will merely side-track from the essay question in hand. (Moreover, if your essays are subject to a word count, as most are, then every word focused on unimportant matters is one word fewer that is targeted on the essay question.) Remember that writing that is clear and crisp will impress the marker far more than florid prose that is difficult to follow. (Philosophers may have a reputation for being obscure, but actually the very best philosophy is usually crystal clear.)

Third, make sure that you *argue for your points*, and that you don't simply state them without support. In general, it isn't a good idea to state one's opinions in essays, as it's not relevant to the task in hand. We want to know what the right position is, and that means not only describing the view you favour, but also explaining why you think it is right. A related point here is that students often get themselves into the awkward position of being impartial referees on a debate in which they don't take sides. This leads them to conclude with something very wishy-washy, along the lines of 'there are lots of viewpoints, and this issue isn't going to be settled soon'. If philosophy were journalism, then this might be good philosophy, but it isn't. That is, good journalism may well be about explaining both sides to an issue without taking a stance yourself (though this is of course disputable), but philosophy is not so even-handed. We want to know what you think the right position is, and to hear your arguments in defence of this claim. (In this respect, a better analogy for philosophy may be the law, such as the legal reasoning offered by a judge, rather than journalism.)

Usually, explaining why your view is right also involves explaining why the competing views are wrong. A good point to bear in mind here is that you should always *describe the opposing views as charitably as possible*. What you don't want to do is score a cheap victory over the opposition by describing their position in such crude terms that it is manifestly untenable (this is what is known as 'arguing against a straw man'). Indeed, being charitable to the opposition can sometimes mean considering ways in which the opponent's viewpoint can be improved even where these are not improvements that the proponents of the position considered themselves. A related point in this regard is to be wary of opposing positions which, on your construal anyway, are obviously false. As a general rule (though it is far from infallible), if a philosophical position as you describe it is obviously false, then you haven't described it correctly.

Fourth, *use examples* to illustrate your points. Examples are a great way of both clearly explaining a point and also demonstrating to the marker that you understand what you are proposing. Indeed, if you don't really understand what you are proposing, then it may only be via the process of trying to come up with a good example to go with your point that you will realise this, which is another good reason always to use examples where possible. Of course, you also need to make sure that the examples you use really do illustrate the point in hand!

We now come to a fifth and more general piece of advice, one that builds on several of the earlier points. This is that you should remember that you are *making a case* for a particular answer to the question. This is more than just a matter of writing clearly and concisely, and offering arguments in support of your view. It is in addition a matter of *structure*, of how you bring everything together to motivate your conclusion. One way to think about this is that you are in effect telling a story when you answer a question. Not in the sense that you're making things up of course, but rather in the sense that you are gradually building a case for a particular view, with every element of your essay leading to that conclusion. This means that a well-crafted essay is likely to have the same kind of narrative arc that a good story has. So, the introduction to the essay will set the scene for the debate and explain why the issues in hand are important. You'll then move on to considering various points relevant to the essay, such as considerations for and against a particular viewpoint. And all along you are building a case in support of the view you defend, something that you can summarize in the conclusion. (I noted above the similarities between philosophy and legal reasoning, and this analogy is also applicable here.)

In order to achieve this end it is a good idea, when drafting your essay, to take some time to try to read your essay with a detached eye. Does your essay really make the case for your thesis that you think it does? In particular, do you explain each point properly, and is it clear how all the points you make intersect with one another to make an overall case for your conclusion? In my experience, the best way to do this is leave a decent gap between the drafting of the essay and the final fashioning of the essay. This will afford you some intellectual distance on your writing, and therefore make it easier to read it in a detached way.

I will close with some general points about essay writing. To begin with, the question of *referencing*. In my experience, the referencing style rarely matters at an introductory level, so long as you list all the relevant details. But this is clearly something worth checking with the person marking the essay. I give some links to the two main referencing styles, Harvard and Chicago, below.

A more important issue is that of *plagiarism*. Plagiarism is when you pass someone else's work off as your own, and the penalties for plagiarism can be very harsh, in some cases including exclusion from the course in question. Note too that these days it is common for an essay to be examined by sophisticated software that can pick up signs of plagiarism very easily, and so this is effectively a crime that is doomed to fail. In order to avoid this problem, the key thing to remember is always to express your points in your own words. That doesn't mean that you can't cite the words of others, but when you do make sure that you reference their contribution properly so that there can be no doubt that you are trying to pass off another's work as your own.

A final point I want to make about philosophical writing is that once you get the hang of it you'll find that it is a very liberating experience. Life is full of differing viewpoints, and also full of appeals to everything other than your rational faculties (think, for example, about how most advertising works, which is in effect an attempt to circumvent your rational self by appealing to your baser motives, such as vanity or avarice). Once you get into the knack of learning how to argue for a position clearly and concisely, you'll find that this is a wonderful skill, one that is applicable to lots of areas of your life. Indeed, I predict that before long you will find yourself appealing to your critical faculties, honed by doing philosophy, in lots of ways that you didn't do hitherto. For example, rather than just listening to a commentator on the television present their viewpoint, and wondering why in general you don't find it persuasive, you'll find yourself sifting through what they say to determine what part of it counts as a genuine argument and what is mere rhetoric. In so doing, you'll either find that you were right to be sceptical about the position being offered, or else find yourself endorsing that position. Even in the latter case, you'll be discovering a route to that viewpoint which is via your own intellectual energies. And either way, you'll be exercising your intellectual capacities in entirely new ways. This kind of critical engagement is one of the most important off-shoots of doing philosophy, and thus of composing philosophy essays.

• FURTHER INFORMATION

For some general advice on writing philosophy essays, see:

Martinich, A. P., *Philosophical Writing: An Introduction* (Oxford: Blackwell, several editions).

There is also lots of guidance on essay writing available on the internet. Here I select some of the highlights:

- http://www.jimpryor.net/teaching/guidelines/writing.html [In this essay, Jim Pryor, a philosopher at New York University, offers some very useful general advice on essay writing.]
- http://www.public.asu.edu/~dportmor/tips.pdf [A very detailed account of good philosophy essay writing, written by Doug Portmore, a philosopher at Arizona State University.]
- http://prezi.com/z4h1_fwilbxj/a-sample-philosophy-paper/ [This offers an interesting take on the subject, in the form of a 'prezi' presentation on what constitutes a good essay, written by Angela Mendelovici, who is a philosopher at the University of Western Ontario.]
- http://web.uct.ac.za/depts/philosophy/James%20Lenman%20-%20How%20to%20Write%20a%20Crap%20Philosophy%20Essay.pdf [Jimmy Lenman, a philosopher at the University of Sheffield, approaches the problem of how to write a good philosophy essay by offering advice on how to write a truly terrible philosophy essay. Very funny.]
- http://www.davidbain.org/teaching/essay-writing [A helpful webpage of advice on essay writing by David Bain, a philosopher at the University of Glasgow.]

Finally, you can find details about the two of the main referencing systems, Harvard and Chicago, here:

- http://www3.imperial.ac.uk/library/subjectsandsupport/referencemanagement/harvard [A very helpful overview of the Harvard referencing system offered by Imperial College London.]
- http://www.chicagomanualofstyle.org/tools_}itationguide.html [A canonical guide to the Chicago system of referencing.]

glossary of terms

Ability knowledge: This is often referred to as 'know-how', since it involves knowing how to do something, such as ride a bike or swim. It is usually contrasted with propositional knowledge, which is knowledge of a proposition. The two types of knowledge are treated differently because, intuitively at least, one might know how to do something (e.g. swim) without having any relevant propositional knowledge (e.g. without knowing that you can swim, perhaps because you forgot that you could until you fell in the water). *See also* **propositional knowledge**.

Abstract objects: Objects that do not exist in space or time and which are not composed of matter.

Adaptation: Adaptation is a position in climate change justice. Adaptation proponents argue the best way to prepare for climate change is to adapt to changing future conditions. These adaptations normally consist in uses of technology and scientific advancements.

Aesthetic experience: An allegedly distinctive sort of experience, had in relation to (for instance) works of art, and perhaps also beautiful man-made and natural objects.

Aesthetic formalism: A theory of aesthetic experience which says that aesthetic experience exclusively depends on properties perceived by the senses (e.g. shape, colour, line, rhythm, tone, texture and so on). The associated theory of art tries to define art in terms of that which produces aesthetic experience, conceived in this way.

Aesthetic judgement: An evaluative judgement, paradigmatically made in response to artworks but also to other objects. For instance: judging something as beautiful, ugly, vibrant, graceful, clumsy, harmonious, pallid, or bold would all count as aesthetic judgements in the right context.

Agency: The capacity of an agent to act in the world.

Agnosticism: A standard definition would have it that agnosticism is the thesis that we cannot know that there is or that there is not a God of the classical theistic sort. It is worth noting that it would be quite possible to be an agnostic in this sense yet also a theist, someone who believes that there is a God. We all believe things which, on reflection, we don't want to say we know. Another standard definition has it that an agnostic is simply someone who fails to believe that there's a God and also fails to believe that there's not a God. In that sense of agnostic, it would not be possible to be an agnostic and yet also a theist (or indeed also an atheist). *See also* **theism** and **atheism**.

Animal rights: In ethics this is the position that we owe moral consideration to animals. Since we have obligations not to treat animals in certain ways, then animals have rights not to be treated in those ways. Some philosophers, such as Peter Singer, ground animal rights in the capacity to suffer: it is the fact that humans and nonhumans are capable of enjoyment and pleasure that brings them into our sphere of moral consideration. Proponents of animal rights oppose raising animals for food and animal experimentation, on the grounds that these fail to give equal consideration to animals.

Anomaly: An anomaly, in Thomas Kuhn's account of science, is a puzzle that resists resolution by the means available within **normal science**. Some such anomalies – for example, the inability of Newtonian physics to explain the orbit of Uranus – can be ignored (or 'quarantined') for a long time, but may ultimately lead to a **scientific revolution**.

Anti-essentialism: The view that the concept of art is not governed by either individually necessary or a small set of jointly sufficient conditions.

a posteriori **knowledge**: A piece of knowledge that we can only come to know by empirical investigation.

a priori **knowledge**: A piece of knowledge that one can come to know by reason alone, without empirical investigation of the world.

Applied ethics: Sometimes called *practical ethics*, this is the study of particular and difficult ethical issues, including those to do with abortion, euthanasia, animal rights, conduct in wartime, and famine. Although normative theories inform our thinking about such things, applied ethics isn't simply the application of theory to such matters; instead, applied ethics involves close scrutiny of the issues to see the principles, values, and structures involved, and where understanding of these is necessary for clear thinking about the issue itself.

Artefact: A man-made object.

A-series: An ordering of events in terms of whether they are past, present, or future.

Asymmetric: A relation, R, is asymmetric just in case if A Rs B, then it is not the case that B Rs A.

Atheism: Atheism is the thesis that there is no God of the classical theistic sort. This definition is a standard one but, as mentioned in text box 25.2, others are available in the literature. One defines atheism as the thesis that we can know that there is not a God. Obviously, in asserting that the non-existence of God is something knowable, Atheism so defined inherits a good number of contested issues in Epistemology. *See also* **agnosticism** and **theism**.

A-theorists: Those who think that time is dynamical. A-theorists think that events change from being future, to being present, to being past, and it is this that characterises the flow of time.

Atonal music: Music that does not possess a clear tonal centre, as most classical Western music does prior to the twentieth century.

Auditory experience: Perceptual experience that either was or appears to the subject to be the result of actually hearing sounds.

Avant-garde: Within a cultural or artistic movement, that which is experimental and innovative.

Axiomatisation: Axiomatisation is a formal approach to scientific theories, whereby certain axioms are posited, from which the rest of the theory can be logically deduced as theorems. On this account, the theory itself consists of the axioms and all that follows from them.

Basic emotions: Emotions that are not analysable in terms of other simpler emotions and that compose more complex emotions. They are also associated with facial expressions that can be recognised by people from all cultures. American psychologist Paul Ekman argued that there are six basic emotions: joy, surprise, anger, fear, sadness and disgust.

B-series: An ordering of events in terms of whether those events are earlier-than, later-than, or simultaneous-with, one another.

B-theorists: Those who think that time is not dynamical. B-theorists think that temporal relations are characterised by the relations of being earlier-than, later-than, and simultaneous-with, and that these properties of presentness, pastness, and futurity can be reduced to these relations and indexical facts.

Capabilities approach: A capability is the ability to do or be. It used to identify liberties that should be secured for each individual. We need not exercise our capability at every turn, but they must be available for us at any time on this view. Amartya Sen defends a capability approach along a continuum where our goal is to increase capability attainment. Martha Nussbaum defends a capabilities approach that highlights the multiple capabilities we have. She argues capabilities must be maintained above a minimum threshold that guarantees a decent human life.

Causation: A relation that obtains between events where one is the cause of the other.

Classical account of knowledge: According to the classical account of knowledge, knowledge is defined as justified true belief. This view is often credited to Plato, and is sometimes referred to as the 'tripartite' (i.e. three-part) account of knowledge. *See also* **Gettier cases**.

Closure principle: This principle states that if one knows one proposition, and one knows that this proposition entails a second proposition, then one knows the second proposition as well. So, for example, if I know that Paris is the capital of France, and I know that if Paris is the capital of France then it is not the capital of Germany, then I also know that Paris is not the capital of Germany.

Cognitive theories of emotion: Cognitive theories of emotion maintain that emotions are cognitive states of appraisal. For example, fear may be the state of rendering a thing or a kind of thing dangerous. Advocates of this theory normally deny that emotions involve feelings or experiences of changes in the body.

Combination problem: A problem of explaining how many micro-subjects can add up to a single conscious person. The problem arises for panpsychism, which holds that all bits and pieces of the external world are conscious.

Composition: A relation that obtains between some things, such that those things are parts of a composite object.

Conceivable: A sentence is conceivable just when it cannot be ruled out on a priori, or logical, grounds. Discovering whether a conceivable sentence is true or false requires exploring the external world. 'Water is not made of H_2O', for example, is false but it is conceivable, as we cannot figure out whether it is true or false simply by thinking really hard about it. An empirical discovery was required to figure this out.

Conceptual analysis: An account of the content of a particular concept. Usually this involves specifying what it would take for a concept to pick out something in the world.

Conceptual art: Twentieth-century artistic movement which prioritised thought and idea over material means of expression, and traditional notions of aesthetic effect.

Consequentialism: This is a moral theory that makes the rightness of actions (and the goodness of people, institutions, etc.) depend upon the value of the consequences that the actions (people, institutions) bring about. Consequentialist theories typically have to parts: a value theory, telling us what it is about an outcome that makes it valuable; and a standard of rightness, telling us how actions (people, institutions) are to be related to the outcomes in order to be right. A standard consequentialist theory says that right acts are ones that maximise value.

Conservationism: Conservationism is a position in climate change justice. Proponents of conservationism argue that the best way to solve the problem of climate change is to end it by reducing carbon emissions to sustainable levels. Ecological footprint defenders argue we should each have an equal share of the Earth's carrying capacity as a limit to ensure a fair and equal measure of guaranteeing future sustainability. The polluter pays principle approach argues that polluters should pay compensation for the pollution they create. The higher costs are aimed to produce incentives for lowering carbon emissions to sustainable levels and the income generated spent to compensate for pollution damage.

Contextualism: Contextualism is the view that 'knowledge' is a highly context-sensitive term, and that this can help us resolve certain fundamental problems in epistemology, such as the problem of radical scepticism. More specifically, contextualists argue that 'knows' picks out quite demanding epistemic standards in some contexts, but quite weak epistemic standards in others. Applied to the problem of radical scepticism, contextualism is the thought that the sceptic is using the term 'knows' in a more demanding way than we usually use it. Accordingly, we can, it seems, grant that we know an awful lot relative to our everyday standards even while simultaneously granting that we may not count as knowing very much relative to the sceptic's more exacting standards. *See also* **radical scepticism**.

Contingency: Contingency concerns the 'could-have-been-otherwise-ness' of things. It is contingent, for example, that I am wearing a blue shirt today; I have shirts of other colours that I could easily have selected. Some philosophers have argued that it is a contingent fact that the universe exists – i.e. that it could have been the case that it did not come into existence. That it is metaphysically contingent is a crucial premise of the Cosmological Argument. *See also* **Cosmological Argument** and **Necessity**.

Cosmological Argument: This is the general name given to arguments for the existence of God that proceed from very general features of the universe, for example the alleged fact that it is contingent (could have been otherwise). The account in chapter 24 focuses on the contingency version of the Cosmological Argument, but other arguments that are usually listed as versions of the Cosmological Argument would use the alleged fact that the universe began to exist, for example, as the fact that implies a God behind it. *See also* **Contingency**.

Cosmopolitanism: Cosmopolitanism is the view that every human being has equal moral worth. This leads some to argue that we have general duties extending to every individual because of their equal moral worth. Cosmopolitanism is generally in criticism of – if not in opposition to – nationalist and statist views claiming our group membership gives rise to special duties among members. While some cosmopolitans are sympathetic to part of this argument, it is often highlighted how group memberships and state boundaries can be arbitrary and so should not outweigh general duties to all because of their equal moral worth.

Counterfactual theories of causation: Theories of causation according to which c causes e is true, just in case had c not occurred, e would not have occurred.

Covering-law model: *see* **deductive-nomological model**.

Death: Unless qualified to be about one's body alone, this word refers to the permanent cessation of one's existence. Hence, it does not (unless qualified) simply mean that one's body has died, but also means that a person's self has perished, never to return.

Deductive-nomological (D-N) model: An account of scientific explanation which holds that, in order to explain something, we must be able to deduce logically the **explanandum** from premises that include a description of the case at hand and at least one (explanatorily relevant) statement of a law of a nature. In other words, we must be able to subsume the particular situation under a more general ('covering') law of nature.

Demarcation criterion: A demarcation criterion would be a criterion that allows us to distinguish between science and **pseudo-science** (or non-science). Karl Popper thought that **falsifiability** constituted a demarcation criterion. While the demarcation problem continues to be relevant – not least since many pseudo-sciences try hard to emulate the hallmarks of science – it is now believed that no single (e.g. logical) characteristic can be isolated as 'the' distinguishing feature of science.

Deontology: A moral theory that is characterised by constraints on our behaviour – there are certain things that we must not do, even if these things maximise happiness – and permissions – we are not necessarily immoral if we don't act to bring about the best outcomes. Kantian deontology justifies constraints by proposing that immoral actions are, in some sense, irrational; other deontological theories hold that immoral actions – and demands that we always maximise happiness – violate the dignity or autonomy of a person.

Derivative: An object or property is said to be derivative if there is some other object or property upon which it depends, or some other object or property that grounds it.

Design Argument (from fine-tuning): The name 'Design Argument' is given to any argument for the existence of God which proceeds from a feature of the natural universe which is taken to be ordered in such a way as to be evidence of (divine) design. So, until the theory of evolution came along and explained this appearance of design naturalistically, one might have taken as one's starting point for a design argument the amazing construction of the human eye; that does prima facie seem to be evidence of design. In the main text, I focus on a phenomenon called the 'fine-tuning' of the universe as – I maintain – evidence of design. 'Fine-tuning' is the name given to the fact that various features of the laws of nature could not have had values much different from those that they do and yet the universe have been life-permitting. This is also sometimes offered as evidence of (divine) design.

Direct realism: Direct realism about perception is the view that it is essential to accurate perceptual experience that it involves direct awareness of an external object and its perceptible property instances.

Disjunctivism: A view about perception that maintains that accurate perception and misperception are of fundamentally different kinds. The standard form of disjunctivism holds that accurate perception is fundamentally a matter of being related to an external object and some of its perceptible properties.

Divine command theory of morality: The view that moral rules that apply to at least all human persons are identical to the expression of God's will, such that wrong actions are those that God has forbidden and right ones are those that God has permitted. This view entails that if God did not exist, then there would be no universally binding moral rules on us.

Doctrine of Divine Simplicity: This would have been understood differently in the Middle Ages from the way that I understand it in the main text, where it is simply the thesis that God is (or would be, were He to exist) a relatively simple entity.

Dualism: Dualism is the view that there are two fundamental (or primitive and unanalysable) types of properties in the universe: mental properties and physical properties.

Empirically equivalent: Two theories are empirically equivalent just in case they make all of the same empirical predictions in this, and every other, possible world.

Empiricism: Empiricism refers to the broad class of philosophical positions that take sensory experience to be the ultimate source of all knowledge. One challenge for empiricists is to show how complex knowledge claims – including many scientific claims – can be traced back to sensory experience.

Epiphenomenalism: In the consciousness literature, epiphenomenalism is a view, or a consequence of a view, that states that consciousness plays no causal role.

Epistemology: This is the name given for the theory of knowledge. Those who study epistemology, known as epistemologists, are also interested in those notions closely associated with knowledge, such as truth, justification and rationality.

Eternality: This is the property traditionally attributed to God of being without temporal limit, either because He is inside time but everlasting or because He is outside time.

Evolutionary psychology: The expression refers broadly to psychologists who hold that evolution is largely responsible for how we sense, think, feel and act. In the literature on emotions evolutionary psychology is the view that emotions are evolutionary adaptations that helped us pass on our genes.

Existentialism: A branch of philosophy typified by the French philosophers Albert Camus and Jean-Paul Sartre that was most influential in twentieth-century Europe, and was characterised by a focus on the individual person. It sought to comprehend the fundamental nature of one's existence and addressed one's need to take responsibility for one's life in the face of unavoidable scepticism about God and objective values.

Explanans, explanandum: In the search for an explanation, the **explanandum** is that which stands in need of explanation, whereas the **explanans** (e.g. the premises in a **deductive-nomological** argument) is that which 'does the explaining'.

Explanatory gap: There is said to be an explanatory gap between mental and physical properties when no amount of third-person physical data would suffice to give us full knowledge of the mind, even if we had perfect logic skills. The term originated with Professor Joseph Levine.

Explanatory power: One of the theoretical virtues. A theory is typically said to have greater explanatory power either if it better explains some set of phenomena than does its rival, or if it explains a wider range of phenomena than does its rival.

Expressivism: A theory in metaethics that says that moral judgements *express* feelings or desires, rather than *describe* objective facts. Moral language, on this view, has the function of expressing our feelings. Expressivism is well placed to explain internalism, since if moral judgements express feelings or desires, and if feelings or desires are motivational states, then it is obvious why moral judgements would have a necessary connection with motivation and action.

Faith: The nature of faith is a controversial topic. Typically, it is understood as an amalgam of what we can call *belief in* and *belief that*. In the case of faith in God, faith is *belief in* God, in the sense of an existential commitment to God, and also *belief that* there's a God, in the sense that one's list of what one believes exists includes God as a member.

Falsifiability: For a statement (e.g. a prediction) to be falsifiable, it must have the potential to be refuted by empirical evidence – that is, by some possible **observation**. Falsifiability, according to Karl Popper, is a central feature of science. If a claim, or theory, is falsifiable, this does not mean that it is false, merely that it could be seen to be false if certain observations were to occur.

Family resemblance concept: A concept not governed by necessary membership conditions, common to all, but rather by partial similarities between some of the things that fall under it.

Feeling theory: A theory about emotions that states that emotions are feelings, or perceptions, of changes in the body. It originates with American philosopher and psychologist William James and the Danish doctor Carl Lange, who independently of each other developed versions of this theory.

Feminism: There is no one 'feminism': it is best characterised as a diverse tent. A possible thread connecting most feminist approaches is a concern about power and gender inequality. Liberal feminists emphasise the importance of consent and individual rights. Radical feminists emphasise structural inequalities.

Fictionalism: An umbrella term that includes many different views. These views share the core idea that to be a fictionalist about some particular discourse (such as mathematical discourse) is to think that strictly speaking that discourse is false, but that there is a fictional version of the discourse such that claims made within that fiction are true.

Fine arts: Painting, sculpture, architecture, music, and poetry.

Formalism: *see* **Aesthetic formalism**.

Freedom: Freedom is a contested idea about individual action. Positive freedom claims we are free when we can achieve some end or goal. Negative freedom claims we are free when we are not coerced or interfered with by others. Republican freedom claims we are free when not subjected to domination. Each defends freedom as a special area of concern to inform our views about political justice and rights.

Free will: The capacity of an agent to choose between options in a way that freely exercises the will of the agent and such that the agent can be held responsible for that action. It is controversial in what free will consists, for instance, in whether it requires that causal determinism is false, or instead requires that the action somehow issues from the agent in an appropriate manner.

Functional definition of art: A definition of art which cites some function(s) as necessary and/or sufficient conditions for something counting as an artwork.

Functional role property: A descriptive property that states a function. For example, if pain is a functional role property, then pain may be the property of producing the belief that something is wrong with the body and a desire for the state to disappear and having a tendency to trigger anxiety, moaning, whining or screaming.

Functionalism: Functionalism about consciousness is the view that consciousness is to be defined in terms of the role consciousness plays. The most common versions take consciousness to be definable in terms of behaviour or other third-person observable features.

Fundamental: An object or property is said to be fundamental if it does not depend on any other object or property. For example, a fundamental property is a primitive property that cannot be analysed in terms of something else.

Gettier cases: Gettier cases are scenarios in which an agent has a justified true belief and yet lacks knowledge because it is substantially due to luck that the belief in question is true. Imagine someone who forms her belief about what the time is by looking at a stopped clock that she has every reason for thinking is working. Crucially, however, she happens to look at the clock at the one time in the day when it is showing the right time, and so forms a true belief as a result. Her belief is thus both true and justified, yet it isn't a case of knowledge since it is just luck that her belief is true given that the clock is not working. Gettier cases show that the classical account of knowledge that analyses knowledge into justified true belief is unsustainable. *See also* **Classical account of knowledge**.

Global Justice: Global justice is a field of political philosophy that examines justice between and among states. Major concerns are climate change, international distributive justice and just war theory.

God (of classical theism): This is the sort of God that philosophers of religion debate the nature and existence of. Of course there are other gods (usually the 'g' is not capitalised) – e.g. Zeus, Loki – that people have believed in and perhaps still do believe in. But it's widely held, even by the staunchest of atheists, that these are even less likely to exist than the God of classical theism, which is why no-one debates their existence. That said, there are some borderline cases. For example, whilst it's pretty plausible that the God of classical theism is the God believed in by religious (rather than merely 'cultural') Jews, Christians and Muslims, it's less clear whether He is the Brahman of Hinduism.

God-based theory: A supernaturalist conception of meaning in life according to which it is solely a matter of relating to God, as conceived in the monotheistic tradition, in a certain way. This theory does not posit anything about whether God in fact exists, but does entail that if God does not exist, then no one's life is meaningful.

Grounding: A dependence relation posited by certain metaphysicians. This relation is typically held to be primitive (it cannot be defined in terms of other relations). It is usually thought to be characterised by being asymmetric, transitive (if x grounds y, and y grounds a, then x grounds a) and irreflexive (nothing grounds itself).

Gustatory experience: Perceptual experience that either was or appears to the subject to be the result of actually tasting a solid or liquid.

Hallucination: An experience in which the experienced object is not causally related to the external object (if any). Hallucinations are not normally veridical.

Happiness: To inquire into the nature of happiness is roughly a matter of asking what is good in itself for an individual, with many contending that this is a matter of her experiencing pleasure or being pleased by her condition. Very few philosophers believe that happiness and meaningfulness are one and the same thing.

Hard problem: The hard problem was introduced as a term with a specific meaning into the philosophy of mind literature by David Chalmers. It is the problem of explaining why and how we have experiences with a distinctly subjective element. The problem should be distinguished from the standard scientific problems, such as that of showing how consciousness evolved or that of showing which neural correlates underlie which kinds of conscious states.

Harm principle: The harm principle is defended by J. S. Mill. The principle argues that the only legitimate constraint on individual freedom is to prevent harm to others. This is one of the most famous and influential principles in philosophy, but it is also controversial as much depends on what we consider (or do not consider) to be a relevant 'harm'.

Hybrid theory: A naturalist conception of meaning in life according to which neither subjective conditions nor objective ones are sufficient on their own for a meaningful life. By this view, a meaningful life is one in which a person is attracted to goods that in fact merit attraction.

Hypothetico-deductivism: Hypothetico-deductivism refers to an account of science that emphasises the conjecturing of hypotheses and their subsequent **testing** against **observations**. Scientific theories, according to hypothetico-deductivism, are sets of hypotheses, from which testable predictions are derived through logical deduction, which are then checked by comparison with observable facts. It is often assumed that, even before testing, some gathering of empirical data must have gone into the formulation of a theoretical hypothesis.

Illusion: An experience in which not all of the experienced properties are relevantly causally related to property instances of the external object. Illusions are not normally veridical.

Immortality: The condition of being able to live forever, i.e. of being able never to undergo death.

Incommensurability: Incommensurability, in Thomas Kuhn's theory of science, refers to our inability, following a **paradigm shift**, to grasp fully the content of previous scientific theories and practices. On a broad interpretation of 'incommensurability', this would affect our view of scientific practices in general – e.g. divergent views on what constitutes a scientific problem or an adequate experimental method. On a narrow interpretation, incommensurability renders the meaning of scientific terms untranslatable across theory changes, since a paradigm shift affects not only the explicit theoretical content of science, but also tacit assumptions, expectations, and conventions. As a result, comparisons between past and present scientific theories may be rendered inconclusive or even impossible.

Incorporeality (transcendence): Insofar as one holds that God is not spatio-temporally located within the universe because the universe as a whole is God's body, then the term 'transcendence' is more apt. *See also* **Omnipresence (immanence)**.

Indirect realism: The view that perceivers are not directly aware of external objects and their perceptible property instances but are only aware of them by being aware of something else.

Indispensability arguments: Arguments that attempt to show that because some entity, E, is indispensable to our best theory of some phenomenon, we should be committed to the existence of E.

Inductive inference: Inductive inference is a mode of reasoning that generalises from past instances to future instances of the same kind. For example, having observed pink blossoms in ninety out of a hundred pea plants that have resulted from cross-breeding white-flowering with red-flowering plants, I might infer that the next pea plant about to flower from the same batch will also have pink blossoms. Whereas deductive inference 'preserves truth', since the conclusion of a logically valid argument cannot be false if its premises are true, inductive inference is fallible: it might be that the next pea plant about to flower has suffered a mutation, turning its blossoms red instead of pink.

Infallibilism: Infallibilism is the view that in order to have knowledge one must have a belief which is formed in such a way that it simply could not have led to error.

Instrumentalism: In the philosophical debate about whether science gives us a true, or approximately true, account of the world, instrumentalism designates the opposite view to **scientific realism**. On the instrumentalist view, scientific theories and claims are instruments for explaining and predicting phenomena rather than a way of approximating to objective reality.

Instrumental value: This is a kind of value that accrues to something in virtue of the fact that it serves some valuable goal. A thermometer is instrumentally valuable, for example, because it helps us to find out something of importance to us (i.e. what the temperature is). *See also* **non-instrumental value**.

Internalism: The position in metaethics that holds that there is a close – indeed, a necessary – connection between morality and action. There are a number of internalist positions, but a popular one is called judgement internalism, and holds that if you make a sincere moral judgement – for example, that eating meat is wrong – then you will be motivated to act accordingly – for example, to not eat meat, to protest against factory farming, and so on.

Introspectively indistinguishable: Two experiences are introspectively indistinguishable if you cannot tell them apart in terms of their internal features.

James–Lange theory: A theory of emotions that maintains that emotions are feelings or experiences of changes in the body. This theory is also known as 'the original feeling theory' or just the '**feeling theory**'. Contemporary versions of the theory tend to require that emotions also involve a perception or a directedness toward an external object or event.

Justice: Justice concerns the legitimate distribution of things we value, such as opportunities and wealth.

Justice as fairness: Justice as fairness is the name that John Rawls gives to his influential theory of justice. It is built on a social contract model where citizens imagine they are in an original position behind a veil of ignorance. The veil masks their knowledge of morally arbitrary features about themselves and others: none know their age, gender, sexual orientation and other features. They consider principles of justice that all can affirm that will attach to the basic structure of society. Citizens then remove the veil. There remains the issue of how to respect the equality of citizens who each accept different views about meaning and value (which Rawls calls comprehensive doctrines). Justice as fairness addresses this by claiming citizens should employ public reasons (reasons accessible to everyone) to forge an overlapping consensus to determine policies within the constraints of Rawls's two principles of justice.

Laws of nature: A law of nature describes some generalisation or regularity that is typically thought to hold at all times and places and describes some physical or metaphysical aspect of the world. It is controversial what makes a regularity or generalisation a law.

Logical empiricism: Logical empiricism was based on the conviction that the formal tools of logic made it possible to firmly ground science in experience. One goal, among others, was to eliminate any theoretical (= non-observational) scientific terms – in particular, any talk about unobservables or hidden structures – reducing them instead to observational facts.

Logically possible: Something is logically possible if it obtains at a possible world. Alternatively, something is logically possible if its obtaining does not entail a contradiction.

Mary argument: An argument against physicalism due to Frank Jackson. A colour scientist named 'Mary' has spent her whole life in a black-and-white room. During her time on the inside she has come to know all physical facts about colour. Yet when she is released and she sees a red flower for the first time, she learns some new fact. Since she already knew all physical facts prior to her release, facts about conscious colour perception are not reducible to physical facts. So, physicalism is false. The argument is also known as 'the knowledge argument'.

Meaningfulness: A good that can be exemplified to a certain degree in an individual person's life and that is thought to merit substantial pride or admiration and normally to be of greater value than physical pleasure.

Mental paint view: A representational view of perception that holds that perception has representational content but denies that the representational content fully determines the phenomenal character. The phenomenal character does not flow from the representational content. For example, two perceptual experiences may represent the same ripe tomato but the tomato may be presented more or less saliently in the two experiences. The view is sometimes referred to as 'the qualia view'.

Mereology: The theory of parthood relations. Mereology aims to offer a comprehensive account of the relations between parts and wholes, and wholes and parts.

Mereological nihilists: Those who think that there are no conditions under which some xs compose a y. Mereological nihilists think that there exist only simple objects and no composites.

Mereological restrictivists: Those who think that there are some conditions under which some xs compose a y, and some conditions under which some xs do not compose a y.

Mereological universalists: Those who think that for any xs, those xs compose a y.

Metaethics: A subdivision of ethics that attempts to make sense of ethical thought and practice, by trying to explain and therefore capture some essential features that such thought and practice are supposed to have. In this metaethics resembles philosophy of religion, insofar as the latter can be viewed as trying to make sense of another distinctively human endeavour – religious belief and ritual.

Metaphysical necessity: Something is metaphysically necessary just when it could not have been differently, not even if the physical laws were different. For example, it is metaphysically necessary that nothing is red and green all over at the same time, that squares are not circles and that bachelors are unmarried. But it is not metaphysically necessary that speed of light is constant, that Santa Claus does not exist or that there are no blue swans.

Metaphysical possibility: By definition, something is metaphysical possible just when its negation is not necessary. For example, it is metaphysically possible that there are unicorns but not that $2 + 2 = 5$, or that there are round squares.

Miracles: The most influential definition of miracles goes back to Hume, who defined them as transgressions of the laws of nature brought about by the direct action of a supernatural agent. So, on this definition, naturally explicable lucky coincidences, however religiously striking they might be, would not be miracles; many of the healings that Jesus is reported to have performed, most obviously resurrections from the dead, would be.

Modality: Modality is concerned with what is possible (what could be the case), necessary (what must be the case), or impossible (what could not be the case).

Monism: The view that the whole is more fundamental than its parts.

Moore, G. E. (1873–1958): *See* textbox on p.149.

Mooreanism: Mooreanism is the name given to the strikingly direct response to the problem of radical scepticism sometimes attributed to, and certainly inspired by, the writings of G. E. Moore (1873–1958). This response involves arguing that since we do indeed know a great deal about the world, it follows that we must also know the denials of sceptical hypotheses as well, since such hypotheses are known to be inconsistent with most of our knowledge of the world. So, for example, since I know that I have two hands, and I know that if I have two hands then I cannot be a (handless) brain in a vat, it follows that I must also know that I am not a brain in a vat. So construed, Mooreanism seems to be making use of the principle of closure. What is problematic about the view, however, is that many find it highly intuitive to suppose that we can't know the denials of sceptical hypotheses. It is thus incumbent on the proponent of Mooreanism to explain how this could be possible after all. To this end, recent defences of Mooreanism have appealed to the safety principle as a way of explaining how we could know the denials of sceptical hypotheses. See also **radical scepticism**.

Moral relativism: This is the view according to which morality isn't objective but is rather 'relative' to particular cultures, societies, or other such groupings. For example, suppose that one culture regards infanticide as morally permissible, while another culture regards it as morally repugnant. According to moral relativism, there is no objective way of adjudicating in favour of either moral claim. Instead, they are *both* treated as correct, albeit, of course, relative to the culture in question.

Morality: Behaviour that conforms to requirements, the violation of which merits guilt, censure and other negative reactions to some degree.

Multiculturalism: Multiculturalism covers a diverse set of contrasting views. A common thread is that cultural diversity is not a problem to be overcome, but something of value to be celebrated. Multiculturalists generally argue that group membership in a culture can give rise to special rights or exemptions.

Naive realism A view about perception that maintains that perception is fundamentally a matter of being related to an external object and some of its perceptible properties.

Nationalism: Best understood as 'ethical nationalism'. This is the view that membership in a nation can have normative value and so this membership can give rise to special duties that extend only to fellow group members.

Naturalism: A broad category of conceptions of meaning in life according to which it can be realised in a world that lacks anything spiritual. The view that a meaningful life is possible for us if the world is purely physical and neither God nor a soul exists.

Necessary: Something is necessary if it obtains at every possible world. Alternatively, something is necessary if its negation entails a contradiction.

Necessity: This is the property of 'could-not-have-been-otherwise-ness' that God has, pertaining to His existence (according to Classical Theism). *See also* **Contingency** for the contrasting notion. According to Classical Theism, whilst the universe might not have existed (it's contingent), God could not but have existed (He's necessary).

Negative freedom: Negative freedom is an understanding of freedom in terms of the absence of coercion or interference by others. It is 'negative' insofar as it defines itself in terms of what it is not. To be free on this view is to be free from constraint or imposition by other people.

Neural correlates of consciousness: A neural region is said to be a neural correlate of a particular type of conscious experience when increased activity in this region is minimally sufficient for generating consciousness, that is, increased activity in that area together with all sorts of enabling factors suffice for generating that particular type of consciousness.

Nomic necessity/possibility: A nomic necessity is what is necessary given the laws of nature. X is nomically possible if x obtains in a world that shares the same laws of nature as the actual world.

Nominalism: The view that there are no abstract objects.

No-miracles argument: The no-miracles argument asserts that the truth, or approximate truth, of our current scientific theories is the best explanation of their explanatory, predictive and technological success. If our theories had no basis in objective reality, their success would be a 'miracle'.

Non-instrumental value: To say that something is non-instrumentally valuable is to say that it is valuable for its own sake, and not merely for the sake of something else. A plausible example of non-instrumental value is friendship. We don't value our friends because they are useful to us (though having friends is undoubtedly useful), but simply because they are our friends; that is, we value our friends for their own sake, and not merely because they serve some further purpose (such as making us happy). *See also* **instrumental value**.

Nonsymmetric: Any relation, R, is nonsymmetric just in case when A R's B sometimes it is the case that B Rs A, and sometimes is not the case that B Rs A.

Normal science: Normal science, in Thomas Kuhn's account of scientific change, refers to the bulk of ordinary scientific activity that takes place within a given **paradigm**. Such research draws on widely accepted methods, tools and principles, and is marked by incremental rather than revolutionary change (*see also* **scientific revolutions**). It is sometimes said that normal science consists largely of 'puzzle-solving', but this is not meant to belittle the extent to which attention to detail and the pursuit of accepted theoretical principles can generate insight and understanding.

Normative ethics: Sometimes called *moral theory*, this is the attempt to construct systematic theories that aim to explain what it is that right actions have in common. Moral theories typically appeal to, and defend, a fundamental moral principle that underlies the more particular principles and rules we use in our everyday moral thinking.

Objectivism: A naturalist conception of meaning in life according to which a life is meaningful just insofar as it engages with conditions that are good in themselves, apart from whether anyone thinks they are good, likes them or decides to pursue them. The view that one's life can be meaningful in virtue of mind-independent features, i.e. not because of one's believing that it is meaningful, desiring it or having chosen it.

Objectivity: The term 'objectivity' has been defined in various ways, for example as the absence of prejudice and bias (and other 'subjective' factors), or as the adherence to certain reliable methods and procedures of inquiry. In phrases such as 'objective reality', the implicit appeal to objectivity also expresses a commitment to the existence of some sort of mind-independent, external reality that resists us and cannot be altered simply by altering what we think about it.

Observation: Observation is based in our sensory experience of the world and is also commonly thought to form the basis of our scientific knowledge of the world. As such, its function is to bridge the gap between individual psychological states and the shared, public world of scientific knowledge. Proponents of **logical empiricism** suggested that observation statements could be recorded in the form of **protocol sentences** and could form the basis of more complex knowledge claims. (*See also* **theory-ladenness of observation**.)

Olfactory experience: Perceptual experience that either was or appears to the subject to be the result of actually smelling an odour.

Omnipotence: Literally, all-powerfulness. The God of classical theism is conceived of as the most powerful being that there could be.

Omnipresence (immanence): Whilst not being in any way constrained within the universe to a particular time or place, God is supposed to be ever and everywhere present in it. This property is called 'omnipresence' or 'immanence'. *See also* **incorporeality (transcendence).**

Omniscience: Literally, all-knowingness. This is the divine property of knowing everything that it's logically possible might be known.

Ontological Argument: This is the name given to an argument which seeks to show from the mere concept of God that He must exist, drawing on no supposed facts about the universe that (on Classical Theism) He created. The original version of it was propounded by St Anselm, but there are other versions, most notably the modal ontological argument (and indeed there are distinct versions of the modal argument).

Ontological gap: There is said to be an ontological gap between mental and physical properties, when there could be two possible scenarios that are physically and functionally indistinguishable yet vary with respect to the mental properties that are instantiated in those scenarios.

Open-question argument: G.E. Moore proposed this argument against 'naturalistic' definitions of moral terms such as goodness. For Moore, no such definition is plausible, since we can always ask, of any attempt to define goodness in terms of natural property, whether actions that display that natural property are in fact good. Such questions are, for Moore, 'open' questions, ones that make sense. This showed, for him, that good cannot *mean the same thing as* having the natural property. Because this argument seems fatal to any naturalistic definition, Moore thought that moral properties were *non-natural* properties.

Panpsychism: Panpsychism is the view that everything, including rocks, bicycles and television sets, has at least a minimal form of consciousness. Many traditional panpsychists argued that mental properties are the only fundamental properties and that physical properties are derived. However, a panpsychist can also hold that there are two types of fundamental properties: physical and mental.

Paradigm: The term 'paradigm', in Thomas Kuhn's theory of science, refers to a set of practices, methods, theoretical principles, scientific theories and judgments (e.g. concerning what constitutes a valid scientific problem), which is shared by scientists in a given (sub)discipline at a given time under conditions of **normal science**. Agreement on these elements of scientific practice need not be explicit, but may be tacit; it is usually associated with contingent ways of organising scientific research and is subject to change (*see* **paradigm shift**).

Paradigm shift: After a **scientific revolution**, scientists typically regroup around a new shared **paradigm** that displaces its predecessor; in Kuhnian terminology this is referred to as a 'paradigm shift'.

Paradox: A paradox is an apparently valid argument which proceeds from premises which seem entirely intuitive, but which generate an absurd conclusion.

Paradox of Fiction: An argument for the paradoxical conclusion that we don't have emotions in response to fictional characters and fictional events.

Parsimony: One of the theoretical virtues. A theory is typically held to be more parsimonious if its posits a more limited ontology than its competitors. It is controversial what this amounts to. Does it require that the theory posits fewer objects, or fewer kinds of objects, or fewer fundamental objects? Metaphysicians are divided on this.

Perfect freedom: We are more or less free in our actions from day to day; lack of power, ignorance, weakness of will and so forth detract from our freedom. God, according to classical theism, suffers from none of these liabilities and thus is called perfectly free.

Perfect goodness: We are more or less good in our actions from day to day; again in contrast to us, God always does whatever it is that would be best.

Personhood: The divine property that makes it the case that God is not just a supernatural force, such as karma is often supposed to be, a something that is merely in states and undergoes only events; rather He is a supernatural person, a some*one* with beliefs who performs actions.

Pessimistic meta-induction: Some opponents of **scientific realism** have argued that the repeated failure of (past) scientific theories allows us to make an **inductive inference** to the effect that our present scientific theories, too, will turn out to be false. This inference is called 'pessimistic meta-induction'.

Phenomenal: In the philosophy of mind, the phenomenal character of an experience describes what it is like subjectively to undergo that experience. Relatedly, *phenomenal properties* are those qualitative properties that determine the subjective character of experience.

Phenomenal character: The conscious aspect of experience together with any representational properties that the experience may have.

Phenomenal consciousness: What it's like to have experiences from an internal perspective.

Philosophy of religion: That branch of philosophy which considers the claim that the God of classical theism exists, in particular whether or not it makes sense and, if it does, whether or not we have reasons for believing it true or believing it false. The discipline also encompasses other related issues, some of which are at least mentioned in chapter 25.

Physicalism: This is the view that all fundamental entities are physical.

Plato (c. 427–c. 347 BC): *See* textbox on p.127.

Platonism: The view that there exist abstract objects. For example, mathematical Platonism is the view that there exist abstract mathematical objects, like numbers.

Pluralism: The view that the parts are more fundamental than the whole.

Political philosophy: Political philosophy is a branch of philosophy focusing on power and institutional relations between individuals and groups. It relates to issues concerning freedom, justice, rights and global justice among others.

Positive freedom: Positive freedom is an understanding of freedom in terms of its achieving some goal or end. It is 'positive' insofar as it is about achievement. So to be free on this view is to be able to pursue some goal or end, such as receive an education or access to health care.

Problem of Evil: This is the name given to the argument from the existence of evil – e.g. suffering, ignorance and death – in the world to the non-existence of God.

Procedural definition of art: A definition of art which cites some procedure(s) as necessary and/or sufficient conditions for something counting as an artwork.

Process theories: A set of similar views about the nature of causation according to which what it is for c to cause e is for c's worldline to leave a mark on e's worldline.

Proposition: A proposition is what is stated by a declarative sentence. For example, the sentence 'The cat is on the mat' states that something is the case; namely, that the cat is on the mat, and this is the proposition expressed by this sentence. Notice that the same proposition will be expressed by an analogue declarative sentence, which is in a different language, such as French, just so long as what is stated by that sentence is the same.

Propositional knowledge: This is knowledge that something (i.e. a proposition) is the case. It is typically contrasted with ability knowledge, or know-how. The two types of knowledge are treated differently because, intuitively at least, one might know how to do something (e.g. swim) without having any relevant propositional knowledge (e.g. without knowing that you can swim, perhaps because you forgot that you could until you fell in the water). *See also* **ability knowledge**.

Protocol sentence: A protocol sentence, within the framework of **logical empiricism**, was thought to be a statement that describes immediate experience in a way that is irrefutable and allows for no further analysis, thereby providing the justificatory basis for more complex claims.

Pseudo-science: Pseudo-sciences such as astrology, homoeopathy or creation science typically emulate certain 'surface features of science' – such as an elaborate terminology and an interconnected system of hypotheses – but often aim at shielding certain central dogmas from empirical challenges. According to Karl Popper, pseudo-sciences lack **falsifiability**; that is, they make claims that cannot in principle be tested against empirical observations. However, a fuller analysis of pseudo-sciences would require looking at their historical origins, which are often motivated by non-scientific concerns (e.g. the introduction of quasi-religious content into the classroom, as in the case of 'intelligent design theory').

Purpose theory: A God-based theory of meaning in life according to which one's life is meaningful to the degree that one fulfills a purpose that God has assigned to one. This theory does not posit anything about whether God in fact exists or has assigned a purpose to human beings, but does entail that if God does not exist (or has not assigned a purpose), then no one's life is meaningful.

Radical scepticism: Radical scepticism is the view that we do not know very much, particularly when it comes to our beliefs about the external world (i.e. a world that is 'external' to our experience of it). Although it is natural to speak of radical scepticism as being a philosophical position, it is not usually advanced in this way but is rather put forward as a challenge to existing theories of knowledge to show why they exclude the type of radical scepticism in question.

Readymade: Mass produced or otherwise antecedently manufactured objects, incorporated into artworks, often with little or no alteration. The art of readymades was most famously practised by Marcel Duchamp (1887–1968).

Religious experience: There are issues surrounding how best to define 'religious experience'; for various reasons, it is best to define it as an experience which seems to the subject to be of a supernatural being or directly imply a supernatural being. So defined, religious experiences need not be or even be taken to be of God.

Replication: Replication refers to the repetition of an experiment under the same conditions as the original experiment, and with the same quantitative or qualitative outcome. It is often assumed that, for an experimental finding to be valid, it must be replicable; such replicability is usually assumed, yet actual replication of experiments is rarer than is commonly thought.

Representation: Scientific representation is a relation between a representational vehicle (e.g. a **scientific model**) and a target system. The vehicle allows its user to gain information, draw inferences, and generally learn about the target system in an indirect way, by engaging with the vehicle rather than directly with the target system.

Representational content: A content, or proposition, associated with a perceptual experience that represents, or stands for, objects and properties in the external world. On the extreme view, representational content represents objects and properties in the external world by having these entities as its constituents.

Representationalism: A view about perception that states that there is a necessary connection between the phenomenal character of experience and the content of the experience. Strong representationalism maintains that to have a particular phenomenal character just is to have a particular content. The two weaker forms hold either that content supervenes on phenomenal character, or that phenomenal character supervenes on content.

Republican freedom: Republican freedom is an understanding of freedom in terms of non-domination. Its roots are in the republican tradition dating back to ancient Rome. To be free from non-domination is to ensure that any interference is not arbitrarily imposed. Republicans argue that citizens should engage in public deliberation – to provide 'discursive control' – over the kinds of interference legitimated.

Research programme: Suggested by Imre Lakatos as the appropriate unit for analysing scientific change, a research programme consists of a 'hard' theoretical core (e.g. central theoretical tenets or assumptions about nature) and a 'protective belt' of auxiliary hypotheses. When scientists come across potentially falsifying data, they will first attempt to modify the auxiliary hypotheses; only if empirical challenges cannot be resolved in this way will they begin to question the hard theoretical core of a research programme.

Restitutive justice: A condition in which those who have undergone wrongful harm have been compensated for it, ideally by those who were responsible for the wrongful harm.

Retributive justice: A condition in which happiness is proportionate to morality, i.e. in which those who have lived morally upright lives flourish or are rewarded and in which those who have not undergo harm such as suffering or punishment.

Russellian monism: A view closely related to panpsychism, according to which physics only concerns the dispositional and relational properties of matter but not the intrinsic nature of things. The intrinsic nature of things may consist in conscious matter.

Safety principle: The safety principle holds that if an agent knows a proposition, then that agent's true belief in that proposition must be safe in the sense that it couldn't have easily been false. For example, provided circumstances are normal, your belief right now that you are reading this book is safe, since it is a belief that couldn't have easily been false (since if you weren't reading a book, then you wouldn't believe that you were). That is, it is not just that you happen to have a true belief in the particular circumstances in which you find yourself; instead, you would tend to form true beliefs about this subject matter across a range of relevantly similar circumstances. What is striking about the safety principle is that our beliefs in the denials of sceptical hypotheses may well be safe, and so if safety is (at least sometimes) all there is to knowing, it follows that it might be possible to know the denials of sceptical hypotheses after all, contrary to intuition. For example, my belief, in normal circumstances, that I am not a brain in a vat seems to be safe, since there is no relevantly similar situation to this one in which I believe this proposition and yet what I believe is false. *See also* **Mooreanism**.

Sceptical hypotheses: A sceptical hypothesis is a scenario in which you are radically deceived about the world and yet your experience of the world is exactly as it would be had you not been deceived. Consider, for example, the fate of the protagonist in the film *The Matrix*, who comes to realise that his previous experiences of the world were in fact being 'fed' into his brain whilst his body was confined to a large vat. Accordingly, whilst he seemed to be experiencing a world rich with interaction between himself and other people, in fact he was not interacting with anybody or any thing at all (at least over and above the tubes in the vat that were 'feeding' him his experiences), but was instead simply floating motionlessly. The problem posed by sceptical hypotheses is that we seem unable to know that they are false. After all, if our experience of the world could be exactly as it is and yet we are the victims of a sceptical hypothesis, then on what basis could we ever hope to distinguish a genuine experience of the world from an illusory one? Sceptical hypotheses are thus used to motivate scepticism. *See also* **radical scepticism**.

Scientific method: Rhetoric about science often includes talk of 'the scientific method', but the search for a single such method (similar to that for a **demarcation criterion**) may be futile. Science consists of many coexisting approaches, which may bear a 'family resemblance' to one another without sharing a particular set of features. However, it may be useful to think of the phrase 'the scientific method' as emphasising evidence-based reasoning and **hypothetico-deductivism**.

Scientific model: Scientists often use simplified models as 'stand-ins' for more complex systems. On an inclusive understanding, the term 'scientific model' would encompass material models (e.g. scale models) as well as theoretical models (e.g. a set of mathematical equations that simplifies, or approximates, the full theoretical description). On a narrower interpretation, the term 'model' has been used to refer to an interpretation of an axiomatic system (e.g. the **axiomatisation** of a scientific theory), such that all the theorems of the system automatically turn out true.

Scientific realism: Scientific realism asserts that science gives us a by and large true, or approximately true, account of the structure of the world as it is independently of what we think about it. If well-confirmed theories make irreducible use of unobservable entities (e.g. electrons), then this gives us good reason to believe such entities exist and have the properties that the theory says they have (e.g. spin-{1/2} and negative electrical charge). In other words, scientific theories are to be taken literally and are to be assessed in terms of their truth or falsity. Regarding the history of science, scientific realists are typically committed to the thesis that, over time, science converges upon a true account of the objective world.

Scientific revolutions: According to Kuhn's theory of science, scientific revolutions are a more or less frequent occurrence in the history of science. They separate periods of **normal science** and occur when scientists working within an earlier **paradigm** can no longer ignore a mounting number of **anomalies** and when an emerging new paradigm holds out the promise of more successful alternative theories and methodologies. Scientific revolutions are thus associated with **paradigm shifts**.

Scientific theory: In science, the term 'theory' is reserved for an integrated body of explanatory hypotheses, which are capable of unifying disparate phenomena and which typically enjoy considerable empirical support. Within **hypothetico-deductivism**, a theory is typically thought of as a set of hypotheses, from which testable predictions are derived through logical deduction, which are then tested by comparison with observable facts.

Sense-datum theory: A form of indirect realism about perception that maintains that perceivers perceive the world by being directly aware of mind-dependent entities called 'sense data'. Sense data have ordinary properties, such as red and round.

Sensitivity principle: The sensitivity principle states that if an agent knows a proposition, then that agent's true belief in that proposition must be sensitive in the sense that, had that proposition been false, she would not have believed it. For example, provided circumstances are normal, your belief that you are reading this book right now is sensitive since, had this not been true (but everything else remained the same), then you wouldn't believe that you were reading this book, but would believe that you were doing something else instead (e.g. reading another book or taking a nap). Some beliefs, in contrast, seem to be by their nature insensitive. Consider my beliefs in the denials of sceptical hypotheses, for example, such as my belief that I am not a brain in a vat. Were this belief to be false (i.e. were I to be a brain in a vat), I would be in a situation in which I would be deceived about whether I was a brain in a vat, and so would continue to believe that I wasn't a brain in a vat regardless. Thus, if sensitivity is a prerequisite of knowledge, it follows that we are unable to know the denials of sceptical hypotheses.

Simplicity: One of the theoretical virtues. Exactly what simplicity consists in is controversial. On some views, simplicity concerns the number and conciseness of the theory's basic principles. On other views, it concerns the number of kinds of entities postulated by the theory (in which case simplicity isn't very different from *parsimony*, listed above).

Singleton set: A set that has a single member.

Social contract: The social contract is an idea with roots at least as back as Plato's work. The social contract is usually understood as a hypothetical agreement between contracting parties. It is meant to demonstrate how and why political obligations arise and a central concept in political philosophy. Philosophers defending social contract theories are called contractarians.

Social constructionism: A view about emotions that take culture to be the main decisive factor in determining which emotions we experience.

Soul-based theory: A supernaturalist conception of meaning in life according to which it is solely a matter of one's soul being in a certain state, where a soul is an immortal, spiritual substance constitutive of one's identity that can live apart from one's current body. This theory does not posit anything about whether a soul in fact exists, but does entail that if one lacks a soul, then one's life is meaningless.

Statism: This is the view that membership in a state can have normative value and so this membership can give rise to special duties that extend only to fellow group members.

Structural identity thesis: An interesting consequence of the **deductive-nomological (D-N) model** is that explanations are logically indistinguishable from predictions. This gives rise to the structural identity thesis, according to which every explanation is a potential prediction and vice versa.

Sub specie aeternitatis: The Latin phrase for the standpoint of eternity, or the point of view of the universe. When taking up this perspective, one is to move as far away as one can from the 'here and now' and instead consider one's life in the context of an infinite, or at least extraordinarily huge, amount of time and space.

Subjective perspective: The perspective of a particular subject from a particular location in space and time.

Subjectivism: A naturalist conception of meaning in life according to which a life is meaningful just insofar as it engages with conditions that are thought to be meaningful, liked or chosen. The view that one's life can be meaningful solely in virtue of mind-dependent features, such as one's believing that it is meaningful or desiring it.

Supernaturalism: A broad category of conceptions of meaning in life according to which it can be realised only in a world that includes a spiritual dimension. The view that a meaningful life is impossible for us if the world is purely physical and neither God nor a soul exists.

Supervenience: A relationship that obtains between properties which co-vary. The A-properties supervene on the B-properties if fixing the B-properties fixes the A-properties.

Symbolism: Late-nineteenth-century poetic movement with a great emphasis on indirect description, metaphor and imagery. Prominent practitioners were Baudelaire, Mallarmé and Verlaine.

Synesthesia: Experience or thought that involves usual but involuntary combinations of features in a systematic way. For example, the musical note D may always be experienced as red, whereas E-flat is experienced as blue. Or the numeral 3 may always be experienced as green, whereas the numeral 7 is always experienced as purple.

Tactile experience: Perceptual experience that either was or appears to the subject to be the result of actually touching an object.

Temporal relations: The relations that hold between events, or between moments, such that those moments are moments in time.

Testing: Testing a theoretical hypothesis requires deriving observable predictions and comparing them with actual observations. If the prediction does not match the observations, the original hypothesis may need to be discarded or modified, although there is usually more than one way of responding to observational mismatches. Tests differ in their severity: a test is the more severe, the more likely it is that it will reveal an error in the hypothesis, provided that error really exists.

Theism: This is the thesis that there is a God of the classical theistic sort. *See also* **agnosticism** and **atheism**.

Theoretical virtues: Features of a theory that make that theory desirable. It is typically held that, other things being equal, of two theories the more virtuous should be preferred over the less virtuous.

Theory-ladenness of observation: The term 'theory-ladenness' refers to the thought that our observations are not solely determined by the external world and our biologically hardwired perceptual apparatus, but are also shaped by background knowledge, expectations, and the theoretical and conceptual framework with which we approach the world. (*See also* **observation**.)

Transparency: Experience is said to be transparent when it seems to the perceiver that an external object and its perceptible properties are presented directly to her, whereas the experience itself isn't itself noticeable. Most cases of normal visual experience are transparent.

Tropes: Individuals located in space and time that are non-repeated; it is in virtue of two objects each having tropes that are exactly similar that the objects in question appear to share a property.

Underdetermination of theory by data: The underdetermination thesis states that, for any finite set of observations, we can always entertain different, incompatible theories which would nonetheless be equally able to account for what we have observed. This would mean that we can never be sure that the scientific theories we take to be well-supported by the observational data are, in fact, unique. (*See also* **observation**.)

Universals: Abstract objects which, according to some views of properties, are instantiated by objects; it is in virtue of instantiating these universals that the objects have the properties that they do.

Veridical experience: Accurate experience, i.e. experience that does not involve any misperception.

Virtue ethics: This is a normative theory that puts much more prominence on agents, their characters, and their motives. Virtue ethics maintains that virtuous motives either make actions right, or are needed in order for us to see and be moved to do what is right. Virtues are regarded as excellences – of character and of the intellect – that can be developed through education and training. For Aristotle, virtues were a mid-point between excesses of feeling or desire.

Zombie argument: An argument against physicalism due to David Chalmers. The argument attempts to establish that there can be creatures just like you and me physically and functionally but with no consciousness. As physicalism holds that consciousness arises from physical matter as a matter of necessity, this claim is incompatible with physicalism. The argument is also known as 'the conceivability argument'.

Zombies: A philosophical zombie is a creature that is physically and functionally indistinguishable from you, yet has no inner mental life.

index